THE SCIENCE OF
VIRTUAL REALITY
AND VIRTUAL ENVIRONMENTS

THE SCIENCE OF
VIRTUAL REALITY
AND VIRTUAL ENVIRONMENTS

A Technical, Scientific and Engineering Reference on Virtual Environments

Roy S. Kalawsky

British Aerospace PLC
and
University of Hull

Addison-Wesley Publishing Company

Wokingham, England • Reading, Massachusetts • Menlo Park, California
New York • Don Mills, Ontario • Amsterdam • Bonn • Sydney • Singapore
Tokyo • Madrid • San Juan • Milan • Paris • Mexico City • Seoul • Taipei

© 1993 Addison-Wesley Publishers Ltd.
© 1993 Addison-Wesley Publishing Company Inc.

The programs in this book have been included for their instructional value. They have been tested with care but are not guaranteed for any particular purpose. The publisher does not offer any warranties or representations nor does it accept any liabilities with respect to the programs.

Many of the designations used by manufacturers and sellers to distinguish their products are claimed as trademarks. Addison-Wesley has made every attempt to supply trademark information about manufacturers and their products mentioned in this book. A list of the trademark designations and their owners appears on page xviii.

Cover designed by Pencil Box Ltd, Marlow, Buckinghamshire
and printed by The Riverside Printing Co. (Reading) Ltd.
Camera-ready copy prepared by the author.
Printed and bound in Great Britain by The University Press, Cambridge.

First printed 1993

ISBN 0-201-63171-7

British Library Cataloguing-in-Publication Data
A catalogue record for this book is available from the British Library.

Library of Congress Cataloging-in-Publication Data is available

Foreword

Pictures have been used as a medium of communication for thousands of years. But the canvases and techniques for drawing them have changed radically since the time of the first images in the caves of Lascaux, France. Modern computer graphics have provided for many years the newest and potentially most expressive media for pictorial communication, but improvements in the power and accessibility of interactive 3D graphics systems have recently added a new dimension.

It is now possible to draw computer graphics images at rates sufficient that, if they are viewed by a person whose head position is automatically tracked, the viewpoint for the graphic image may be slaved to follow that person's head orientation. This format has variously been termed cyberspace, virtual reality, or artificial reality. But whatever oxymoronic neologism is used, the basic underlying feature is that the viewers of such a display system can be made to experience the interactive image as a synthetic or virtual environment with which they may interact in a potentially natural way.

This possible natural interaction has suggested that these virtual environments might provide an ideal human–computer interface for a wide variety of applications, such as procedural training, computer aided design and manufacture, teleoperation simulation, laparoscopic surgery, computer animation and so on. Since this interface amounts to a new communications medium, the list of applications could be extended almost indefinitely. *The Science of Virtual Reality and Virtual Environments* provides the first comprehensive, technical review of the engineering details underlying the development of virtual environment displays.

As pointed out in Chapter 2, the technologies to produce virtual environment interfaces date from developments in flight and teleoperator simulation made during the last 25 years. Virtual environments are, however, special simulators that are generally worn rather than entered. They are personal simulators. They aim to provide an unmediated, immediate sense of presence in a world or space other than the physical one in which their users actually are. Their users are not in a cockpit that is within a synthetic environment, they are in the environment themselves. In this environment abstract or concrete computer databases can be reified for manipulative or other concrete modes of interaction.

Until the last few years, access to these personal simulation systems – pioneered by Ivan Sutherland in the late 1960s – had been restricted by cost and the limited availability of the necessary hardware. However, now that relatively inexpensive systems costing in the order of $50–100,000 have become available, public anticipation of great new adventures in virtual worlds has been encouraged by widespread media interest.

Despite the engineering history and in contrast to the impression generally given by the press coverage, the performance of these more widely available, lower priced systems is quite poor. Current users of cyberspace are generally legally blind, headed for a stereoscopic headache, about to be motion sick, and soon to be struck by a pain in the neck due to the helmet weight. *The Science of Virtual Reality and Virtual Environments* collects for the first time the necessary technical information needed for improvement of the performance of these cheaper virtual environment systems and the diffusion of this display technology away from the traditional applications in flight and teleoperator simulation and training.

Despite the poor performance of the more widely available displays, a fledgling industry has begun to develop around them. Commenting on the industry itself an outspoken proponent of 'virtual reality' once described it as a most unusual field: '... it's a field where there are no experts and everyone can be one!'

As the technical content of *The Science of Virtual Reality and Virtual Environments* attests, nothing could be farther from the truth. Though some may reasonably doubt that the research area is, in fact, a distinct science, scientists and engineers such as Professor Roy Kalawsky have been designing virtual environment systems as parts of flight simulators for years, and have been disseminating their knowledge in courses on flight simulation like those periodically offered at MIT and SUNY Binghampton. Readers of this book will be empowered to pass beyond the hyperbole of 'virtual reality' to the design of virtual environments for useful work.

Probably the most important contribution of this book is its collection and analysis in one place of the varied fields of science and engineering on which the synthesis of a virtual environment depends. Mechanical and electrical engineering form a basis for the design of the hardware substrate of the synthetic environment. Human sensory and motor physiology identify the phenomena that constrain successful design. Human factors design principles and control engineering help establish the specific design targets and assessment procedures. All of these key areas are addressed in this book, which provides not only commentary but an extensive collection of key references.

The application of virtual environment technology directly to simulation of human experience for either engineering, scientific or recreational ends has concerned some who have contemplated the future of the field. There is certainly potential for significant negative social impact if the high level of violence in video games is recreated in virtual environment displays. Similarly, due to unnatural visual–motor and visual–vestibular adaptation, users of virtual environments should probably not immediately hop into their cars after protracted time in 'virtual land'. However, the danger that this technology may be abused is probably no greater than that posed by other powerful technologies which may be used for good or ill. Nevertheless, the close linkage between this technology and the control of individual behaviour should alert those concerned with the social impact of technology that new analysis might be needed.

There should be no question, however, that new forms of individual expression and control will be possible through the maturing of virtual environment technology. The tasks most likely to uniquely benefit are those that are highly interactive and require multiple, simultaneous, coordinated foci of control within natural or synthetic 3D environments.

In fact, however, the future uses for virtual environments are hard to foresee accurately since the situation is probably parallel to the introduction of the first personal computer, the Altair. At its introduction its current practical uses – word processing, databases and spreadsheets – seemed well beyond its reach. In fact, spreadsheet programs like VISICALC had not even been foreseen!

Accordingly, the most prominent application of virtual environments is possibly today unknown, but it may well be made by a reader of this book.

Stephen R. Ellis
Group Leader: Advanced Displays
NASA Ames Research Center

Preface

By sensing the position and orientation of the human head and coupling the resulting data into a high performance computer graphics system it is possible to generate a computer synthesized view of a virtual world wherever the user is looking. This is the essence of visually coupled systems now popularly known as Virtual Reality. What does this mean to the user and why all the excitement?

Virtual reality has emerged almost overnight from various secret laboratories throughout the world, mainly because of the high profile it has gained from press and media exposure. Unfortunately, the general public's exposure to the concept of virtual reality has come when not all the necessary technologies are fully mature and fully understood. The demand for products embodying some form of virtual interface is accelerating. This has led to a proliferation of small research groups, desperately attempting to grasp this so-called 'new' technology. Even though the concept of a virtual reality system was first thought of in the 1950s, many researchers claim that there is little serious scientific material available. When one searches through scientific journals for work on visually coupled systems or virtual reality it soon becomes evident that many of today's claims have been tried and tested before. The major difference today is that the technology is available at a reasonable price.

More recently, virtual reality has been split into two distinct groups. The first group, known as immersive virtual reality, is based on helmet-mounted or immersive display technologies. The second group, desktop virtual reality, has emerged from animated computer aided design (CAD). With desktop virtual reality the user views and interacts with the compute-represented image on a traditional computer graphics screen. Whether or not this later group is virtual reality or just a more sophisticated version of CAD is an interesting question, which will not be discussed here. However, desktop CAD or desktop virtual reality will be given a brief mention in this book because the tools used to create a desktop virtual reality system are also used to create the virtual environment for an immersive virtual reality system.

This book provides information and technical detail for those who require grounding in what is regarded as the next generation computer interface – virtual reality or virtual environment systems. Whereas previous books either describe the history of virtual reality or its more abstract applications, this book gives the complete technical detail. It also serves as a comprehensive technical reference for this exciting and important scientific field. The section on virtual reality technology describes how the various technologies work, including their principles of operation, and later chapters highlight where the technology must be developed further. Both the human factors and related engineering issues are discussed in detail. It is anticipated that this book will be used for reference purposes rather than being read from cover to cover. Therefore, some material has been reiterated in one or two places for the convenience of the reader. The structure of the book is quite intentional and makes it easy for the experienced practitioner to find material of specific interest quickly. Equally, it is easy for the new researcher to gain a rapid understanding of the field without being overwhelmed by implementation details.

Recently (1991–1992), virtual reality has received considerable press and media coverage. Ridiculous statements have been made about its origins, and unsubstantiated claims have been made regarding its current capabilities. This book gives true and accurate information and explains in detail, with facts and illustrations, the development of the subject. Virtual reality is not a new concept: the ideas behind virtual displays have been in evidence from the early 1950s. Indeed, many jet aircraft already employ a virtual display as the primary flight instrument – the head up display. It was within the aerospace industry that virtual reality had its origins, and the author and his team of specialist research engineers established a substantial virtual environment research facility at British Aerospace, Brough, UK. Experience gained during the various projects and other related work gave the author a unique insight into this extremely significant technology, which will revolutionize future computer systems and human–machine interfaces. The author has also established a centre of excellence for virtual environments and advanced display technologies at the University of Hull, UK, which researches the fundamental issues behind virtual environment systems.

This book has been written for the scientist, the engineer, the student, the eventual end user and the layman who wants to gain greater understanding of the underlying principles behind this exciting next generation computer interface than is available from the limited information in the public domain. For those interested in either exploiting the technology or developing virtual reality peripheral devices, the section on current limitations will be of particular value. The information given in this book is based on the author's experience in virtual environments, accumulated over many years of research and development work for British Aerospace.

This book is divided into eight chapters covering issues such as how the technology should be used and where limitations exist, both in terms of the technology and the basic human factors.

Chapter 1 gives an overview of the concept of virtual environment systems and forms the framework for the rest of the book, showing how the various elements link to form an integrated virtual environment.

Chapter 2 describes the background behind virtual reality from the very early concept stage and traces the development of several key enabling technologies. Essential background material is presented on visually coupled systems, the forerunner to virtual reality. The performance criteria of these early generation systems are given so that the reader can see where technology limitations impeded the design of early systems. The lessons learnt during the early stages of visually coupled system development are extremely relevant to today's virtual reality technologies.

Chapter 3 is devoted to one of the most fundamental aspects of virtual reality and environment systems, an understanding of relevant human physiology and perception. Virtual reality is intimately bound to both human factors and engineering issues: without this grounding there is a danger that whatever virtual reality system is configured, it will not meet the fundamental requirement of being integratable with a human operator. In the past there have been temptations to separate out the human factors from the engineering requirements. The field of virtual reality is a multidisciplinary subject.

Chapter 4 explains what a virtual reality or virtual environment is, by partitioning the virtual man–machine interface into three worlds: visual, auditory and kinaesthetic (haptic and tactile). The technologies used in each of these worlds are described in terms of theory of operation, physics and actual implementation. Wherever possible, alternative technologies are also described in detail to give an idea of the diverse range of subjects this new technology encompasses.

Chapter 5 discusses the software that is required to support the construction of virtual environments.

Chapter 6 highlights the limitations of current technology and gives specific examples. In the future many of these problems will be overcome by appropriate technological development, but it is necessary to lead or drive this development in a coherent way. It is essential that both the fundamental human factors and the engineering issues are fully understood before an effective virtual reality system can be realized.

Chapter 7 summarizes a range of current applications for virtual reality and considers several examples as case studies. It is not possible to describe every potential application for a virtual environment system, and perhaps after reading the previous five chapters the reader may have considered many new applications for himself. The next stage is to quantify the benefits of the application of virtual reality to new ideas; not all applications will be appropriate. Given that the reader has become sufficiently interested in applying virtual reality to a product, it must be considered how this could be undertaken. A virtual environment application development life cycle is described in the following chapter.

Chapter 8 examines the way ahead for virtual environment technologies and recommends the development of a number of fundamental virtual reality technologies. This guidance is beneficial to those wishing to undertake the development of virtual reality technologies to complete virtual reality based systems. An insight is given into where the future might lie and how the technology is likely to develop over the next five to ten years.

A complete bibliography of known scientific papers and other material that relates to visually coupled systems, virtual environments and virtual realities is given, which will be particularly valuable to those wishing to take an active role in virtual environment research and development.

This book should be read along with the following two complementary books:

Ellis S.R., ed. (1991). *Pictorial Communication in Virtual and Real Environments*. London: Taylor and Francis

Foley J.D., Van Dam A., Feiner S.K. and Hughes J.F. (1990). *Computer Graphics: Principles and Practice*. Wokingham: Addison-Wesley

Finally, a detailed glossary of terms that are in use within the fields of virtual reality and virtual environment is provided. This is particularly important because virtual reality is really a multidisciplinary field, and not all of the terminology will be familiar to every reader.

Acknowledgements

In researching, compiling and writing this book, the author has received encouragement and help from various specialists in the field of virtual environments. His gratitude and thanks go to the following:

To British Aerospace Military Aircraft Division for the privilege of freedom while undertaking research for the Company, and for giving the necessary permission to write a technical book on such an exciting subject. Grateful thanks for providing the necessary funding to establish a significant Virtual Environment Laboratory Facility.

To my research team: it is a pleasure to give them special thanks for their constant support and for contributing to the understanding of the technology. Their enthusiasm and expertise turned ideas into reality.

To Sowerby Research Centre, British Aerospace, Filton, UK for providing half the funding for the Virtual Rover 400 demonstration.

To the following people, companies and organizations who have provided me with essential technical detail, much of which has not been published before:

Mr Mike Bevan of *VR News* for giving me encouragement and advice on areas of Virtual Reality not covered by my draft manuscript.

Mr Peter Connor for providing me with a Private Eye display for an extended evaluation period.

Mr Tom Coull of Sense8 for kindly commenting on several aspects of this book.

Dr Stephen Ellis, NASA Ames and U.C. Berkeley, for providing me with very useful data and very helpful constructive comments in the field of virtual environment perception.

Mr Andrew Delgaty and Mr John McKay of British Aerospace for taking many of the superb photographs used in this book.

Mr Kevin Emmons and Mr Jaron Lanier, formerly of VPL Research Inc. USA, for providing technical details.

Mr Scott Fisher of Telepresence Research, USA for providing details of his Company's products.

Mr Chris Gaertner, USA for providing details of his precision optical space tracking system.

Mr Charles Grimsdale of Division Limited for providing me with a wealth of material about his company's products.

Mr John Hough of Virtual Presence for providing me with details of a range of relevant products including WorldToolKit.

Dr Dean Kocian for providing me with details of the latest developments at Wright Patterson Air Force Base.

GEC Avionics, UK for permission to disclose details of their d.c. magnetic tracking system.

Professor Mark Green and Mr Chris Shaw for allowing me to publish details of their MR Toolkit.

Mr Richard Holloway, University of North Carolina, USA for providing details of the research being undertaken there.

Professor Tony Horseman, Hull Royal Infirmary, Kingston upon Hull, UK for many inspirational discussions.

Mr Jim Kramer, Virtual Technologies, USA for providing me with technical and photographic material for his CyberGlove.

Wing Commander Clive Learmonth of British Aerospace for facilitating with the security clearance necessary to publish this book.

Mr Eric Howlett, LEEP Systems, USA for providing details of the LEEP Optical Systems, which are integrated into most virtual reality headsets.

Mr Bob McFarlane of GEC–Marconi Aerospace, UK for providing additional material concerning their modification to Gaertner's Tracker.

Dr Mike McGreevy NASA Ames for providing me with material about his work at NASA Ames.

Mr Kenney Meyer, Piltdown Corporation, USA for disclosing early details of their high performance acoustic space tracking system.

Mr D. Orton, Mr J. Knowles, Mr I. Reddy and Mr J. Forston of Silicon Graphics Inc. for providing excellent support.

Mr Greg Paul of ISG Technologies Inc., UK for providing details of his company's Magnetic Resonance Imaging System.

Mr Bill Polhemus of Polhemus Laboratories Inc., USA for kindly providing me with details of his fibre optic coupled helmet-mounted display and for his encouragement.

Mr Jack Scully, Ascension Technology Inc, USA for permission to disclose some of the technicalities of his head tracking system.

Mr Robert Stone of the Advanced Robotics Centre, UK for providing details and information about the Advanced Robotics Centre's research programme.

Dr Ivan Sutherland for kindly taking the time to find one of the original photographs showing his ultimate display in operation.

Professor Bill Wright, University of North Carolina for providing me with additional details of his work on force/haptic display systems.

Dr Michael Zyda of the Naval Postgraduate School, Monterey, CA., USA who has provided me with useful advice.

Professor Graham Brookes, Dean of Science, the University of Hull, UK for recognizing my achievements in the field of virtual environments. He also proposed me for the honorary position of Visiting Professor of Virtual Environments and Advanced Display Technologies at the University of Hull.

The press and media: while I have been rather critical of the reports they have made about virtual reality, it has been these reports that have advertised and promoted the subject. They captured the public's attention with their words and took virtual reality out of the laboratory and into the street.

While preparing and researching my book I have had the pleasure of meeting, speaking on the telephone with, and communicating by email with many leading figures in the exciting and new scientific field of virtual environments. Without exception everyone has been most helpful and encouraging.

I would like to express my sincere gratitude to the following people who had the patience to review my book prior to publication:

Mr Mike Bevan, *VR News*
Mr Dave Beck, British Aerospace PLC
Mr Lambert Dopping-Hepenstal, British Aerospace PLC
Dr Steve R. Ellis, NASA Ames and U.C. Berkeley

Mr S. Fisher, Telepresence Research
Mr Mel Slater, Queen Mary College, London
Professor John Vince

I am convinced that the comments and suggestions made by these people have improved the quality of this book.

I would also like to thank Addison-Wesley for their encouragement and advice during the preparation of this book, in particular Alan Grove and Nicky Jaeger.

Finally, a special mention must be given to those closest to me – my family. To my wife Christine and children Jason, Sallyann, Anna and Katryna who have always been supportive, understanding and patient. Their encouragement was always at hand while I researched at home for my MSc and PhD. This book would not have been possible without their further encouragement, support and love. I must admit that at the beginning of this book I had completely underestimated the amount of effort that would be required to bring together a detailed scientific reference on virtual environments. My wife has been instrumental in bringing together my many thoughts and vast collection of data into a coherent reference. This book would not have been completed without her guidance and continuous review of the manuscript. I shall always be indebted to my wife for the love she has shown me while I worked many long hours. Without my wife and children I certainly would have lost sight of life's realities.

Figure Acknowledgements

Figure 2.2 Dr Ivan Sutherland, Sun Microsystems Laboratories, Incorporated
Figures 2.9 and 2.10 Dr Dean Kocian, Wright Patterson Air Force Base
Figure 2.12 British Aerospace, Military Aircraft Division
Figure 2.13 Advanced Robotics Research Centre
Figure 4.12 Richard Osborn, Tektronix
Figure 4.26 Eric Howlett, LEEP Optics
Figure 4.30 Bill Polhemus
Figure 4.31 and 4.32 Reflection Technology
Figures 4.38 and 4.39 GEC Avionics
Figures 4.40 and 4.41 Ernie Blood, Ascension Technology Corporation
Figures 4.49 and 4.50 Charles Grimsdale, Division Limited
Figure 4.52 *Scientific American*
Figures 4.57 and 4.58 Exos Incorporated
Figure 4.59 Bob Stone, Advanced Robotics Research Centre
Figure 6.6 Eric Howlett, LEEP Optics
Figure 6.12 Polhemus Incorporated
Figure 7.1 Alan Mawdsley, ISG Technologies Incorporated
Figure 7.2 Andrei State, Department of Computer Science, University of North Carolina at Chapel Hill
Figure 7.3 Bob Stone, Advanced Robotics Research Centre
Figure 7.5 British Aerospace, Military Aircraft Division
Figure 7.9 Andrei State, Department of Computer Science, University of North Carolina at Chapel Hill

CONTENTS

Trademark Notice

Flight Helmet™ is a trade mark of Virtual Research.

Private Eye™ is a trademark of Reflection Technology.

BOOM™ (Binocular Omni-Orientation Monitor) is a trademark of FakeSpace Incorporated.

SPASYN™, 3Space™ Tracker, Isotrak™ and Fastrak™ are trademarks of Polhemus Navigation Systems Incorporated.

Bird™, Flock of Birds™ and Extended Range Transmitter™ are trademarks of Ascension Technology Corporation.

Lincoln Wand™ is a trademark of Lincoln Laboratory.

Space Pen™ is a trademark of Science Accessories Corporation.

SELSPOT™ is a trademark of Selective Electrical Corporation.

Rotating Beam™, Videometric™, LED Array and Integrated Helmet and Display Sighting System (IHADSS™) are trademarks of Honeywell.

SkyWriter™, RealityEngine™, PowerVision™, Graphics Library (GL™), Geometry Engine™, PowerLock™, REACT™ and POSIX™ are trademarks of Silicon Graphics.

ProVision™, SuperVision™ and Distributed Virtual Environment System™ (dVS) are trademarks of Division Limited.

Convolvotron™, Audiosphere™ are trademarks of Crystal River Engineering Incorporated.

RB2™, Swivel, Body Electric™, DataGlove™, EyePhone™ and FMT Optics™ are trademarks of VPL Research Inc.

Dexterous Hand Master™ is a trademark of Exos Incorporated (under licence from Arthur D. Little Inc.).

PowerGlove™ is a trademark of Mattel.

CyberGlove™, CyberCAD™, Virtual Hand™ and Gesture Glove™ are trademarks of Virtual Technologies.

Virtual Environment Operating Shell™ (VEOS) is a trademark of Geoffrey P. Coco Human Interface Technology Laboratory.

WorldToolKit™ is a trademark of Sense8 Corporation.

DXF™ is a trademark of Autocad.

MultiGen is a trademark of Software Systems.

Generic Visual System (GVS™) is a trademark of Gemini Technology Corporation.

Viewing Wand™ is a trademark of ISG.

Teletact™ is a trademark of Advanced Robotics Research Centre.

Headsight™ is a trademark of Philo Corporation.

LEEP™ Optical System is a trademark of LEEP Optics.

HP-UX and HP Turbo SRX™ are trademarks of Hewlett-Packard.

UNIX™ is a trademark of AT&T.

Macintosh™ is a trademark of Apple Computer Incorporated.

ESQ-M™ is a trademark of Ensoniq.

VocaLink™ is a trademark of IBM.

Super Cockpit™ is a trademark of US Air Force.

Vituality™ is a trademark of W Industries.

Plates

In Memoriam

The early part of my life was influenced by one man, Mr Reginald Sheldrake, a pharmacist and herbalist who lived in my home town of Newark upon Trent, Nottinghamshire. When I was a schoolboy he provided me with chemicals for home experiments, and we spent many hours together discussing our mutual interest of microscopy. In my youth, he and his wife took me on a trip to Cambridge University where their son Rupert was a researcher. This was my first visit to a university and it made me realize that if I were to fulfil all my ambitions I must set my sights on gaining a place at a university.

Mr Reginald Sheldrake moulded much of my inquisitive and enquiring mind. He showed me university life and guided me. He was my friend and mentor. I dedicate this book to his memory.

1   Virtual Environment Systems: An Introduction

Objectives

The main objective of this chapter is to give an overview of the concepts of virtual environment systems. A discussion of the types of technology that apply to this emerging field is presented and the major issues which complicate it are highlighted. (More detailed information about the enabling technologies and techniques is discussed in subsequent chapters.) In order to whet the reader's appetite, some potential applications of a virtual environment system are proposed. In common with following chapters, the final section of this chapter highlights the main points. It is important to show how the various elements link to form an integrated virtual environment system that serves man's desire to build the ultimate man–machine interface.

1.1 Introduction

Virtual reality, or virtual environment techniques, will change the way in which man interacts with computer systems.

The underlying ideas of virtual reality emerged almost twenty-five years ago when researchers began immersing human participants (operators) in visually coupled teleoperated environments. A teleoperated system is one that operates on an environment and is controlled by a human operator who is at a remote location from that environment. A visually coupled system implies that the observer wears some form of display device on his head, which is updated whenever the head is moved. Early visually coupled systems were based on a remote television camera system that could be panned and tilted in relation to the head of the operator. In these systems the orientation of the operator's head was sensed by a simple tracking device that supplied information to the pan and tilt mechanism of the television camera. To provide a closed loop between the operator's visual system and the television camera, the operator was required to wear a head-mounted display that presented imagery from the television camera. Teleoperated systems developed as a result of the need to interact with environments from a distance. Examples of such environments include space exploration and the handling of hazardous materials. Figure 1.1 illustrates the principle behind a visually coupled teleoperated camera system.

The operator conveys instructions via a communication link to a robot (teleoperator) that is typically equipped with an end effector. The operator obtains some form of visual feedback, either directly or remotely coupled, of the actions of the teleoperated robot.

The visually coupled system described above provides the operator with a remote view of the teleoperator's environment. This leads to a sense of telepresence. Sheridan (1992) defines telepresence as meaning that the 'human operator receives sufficient information about the teleoperator and the task environment, displayed in a sufficiently natural way, that the operator feels physically present at the remote site'. Closer examination of Sheridan's statement raises two questions: firstly, what is meant by 'receives sufficient information', and secondly, what is meant by 'displayed in a sufficiently natural way'?

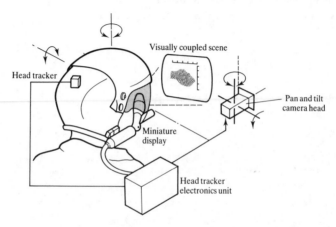

Figure 1.1 Principle behind visually coupled teleoperated camera system.

The visually coupled system is one in which the operator is immersed in a real environment. However, by sensing the position and orientation of the operator's head with a tiny sensor and coupling the resulting data into a high performance computer graphics system it is possible to generate a computer synthesized view of a virtual environment. This synthetic view can be seen by the operator in whichever direction they look.

Both teleoperation and virtual environment systems convey a level of personal presence within the synthetic or remote environment. Many people who have tried out such systems claim that they felt as though they were 'immersed' or 'present' in the virtual environment. Currently, there are no metrics that help to define the level or degree of presence conveyed by a virtual environment system. Of particular interest to the scientist is how this sense of presence relates to the sensorimotor and cognitive performance of the operator. The basic question is: does a sense of presence or immersion actually improve the performance of an operator? In order to develop telepresence or virtual environment systems it will be important to determine their effectiveness. It will also be necessary to link conveyors of presence with measures of human performance. Sheridan (1992) notes that 'presence is a subjective sensation, much like mental workload and mental model – it is a mental manifestation, not so amenable to objective physiological definition and measurement'.

Unfortunately, the general public's exposure to the idea of virtual reality or virtual environments has come when our fundamental understanding of the field is relatively immature. Furthermore, the demand for products embodying some form of virtual interface is accelerating at such a pace that our existing knowledge base has been outstripped. The original aim behind preparing this book was to provide a scientific and engineering reference basis for practitioners in the field of virtual environments. However, it is hoped that the book will fulfil the needs of other researchers, scientists, engineers and students, who consider applying this important interface or communication technique to their problem domain. The chapters on virtual environment systems describe the principles of operation of the enabling technologies and how they integrate together. The relationship between the hardware and software components of a virtual environment system are discussed. Later chapters highlight areas where the underlying technology must be developed. Related human factors and engineering issues are reviewed at length throughout the book.

Press and media speculations about virtual reality provided the platform for its worldwide exposure. However, these speculations were in danger of 'overclaiming' what could be delivered with existing technology. Moreover, the press coverage encouraged many laboratories throughout the world to rush ahead and invest in the enabling virtual environment technologies. Apart from giving the manufacturers of this technology a false sense of security, this also led to duplication of effort in the various research laboratories. Many manufacturing companies simply responded to market demands and produced a variety of products that enabled simple systems to be produced. The resulting concentrated effort devoted to turning research standard devices into products without any further development led to a slowing down in the optimization of these devices. In many instances virtual environment peripheral devices were being bought without any form of specification being agreed. Indeed, a situation developed where different manufacturers were employing ambiguous definitions regarding the performance of their products, which makes it very difficult to form a comparison between different products. Clearly, a more structured approach is required to develop the background research if we are to exploit this important technique.

1.2 What are virtual environments?

Virtual environments are synthetic sensory experiences that communicate physical and abstract components to a human operator or participant. The synthetic sensory experience is generated by a computer system that one day may present an interface to the human sensory systems that is indistinguishable from the real physical world. Until then we have to be content with a virtual environment that approximates several attributes of the real world. However, it is feasible to synthesize a suitable facsimile of a real environment or some form of abstract environment. Figure 1.2 conveys the concept behind a virtual environment system.

Human beings have evolved an auditory system which augments the visual system as well as providing a means of communication. Employing the auditory system in a virtual environment could increase situation awareness by supplementing visual information. Technology is available that allows sound to be electronically spatialized in three dimensions: this is not stereo sound that operates in a frontal plane, but is instead sound covering a full 360° sphere. This means that an operator in a virtual environment could be presented with a realistic sound environment. As with the visual system, the degree to which the auditory system needs to mimic the real world by emulating effects such as reverberation and absorption will depend on the task. The addition of a synthetic sound system further adds to the realism of the computer-synthesized world.

Using similar technology to that used for head tracking, it is possible to track the position of the operator's hands and feed this information into the graphics computer. This will then allow the observer to see an image of their hands in the virtual environment that corresponds to their actual hand position. Additional hardware could be used to determine the position and orientation of individual fingers. The combined hand tracker and finger tracking system is known as a virtual hand controller. Software can be written to perform collision detection and in this way allow the operator to interact with objects in the virtual environment: this interaction extends to manipulation of objects. Figure 1.3 shows the principle behind the operation of virtual controls and a virtual hand controller.

The user is presented with an image of a space stabilized virtual control panel with an image of their hand in the head-mounted display. As the hand is moved the virtual hand image also moves. Collision detection software in the graphics computer detects when the user's hand penetrates the virtual control volume. Therefore, the user can interact with virtual switches or objects to control events or manipulate objects. When we interact with objects in the real world we experience things such as resistance to movement, texture, mass, compressibility, and so on. In a virtual environment these attributes of the environment will not be experienced unless haptic (tactile) and force feedback systems are employed. For some applications a lack of tactile feedback can cause the operator difficulties and lead to a reduction in performance. However, it is possible to synthesize a sense of interaction by using both visual and auditory cues to augment the visual information. Figure 1.4 shows the link between the visual, haptic/kinaesthetic and auditory system.

Examples of typical auditory cues include a 'squelch' sound when an object is grasped, a rasping sound when an object is dropped and a click when a virtual switch is operated.

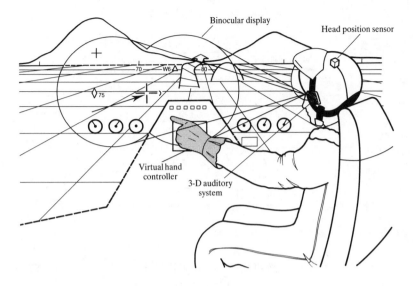

Figure 1.2 Underlying principle behind a virtual environment system.

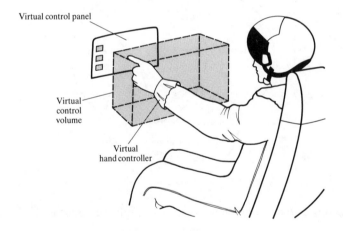

Figure 1.3 Principle behind a virtual hand controller.

Obviously not all interactions result in an auditory signal in the real world. Therefore, it will be necessary to develop a series of auditory metaphors to communicate the appropriate tactile or haptic action/reaction.

To deal with a complete virtual environment, it is sensible to partition the full environment into smaller separate but related environments. In this book the virtual environment has been partitioned into visual, auditory and haptic/kinaesthetic environments. Figure 1.5 shows the interrelationship between the different environments.

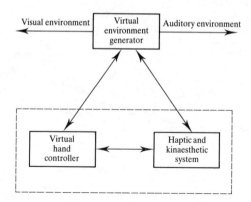

Figure 1.4 Possible link between the visual, haptic/kinaesthetic and auditory systems.

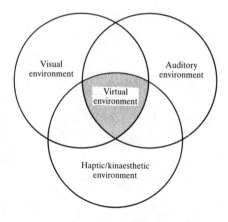

Figure 1.5 Interrelationships between a partitioned virtual environment.

The significance of the shaded region in Figure 1.5 is that it shows a fully interactive virtual environment embodying visual, auditory and haptic/kinaesthetic interactive component environments. However, a much smaller virtual environment system can be created by using subsets of the three component environments.

As mentioned above, it may ultimately be possible to generate a synthetic environment that is indistinguishable from the real world. Whether this level of realism is desirable, let alone achievable, will be discussed in the concluding chapter. However, there is potential for considering the application of lesser virtual environment systems to existing problems. Careful examination of any real-world situation reveals an extremely rich sensory environment for the human perception system. Even so, our perception system makes use of only a tiny part of the total information available: consider the extent of the electromagnetic spectrum and the very narrow region where our visual senses operate. Nevertheless, the human perceptual system is quite remarkable in the fineness, or resolution, of detail that it can resolve. The dynamic range of our sensitivity to external stimuli is indeed extraordinary. Perhaps even more remarkable is our ability to process internally information from our senses and couple this with existing knowledge of our world. In this way we can take incomplete information from several senses and integrate the data together to give a more accurate representation of the world. A key element of this internal data fusion processing is that our knowledge base is being constantly calibrated through various feedback processes. A noteworthy account of these processes is given by Ellis (1991). He reports that our knowledge is being updated by behavioral plasticity of visual–motor coordination and vestibular reflexes, and states, 'thus, a large part of our sense of physical reality is a consequence of internal processing rather than being something that is developed only from the immediate sensory information we receive'. This statement is quite significant in that it highlights the need to be aware not only of the information being presented to a human operator but also of the way in which it is internally processed by the human operator. It is very easy to overlook the latter aspect in a human–machine interface and then wonder why the resulting system is unusable or, at best, difficult to use. Equally, it is possible to deal with the human factors issues without considering the limitations of the technology employed in the interface. To do so results in an interface that cannot be engineered by even the very best technology solutions available today. What we must do is to take nature's approach and slowly evolve our understanding of the human–machine interface. This means taking cognizance of the developing technology, and direct its development in step with our understanding of human factors issues. Close coupling of the engineering with human factors will enable us to make appropriate compromise decisions.

1.3 Terminology in common usage

Virtual reality is perhaps an unfortunate term. The word 'virtual' is correct in the sense that we are dealing with virtual optical images but the word 'reality' is quite an all embracing claim. At most conferences on the subject someone attempts to define what they mean by virtual reality. There are probably as many definitions for virtual reality as there are people in the field! Sometimes this can lead to quite lengthy and heated debates. While it is not important what we call 'the subject', it is important that we understand the limitations of the technology we are dealing with. Personally, I prefer the description 'Virtual Environments' but I recognize that 'Virtual Reality' is a term that is here to stay because that is the description used by international press coverage. In a virtual environment the human is immersed in a computer simulation that imparts visual, auditory and force sensations. The computer simulation can present conventional real-world environments without modification or entirely new environments where different (or no) physical laws exist. The human operator is allowed to interact with components of the virtual environment through his/her responses being sensed appropriately and coupled into the virtual environment simulation. Irrespective of the linguistically self-contradictory nature of the term virtual reality, it is perhaps sensible to think of different classes of virtual environments. The subject can be further confused when we speak of immersive and non-immersive virtual environments.

Terms that have emerged over recent years include: visually coupled systems, artificial reality, cyberspace, virtual presence, telepresence, and desktop virtual reality.

However, this list is not exhaustive. New terms and descriptions are appearing all the time; for instance I recently came across the term 'quasi-virtual reality'. These terms have been defined in the glossary at the end of the book.

1.4 Classification of virtual environments

One way of dealing with the debate about virtual reality versus all the other terms is to try to classify or categorize what we mean. When faced with the debate I often say that virtual reality is the pinnacle of what we are ultimately trying to achieve. This presumes that we need a high fidelity, photorealistic environment for our application. Many applications will be more viable if we can offer a simpler environment with fewer ambiguities. When attempting to categorize a virtual system it is convenient to try to place the system into some form of hierarchy. We can immediately think of being immersed in a completely real world or in a virtual environment. The latter need not be restricted to phenomena that obey the laws of physics. There is also an intermediate subset where aspects of a virtual environment can be used with a real world; for example, the use of a see-through head-mounted display where virtual images are overlaid onto the real world.

In dealing with the real-world case we are viewing the world either directly or indirectly. Indirect viewing means that we are allowing the participant to view real-world objects via a relay system. This could be a television camera and associated television monitor. Interaction in an indirectly coupled real-world system could be achieved by teleoperated robots. The term teleoperation is often used in this context. The level of immersion or presence is governed by the manner in which the participant interacts with the indirectly coupled real world. If a large television display is used then the level of immersion will be low. However, if a head coupled or visually coupled system is used then the level of immersion will be much higher.

On the other hand, when the participant is dealing with a synthetically generated environment there are two ways of viewing the images. These are a non-immersive technique where a large display is used, and an immersive solution where a head-mounted display is used. It would be tempting to say that the immersive system offers a higher degree of virtual presence than the non-immersive system. However, to make a scientific judgement of the degree of immersion it is necessary to define what we mean by immersion or virtual presence. It is reasonable to assume that the level of presence depends on many factors, including field of view, display resolution, level of physical interaction, and so on. The level of task involvement will have a bearing on the sense of immersion. These issues are dealt with in more detail in Chapter 3. The point to note is that if we could define what we mean by virtual presence and actually specify how much immersion is required to undertake a specific task, then we would have a means of identifying what type of virtual environment or virtual reality system is required.

1.5 Are we dealing with a science?

I recall a telephone conversation I had with Dr Ivan Sutherland, where he challenged the title of this book and questioned whether the subject of virtual environments was indeed a science. Since then I have thought long and hard about his question.

Throughout the preparation of this book Dr Sutherland's question and other difficult problems have made me think very carefully about the subject. There is little doubt that the field of virtual environments has grown to include the creation, storage, and manipulation of models and images of virtual objects. These models are derived from a variety of scientific and engineering fields, and include physical, mathematical, engineering, architectural and abstract structures, and natural phenomena. Because of the need to develop new technologies that allow the human operator to become immersed and interact with virtual worlds, developers of these systems must be multidisciplinary in their approach. This means that they will have to cross into many scientific fields. Upon reflection I would probably answer Dr Sutherland's question by saying that the field of virtual environments is a multidisciplinary science that, to be effective, needs to take account of the engineering compromises.

1.6 System architecture overview

Figure 1.6 illustrates a generic immersive virtual man–machine interface, showing the basic components used to realize a virtual environment system.

1.6.1 Virtual environment generator

The virtual environment generator is probably best described as a large high performance computer system that contains a database of the required virtual world. This database contains a description of the objects in the virtual environment, together with descriptions for object motion, behaviour, effect of collision, and so on. The memory size required to contain even the simplest virtual environment must not be underestimated. Database compression techniques can be used to reduce this requirement, but care must be taken not to compromise access time to the database. Some very efficient data packing algorithms are inefficient for real-time operation. Therefore, a compromise has to be made of packing efficiency versus real-time access. A second role for the virtual environment generator is to generate and render the images for display. These images must be computed taking into account head position and orientation with the minimum of delay. Any communication delays inherent in the virtual environment generator will inevitably show up as visual lags. If these are perceptible, they can under certain conditions induce nausea. This means that it is not a simple matter of 'stringing together' a series of virtual environment peripherals. A careful analysis of component and system throughput delays must be undertaken if these inherent lags are to be kept to an acceptable value.

1.6.2 Auditory synthesis

The human being is remarkably good at dealing with several tasks at once. For instance, while the visual system is dealing with one task the auditory system can be operating in the background. The auditory system operates at a much lower bandwidth than the visual system. Nevertheless, the human auditory system is good at picking out a particular sound from many others. It seems sensible to incorporate synthetic audio cues and speech into the virtual man–machine interface.

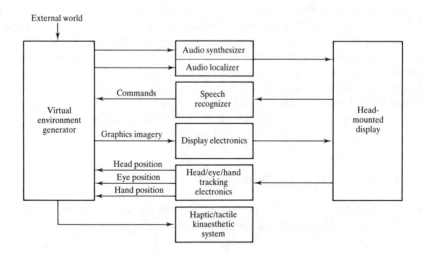

Figure 1.6 Immersive virtual man–machine interface.

1.6.3 3-D audio localization

An audio localization system takes either real or synthetic audio signals and applies specialized processing techniques to spatialize the signals in a 360° sphere. These spatialized cues can be made to appear space stabilized or moved around in accordance with an external motion signal. For instance, it is possible to generate a sound such as a ticking clock and place this in a precise position in the virtual environment. The sound appears to the listener to remain stationary even when he moves his head. To achieve this effect the audio localization system must consider the high frequency filtering of the listener's pinnae, the interaural comparison of the complex frequency spectra (amplitude and phase) between the signals received by the two ears, and a factor known as the head related transfer function (HRTF). Other factors associated with audio localization will be discussed in Chapter 3. For the purposes of this introductory chapter, it is sufficient to point out that the computation of transfer functions, to allow reliable audio localization, requires very sophisticated digital signal processing techniques and hardware. To provide accurate localization it is necessary to compute the specific HRTF because the human pinnae are different in every individual. For convenience many 3-D sound systems use a generalized HRTF. The orientation of the listener's head plays an important role in correctly spatializing audio signals. The virtual environment generator must supply head position and orientation signals to the audio localization equipment to enable localization to take place. Since the audio localizer considers the interaural phase it will be necessary to pass head position and orientation data with minimal delay, otherwise the effect will not work.

1.6.4 Speech recognizer

A speech recognizer has been shown on the virtual man–machine interface to indicate that other user modalities can be incorporated. Speech recognition can be effectively used for low mental workload situations where lengthy data input is required. Under extreme workloads it is known that human operators will temporarily shut down their auditory channels. This obviously affects the use of speech recognition.

1.6.5 Display electronics

The display electronics unit has been shown as a separate system because of the need to keep the weight of the head-mounted display as low as possible. Obviously this depends on the technology used for the display. For a cathode ray tube the weight of the associated electronics assembly can be quite considerable. As will be described later it is not always that easy to split the system down. For example, a cathode ray tube requires an extra-high voltage source. If this is not mounted on the head, then very high voltages must be supplied through an umbilical cable, which, in turn, requires thought on the safety aspects.

1.6.6 Head/eye/hand tracking electronics

In order to interact with the virtual environment it is necessary to sense where the operator is looking. This means that the position and orientation of the head must be tracked. More sophisticated virtual environment systems may even employ special sensors to determine where the observer's eyes are looking. To move objects around in the virtual environment or even to move the torso around, it is necessary to track the position of the observer's limbs. This can range from tracking the position of the hand through to a full body suit where the positions of all the limbs can be determined.

1.6.7 Haptic/kinaesthetic system

To improve the sense of immersion or presence in the virtual environment it may be necessary to provide some form of physical feedback to the operator. Without this feedback all that can be done is to change the appearance of an object or generate a sound to signal that an object has been touched. Haptic feedback means that the virtual environment system provides tactile cues about the object that has been touched such as surface texture or even an indication that a switch has been selected. It is difficult to separate haptic sensations from force reflective feedback because the two are inextricably linked. When we feel the surface texture of an object this is also coupled with a resistance to motion. There is no doubt that haptic/kinaesthetic feedback in a virtual environment system will be very difficult to achieve. When this is eventually mastered then the degree of virtual presence may improve dramatically. The human proprioception system relies on integrating the forces that our whole body experiences to maintain a mental model of our surroundings. At the moment the only way of producing this is to design some form of whole body exoskeleton. The use of force reflecting systems will change the way in which we write the software for the virtual environment system. If a force reflecting system is to synthesize representative forces, then these forces could be hazardous if applied incorrectly.

1.6.8 Head-mounted display

The role of the head-mounted display is to provide the means of seeing the virtual environment. This means that it has to support usually two display sources along with a set of optical elements. The optical elements project the image at some predetermined distance in front of the observer, and magnify the image so that it fills a wide field of view. However, the display source is limited in size because of weight considerations. The human visual perception system is very sensitive to misalignment errors between images presented to the left and right eyes. This means that whatever arrangement is used to hold display sources and optical elements, it must do so without introducing alignment errors. This aspect is discussed in Chapter 6. The head-mounted display also provides the means of locating the head position sensor so that the visuals can be referenced to the head line of sight. If an auditory system is used then this is attached to the head-mounted display. All this has to be achieved without increasing the weight of the assembly to a point where it becomes unbearable. The major design issues of the head-mounted display are discussed throughout this book.

A range of different technologies can be used to present an image on the head-mounted display. An appropriate choice is made after the potential application has been considered. For initial research, or for low cost applications, the liquid crystal display is the most popular solution.

1.7 Synthesis of virtual environments

The synthesis of a virtual environment is not just a question of defining a series of objects and their spatial relationships. Ellis (1991) suggests that it is necessary to consider the synthesis of a virtual environment as three parts: a content, a geometry and a dynamic relationship.

1.7.1 Content

Objects in the virtual environment are described by parameters that define position, orientation, velocity, acceleration, colour, texture and energy. These parameters are sometimes called state vectors. A special type of object can also exist, and is known as an 'actor' because it has the ability to interact with other objects in the environment. There is usually at least one unique actor in the system that provides the point of view from which the environment is constructed. At least one software development environment that is available uses the principle of objects and actors to build up a virtual environment. Another package uses the term 'camera' to specify the point of view camera. In a sense, these terms are just abstract names that allow us to define a virtual environment.

1.7.2 Geometry

Ellis (1991) defines an environmental field of action that comprises objects and actors, except when the actor represents a view point. However, this definition only seems valid for single point of view actor, that is a single participant in a virtual environment. The geometry has dimensionality, metrics and extent. Dimensionality refers to the number of independent descriptive terms needed to specify the position of every element of the environment. Metrics refers to the rules specifying the ordering of the contents. Extent refers to the range of values for the positions of every element in the environment. The environmental field of action can be defined in Cartesian coordinates though this is not always the best form for certain applications. Given starting conditions and dynamic relationships it is possible to compute an environmental trajectory of an object through the environmental frame of action.

1.7.3 Dynamics

The dynamics of a virtual environment define the interactivity between objects and actors. The usual outcome of a dynamic behaviour is an exchange of information or an exchange in energy. Dynamics include classical laws of motion and the way in which objects or actors behave upon collision.

Additional factors must also be considered, such as the architecture of the virtual environment system. A poorly developed set of hardware components will lead to many inefficiencies that could make the system unusable. Before even considering the synthesis of a virtual environment it is very important to understand the task requirements of the application.

1.8 Applications: An overview

It is difficult to predict exactly where the greatest benefits will occur and in which field, simply because there are so many potential applications for virtual environments. Possible application areas are likely to include those shown in Table 1.1.

Table 1.1 is not intended to be exhaustive but merely serves to illustrate the enormous possibilities. However, before racing ahead and trying to apply virtual environments to every problem domain, it is more prudent to analyse exactly what the problems are and where the benefits would come. It is tempting to jump onto the virtual reality band-wagon without first considering alternative, less expensive, solutions. This does not necessarily imply that benefits cannot be accrued from the introduction of virtual environment techniques – far from it. One clear recommendation is to undertake a careful task analysis of the application domain. When the question of level of presence is addressed this will provide firm indications of the type of technology that is appropriate. The applicability of virtual environments to the rapid prototyping field will be a key driver in its early introduction. The flexibility offered by the technology is second to none. Provided that appropriate tools and software environments are available at a reasonable cost then the move into a virtual environment prototyping system will be relatively easy.

Table 1.1 Possible application areas for virtual environment systems.

Application area	Description
Air traffic control	Improved situation awareness for air traffic controllers.
Architectural design	Design and visualization of buildings and impact on city layout. The technology can allow a virtual walk-through to be made.
Aircraft design	The paperless aircraft. The traditional drawing board could be replaced and the whole design process undertaken in an electronic form, from initial design through to rapid prototyping and system evaluation.
Acoustical evaluation	Soundproofing and room acoustics.
Computer aided design	Design of complex objects with a high degree of designer interaction.
Education	Virtual science laboratories. Cost-effective access to sophisticated laboratory environments. Virtual planetariums.
Entertainment	Wide range of immersive games such as those produced by W Industries.
Legal/police investigations	Re-enactment of accidents and crime.
Medical applications	Radiation therapy treatment planning. Medical training – virtual cadavers. Ultrasound imaging. Molecular docking – drug synthesis.
Scientific visualization	Aerodynamic simulation. Computational fluid dynamics. Planetary investigations.
Telepresence	Robot operation in hazardous environments.
Training/simulation	Flight simulation.
Virtual manufacturing environments	Ease of assembly and maintainability evaluations.

In many applications the associated benefits in cost and time-scale to market reductions will more than justify its use. The next stage that any intending user of the technology should go through is to establish the type of virtual environment that will satisfy their requirement. To some extent this process will narrow down the candidate technologies and help to identify any risk. I remain firmly convinced that virtual environments of all classes will find their way into our lives.

1.9 Advantages of virtual environment systems

Given the right level of development, virtual environments arguably provide the most natural means of communicating with a computer. They match the computer's representation of an environment with the 3-D spatial processing capability of the human being that has evolved over thousands of years.

Virtual environment display systems provide a wide field of regard visual/auditory portrayal medium that can present information to an operator wherever he/she looks. This means that it is no longer necessary to condense all the information onto a small display in front of the operator. Information can be taken to the operator's workplace and even overlaid onto the work area. Correct use of auditory displays can greatly enhance the operator's ability to deal with complex situations where considerable amounts of information have to be processed. For some tasks it is essential to employ the 3-D spatial processing capabilities of a human operator. Examples include vehicle training, where awareness of the objects surrounding the operator is very important. Some tasks would benefit from the provision of an immersive environment where cues from the outside world could affect the operator. Some virtual environment systems can present information where structural supports would prevent information being displayed. For example, with proper use of sensors and computer generated imagery it is feasible to give a tank commander an all-round view, compared to the current very restricted field of view. Most human operators communicate and control systems by voice- and hand-initiated activities. When we speak we often use gestures to reinforce what we are saying. With some manipulative tasks it is very difficult to design alternative input systems that replace the human hands. The resulting systems also tend to affect the operator's performance. Therefore, a virtual environment system can provide natural control interfaces. This issue is extremely important for operations in hazardous environments where it would be dangerous for personnel to work. The provision of effective control over a teleoperated robot in a manual dextrous task can involve some very complicated mechanisms. By using a virtual hand controller with proper haptic feedback the operator's task can become more straightforward.

At the moment the cost of the associated hardware to construct a virtual environment system is rather high compared to current 2-D display systems. However, the cost versus performance of modern computing systems is decreasing at a dramatic rate. It will only be a matter of a few years before today's very high performance graphics systems are available at a modest sum. Perhaps fortunately for the virtual environment field, the enabling technologies are also being driven by other consumer demands. For instance the high resolution displays that are so desperately needed for head-mounted displays are also required for a range of domestic consumer products. There is little doubt that the price of virtual environment systems will come down as the technology matures.

One key feature of a virtual environment system is that it is a software driven environment: the software defines its operation. Therefore, by loading in different database and software control structures it is possible to convert one virtual environment system into any other. This flexibility offers definite advantages to owners of such systems because they can be updated quickly and without incurring expensive hardware changes. They can also be modified to suit different roles or tasks. This latter feature is responsible for the wide range of applications for virtual environment systems.

1.10 Summary

This chapter has introduced the reader to some of the basic ideas behind the exciting field of virtual environments. It is now possible to begin to examine the underlying scientific and engineering principles and how they must be matched to the capabilities of the human operator.

A few key points are worth remembering from this chapter:

- Virtual environments are synthetic sensory experiences that communicate physical and abstract components to a human operator or participant.

- Ellis (1991) stresses that 'a large part of our sense of physical reality is a consequence of internal processing rather than being something that is developed only from the immediate sensory information we receive'.

- Virtual environments provide a wide field of regard visual/auditory portrayal medium.

- Virtual environments employ the 3-D spatial processing capabilities of a human operator.

- A virtual environment system can provide natural control interfaces.

- A virtual environment user can be remote.

- Virtual environment visual systems are unconstrained by structures.

- A system based on a virtual environment has the potential for low cost.

- Virtual environment systems are software reconfigurable.

- Virtual environments have a potentially wide range of applications.

Recommended further reading

Krueger M.W. (1991). *Artificial Reality* 2nd edn. Reading MA: Addison-Wesley

Rheingold H. (1991). *Virtual Reality.* London: Secker and Warburg

2 The History of Virtual Environment Systems

Objectives

The objective of this chapter is to highlight the history of virtual environment systems and some of the major milestones that have been achieved in this exciting field. The chapter provides a review of the variety of ideas that have evolved over a period of forty years. Examples are illustrated by a series of tables showing specification and performance information for the early generation systems. The future user of virtual environment systems should be reassured that this is not a totally unknown field. As the bibliography at the back of the book will confirm, there is a wealth of relevant scientific/engineering material available.

2.1 Introduction

This chapter highlights a few of the most significant developments or milestones in the field of virtual reality or virtual environments. Readers who wish to learn about the history behind virtual reality are referred to Rheingold (1991), which is a journalistic account of some of the historical aspects of virtual reality and the people in the field, without any technical detail. In this book the author deals with the scientific and technical aspects of virtual reality and virtual environments. He cannot mention all major accomplishments or all the scientists and researchers involved in this exciting field. However, he does recognize the contribution other scientists and researchers have made.

Virtual reality is a recent description for a technology that had for many years been known as visually coupled systems. The roots of visually coupled systems can be traced back to the aerospace and defence industries. Two different requirements led to the development of head tracking systems and helmet-mounted displays, which form the basis of today's virtual environment technologies. Aerospace products demand some form of cost-effective training in a safe environment. This led to the development of the familiar flight simulator which is a subtle integration of virtual and real-world systems. Flight simulator developments tended to drive the development of high speed, high resolution computer graphic systems for projection onto large simulator domes. The other aerospace requirement that led to visually coupled system development arose out of the need to take the information presented on a head up display (HUD) to wherever the pilot was looking. The HUD is an example of a virtual display that presents computer generated information. This information is overlaid onto the real world in a fixed position, relative to the centre line of the aircraft, known as the longitudinal fuselage datum. Figure 2.1 shows the schematic diagram for a refractive optics HUD.

In the HUD the image is usually generated by a high brightness cathode ray tube (CRT). It is relayed via a small front silvered mirror (to avoid double reflections) through a relay lens system to a large collimating lens, which produces the virtual image via the glass plate combiner. The combiner acts to overlay the virtual image onto the real world. The pilot views the combined image by looking through the combiner plate from a precisely defined position known as the design eye position or entrance pupil. If the eye is positioned outside this region, the virtual image cannot be seen. The HUD's combiner plate and collimating lens dimensions are governed by how far away the HUD is from the pilot. Obviously, this is for safety reasons. The HUD must be positioned outside the ejection line of the pilot. The total field of view of the HUD is determined by the distance from the pilot's eyes, which in turn determines the size of the combiner plate and the diameter of the collimating lens.

As CRTs became smaller the aerospace industry developed versions of the HUD that were head-mounted. These are now known as helmet-mounted displays. Initially these were simple affairs based on low resolution CRTs and had the disadvantages of being rather heavy and unsuitable in the event of emergency ejection.

Space tracking systems were also being developed that could measure the position and orientation of the pilot's helmet line of sight. The early space tracker systems were integrated with the helmet-mounted display to produce what was known as a visually coupled system, the forerunner to what is now known as virtual reality.

Visually coupled systems were seen as the next generation of simulation system, with applications as off-boresight weapon aiming aids and steerable night vision aids.

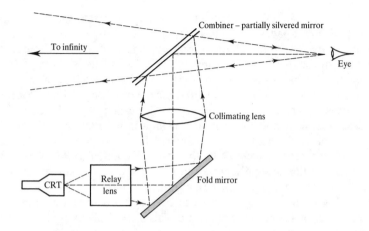

Figure 2.1 Conventional refractive optics head up display.

Unfortunately, the technology has been slow to mature because of the problems posed by various safety and biomedical issues. Today, the only helmet-mounted display that is being produced in reasonable production quantities is Honeywell's Integrated Helmet and Display Sighting System (IHADSS) fitted to the Apache AH64 helicopter. However, research continues to be conducted at a great rate into the next generation of visually coupled systems, the developing technologies being considerably superior to the modest virtual environment technologies available in the commercial sector. Depending on one's definition, it is possible to trace the development of virtual displays even further back. Physics text books define a virtual image as one that cannot be formed on a screen because the rays that make the image are diverging and do not come to focus at any point. Virtual images are formed by mirrors, lenses and other optical systems.

Most optical systems generate a virtual image of some description. The principles behind the generation of a virtual image from a real image, whether it is based on a computer image or an optical image, are generally well understood. Difficulty arises when high resolutions or very wide fields of view are required. These requirements demand specialist knowledge in optical design.

2.2 Sensorama: Multisensory artificial experience machine (1956)

In 1956 Morton Heilig developed a simulator called Sensorama, which provided the user with a unique combination of 3-D visuals, stereo sound, vibration, wind sensations and city smells. The user sat on a seat and underwent a simulated motor cycle ride through Manhattan. Not only were the visuals compelling, the sounds realistic and the vibration effects convincing, the introduction of smells such as exhaust fumes and food smells added to the realism. Unfortunately, Sensorama was not a commercial success. A photograph of Sensorama appears in Krueger (1992).

2.3 Philco Corporation's Headsight television surveillance system (1961)

Many people believe that Ivan Sutherland produced the first visually coupled system way back in 1968, but a paper by Comeau and Bryan (1961) describes an even earlier system developed by the Philco Corporation, consisting of a closed circuit television surveillance system used with a helmet-mounted display. (This is not the first reference to a helmet-mounted display, see Stanton, 1956.) A miniature CRT was mounted on the helmet with lightweight optics. A half silvered mirror was used, with a spherical mirror producing a virtual image in front of the user. The wearer's head was sensed with a magnetic tracking system and the resulting data was used to control the directional positioning of a remote vidicon television camera. The angle of view of the camera was adjusted to match the angle subtended by the image presented to the user. Comeau and Bryan explained that this system gave a sense of presence in the environment of the remote camera. The system was called Headsight.

The head position sensing system was based on a pair of coils mounted rigidly on the helmet. A set of Helmholtz coils were placed in a cube around the helmet. The coils mounted on the head detected the orientation by sensing the phase of three magnetic fields rotating in azimuth, elevation and roll directions. Precise details are given in Comeau (1961).

The Headsight system allowed an observer to view dangerous operations from a safe remote location. Applications were suggested for ocean or space exploration, radioactive areas and military surveillance. Comeau even suggested that the effective resolution of the Headsight system could be improved by matching the resolution of the system to that of the human eye. In other words, the resolution of the CRT should be made higher at the centre (in the fovea of the eye) and lower at the edge. Table 2.1 shows the quoted specifications of the Headsight system.

Table 2.1 Specifications of the Philco Corporation helmet-mounted display.

Display source	CRT
Mode	Monocular
Field of view	Not specified
Display size	1" × 1¼"
Resolution	525 line
Image distance	1' 6"
Image type	Raster display
Weight	Claimed 2 lb (?)

2.4 Ivan Sutherland's Ultimate Display (1965)

In 1965 Ivan Sutherland suggested that a display could be built that would ultimately provide computer generated images so realistic that they would be indistinguishable from the real thing. In 1968 at Harvard University he produced the first computer graphic driven helmet-mounted display. He based his design around two small CRTs mounted on a head band (see Figure 2.2). Sutherland's system was unique in that it also incorporated a head position sensing system.

Table 2.2 Characteristics of Ivan Sutherland's helmet-mounted display.

Display source	CRT
Mode	Binocular 100% overlap
Field of view	40°
Display size	1/2" square
Display resolution	6/10 mm spot size
Operating mode	See-through half silvered mirrors
Adjustments	Eye separation
Image distance	18"
Image type	Cursive display

The complete helmet-mounted display system allowed a user to see 'wire-frame' three-dimensional objects that could be overlaid onto the real world. The wire-frame objects could be fixed to positions in the room or moved with the user's head. Considering the level of technology available during the late 1960s, Sutherland's feat was quite impressive. The characteristics of Sutherland's helmet-mounted display are given in Table 2.2.

2.4.1 Sutherland's head position sensing system

Sutherland used two approaches to determine the position and orientation of the head. To generate images consistent with the orientation of the user's head it was necessary to determine head translation in x, y, z coordinates and head rotation in azimuth, elevation and roll. The characteristics of Sutherland's mechanical tracking system are given in Table 2.3.

Sutherland's first head position sensor was based on a mechanical arm consisting of two universal joints and a sliding joint. Digital shaft position encoders were used to determine the head position and orientation to six degrees of freedom. Despite being carefully balanced and supported the complete assembly was very heavy. Features of the mechanical head position sensor are given in Table 2.3.

Table 2.3 Characteristics of Ivan Sutherland's mechanical head tracking system.

Sutherlands's head position tracker	Specification parameter
Translation range	1.8288 m (6') diameter × 0.914 m (3') high
Translation accuracy	2.54 mm (0.1")
Angular range	± 180° azimuth, ± 40° elevation, roll not specified
Angular accuracy	1:10,000 of rotation
Phase lag	Not specified but assumed to be zero

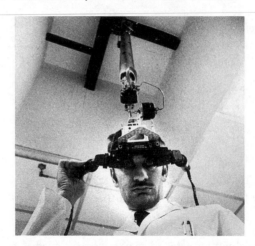

Figure 2.2 Ivan Sutherland's head-mounted display.

Sutherland's second head position sensor employed a Seitz–Pezaris continuous wave (phase coherent) ultrasonic position tracker. Three ultrasonic transmitters were fitted onto the head and emitted three unique frequencies, 37.0, 38.6 and 40.2 kHz. Four ultrasonic receivers were fitted into the ceiling above the user's head and the phase changes in ultrasound transmitted over the twelve paths were measured. By feeding the resultant data into a computer it was possible to calculate head position and orientation. The system could track changes within one wavelength to approximately 0.3 inch, but there was an ambiguity about which wave number the data represented. Sutherland called this 'initialization error'. Sutherland, Seitz and Pezaris attempted to solve the ambiguity by using redundant data. In 1968 Sutherland reported that his team had achieved promising results but had not finished their experiments. Unfortunately, no performance figures have been quoted for Sutherland's ultrasonic system. Figure 2.2 shows the ultrasonic head position system. It has been reported that the system worked well for several minutes until cumulative errors became objectionable. Phase lag response would have been rather high owing to the slow computer systems then available.

2.5 Haptic display augmentation for scientific visualization (1967)

Few people deserve more credit than Fred Brooks of the University of North Carolina for pioneering some key aspects of virtual environment systems. Brooks, who directed the IBM team that designed the operating system for the IBM 360 series of computers, had a unique insight into what was required to lead a pioneering virtual environment research team.

In 1967 the University of North Carolina began a project to investigate a haptic/kinaesthetic display system that could present the 6-D force field of a molecular structure. The research programme was partitioned into four phases: 2-D system, 3-D system, 6-D system and finally a 6-D system with full molecular docking. The project, known as Grope, led to three development systems.

The Grope I system allowed simple force fields to be examined by moving a probe particle and seeing and feeling the force on the probe. Grope II allowed a user to manipulate children's building blocks on the surface of a virtual table. Early results indicated that the haptic display seemed to improve the performance and perception of simple motor tasks. The force cue appeared to be better than a stereoscopic display. The more recent Grope III system was based on Model E-3 Argonne Remote Manipulators (ARMs) and employed a full 6-D system. Grope IIIA allowed the user to find minimum energy positions of a virtual arm that was suspended in space by six virtual springs. This experiment was less than satisfactory since the ARM would find its own position of minimum energy level.

A display combining visual, haptic and kinaesthetic aspects of a computer model of a molecular structure helps a scientist to understand its behaviour and function. Plate 1 shows graduate student Ming Ouh-Young using a force-displaying remote manipulator to dock a virtual drug molecule in the receptor site of a protein enzyme. Both the visual display and the force and torque vectors are updated in real time, enabling the user to test for favourable binding. This project is supported by the National Center for Research Resources of the National Institutes of Health, USA.

Real breakthroughs came when Grope IIIA was modified to the Grope IIIB standard. This system allowed a user to dock four drugs into an active site of a protein molecule. Apparently users were unaware of the haptic forces until the force feedback system was switched off. There is little doubt that haptic displays enhance the performance and understanding of the human operator. Little work has been undertaken with haptic display systems, despite their obvious importance in manipulative tasks. While this may be attributed to the rather complex electromechanical structures, the gains demonstrated by researchers at the University of North Carolina must not be overlooked.

2.6 Knowlton's virtual push button system (1975)

During 1975 a very interesting virtual display system appeared in the press. Knowlton (1977) proposed a new type of computer console consisting of an array of unlabelled black push-buttons. A semi-transparent mirror was placed above the keyboard so that information from a television monitor could be overlaid onto the push-buttons. In this way computer generated (virtual) legends could be placed on top of the push-buttons.

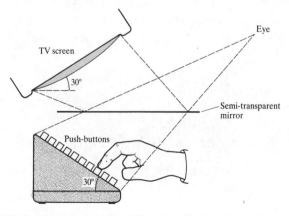

Figure 2.3 Basic arrangement of Knowlton's virtual push-button system.

The keyboard could be 'programmed' to be, for example, a typewriter keyboard, or a telephone operator's console. The individual push-buttons could be labelled, made invisible or even reprogrammed under computer control. The user had the feel of a conventional keyboard. Figure 2.3 shows the basic arrangement of Knowlton's virtual keyboard. The virtual push-button idea offers a few pointers to today's designers of virtual environment systems. One technological limitation of existing virtual environments is the lack of tactile feedback. Apart from the physiological problems that have to be overcome no really effective solution has emerged. Perhaps Knowlton's approach of using a real keyboard under the virtual image is an interim solution until we can achieve tactile feedback in a virtual environment.

2.7 LEEP Optical System (1975)

A company called LEEP Systems Inc. (formerly known as Pop-Optix Labs) was founded by Eric Howlett to develop wide angle lenses for 3-D still photography applications. Howlett admitted that during the early years he was 'turned off' by computers, seeing them as no more than automated accounting and bookkeeping devices. However, the ray tracing calculations involved in designing his lenses became too complex and manual calculations proved to be too time consuming. Howlett decided to use early programmable calculators and microcomputers to model his designs for 3-D lens systems. Eventually, in 1979 Howlett designed the Large Expanse, Extra Perspective (LEEP) optical system. In 1985 he was approached by the NASA Ames Research Center and contracted to supply a set of lenses for NASA's first virtual environment system. The standard LEEP optical system is shown in Figure 2.4. The initial LEEP optical system was designed so that photographs taken by special 3-D cameras could be viewed. The combined system gave a very wide field of view stereoscopic image. The LEEP optical system and 3-D cameras were intended to be used as a pair because the distortion introduced by the camera is compensated for by the lens design of the viewer. Ideally, anyone using the LEEP optical system for other applications should predistort their images before display. Figure 2.5 shows the extent of the image produced by the LEEP optical system. Anyone who has viewed one of Howlett's colour slides through the LEEP optical system would have been extremely impressed by the sensation of depth in the scene and the corresponding realism.

LEEP optical systems are now used in almost every virtual environment headset manufactured in the world today. Further details are given in Chapters 4 and 6.

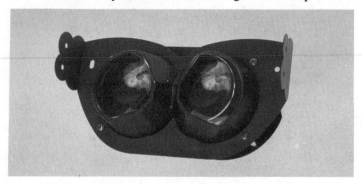

Figure 2.4 Standard LEEP optical system.

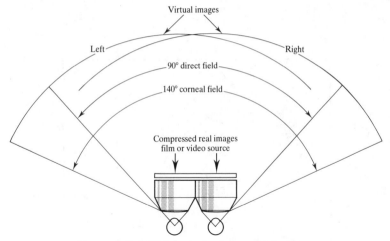

Figure 2.5 LEEP optical system: field of view.

2.8 Birth of the DataGlove (1981–1982)

Many people think that the VPL DataGlove was the first glove-like device to be made, but an earlier bend-sensing glove called the Sayre Glove was invented by Dan Sandin, Richard Sayre and Thomas Defanti at the University of Illinois, Chicago in 1977, under a grant from the National Endowment for the Arts (DeFanti and Sandin, 1977).

In 1982 Thomas Zimmerman patented an optical flex sensing glove (US Patent no. 4,542,291). Early generation exoskeleton devices were too clumsy for Zimmerman so he developed a system based on hollow plastic tubes that could conduct light. The plastic tubes were attached to a glove, then attached to a light source and light sensor. As the hands were flexed it was possible to measure the change in light level and relate this to actual finger position. Alternative devices for measuring finger flexion were developed by other researchers, such as the one made by Gary Grimes of Bell Laboratories (Grimes, 1983). According to Rheingold (1991), while Zimmerman was waiting for the patent to be granted he went to work at Atari's Sunnyvale Research Laboratory, USA. There he met Jaron Lanier and Scott Fisher. As a result, Zimmerman became one of the founders of VPL Research Inc. and assigned the glove patent to the new company. Jaron Lanier suggested mounting a space tracking system on to the glove to give hand orientation and position as well as finger flexure. Charles Blanchard, Young Harvill and Steven Bryson worked with Zimmerman and Lanier to develop the software behind the DataGlove. Interestingly, Harvill and Blanchard's software evolved into VPL's RB2 Swivel and Body Electric, described in Chapter 5. However, it was not until 1987 when *Scientific American* featured the DataGlove that the world became very excited by 'Virtual Reality'.

2.9 Krueger's Videoplace (1983)

A visionary figure, Myron Krueger spent years working on artistic expression in human–computer interaction. He took the view that immersive helmet-mounted displays were not the only means of entering computer generated artificial worlds.

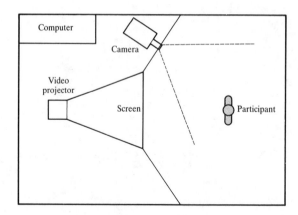

Figure 2.6 Krueger's Videoplace.

In his book *Artificial Reality*, Krueger (1983) describes the work he undertook on mixing computer graphics and gesture/position sensing technologies. By the mid 1970s he had established a full-blown artificial laboratory called Videoplace at the University of Connecticut, USA (see Figure 2.6)

An extension to the Videoplace idea resulted in the creation of a desktop version called Videodesk where the user sits at a desk and places their hands on it. A television camera captures a silhouette image of the user's hands and relays this to another participant, who is sitting at a similar desk, some distance away. The participants are able to communicate with each other using natural hand gestures. A computer system extracts gestures from the silhouette images and uses them to provide control over the computer graphics presented to the user. In this way it is possible to paint, draw and even make menu selections by hand position.

Whether or not Krueger's idea of Videoplace or its derivatives will find a place in society remains to be seen. He himself is only too aware of the restrictions of some of today's technology, but many of the provocative ideas presented in his second book (Krueger, 1991) will find a place in the field of virtual environments in the future.

2.10 MIT Media Laboratory animation research (1984 onwards)

Long before virtual reality, as we now know it, emerged, many researchers and in particular those at the Massachusetts Institute of Technology (MIT) Media Laboratory had as their goal realistic animation in real time. David Zeltzer, formally of Ohio State University, designed and programmed a computer synthesized skeleton, named George, for his PhD. Zeltzer had achieved a sense of realism in his animation that mimicked the real world. He realized that the key to realistic animation was to encapsulate within the computer graphics system certain behaviourial issues such as knowledge, ranges of movement and how joints relate to other joints. He then related these low level issues into higher level behaviour, such as a stance phase or a swing phase in a walking motion. While Zeltzer's work is legendary in the animation field, the full potential of his work in the virtual environment field has still to be realized. Perhaps one reason why current virtual environment systems have an unnatural feel about them, despite some very powerful graphic systems, is the unnatural movement or behaviour of the virtual objects. It might be that virtual world object motion behaviour is a more powerful and convincing visual cue than high definition textures. Zeltzer's more recent work considers the environment and terrain of the computer world. He has developed a conceptual tool for dealing with classification of virtual environments, which is described in Chapter 3. He, like Ellis (1991), points out that virtual environments need content, geometry and dynamics. Consequently Zeltzer's animated creatures move within the computer generated world in a realistic manner.

2.11 NASA Ames Research Center helmet-mounted display (1984)

In 1984 at the NASA Ames Research Center McGreevy and Humphries built the first non-see-through helmet-mounted display (known as the Virtual Visual Environment Display) from monochrome LCD pocket television displays (see Plate 2 and Table 2.4).

The key to the success of this display was the use of wide angle stereoscopic optics produced by Howlett of LEEP Systems. This research led to the establishment of a Virtual Interface Environment Workstation (VIEW) for use as a multipurpose interface environment (McGreevy *et al.*, 1990). The workstation provided a multisensory, interactive display environment in which the user could virtually explore a 360° synthesized or remotely sensed environment and interact with its components. The virtual display consisted of 3-D stereoscopic visuals as well as an auditory simulation. The user could interact with the virtual environment by glove–like devices – the forerunners to the DataGlove (see Plate 3).

2.12 NASA Ames Research Center Virtual Interactive Environment Workstation (1985)

The Virtual Interactive Environment Workstation (VIEW) project developed a general purpose, multisensory, personal simulator and telepresence system. The initial operating configuration included head and hand tracking by a Polhemus Space Tracking System, wide field of view stereo head-mounted displays by LEEP optics and monochrome LCDs, 3-D audio output by Crystal River's Convolvotron, gesture recognition by a VPL DataGlove, a BOOM-mounted CRT display by Sterling Software, and a remote camera platform produced by Fake Space.

The VIEW project was led by Scott Fisher. Some of the hardware development, and almost all the software development and systems integration were undertaken by Sterling Software, a contractor to NASA Ames. Some of the initial scenarios developed for VIEW were the teleoperation of a (virtual) Puma robot arm, an astronaut extravehicular (EVA) scenario, and fluid flow visualization. The VIEW laboratory's direction was to focus on a few specific research issues. One project connected the VIEW environment to a real Puma arm to study the effect of improved force–torque displays on teleoperations. Another project, perhaps the most interesting to virtual environment enthusiasts, was a joint study between the VIEW laboratory and the Computational Fluid Dynamics Group at NASA Ames. The project studied human interaction with various virtual control devices.

Table 2.4 Reported characteristics of the NASA Ames VIEW display system.

Display source	LCD monochrome
Mode	Binocular
Field of view	120°
Display size	3.2" diagonal
Aspect ratio	4:3
Display resolution	320 × 220
Operating mode	Non-see-through
Adjustments	Eye separation
Mode	Binocular up to 90° overlap
Optics	LEEP

A third project simply used the VIEW environment as a simulator to study the amount of fuel that would be used by a 'lost' astronaut trying to propel himself back to the space station.

The host computer for VIEW was based on a Hewlett–Packard HP 9000/835 while graphics processing was undertaken by an ISG Technologies graphics computer or the HP SRX graphics system.

Most of NASA Ames work in virtual environments is currently under an 'umbrella group' called Advanced Displays and Spatial Perception Laboratory, headed by Stephen Ellis. Two other laboratories within this group are the Spatial Audio Display Laboratory and the Virtual Planetary Exploration Laboratory. The latter, run by Mike McGreevy, is investigating ways to help planetary geologists remotely analyse the surface of a planet, by applying virtual environment techniques to 'explore' planetary terrains in virtual terms using height field data derived from Viking images of Mars. A typical scene will contain tens of thousands of polygons. Their host computer is a Stardent GS2000, and they are using VPL EyePhones.

The Spatial Audio Display Laboratory, run by Beth Wenzel, is developing digital signal-processing techniques and the technology platform required for three-dimensional auditory displays. The work is based on psychoacoustic principles of auditory localization and there is ongoing supporting research aimed at perceptually validating and improving the display. The real-time hardware, called the Convolvotron, was developed by Scott Foster of Crystal River Engineering with F.L. Wightman and D.J. Kistler (Wightman and Kistler, 1989).

2.12.1 NASA Ames VIEW software overview

This section is an overview of the NASA Ames VIEW software development environment. The VIEW system is a set of computer controlled I/O subsystems. The purpose of the system is to place a user in an artificial, or virtual environment. It is a graphics system that presents predefined, solid shaded objects around the user. It has an audio system that presents synthesized speech, and modulated or constant tones that can be located in space. The orientation and position of the user's head is tracked and is used to control the viewpoint of the graphics system. The user's hand position is tracked and may be used by the system. The positions of the user's fingers are also tracked and can be used to control the computer through gestures. The user can also give voice commands to the system.

Overview of hardware and subsystems

Figure 2.7 shows the architecture of the VIEW hardware. This figure has been derived from various sources and may not be completely correct. The virtual environment hardware consists of a host computer and I/O subsystems. The host computer is based on an HP 9000/835 that runs HP-UX, Hewlett–Packard's version of UNIX. The HP 9000/835 communicates with the subsystems in several ways – through a backplane, parallel communication card, and through an RS232 serial interface. The serial communication can be done in two ways, either though a multiplexer (MUX) card or through a real-time interface (RTI) card.

Graphics systems

There are two graphics systems in the VIEW environment. They are an ISG Technology graphics system (ISG) and an HP Turbo SRX graphics system (SRX). The ISG is a stand-alone Motorola 68020 based computer running UNIX, which has two drawing channels (one for each eye). Each channel has a drawing engine (DEU consisting of 16 TI 320c25s), a display processor (DPU bit-slice processor) and a frame buffer. The frame buffer in use is 640 × 480. There is a 1K × 1K mode that has not been used. The HP 9000/835 and the ISG communicate over a parallel channel (AFI on HP 9000/835, DR-11W on the ISG). There are two SRXs on the HP 9000/835 bus, one for each eye. The SRX frame buffers are 1280 × 1024. The ISG graphics are faster, but lower resolution. The SRX graphics are higher resolution, but slower.

I/O device communication

All other I/O devices communicate with the HP 9000/835 in a serial manner. Both the MUX cards and the RTI cards sit on the HP backplane. The standard MUX interface is probably the easiest to code. However the HP's MUX card is not designed as a real-time interface. The ports are polled and this limits a scene's frame rate to about 11 Hz. The two RTI cards perform as if they were attached co-processors. They are based on an Intel 80c186 with 512 Kbytes of memory and run PSOS. Each RTI has eight serial ports with which to communicate with I/O devices. Programs are downloaded from the HP 9000/835 to the RTI, one for each device with which to communicate, and a main program to gather the device data and send it to the HP 9000/835.

Trackers

There are three different six degree of freedom tracking devices: a Polhemus tracker with a source and two sensors, an Ascension tracker with a source and three sensors, and a BOOM. The Polhemus tracker operates at 18 Hz and is fairly accurate up to 4 feet from its source with two sensors. The Ascension tracker operates at 30 Hz and is fairly accurate up to 6 feet from its source with three sensors. They are connected to an RTI card and used for tracking head and hand glove movement. The BOOM is used to support and track the movement of the BOOM-mounted viewer. There are six potentiometers on the BOOM. The potentiometer's analogue values are converted to digital values on an IBM AT computer and sent to the host computer (HP9000) which computes the position and orientation of the viewer relative to the BOOM base.

Gloves

There are three VPL glove devices, a Macintosh with glove software, and two stand-alone glove boxes. All three are connected to an RTI card. The amount of finger joint flexion is returned to the HP 9000/835 where the gesture software determines which of the eleven gestures is being made.

Audio systems

The audio system consists of two MIDI driven Ensoniq (ESQ-M) synthesizers, a Hinton box (RS232 to MIDI converter), a Dectalk speech synthesizer, a Convolvotron, headphone and headphone amp, speakers and speaker amp and an audio mixer/patch bay. Audio output is either audio cues (discrete or continuous tones) or speech strings. The output is played through room speakers and/or headphones. Audio cues can be convolved (located in 3-D space) or unconvolved. Unconvolved cues are routed to the second synthesizer and then to the mixer. Convolved cues are routed to the first synthesizer and then to the Convolvotron. The Convolvotron output should be routed to the mixer, but because of a Convolvotron/mixer signal matching problem, the Convolvotron is now patched around the mixer and goes directly to the headphones. The system can play eight unconvolved cues and two independently convolved cues at once.

Speech recognition

Speech recognition input is performed by a VocaLink speech recognizer. It is connected to an IBM PC, which is connected to a MUX port. The IBM is needed because it runs some VocaLink supplied software. The VocaLink can understand connected speech, but in a discrete time mode.

Viewing stations

There are two viewing stations for the virtual environment. These are the helmet and the BOOM-mounted viewer. The helmet viewer consists of two back-lit, monochrome LCDs with 320 × 220 resolution and diamond shaped pixels. Tracking the position and orientation of the head is done with a magnetic tracker. The helmet also has earphones for audio output, and microphone for speech input. The BOOM-mounted viewer consists of two black and white CRTs with 400 × 400 resolution. Tracking is done with the BOOM output.

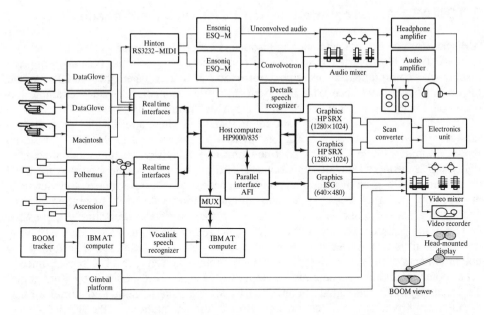

Figure 2.7   Schematic diagram of the NASA Ames VIEW system.

Viewer electronics

The output of the SRX graphics system is an RGB video signal that is passed through a scan converter where it is converted to the NTSC standard. The output of the ISG already conforms to the NTSC standard. The NTSC signal is sent to an electronics unit where it is conditioned for the viewer. For example, the sync signal is changed and the image positioned. The final signal is sent from the electronics unit to the viewer.

Gimbal platform

The gimbal platform is a remotely operated three degree of freedom pointing device. It has two video cameras mounted on the gimbal for stereo video input into the VIEW environment. The gimbal is connected to an IBM AT, which sends orientation data from the BOOM to the gimbal to control where the cameras are looking. The Polhemus tracker can also be switched to the AT so that the helmet's orientation can be made to control the orientation of the gimbal.

Video editing workstation

Output from both the audio mixer and the viewer electronic units are routed in parallel to the user viewer, earphones, and speakers and to the video editing and mixing workstation. Routing to the workstation allows video recording of the research and demonstrations.

2.13 NASA Ames counterbalanced CRT-based stereoscopic viewer

A display for virtual environment applications is generally assumed to be of the helmet-mounted type. However, it is possible to construct a head coupled (visually coupled) display that communicates the same information to a user when the head is moved. Several displays have been built that perform in this manner. One such example has been constructed by the team at NASA Ames (McDowall *et al.*, 1990).

The NASA Ames display is a counterbalanced kinematic linkage, stereoscopic viewer with wide angle optics and a joint measuring system (see Table 2.5). The stereo viewer comprises two CRT based (monochrome) television displays mounted in a lightweight housing with wide angle optics (LEEP). The stereoscopic viewer is mounted on a limited six degree of freedom counterbalanced arm. The user places the viewer to his eyes by means of a pair of handles mounted either side of it. Operating is very similar to a pair of binoculars. To explore a virtual world the user simply moves the viewer in the desired direction. CRTs have been used primarily to overcome the limiting resolution of LCD systems. Viewer position and orientation is determined by potentiometers mounted on the joints of the counterbalanced arm. The potentiometers act as potential dividers, generating an output voltage that corresponds to the joint angle. The resulting analogue signal is converted by an analogue to digital converter so that it can be read by a small microcomputer. Recent implementations of the BOOM system use optical shaft encoders to measure limb joint angle.

2.13.1 Advantages of the counterbalanced CRT-based stereoscopic viewer

The counterbalanced CRT-based stereoscopic viewer now allows fairly high resolution virtual imagery to be presented to a user, although it is limited to the monochrome mode. There is no reason why colour CRTs could not be used although the spatial resolution of such displays may be limited. Improvements in technology will eventually overcome these limitations.

However, one definite advantage lies in the ability of a user to sit at a normal place of work and quickly move a counterbalanced CRT-based stereoscopic viewer display into operation. The user can transfer very quickly between a real environment and a virtual environment (see Figure 2.8).

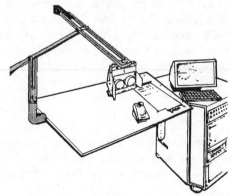

Figure 2.8 NASA Ames counterbalanced CRT-based stereoscopic viewer.

Table 2.5 Reported characteristics of the NASA Ames counterbalanced CRT-based stereoscopic viewer.

Display source	CRT
Mode	Binocular
Field of view	120° per eye
Aspect ratio	4:3
Display resolution	400 lines
Operating mode	Non-see-through
Adjustments	IPD – electronic shift
Mode	Binocular up to 90° overlap
Image type	Monochrome display
Video standard	NTSC
Optics	LEEP

2.14 USAF Super Cockpit (1985)

A revolutionary concept called a virtual crew station was proposed by Furness (1986) of the Armstrong Medical Research Laboratory at Wright Patterson Air Force Base (WPAFB). Furness reported that the US Air Force (USAF) had been conducting intensive research to identify future technologies that would meet the operational needs for the next twenty to thirty years. One of these technologies was the Super Cockpit concept. Concern had been expressed by aerospace scientists that the workload of the future pilot would reach the stage where it would be unmanageable. This led to a crew station concept that would exploit the full perceptual, cognitive and psychomotor capabilities of the pilot. Care was being taken to ensure that the pilot would retain, if not improve, his spatial awareness. The Super Cockpit is based on a virtual environment that comprises visual, auditory and tactile environments with an interactive control environment that uses head, eye, speech and hand control inputs. Current cockpit designs transfer information to the pilot via 2-D display surfaces and a limited field of view head up display. The data presented to the pilot is derived from several inputs and is highly processed. The pilot must assimilate the information and process it mentally to build up his situation awareness. Any form of interaction with the external scene must be based on the information received from the limited bandwidth man–machine interface. Many current display formats are not very intuitive and require considerable amounts of mental or cognitive processing. The human has a high capacity to process 3-D spatial data, as long as it is presented in a way that takes account of his perception processes. Dean Kocian at WPAFB developed a Visually Coupled Airborne Systems Simulator (VCASS). The VCASS is a research tool for addressing fundamental human factors issues of virtual cockpit systems. The VCASS facility employs a monochrome helmet-mounted display with a field of view of 120° horizontal × 60° vertical. Figure 2.9 shows the helmet-mounted display used in the VCASS. The helmet was not designed for airborne applications, because the weight would be a serious problem during ejection. Nevertheless, some very important research was undertaken with this facility.

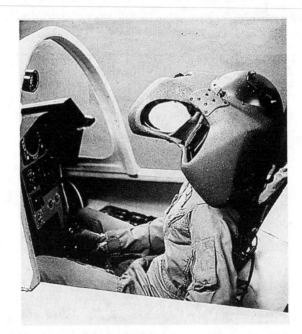

Figure 2.9 Wright Patterson Airforce Base VCASS.

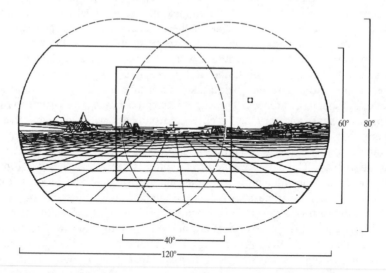

Figure 2.10 USAF VCASS Super Cockpit: typical display format.

The VCASS was developed during 1985 as a first-stage demonstrator for a virtual cockpit. The visuals presented to the pilot were monochromatic wire-grid type display formats. The wide field of view display was presented in a 3-D pictorial manner to convey information about the status of the aircraft and the targets or threats in the outside world. All the cockpit instrumentation, except side panel mounted displays, was represented in virtual space. A typical display format used to evaluate the VCASS concept is shown in Figure 2.10, refer to Wells and Venturino (1990).

Information presented to the pilot was stabilized in one of four ways in virtual space:

- Head stabilized for head pointing of weapons or selection of functions within the cockpit.
- Cockpit stabilized for the display of conventional cockpit instrumentation and switch panels relative to the cockpit reference frame.
- Earth stabilized for display items that relate to actual objects on the ground, for example, navigational reference cues such as churches.
- Space stabilized for aircraft heading and attitude reference information.

To interact with the virtual cockpit the pilot would have access to various input systems such as head pointing, eye pointing, voice input and a hand tracking system. One objective of this research programme was to determine if these interfaces could be used by a pilot. The VCASS programme posed several questions that are still valid in virtual environment systems today. These include:

- What update rate is needed for visual presentation?
- How accurately should information be registered?
- What field of view is required to undertake specific tasks?
- What spatial resolution is optimal for a particular task?
- How should information be displayed to the pilot?

These questions represent only a few of the many questions that remain unanswered today. The human factors associated with a man–machine interface such as that presented by a virtual cockpit should not be underestimated. The super or virtual cockpit is an extreme departure from conventional cockpit design and may be the only solution to the very complex workstation that the future pilot may have to endure. Virtual cockpits may be a way ahead for aircrew station design in the future. Despite the technological problems that must be resolved the hostile environment predicted for future aircraft may make it the only practical solution. The virtual cockpit will be discussed further in Chapter 7, because it presents the greatest challenge for the virtual environment scientist or engineer.

2.15 VPL Research, Inc. (1985)

VPL was founded in 1985 by Jaron Lanier and Jean-Jacques Grimaud. VPL focused on the provision of state-of-the-art human interface tools and is widely renowned for producing the DataGlove device, which appears in almost every 'virtual reality' photograph. Lanier received substantial funding from Thompson–CSF and eventually from NASA. This enabled VPL to take a more serious view of the technology and thus paved the way for them to become known worldwide for virtual environment products. Moreover, it was Jaron Lanier who coined the term 'virtual reality'. VPL manufactured and marketed a range of virtual environment products ranging from interface devices such as the DataGlove to the EyePhone and the Audiosphere.

VPL recognized that people who wanted to investigate virtual human–computer interface devices would also need an underlying software environment. This would be required in order to create virtual worlds, perform low level control of the interfaces and enable a high degree of interactivity with the virtual world. A set of software tools was developed to offer the researcher a complete virtual environment development system. The resulting system was known as Reality Built For Two or, more commonly, RB2. Users could build as much of the virtual world as they wanted by purchasing only those parts of the system they required. The complete system was centred around a high performance Apple Macintosh computer that processed the data from several input peripherals. The processed data was in turn passed onto one, or two, of a range of Silicon Graphics computers for rendering and display. If higher performance was required then the user had to employ higher performance Silicon Graphics computers. The unique advantage of the RB2 system was that it allowed a 'computer literate' person to design and implement a wide range of virtual environments with the minimum of effort and time. A complete RB2 system would allow two users to interact with each other within the virtual environment. In a sense, the RB2 system has become a benchmark with which other virtual environment systems are compared. Full details of the RB2 system are given in Chapter 5.

2.16 British Aerospace Virtual Cockpit (1987)

During the 1970s two head-mounted systems were considered for cockpit application. These were the head tracking system and the head-mounted sight. They were tested in flight, but the accuracy of the head tracker and the resolution of the helmet-mounted sight were not high enough for them to be considered suitable for cockpit application. They were developed, but their development took second place to other emerging technologies such as colour head down displays and wide field of view head up displays. However, in 1987, as technology matured and operational requirements changed, the need for a visually coupled system based around a helmet-mounted display became increasingly important. At the same time technological developments were advancing in aircraft systems functionality.

Together, the emerging technologies presented a new dilemma – pilot workload. The pilot was in grave danger of becoming saturated to the point where he could not possibly perform his mission. Unfortunately, there was not a set of metrics to quantify workload. Considerable research into mental workload and situation awareness conducted at this time could give no clear or consistent definition for these factors (the same situation exists today). Therefore, it was essential that all cockpit technologies were integrated in order to maintain a low workload man–machine interface.

At British Aerospace the emergence of these new technologies and the question of their integration with cockpit development led to the birth of the Advanced Cockpit Research Programme. This programme brought together some of British Aerospace's best engineers, scientists, human factors experts and cockpit specialists drawn from the company's sites at Brough, Warton, Kingston and Sowerby Research Centre. Their prime objective was to deal with the integration of emerging man–machine interface technologies and complex human factors issues. The virtual cockpit research facility developed at British Aerospace, Brough allows the engineering and human factors issues to be evaluated with a pilot in the loop. The facility has been engineered so that a range of cockpit technologies can be evaluated.

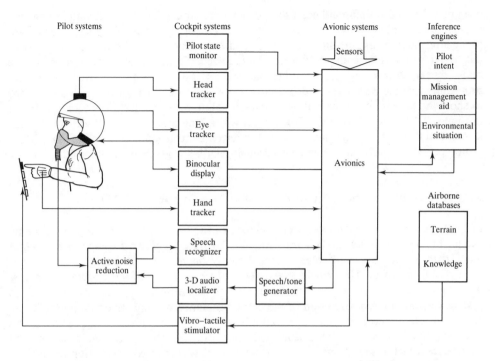

Figure 2.11 British Aerospace virtual cockpit system architecture.

For instance, different head tracking systems can be accommodated and exercised within carefully controlled trials to assess the relative merits of one system compared with another. Similarly, a range of other equipment such as helmet-mounted displays can be evaluated against each other. A key feature of the system is the full colour, high resolution helmet-mounted display that has been developed (see Plate 4). This display can be programmed to emulate all current helmet-mounted display systems and has proved to be invaluable for many studies. Not only can it emulate existing helmet-mounted displays, but it can also present the pilot with the sort of displays required for a full virtual cockpit. While it is tempting to mention only the visual systems of this facility, it is worth noting that it comprises other technologies such as speech recognition and 3-D auditory localization. The Phase III virtual cockpit architecture represents the sort of equipment that a virtual cockpit of the 2010 era might employ (see Figure 2.11).

2.17 British Aerospace Virtual Environment Configurable Training Aids (1990)

At the time of writing it is not possible to build a full virtual cockpit that can be flown in a fast jet aircraft. Factors such as safety and helmet mass prevent current virtual cockpit systems being cleared for flight. However, in 1990, rather than wait for the technology to mature British Aerospace decided to apply current technology to one of the company's products, a cockpit procedures trainer. The cockpit procedures trainer is a ground-based training aid consisting of a wood/fibre-glass structure employing real cockpit instrumentation. Trainee pilots sit inside one of these cockpits and can be taught procedures such as engine start sequences and emergency drill. To understand how to put together a virtual cockpit in terms of required display resolution, system update rates, displayed information and other parameters, a virtual equivalent of the cockpit procedures trainer was developed. Initially this was limited to a concept demonstration, to show the potential of a virtual environment solution. The resulting system is shown in Figure 2.12. Even though the first system was a long way from a full virtual cockpit, it employed some of the latest virtual environment technology, including VPL's prototype HRX EyePhone. Further technical details are given in Chapter 7.

2.17.1 Virtual Environment Configurable Training Aid (VECTA)

In 1991 the VECTA system was used with one of the fastest available graphics systems and the highest resolution LCD helmet-mounted displays to give a display that compared more than favourably with other virtual environment systems being demonstrated throughout the world. Nevertheless, the general performance of the system was below that required for a range of training tasks. The first and most obvious drawback of the system was the limited resolution of the helmet-mounted display. Even though this was based on the highest resolution LCD available, the resolution still proved to be subjectively too low. A second drawback was the inability to see one's hands, and experience a tactile sensation when a virtual control was pressed. The resulting cockpit did not give the user the feeling that they were actually part of the system.

VECTA was introduced and demonstrated to the world at the 1991 Paris Airshow, where it received considerable enthusiastic praise and support from leading users of aircrew training technologies. Significant interest was generated to the extent that funding was released to take the idea one stage further.

The latest generation system is described in Chapter 7. Critical performance parameters of the VECTA system were identified and effort was focused on resolving them.

Figure 2.12 British Aerospace Virtual Environment Configurable Training Aid.

2.17.2 Real and Virtual Environment Configurable Training Aid RAVECTA (1992)

Not surprisingly, VECTA demonstrated that it was not yet possible to build a full virtual cockpit for training applications. The display resolution was more or less adequate for the presentation of outside world visuals (especially when texturing was used) for some training tasks, but a weakness of the system was the inability of the pilot to see his hands and arms. This raised doubt about the use of completely immersive, all computer generated visuals for a training task. A see-through capability was required. Conventional see-through helmet-mounted displays were considered, but these would have overlaid imagery onto the user's hands. A display was required that appeared behind the user's hands in such a way that the hands could be seen at the same time as the virtual imagery. The basic training requirement was for a student pilot to sit inside a representative cockpit and fly segments of a mission. Until this time the outside world presentations were provided by a projected television image (dome simulation) or by one of several television monitors mounted in front of the cockpit. Apart from the cost of ownership, these arrangements were somewhat cumbersome and required large areas of blackened-out laboratory. A means of retaining the look and touch of a real cockpit while providing virtual computer generated imagery for the outside world was required. A technique developed by Kalawsky (1991) achieved all the requirements. The technique relies on mounting a pair of very small television cameras onto a helmet-mounted display and relaying the image from the cameras into the user's eyes. The user obtains an indirect view of the cockpit and can readily see his hands. The integration of the computer generated outside world was the key to the system. By painting the cockpit windscreen and canopy with a specific blue colour (other colours can be used) it was possible to chroma-key the computer generated outside world on to the blue areas (see Plates 14 and 15). Wherever blue areas are seen by the camera's field of view, outside world imagery is substituted for the blue.

The system offers the following advantages:

- No cockpit mapping or registration required.
- Can be used in any cockpit or workplace without modification.
- Users can see and feel real–world objects.
- Very wide application.
- Displays can be collimated to infinity, unlike dome projection systems.

RAVECTA was demonstrated at the 1992 Farnborough International Air Show and even though it was a concept demonstrator for an integrated virtual and real world system it generated considerable interest (Bevan, 1992). Further details of the RAVECTA system are given in Chapter 6.

2.18 W Industries Virtuality System (1990)

In 1987 Dr Jon Waldern founded W Industries, and in 1990 launched the company's Virtuality System, based upon research work that he had undertaken towards his PhD, which he initially called 'Spatial Imagery'. The W Industries Virtuality System comprises three main components:

1. Expality: A computer providing computer generated images of a synthetic database.
2. Animette: A software application programming interface providing the virtual interactive environment. In a sense, this acts as a mini operating system coordinating the run time elements of the virtual environment system.
3. Visette: The helmet-mounted display incorporating low resolution LCDs, head position sensor, four channel audio system and microphone. The interesting feature of the Visette is the ERGOLOK system, which enables a wide range of head sizes and shapes to be accommodated from the age of 10 years to adulthood.

While some researchers buy Virtuality Systems to aid their research, by far the largest number of customers comes from the entertainment and leisure sector. W Industries has captured the entertainment market in the United Kingdom, where the development of the 1000 SD (Sit Down) system and the 1000 CS (CyberSpace) system allows the user to select a range of interactive experiences. W Industries offer:

1. Solo Systems: Stand alone Virtuality 1000 SD or Virtuality 1000 CS.
2. Head 4 Head: A multi-player, four person maximum system.
3. Destination Centre: A fully interactive 'Virtual Reality Centre' employing several 1000 SD and 1000 CS systems.
4. Location Based Entertainment: A dedicated 'Virtual Reality Game Centre' to be used on location, intended to attract the public.

2.18.1 Health and safety issues

One of the key attributes that separate out an entertainment virtual environment system from a scientific/industrial system is the sheer number of people using the former.

The manufacturers have to consider health issues. For instance, a headset in an amusement arcade centre could be used on average by 100 people a day. It will pass from one user to another without being disinfected or hygienically wiped.

Considerations of health and safety issues should include:

- Microbiological cross-infection, particularly affecting the eyes.
- Neck and spine stress.
- Noise induced hearing loss.
- Electrical safety.
- Safety and precautionary measures to avoid accidents when the user enters and leaves the system.

Companies such as W Industries have had to deal with these issues.

2.19 Advanced Robotics Research Centre Teletact Glove I (1991)

In 1988 the Advanced Robotics Research Centre (ARRC) initiated a Virtual Environment Remote Driving Experiment (VERDEX), to evaluate the interactions between semi-autonomous robots and remotely sited human operators. One noteworthy achievement of the ARRC has been the development of a glove incorporating tactile feedback, called the Teletact.

Teletact I (Stone, 1991) was designed as a two-glove prototype (not as a right- and left-hand pair of gloves) and built by Airmuscle Ltd of Cranfield, UK. The input glove consists of a Lycra glove with 20 force sensitive resistors embedded on the underside in strategic positions. As pressure is exerted against the glove the resistors produce a resistive change corresponding to the applied pressure, which is then read by a computer. The output glove contains 20 air pockets embedded in positions corresponding to those of the force sensitive resistors in the input glove. Each air pocket is connected to 20 pneumatic pumps via microcapillary tubing. Each pneumatic pump is under proportional control by a computer. As pressure is increased on a given resistor, the resistive change is sensed by the computer, which in turn causes the pneumatic pump to increase the air pressure in the corresponding air pocket. In this way pressure experienced by the input glove is transmitted to the Teletact glove (see Figure 2.13).

Since the development of Teletact I, several evaluations have been undertaken, leading to considerable refinement of the tactile feedback system. Teletact II incorporates additional air pockets, which give improved tactile feedback to the user. Other tactile feedback devices have been developed by ARRC, including a free joystick called Teletact Commander, which is discussed in Chapter 4.

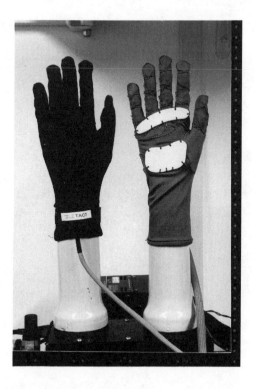

Figure 2.13 Advanced Robotics Research Centre Teletact I tactile feedback glove.

2.20 Summary

Virtual environment system concepts have been around for many years. Early researchers tried to produce visually coupled systems to convey a sense of remote presence. However, the technology available to them was rather crude, and could allow only limited experiments to be performed. Today, modern electronics and computer technology have made it possible to synthesize a computer generated virtual environment that can immerse the user. This chapter has described some of the major milestones of recent years. No attempt has been made to describe every event, because so many have contributed to the position that we are in today. The recommended reading list gives good reference material for those wanting to find out more about the roots of this exciting field.

The remainder of this book describes the underlying human perception issues relevant to the field, and the hardware and software systems required to build a virtual environment system. A chapter is also devoted to discussing the realities of a virtual environment system.

Recommended further reading

Ellis S.R. (1991). Nature and origins of virtual environments: A bibliographical essay. *Computer Systems in Engineering*, **2**(4), 321–47

Krueger M.W. (1991). *Artificial Reality* 2nd edn. Reading MA: Addison-Wesley

Rheingold H. (1991). *Virtual Reality*. London: Secker and Warburg

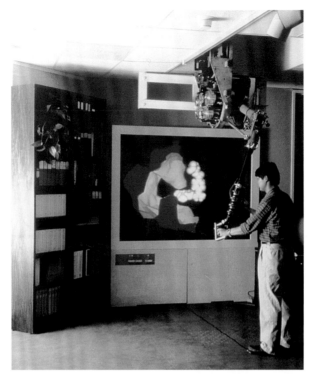

Plate 1   University of North Carolina haptic display Grope III.

Plate 2   First generation NASA Ames helmet-mounted display.

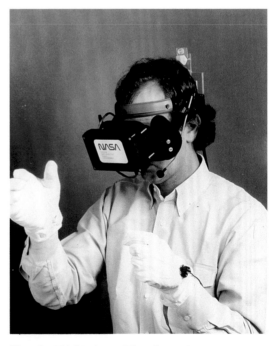

Plate 3   NASA Ames Virtual Interface Environment Workstation (VIEW).

Plate 4 British Aerospace full colour high resolution helmet-mounted display.

Plate 5 High resolution imagery displayable on British Aerospace high resolution helmet-mounted display.

Plate 6 British Aerospace Brough virtual cockpit facility.

Plate 7   British Aerospace Virtual Environment Configurable Training Aid (VECTA) as exhibited at the 1992 Farnborough International Air Show.

Plate 8   Virtual cockpit used in Virtual Environment Configurable Training Aid (VECTA).

Plate 9   Virtual aircraft incorporated into the virtual world as used in the British Aerospace Virtual Environment Configurable Training Aid (VECTA) as exhibited at the 1992 Farnborough International Air Show.

Plate 10   British Aerospace virtual environment laboratory facility.

Plate 11   British Aerospace virtual environment laboratory facility showing part of the computing facility with the Silicon Graphics Skywriter in the background.

Plate 12   British Aerospace virtual environment laboratory facility showing the Rover 400 demonstrator system.

Plate 13   British Aerospace Rover 400 virtual car interior rapid prototyper.

Plate 14 British Aerospace Real and Virtual Environment Configurable Training Aid showing the exterior of the cockpit. The virtual environment display appears superimposed on blue features in the real world.

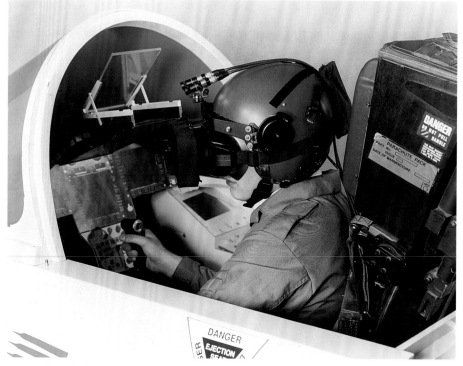

Plate 15 British Aerospace Real and Virtual Environment Configurable Training Aid showing pilot sitting in a real cockpit.

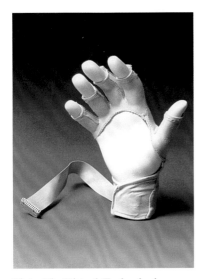

Plate 16 Virtual Technologies CyberGlove (Photo by Mitch Meynick, courtesy of Virtual Technologies).

Plate 17 Virtual Technologies 'Talking Glove'. Cathy Haas (right), teacher of American Sign Language at Stanford University, shows how a non-speaking deaf person communicates with a hearing person, Jim Kramer (left), using the Talking Glove. Cathy, who lost her hearing to a high fever when she was two, is wearing the instrumented glove on her right hand, a speaker pendant around her neck (normally worn under the shirt) and an alphanumeric LCD wristwatch display on her left wrist for visual feedback. As she quietly fingerspells, her hand formations are converted into words and transmitted as synthezised speech via the speaker pendant.

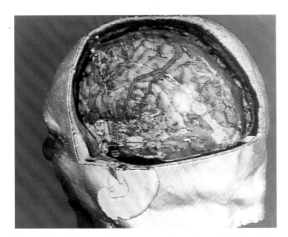

Plate 18 Magnetic Resonance Imaging display. An example of the high quality of display achievable today.

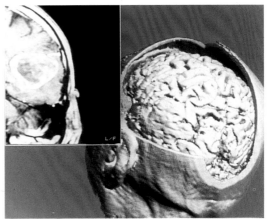

Plate 19 Magnetic Resonance Imaging display. An example of the high quality of display achievable today.

Plate 20   The pilot station aboard the simulator complexity test bed with the fibre-optic helmet-mounted display (FOHMD) manufactured by CAE Electronics Ltd of Saint-Laurent, Quebec, Canada for the US Army Research Institute.

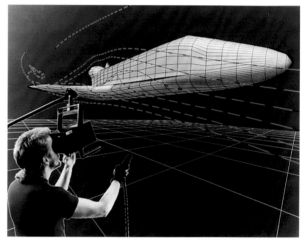

Plate 21   NASA Ames Research Centre virtual windtunnel showing a user employing the BOOM display system.

Plate 22   Latest visually coupled airborne systems simulator, at Wright Patterson Airforce Base.

3   Physiology and Perception in Virtual Environments

Objectives

The objective of this chapter is to cover one of the most fundamental aspects of virtual environment applications – an understanding of the physiology and perception issues. Without this grounding there is a danger that whatever virtual environment system is being configured it will lack the fundamental requirement of being compatible with the human being. It is often tempting to separate out the human factors issues from the engineering requirements. However, virtual environments is one of those subjects that is intimately bound to both the human factors and the engineering requirements. In many instances it is impossible to separate the two. To limit the extent of this chapter, only those issues that have a direct impact on the design of a virtual environment will be discussed. This will largely be confined to the special senses and related human perception system.

3.1 Introduction

This chapter has been organized into four sections, visual, auditory, haptic/kinaesthetic perception and virtual presence, for easy reference.

3.2 Physiology of visual perception

The visual channel is the most important interface in a virtual environment system. The relative bandwidth of the visual channel is many orders of magnitude greater than that of any of the other senses. Consequently, the human observer has an extremely sensitive and critical vision system. In terms of the actual sensor, the eye, the physiology may seem straightforward but when one probes further into the science of visual perception one soon realizes that the topic of visual perception is incredibly complex. The use of virtual environment systems is complicated because the human visual system is very sensitive to any anomalies in the imagery presented to a user. The smallest, almost imperceptible, artefacts of a computer graphics system can become very apparent when motion is incorporated in the scene. The actual mechanisms for visual perception are not yet fully understood. Another aspect of visual perception which must be dealt with is visual performance because it allows us to determine the effectiveness of the virtual environment visual channel. Without this understanding of the human visual perception system it is difficult to work out where improvements must be made and in particular how they must relate to a specific task.

3.2.1 The Eye

This section deals with the eye and how it works in terms of image formation and image quality. Later sections will describe the process of perception.

The human eyes are protected by a pair of bony cavities in the skull called the orbits. Further eye protection is provided by large amounts of fatty material surrounding the bony orbits. Each eye is further supported by six extraocular muscles which allow a range of movement of 50° to either the left or right of the resting position and approximately 40° above and 60° below the straight ahead position. A further movement in torsion about the optic axis can be achieved, but this is typically limited to less than 6°. The eye is kept clean and moist by the eyelid. Special glands under the upper eyelid secrete oils and other compounds to lubricate and wash away any foreign particles that inadvertently enter the eye. A secondary role of the eyelid is to provide protection against bright lights or objects that move rapidly towards the eye. The first optical surface of the eye is the cornea. That is the transparent bulge at the front of the eye (see Figure 3.1). The corneal bulge has a horizontal radius of approximately 8 mm and a vertical radius of 6 mm. Behind the cornea lies the anterior chamber that leads onto the iris. The anterior chamber is filled with fluid called the aqueous humour which has a refractive index almost the same as the cornea, hence the light leaving the cornea does not deviate very much. The iris is an extremely delicate membrane with a circular opening (the pupil) at the centre. The pupil is dilated in accordance with the amount of light that enters the eye. The diameter reduces as the light level increases. In the normal human the pupil diameter varies between 2 and 8 mm.

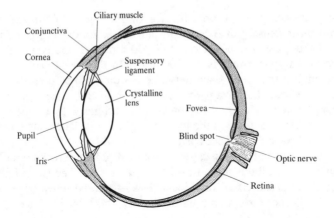

Figure 3.1 Cross-section of the human eye.

Behind the iris lies the crystalline lens, which provides variable focusing to bring images into focus on the back face of the eyeball, the retina. The rear surface of the lens leads into a larger cavity called the posterior chamber which is filled with vitreous humour. The vitreous humour gives strength to the eye and helps to absorb heat.

The back face of the eye is covered with the photosensitive lining called the retina. The retina is a complex structure containing nerve cells, blood vessels and connective tissue. Its role is to convert incident electromagnetic radiation (in the visible region) into nerve impulses. The whole retina is composed of a layer of photosensitive receptors, two layers of neural connections and a neural fibre pathway from the retina. Overall, ten layers can be identified in the retina. The neural receptors are divided into two groups: the rod system, and the cone system.

Rod system

Rod receptors are unevenly distributed in the retina. They are absent from the small central area called the fovea which subtends about 1° of visual angle (Barlow and Mollon, 1982). Outside this area the rod concentration builds up until it reaches a maximum density of between 150,000 and 170,000 mm^{-2} at about 18 to 20° from the fovea. Several rods tend to be linked to a single nerve cell that in turn is connected to another nerve cell. Rod receptors react to light of a lower intensity than the cone receptors. The rod receptors contain a photosensitive material called rhodopsin that breaks down when exposed to very low levels. If the incident light level is high then the rhodopsin lowers its concentration due to photobleaching causing the rods to become less sensitive. To enable maximum sensitivity to be reached it is necessary for the rod system to be dark-adapted for about 35 minutes. The sensitivity of the rods varies across the eye and is at a maximum in the region about 18 to 20° from the fovea.

Cone system

Cone receptors, the receptors responsible for bright light, colour and visual acuity (sharpness), are most densely distributed in the fovea. At the centre of the fovea the concentration of the cones reaches about 147,000 mm^{-2}. At the edge of the retina the cone concentration is approximately 16,300 mm^{-2}. In the fovea each cone receptor is connected to a single nerve cell. Each nerve cell is then linked directly to the brain.

Figure 3.2 shows the arrangement of the rod and cone systems, with their underlying neural system. The cone receptors react to light with a wide dynamic range (typically 10^{13}) and can adapt to suit the incident light levels. The cone receptors contain a photochemical substance called iodopsin.

The retina has a small region called the optic disc where receptors of neither type are found. This is where all the nerve fibres leave the retina. The lack of photoreceptors produces a blind spot in the visual field located 15° from the fovea on the nasal side of the retina. The blind spot covers an area of about 7° high by 5° wide.

Optic nerve

The optic nerves from each eye intersect at a point called the chiasma, then divide. The nerve fibres from the right-hand side of each eye form an optic tract that passes to the right-hand side of the visual cortex of the brain. Similarly, the nerve fibres from the left-hand side of the eyes form a second optic tract and pass to the left-hand side of the visual cortex. Each neural fibre from the fovea maintains its uniqueness, ensuring a point–to–point correspondence between the retina and the visual cortex of the brain. Neural fibres from rod and cone receptors outside the fovea are combined onto neural fibres.

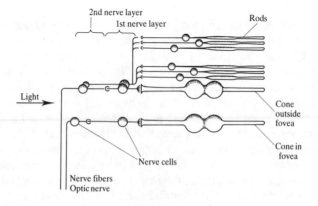

Figure 3.2 Arrangement of the rod and cone system.

Adaption

The human eye is very sensitive to extremely small variations in light intensity over a wide dynamic range of approximately 10^{13}, from light levels where vision is just about perceptible to levels where the energy is so intense that it can burn the retina. The lowest level (rod vision) is almost at the theoretical limit of any light sensing device while the highest level is 10^{13} times brighter (cone vision). No man-made sensor has as wide dynamic range and wavelength coverage as the eye.

Accommodation

The resting eye has a depth of field of 6 m to infinity. Pupil diameter is a controlling factor on the depth of field. For example, with a pupil size of 4 mm the depth of field at infinity extends to about 3.5 m in front of the eye. At 1 m the depth of field varies from 1.4 to 0.8 m. When the light level increases such that the pupil diameter is 2 mm the depth of field at infinity extends to 2.3 m whereas at 1 m the depth of field varies from 1.8 to 0.7 m. In order to bring objects that are within 6 m it is necessary to alter the optical system of the eye. The eye does this by altering the curvature of the crystalline lens by means of the ciliary muscles. This process is called accommodation. Accommodation is expressed in dioptres, the unit for specifying the refractive power of a lens. The power of a lens is the reciprocal of its focal length in metres.

3.2.2 Visual field

The ability to see an object depends, first, on whether the object is in the image on the retina and, second, on where on the retina it appears. Charts are constructed that show the visual field, covering both foveal vision and the part of space that can be seen without moving the eye or head. Several graphical techniques have been devised to represent the field of view of the human being. To determine what an operator can see it is very important to overlay this information on obscuration plots. For example face masks or protective goggles will reduce the field of view and have a marked effect on the detection of moving objects in the periphery vision region. Such losses can affect the safety of the operator. The graphical techniques include polar plots, equal area projection plots, rectilinear plots, and so on. Although all of these techniques offer certain advantages, they are not always easy to interpret and relate to the real world. The polar plot or perimeter charts (see Figure 3.3) are often used, but one really has to stop and think about the information. At one time the Aitoff Equal Area Graph was used quite frequently but it has now fallen out of favour because of the difficulty of generating the distorted grid on a computer.

The perimeter chart is a polar representation of a viewing sphere. The observer is assumed to be at the centre of the perimeter chart with a straight-ahead view shown by the 90° radial line. Objects appearing within the forward hemisphere are drawn on radial lines 0° to 180° (representing azimuth). An object appearing in the hemisphere behind the observer would be drawn on the radial lines 180° to 359°. The position of the object in elevation is shown on the circles of constant elevation 0° to 100°. One should be wary when extracting data from other perimeter charts because some authors have reversed the numbering of the radial lines from the standard convention.

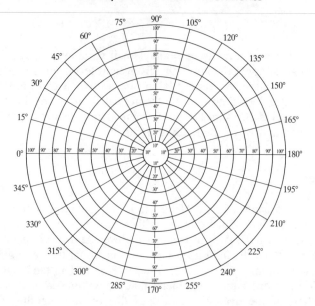

Figure 3.3 Perimeter chart used for displaying visual field.

Comparing systems in the virtual environment field is very difficult, because there are no real definitive standards.

The human eye has an instantaneous field of view of approximately 120° vertically by 150° horizontally. When two eyes are used the total field of view measures approximately 120° vertically by 200° horizontally.

Each eye has its own monocular instantaneous field of view that extends from the forward view to approximately 100° on the temporal side and to about 60° on the nasal side of the eye (see Figure 3.4). The facial structure, particularly the extent of the nose bridge, affects the actual field of view. The two monocular fields of view overlap to form a region of binocular overlap where stereoscopic vision is achieved. The field of view in the binocular region is generally defined as the total field of view as seen by both eyes directed to a distant fixation point. The binocular field of view is used for central vision. With the head fixed, left and right eye movement gives a binocular field of view that covers approximately 20° either side of the centre line between the two eyes. With no eye movement and looking straight ahead, the binocular field is reduced to about 15° either side of the centre line. The field of view in the vertical plane is about 60° above the horizontal plane and about 70° below. As will be described later, the visual acuity or resolution of the eye varies considerably over its field of view, the finest detail being resolved within a field of view of only 2° in the fovea region.

The visual field can be extended by eye movements, head movements and body movements (see Table 3.1). To resolve the object with the highest acuity the observer keeps his central vision on the object (the observer is said to be fixating on a point). This fixation point appears to be at the precise centre of the visual field. The position of any other point in the visual field is then expressed as an angle (eccentricity angle) between the visual axis and a line between the point and the eye.

Table 3.1 Visual field limits.

Field type and limiting factors	Movement	Horizontal limits		Vertical limits	
		Temporal field	Nasal binocular field	Field angle up	Field angle down
Peripheral vision (foveal fixation)	Head fixed (eyes fixed straight ahead)	95°	60°	46°	67°
Limits of eye displacement	Head fixed	74°	55°	48°	66°
Peripheral field	Eyes maximum displacement	91°	5°	18°	16°
Total peripheral field		167°	60°	66°	82°
Limits of head movement	Head maximum displacement	72°	72°	80°	90°
Peripheral field	Eyes fixed	95°	60°	46°	67°
Total peripheral field		167°	132°	126°	157°
Fixation range	Moderate movements of head and eyes	60°		45°	
Eye displacement	Eyes: 15° left or right	15°	15°	15°	15°
	15° up or down	95°	45°	46°	67°
Net peripheral field	Head: 45° left or right	110°	60°	61°	82°
	30° up or down	45°	45°	30°	30°
Total peripheral field of view		155°	105°	91°	112°
Limits of head movement	Maximum movements of head and eyes	72°	72°	80°	90°
Maximum eye deviation		74°	55°	48°	66°
Range of fixation		146°	127°	128°	156°
Peripheral field		91°	~5°	18°	16°
Total peripheral field		237°	132°	146°	172°

Vision disorders of the eyes or the presence of objects such as face masks in front of the observer will lead to a reduction of visual field. In later chapters the fields of view of various helmet-mounted displays will be discussed.

Unfortunately, current technology does not allow us to match the field of view of the helmet-mounted display with that of the observer. Very wide field of views can be made but the overall spatial resolution is very low in the central or foveal vision area. This leads to almost unusable displays. To get around this problem the field of view is reduced to a point where the resolution in the foveal vision region is acceptable. An obvious question is: what is an acceptable resolution? Helmet-mounted display manufacturers (aerospace equipment manufacturers excepted) rarely give accurate figures for their field of view. This leads to disappointments when their systems are integrated.

Visual angle

Dimensions of objects are usually expressed in terms of the visual angle, that is, the angle subtended by the eye. The further an object is from the eye, the smaller the visual angle it subtends. It is common practice to relate the extent of an object in a visual field to visual angle. The advantage of doing this is that visual angles form a constant relationship to retinal distances in the eye.

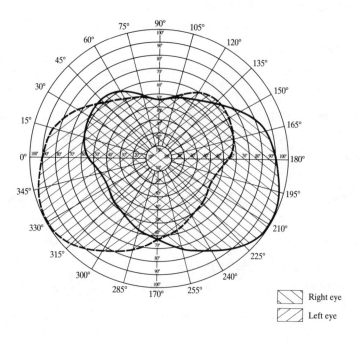

Figure 3.4 Visual field of a normal human observer.

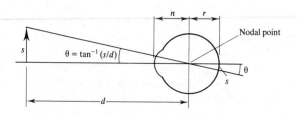

Figure 3.5 Visual angle.

The visual angle of an object projected onto the retina is given by:

$$\theta = \tan^{-1}(s/d)$$

The distance n from the cornea to the nodal point on the eye is about 7 mm for most people. Visual angle is used to express positions on the retinal surface. For instance, the diameter of the fovea is expressed as 30 arc min. When it is necessary to express retinal extent in conventional units, the distance from the retinal surface to the nodal point must be considered. This is about 17 mm for most people. When the eye is focused at infinity the focal length is approximately 17 mm, whereas for near-field objects this decreases to about 14 mm.

3.2.3 Stereopsis (binocular vision)

Many animals share a large portion of the visual field with both eyes. This is known as binocular vision. Binocular vision relates to the neural and physiological interaction of the two eyes in the overlap region. While the human visual system has two distinct optical channels, from a neurophysiological point of view it is considered as a single sensory system. The term stereopsis is often used to describe the perceptual transformation of differences between the two monocular images seen by the eyes.

When two very different images are presented to an observer, the visual system often suppresses one of the images. Occasionally, the dominant image alternates from one eye to the other. This phenomenon is called binocular rivalry. Differences in size, brightness and hue can all lead to rivalry effects. Rivalry effects are generally rare in natural scenes but with synthetic computer generated images it is possible to generate such effects very easily. When an observer is presented with a display that exhibits binocular rivalry, it can be extremely disturbing, and almost certainly affects the user's performance.

It is interesting that stereopsis is not always necessary for depth perception. Some people without stereopsis (or those having sight in one eye) can often perceive depth very well.

Partial binocular overlap

An alternative to a fully overlapped binocular display is to displace the monocular image inwards or outwards to create a partial binocular overlap. A partial binocular overlap enables a smaller and lighter optical system to be produced. An additional benefit is an improvement in effective resolution, because for a given cathode ray tube, the angular substance of each display element is proportionally reduced.

As an example, a 60° horizontal field of view system can be produced from two 40° optical systems – this produces a 20° overlap region (see Figure 3.6).

The average human has a binocular overlap (between the two eyes) of approximately 120° with about 35° monocular vision either side of the overlap region. This is principally determined by the optics of the eye and the bridge of the nose. The binocular overlap can be convergent or divergent, depending on whether the optical systems are mounted inward or outward. When the two images are displaced outward this leads to a divergent system, as shown in Figure 3.7.

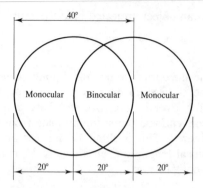

Figure 3.6 Partial binocular overlap.

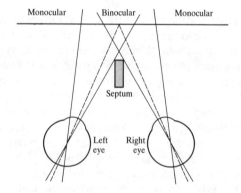

Figure 3.7 Divergent partial binocular overlap.

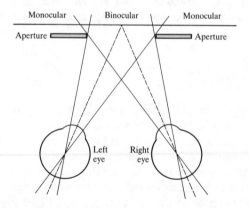

Figure 3.8 Convergent partial binocular overlap.

Divergent binocular overlap optical systems are generally preferred because this allows the combining optics to be tilted outwards. This gives the advantage of allowing the range of inter-pupillary adjustments to be extended (see Figure 3.8). Certain partial overlap systems suffer from binocular rivalry and binocular/monocular edge effects.

Binocular rivalry effects

Nearly all observers have a dominant eye, and the brain suppresses the disparate image on the other eye. For example, if a finger is pointed to a distant object, images of the finger and object coincide on the fovea of one eye. The dominant eye is defined as the eye whose image is perceived for a greater period of time. Researchers have found that sighting dominance and rivalry dominance can occur.

Rivalry effects in helmet-mounted display are complex and not fully understood. If one channel is brighter than the other, the brighter field will dominate and the brain can suppress the dimmer channel. It has been found that factors other than luminance can cause rivalry effects. For example, display scene representation and complexity can induce rivalry effects. In a closed helmet-mounted display (no direct view of the real world) it is easier to control scene information and to avoid rivalry problems. However, in normal helmet-mounted displays that optically overlay the outside world, it is very difficult to control the incidence of binocular rivalry. Clearly, objects in the outside world appear at different ranges to the observer, ranging from several millimetres away to infinity. A helmet-mounted display used in these circumstances will almost always be collimated to infinity. When the helmet-mounted display imagery is overlaid onto an object in the near field, conditions for rivalry exist. During rivalry, the suppressed eye ignores substantial amounts of information.

With a partial overlap binocular system the edge of one monocular image overlaps the other monocular view. When different patterns are displayed on the two channels then binocular rivalry can sometimes be experienced. This manifests itself as a temporal alternation between the two eyes and is often accompanied by dark bands that appear in the image. This effect is more pronounced for raster images than for vector images. Furthermore, the nature of the imagery has an effect. Simple line drawings displayed on raster displays are less prone to binocular rivalry effects than rendered images.

The exact reason for the dark bands is still something of a mystery. These bands vary in brightness over time and the image in the area of these bands can become visually unstable because of sporadic breakdowns of the fusion mechanism. For optical systems with a small overlap region this effect can be particularly distracting. This effect has been evident in helmet-mounted displays for some years and is known as luning (CAE, 1984).

One possible method that may eliminate this effect is to employ a roll-off luminance for each channel that will attenuate the sharp edge. This can be undertaken with a step wedge optical filter or by electronic means (shading). Unfortunately, it is not possible to photograph the binocular rivalry or luning effect because it is a psychophysical phenomenon.

Stereopsis: Limit of depth cue

Stereopsis effects operate over a limited range in terms of giving depth perception. However, it should be noted that four cues in particular are responsible for giving depth perception. These are lateral retinal image disparity, motion parallax, differential image size and texture gradients. The geometrical relationship behind stereopsis is shown in Figure 3.9.

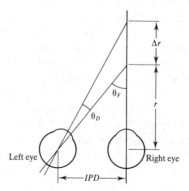

Figure 3.9 Geometrical relationship behind stereopsis.

The depth difference between two targets is given by Δr where the angular separation between the targets is given by:

$$\theta_D = \frac{IPD}{r}\left[\frac{\Delta r}{r + \Delta r}\right]$$

where r = fixation distance, Δr = depth difference between two targets, θ_D = angular separation between targets, θ_F = convergence angle to fixated target IPD = interpupillary distance.

Under optimal conditions, very small disparities can be detected. These disparities correspond to a depth difference of less than 0.05 mm at 500 mm or 4 mm at 5 m. This high stereo is an example of the positional accuracy of the visual system. Unfortunately, perceived depth does not increase indefinitely with disparity. Only a qualitative sense of 'in-front' or 'behind' is achieved for disparities exceeding 1°. Most real scenes produce disparities exceeding 2° and the limits quoted apply to the foveal region. However, the limits tend to increase towards the periphery of the visual field.

Stereoscopic cues operate to 9.2 m for peripheral viewing of static scenes, while retinal size becomes the dominant factor beyond that range. To be strictly correct, angular rates are important. Stereoscopic cues operate out to 500 m in the fovea. However, for dynamic motions (for example, a target velocity of 1 knot lateral), motion parallax is the dominant factor to a distance of about 49 m. Beyond this point, retinal size takes over. This example merely serves to illustrate that depth perception in a dynamic scene is a complex issue. Other parameters such as perspective, texture and accommodation are related cues. Observers can also be trained to improve their depth perception.

Lateral retinal image disparity

Lateral retinal image disparity (δ) is the difference in relative position of the image of an object on the observer's retinas as a function of the IPD and vergence position. Retinal image disparity is one of the cues that induce depth perception. However, lateral retinal image disparity in the range 0–10° only, results in depth perception. A disparity greater than this limit results in double images (diplopia) and the sensation of depth is lost (see Figure 3.10).

$$\text{Disparity } \delta = \frac{IPDd}{(D^2 + dD)}$$

where θ_1, θ_2 = binocular parallax and θ_1-θ_2 = binocular disparity, independent of vergence.

$$\text{Depth } d = \frac{\delta D^2}{(IPD - \delta D)}$$

Vertical retinal image disparity

Wherever there is a vertical displacement of the retinal image in one of the eyes a condition known as vertical retinal image disparity exists. When vertical retinal image disparity exists in a binocular system it is considerably more objectionable to the user because the eyes cannot make very large compensatory movements in the way they can for horizontal displacement. Vertical disparities do not convey any depth information to the observer and must be avoided. Small amounts of vertical disparity can cause double imagery (diplopia), a very uncomfortable condition. However, most users can adapt to the diplopia after 15–20 minutes. When the user becomes adapted it is necessary to re-adapt to the real world (when the binocular display system has been removed). A similar re-adaption time is required. This effect accounts for some of the criticisms levelled against virtual environment systems.

Some optical designers have introduced unacceptable vertical retinal image disparity into their designs. A secondary cause of vertical retinal disparity is objects in the near field being closer to one eye than the other. There is a small magnification difference between the two eyes that results in the retinal disparity. The amount of vertical retinal image disparity that can be comfortably tolerated increases as a function of target distance from the fixation point.

Many studies have been conducted to verify this point. One study presented either horizontal or vertical parallel lines at a constant separation in one channel of a binocular instrument. The other eye was presented with an identical pattern, except that the separation was varied. Figure 3.11 shows the resulting diplopia thresholds for both vertical and horizontal retinal image disparity as a function of target distance.

From the two curves it can be seen that vertical diplopia thresholds are smaller and increase at a slower rate than horizontal diplopia thresholds.

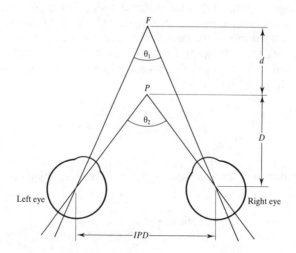

Figure 3.10 Lateral retinal image disparity.

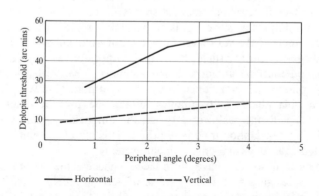

Figure 3.11 Horizontal and vertical diplopia thresholds.

Image rotation misalignment (extortion): Tolerance

A gradual increase in the rotational misalignment between the left and right eye channels quickly reaches the point where double images (diplopia) occur. The point at which this occurs is also a function of target size. The average observer is very sensitive to rotational misalignment effects when viewing simple line structures such as a single line. A misaligned multiple line pattern can be tolerated for a longer period than a single line pattern. In medium term tasks (approximately 2-hour duration) the observer can tolerate a rotational misalignment with no more visual fatigue than occurs during other precise visual tasks. Longer term effects show up as image blurring, tears and accommodation variations, and longer term exposure to rotational misalignment may induce queasiness in some observers. Unfortunately, it is not possible to quote some form of comfort index due to the variability of the observer population and image display characteristics.

Image magnification induced retinal disparity

When a slightly magnified image is presented to one eye, several of the disparities presented earlier can appear together, depending on the nature of the magnification. This defect is known as aniseikonia and is usually introduced by tolerances in optical design. Spectacle wearers sometimes suffer from this defect if they require substantially different corrective prescriptions for each eye. Even people who do not wear spectacles can suffer from a degree of aniseikonia caused by refracture differences between each eye. A consequence of aniseikonia is that one of the visual fields seems much further away than the other. This tends to affect near-field objects more than those in the far field. Extreme effects of aniseikonia can lead to eye discomfort, fatigue, headaches and in some cases motion sickness.

Stereoacuity

Stereoacuity is the ability to resolve small differences in depth between two objects and is expressed in terms of visual angle. When attempting to make such measurements particular care has to be taken to eliminate other cues such as monocular depth cues, inter-position and perspective. These cues can give misleading measurements. A further point to remember is that individuals have a wide stereoacuity capability, which can be improved with practice. Stereoacuity, when measured properly, is a function of binocular retinal disparity.

- Effects of luminance: Stereoacuity increases with increasing illumination up to 3 cdm^{-2}. An individual's response tends to exhibit a discontinuity at about 0.016 cdm^{-2}, where photopic (cone) vision takes over from scotopic (rod) vision. Exposure time at a particular illumination level can have a bearing on stereoacuity.

- Retinal location: Stereoacuity is at a maximum for objects that are in the fovea and decreases as the objects move from the centre of the visual field.

- Field of view: Stereoacuity reduces as the field of view is reduced and applies to stationary and moving objects.

- Object orientations: Stereoacuity is maximum for vertical lines, and decreases slowly as the lines rotate to 45° from vertical and then quickly as the lines approach the horizontal. It is interesting that stereoacuity reduces slightly (declines in proportion to the cosine of the inclination of the head) when the head is tilted and the lines remain vertical rather than the lines themselves being rotated. To some extent cyclorotation or cyclotorsion movements of the eyes can compensate for small angular head movements (see Kertesz and Sullivan, 1978).

- Object lateral motion: The ability to detect a relative depth difference between two momentarily presented objects is not affected, provided the objects do not move laterally with a velocity exceeding $2.5°s^{-1}$, (see Westheimer and McKee, 1978).

- Effect of vertical disparity: Stereoacuity decreases as lateral retinal image disparity increases.

3.2.4 Visual motion perception

Visual motion perception in virtual environments is not properly understood by most people. Some very convincing immersive virtual displays can be produced but when the observer moves relative to the scene, the illusion is instantly destroyed. This is because the visual flow field cues take on an unnatural appearance. Gibson (1950) suggested that the observer's ergo motion can be derived from texture points and their relative motion in a visual field. For straight line motion an optical flow field seems to originate from a focal point, giving an indication of direction of travel. Figure 3.12 shows straight and level motion over flat terrain. The y axis represents the observer's viewing axis parallel to the ground and at a fixed height.

Consider a set of equally spaced (in azimuth) points on the ground at a range of R. The paths of each point relative to the moving reference frame of the observer form straight lines. If the visuals are head coupled, the viewing axis is rotated with respect to velocity vector directions, as shown on the right of Figure 3.12. In either case, mapping the trajectories of each point with respect to the velocity vector gives the line of sight motion streamers shown in Figure 3.13.

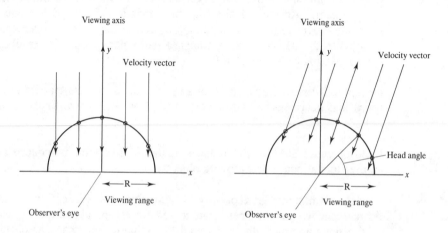

Figure 3.12 Horizontal situation for straight and level motion.

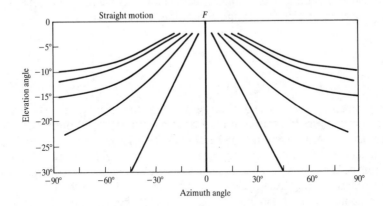

Figure 3.13 Optical streamers appearing from fixation point.

For straight and level motion, the streamers appear to come from a fixed point on the horizon. From a perceptual viewpoint, the optical flow streamers are very important in the judgement of motion, speed, and, to some extent, height above ground. If a virtual environment display system is unable to generate approximate optical flow patterns, then the user becomes very aware that the image is anything but virtual. Early flight simulator displays were limited to large areas of flat ground arranged into regular 'patchwork-like' regions. These were supposed to generate artificial optical flow streamers, but because of the coarse nature of the regions, the effect did not work very well.

Motion parallax

Parallax induced by head movement is a very effective cue to depth perception and works well with just one eye. Motion parallax refers to the relationship between objects in an observer's field of view as the observer moves in relation to the objects. It does not matter if the observer is moving relative to the scene or vice versa; the visual effects do not alter. Motion parallax is very important for depth perception at extended ranges. It is well known that stereopsis fails for most observers at distances exceeding about 500 m (theoretical limit). The fact that we can still judge relative distances is partially due to motion parallax cues (Haber and Hershenson, 1973). The geometric explanation is straightforward (see Figure 3.14). If the observer moves through a distance L, while fixating on the point P, then for small movements the change in angle between the near field and far field points N and F, respectively, is:

$$\theta = L\frac{\Delta D}{D^2}$$

If ΔD is positive for objects beyond P and negative for objects closer than P, a positive angle corresponds to a displacement in the same direction as the head movement. Since we are primarily interested in movement across the scene it is helpful to consider the rate of angular change across the observer's retina. Thus:

$$\omega = \frac{d\theta}{dt} = \frac{L}{D^2}\frac{\Delta D}{\Delta t}$$

For example, consider at a distance of 10 m, the relative velocity induced in an object at 11 m that would be caused by a head movement of 50 mm in 1 second. The relative velocity ω will be about 0.582 mRads^{-1}. This is below the 0.01745 – 0.03491 rads^{-1} for detection by the bar and edge detectors in the visual cortex. The fact that an observer can detect displacements at such low rates suggests that the visual cortex is comparing (or averaging) relative motions between objects. Motion parallax contains information about the direction and the magnitude of the depth relative to the fixation point. Additional depth information is obtained by taking into account the relative size of the object.

3.2.5 Temporal resolution

The eye operates differently from a photographic camera, where the total amount of light falling on the silver grains in the film causes a permanent irreversible effect. The eye responds to changing or varying light levels in order to give dynamic representations of a scene. It integrates the incoming light for a short period. This can be established by noting that the amount of light required at the threshold level is independent of the stimulus, provided that it is less than the integration time. Under certain conditions the integration time can extend for several tenths of a second. To obtain high sensitivity,

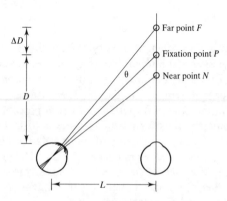

Figure 3.14 Motion parallax.

long integration times are required, while shorter integration times are necessary for rapid responses to changing scene information.

The retina is an efficient mechanism, because it comprises a very sensitive, long latency, slow exposure monochromatic system (rods), and a less sensitive, shorter latency, short exposure colour system (cones).

Perception of flicker in a display device

The majority of display devices produce images that are derived sequentially in a raster–like fashion. Consequently, it is possible that an observer may perceive the display to be flickering on and off. The point at which the brightness variation disappears is known as the critical fusion frequency (CFF) and is affected primarily by brightness levels, field size and retinal location. The critical fusion frequency is reduced outside the foveal region, due to the influence of rod vision. A fairly linear relationship exists for a range of brightness levels and can be expressed by the well–known Ferry–Porter Law:

$$f_c = a \log B_a + b$$

where f_c = CFF; a, b = degree of adaption constants, $a = 12.5$, b $\approx$ 37 photopic, $a \approx 1.5$, b $\approx$ 37 scotopic; and B_a = luminance of test field (average).

Other relationships have been derived and most good visual science text books will give examples.

Critical fusion frequency is also governed by the stimulus area as follows:

$$f_c = C \log A + d$$

where C and d are constants and A is the stimulus area.

These relationships tend to relate to display devices where the image appears and disappears instantaneously. Unfortunately, CRTs and some other display devices have a decay time over which the intensity of the display decays to zero. This decay time can range from a few milliseconds to several minutes, depending upon the phosphor being used. As a result CFF is a difficult effect to quantify precisely and is further dependent upon the observer. Generally though, above 50 ft L a CFF of 50 Hz is probably a good start while below 5 ft L a CFF of 20 Hz might be expected.

3.2.6 Spatial resolution

Display structure effects on perceived eye level

It has been reported by Stoper and Cohen (1989) and more recently by Nemine and Ellis (1991) that a matrix or discrete optical structured array can bias the perception of eye level in the direction of the pitched array. Moreover, there is evidence that a single pitched line can be just as effective at biasing the apparent eye level as a grid structure. An extremely important study conducted by Nemine and Ellis (1991) investigated the influence of a pitched optic array on gravity referenced grids and amounts of optic structure. Nemine and Ellis found definite evidence that a pitched optic array does bias perception of the gravity referenced eye level, such that there is a deviation of apparent eye level from true gravity referenced eye level.

Spatial frequency response of a display system

An optical system can increase the amount of blurring produced by a display system. Blurring of an image can be caused by a small point source in the image plane being reproduced as a spot of finite size. For a CRT this spot will generally be circular, with an intensity fall-off at its edges. The blurring function is often called the point spread function (PSF). Blurring generally occurs for every point in the original image, and one may define the final image as the result of convolving the original image with the PSF.

The more common definition of blurring is derived by taking the Fourier transform of the PSF. The resulting transform is known as the modulation transfer function (MTF). The MTF is used to describe how well the display or optical system reproduces the frequency components of a point source or image line. The frequency components are expressed as a number of cycles per millimetre, or, at a given viewing distance, cycles per degree of visual angle. The modulation depth (MD) at each spatial frequency is the dependent variable. The MTF of any optical system can be determined by its response to sinusoidally modulated gratings with linearly varied MD. The threshold MD (where the grating is just noticeable) is measured for each spatial frequency.

Spatial frequencies relationship to frame rate and bandwidth

The video bandwidth of a CRT or matrix display is proportional to the frame rate and the total number of pixels. For example, in the CCIR 625 line video standard, the writing speed of one television line is 64 μs and the frame period is 25 Hz. Slow frame rates such as this can increase the perception of flicker. An interlacing technique has been developed whereby each frame is split up into two interlaced fields, each field being displaced by one line with respect to the other field. For grey scale (continuous) television pictures this technique is perfectly acceptable but is rather objectionable for high contrast graphic displays, where symbols can appear to flicker on and off.

3.2.7 Visual space perception

The environment surrounding us provides a framework for the perception of spatial relationships between objects. Generally when dealing with human perception it is best to define an axis set that is non Euclidean and more centred on the observer. It is easy to relate spatial data to the observer in this way even though the Euclidean axis set (and any other axis set) is a straightforward transformation of the other. For instance we all know what is meant by straight ahead. Even though an egocentric coordinate system is easy to relate to, at times it is also ambiguous. For some applications it is often desirable to work with a primary and a secondary axis: a primary axis relating to the observer irrespective of his/her orientation in space and a secondary axis that is defined relative to the gravity vector (perpendicular to the horizon). For airborne situations a third axis set is defined that relates to the vehicle – in the case of an aircraft this is called the aircraft axis set. The secondary axis set is very important from a perception point of view because it can be deduced by the way in which visual cues are presented to the user. For example, if trees and buildings are presented as a virtual image the observer deduces that the gravity vector is parallel to the vertical dimension of the object. To some extent, this accounts for some individuals falling over when they stand inside a flight simulator dome and the horizon is progressively tilted. If no other visual cues are available such as fixed mechanical structures, it is very difficult to know which is the right way up. Therefore the visual scene overrides the real vestibular cues.

Space perception: Depth

Many visual cues impart a sensation of depth to an observer that can lead to the awareness of distance in an image. These include:

- Binocular disparity: Stereopsis is very sensitive and reasonably reliable at giving a measure of depth perception. At certain distances, stereopsis is a less dominant cue for depth than the other cues presented below.

- Interposition: Given two objects, if one partially or completely occludes the view of the other, then it is reasonable to presume that the object being occluded is much further away.

- Motion parallax: Motion parallax is probably the most powerful depth perception cue. As the head or body is moved, a relative displacement of objects in the visual field occurs. The manner in which the objects appear to move relative to one another is known as the kinetic depth effect.

- Perspective: If objects of the same size are placed at ever increasing distances from the observer, the size of the object appears to become smaller. Many objects lead to strong perspective cues, including roads, railway lines and any parallel lines. A uniform texture exhibits strong perspective cues.

Constancy scaling

An effect known as constancy scaling can have an interesting and sometimes misleading effect on distance perception. Our perception system processes data such as depth information, surface information, and relative position of other objects and tries to get a scale for the objects in the scene. A whole range of optical illusions can occur when the perceptual system tries to compensate for a difference in distance by making objects or lines appear larger than they are. More than 200 geometric illusions are known to exist. The more well known include Delboeuf, Judd, Lipps, Müller-Lyer, Ponzo, Poggendorff, Titchener and Zöllner.

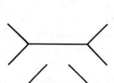 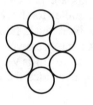 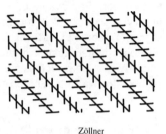

Müller–Lyer   Titchner   Zöllner

Figure 3.15 Geometrical illusion.

Figure 3.15 shows three such illusions. The Müller–Lyer illusion involves two equal length horizontal lines, the upper line appearing larger than the lower line. Similarly, the Titchener illusion comprises two inner circles of the same diameter. The inner circle on the left appears to be much smaller than the one on the right. In the Zöllner figure, the oblique lines are parallel, but appear angled relative to each other.

Rather than present a whole range of illusions and their causes, the author considered it only necessary to draw the reader's attention to the presence of illusions and how the perceptual system can be fooled. Anyone wishing to obtain a fuller account of illusions should consult Gibson (1950) and Rock (1990). The latter book makes fascinating reading.

3.2.8 Colour perception

Colour is an important aspect of visual perception, which describes an observer's ability to discriminate objects or surfaces with respect to spectral composition. Three attributes are applied to colour perception.

- Hue: The correct term to describe a colour by name.

- Saturation: The term used to describe the amount of purity or proportion of pure chromatic colour in the perception.

- Brightness/Intensity: The degree of intensity of a luminous light source.

Intensity

The appearance of a coloured object depends greatly upon the conditions under which it is viewed. Unfortunately, there are large individual differences in the perception of colour, or more correctly, hue. This factor, with the large number of parameters that affect colour perception, makes the subject extremely complex to analyse.

The perception of colour displays in a virtual environment is no different from colour perception in any other application. Therefore, rather than repeat what is available in standard text books, the author decided to provide the interested reader with a pointer to the more detailed text books covering specific issues. An extremely good account of various experiments in colour perception is given in Boff *et al.* (1986, chapter 9, sections 1.1, 3.1).

Tests for colour perception

In order to undertake any form of investigation into colour perception, a series of tests must be conducted. Tests include simple matching of lightness or hue of one test object to that of another object, and more complicated comparisons involving coloured objects on coloured backgrounds. Boynton (1979) and Boff *et al.* (1986) give details of specific tests and summarize appropriate results.

Observers frequently make reference to objects that appear to be the same colour. Unfortunately, it is not possible to extract the spectrum of a coloured light source merely by looking at it.

It is possible for two objects to appear to be the same colour and yet be composed of different wavelength components. Individual differences between observers may mean that a colour match for one person is different for another. However, it is feasible to match to any hue by manipulating the three primary colours.

Variations between individuals come about from the different spectral absorption characteristics of their photoreceptors and to a lesser extent from individual differences in the absorption characteristics of the lens and macular pigment of the eye. Wright (1946) describes ways of normalizing for observer variability.

Each observer will generally have a sensitivity threshold below which chromatic differences cannot be resolved. Wright (1941) shows that an observer's chromaticity sensitivity threshold varies as a function of time and the degree of exposure to other coloured stimuli prior to the test being undertaken.

In optical systems the terms achromatic and monochromatic are often used to describe part of, or a complete, optical/display system. An achromatic response refers to a system that exhibits a certain behaviour for a wide range of wavelengths, usually from blue through to red. Hence, the term 'white light response'. Conversely, monochromatic refers to a narrower spectral response, typically over a few tens of wavelengths. This results in a single colour display. The term monochromatic is often used incorrectly to describe a black and white display. These are subjective terms only and do not necessarily relate to radiometric photometric units. Colour perception is brought about by the stimulations of cone cells in the eye that are sensitive to electromagnetic radiation in the range 400 nm to 700 nm. The minimum radiant energy threshold occurs at about 0.001 cdm^{-2}, below which colour cannot be detected.

Users of colour should be aware that a coloured object when viewed under incandescent lights will appear to have a different hue, lightness and chroma, compared to natural daylight. This is because natural light has a different spectral characteristic from incandescent light sources, and because the eye adapts to shifts in spectral wavelength. It is worth noting that the spectral emission of an incandescent light source is a function of the current passing through (hence temperature) of the tungsten filament (see Table 3.2).

Table 3.2 Factors affecting colour comparison/discrimination.

Factor	Effect
Chromatic adaption	Colour comparisons in the green to blue regions of the spectrum if the background field is desaturated with the addition of more green primary.
	Chromatic discrimination deteriorates above 490 nm by almost 1.5 when equal amounts of white and spectral light are presented. This further increases to about 3.5 if there is an excess of white light relative to the spectral light. However, below 490 nm increasing the amount of white light relative to the spectral light can actually improve chromatic discrimination.
	Chromatic discrimination is greatly affected by previous exposure to coloured lights.
Luminance	Below 3.5 cdm^{-2} (approximately) an observer's chromatic discrimination ability reduces significantly.
Retinal position	Objects in the peripheral field must subtend larger visual angles in order for colour to be perceived. Foveal images generally appear more saturated than those in the peripheral region.
Duration	Increasing stimulation times generally increases chromatic discrimination sensitivity; this only holds for durations greater than 0.02 s. Alternate presentation of test and comparison stimuli causes a decrease in chromatic sensitivity for duty rates ranging from 60 ms to 5 s.
Object size	It is difficult to determine or compare the colours of objects that approach a point source in angular subtense.

Colour specification

The definition of a colour in the form of a hue is very subjective and depends on several factors. To specify accurately a single or range of colours a more scientific and repeatable method is required. The most accurate method of specifying a colour is to plot the radiance of the light source as a function of wavelength. For transparent objects, such as coloured filters, the spectral transmittance distribution is usually specified.

To obtain colour specifications in terms of observers with normal vision, it is necessary to use the tristimulus values. A series of ideal observers have been characterized by the CIE colorimetric system (Wright, 1965).

The colour matching properties of the CIE 1931 standard colorimetric observer are defined by a series of spectral tristimulus values. These are shown in Figure 3.16. These values apply to observer fields of angular subtense of 1–4°. If fields of angular subtense exceed 4° then a modified set of tristimulus values must be used. These are the CIE 1964 supplementary standard colorimetric standard.

In many display systems chromaticity coordinates $x(\lambda)$, $y(\lambda)$, $z(\lambda)$ are quoted to define the whole gamut of reproducible colours. These chromaticity coordinates are derived from the monochromatic tristimulus values by the following relationship.

$$x = \frac{X}{X + Y + Z}$$

$$y = \frac{Y}{X + Y + Z}$$

$$z = \frac{Z}{X + Y + Z}$$

The resulting spectrum locus for the 1931 CIE standard observer is given in Figure 3.17. As with the spectral tristimulus values, there is a CIE 1964 supplementary standard for the chromaticity coordinates (for objects subtending more than 4° at the observer's eye). Full tables are available in CIE (1970).

By taking the chromaticity coordinates for a given display, it is possible to mark on CIE diagrams the exact range of colours reproducible by the display. However, particular care has to be taken to ensure that the correct CIE chromaticity diagram is used.

When using colour displays such as CRT, it is straightforward to determine the spectral tristimulus values x, y and z from the following relationship.

$$
\begin{bmatrix} x \\ y \\ z \end{bmatrix} =
\begin{bmatrix}
\dfrac{x_R}{y_R} & \dfrac{x_G}{y_G} & \dfrac{x_B}{y_B} \\
1 & 1 & 1 \\
\dfrac{z_R}{y_R} & \dfrac{z_G}{y_G} & \dfrac{z_B}{y_B}
\end{bmatrix}
\begin{bmatrix} Y_R \\ Y_G \\ Y_B \end{bmatrix}
$$

where x_R, x_G, y_R, z_R, and so on are the chromaticity coordinates of the display device's red, green and blue primaries, and Y_R, Y_G, Y_B are the luminance values of the red, green and blue primaries.

Therefore, to determine what luminance level is needed to drive each CRT, primarily to achieve a particular colour, it is only necessary to multiply the colour tristimulus value by the inverse of the 3 × 3 chromaticity matrix.

The chromaticity coordinates for a particular display device usually specify a triangular area on the CIE chromaticity diagram. Colours outside this triangular area are not within the gamut of colours reproducible by the display device.

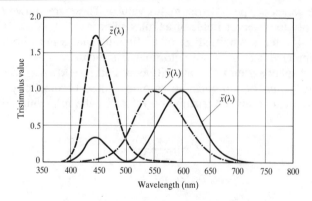

Figure 3.16 Spectral tristimulus values for CIE 1931 standard colorimetric observer.

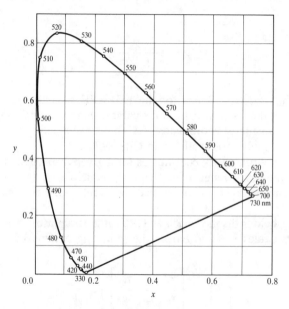

Figure 3.17 Spectral locus for CIE 1931 standard colorimetric observer.

3.3 Physiology of auditory perception

The human auditory perception system has evolved to become an extremely impressive sensory system. The auditory system probably formed part of an omnidirectional early warning system and has evolved as one of the key components of communication between other humans. The auditory system is very impressive when one considers that it is responsive to a wide frequency range with a sensitivity of 0.2%. The wide dynamic range of the auditory system is particularly impressive, with an upper capability of around 110 dB. A sensitivity of a fraction of a decibel at all intensity levels is something that no current electronic system can easily emulate.

To synthesize a realistic auditory environment for the listener, it is important to take account of the acoustic environment and deal with aspects such as echo or reverberation. Moreover, the position and orientation of the listener's head plays a significant role in auditory perception. To highlight the complex nature of auditory perception, consider the following situation.

Imagine one is standing in a room full of twenty or so people who are actively engaged in talking to each other in small groups. It is possible to focus one's attention on to a single group and eavesdrop on their conversation, disregarding what is going on in the other groups, even though they may be closer than the one being listened to. The ability of the human auditory perception system to discriminate in this manner is indeed quite remarkable.

To analyse this sort of situation, it is necessary to find some way of representing the sounds received at the ears by several sound sources in a given real-world environment. As the listener's head moves, the sound source changes in a way that can only be specified with knowledge of the source position and the position and orientation of the head. This is known as the head related transfer function (HRTF). Other factors, including phase differences and overtones, play an important role.

There are essentially two pathways for the reception of sound: the normal air conduction route via the ears, and the bone conduction route in the head. These routes, along with the masking effects caused by the head and inter-aural time delays between the two ears, contribute to the total auditory perception.

3.3.1 Hearing

The ear is divided into three anatomical regions: the external ear, the middle ear and the internal ear. The external ear collects the sound waves with the pinna (auricle), and directs them inward into the external auditory canal and onto the tympanic membrane (eardrum) (see Figure 3.18).

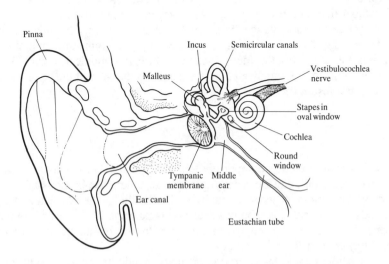

Figure 3.18 Anatomy of the ear.

External ear

The pinna is constructed from a flap of elastic-like cartilage shaped rather like a trumpet and covered by a thick layer of skin. The external auditory canal is essentially a tube about 2.5 cm long lying within the temporal bone. It connects the pinna to the tympanic membrane. The wall of the canal is composed of bone lined with the same cartilage material as the pinna. The surface of the auditory canal is covered with thin, highly sensitive skin. The tympanic membrane is a very thin semi-transparent layer of connective tissue that separates the external auditory canal and the middle ear.

The pinna is interposed into the auditory system before the ear canal and is terminated by the acoustic impedance of the ear canal. It acts as a linear filter whose transfer function is dependent upon the direction and distance of the sound source. The pinna operates by distorting incident sound signals linearly, depending upon the direction and distance of the sound source, hence coding the spatial characteristics of the sound field into temporal and spectral attributes. The pinna experiences a range of acoustical/physical properties including: diffraction, dispersion, interference, masking, reflection and resonance.

The external ear canal is terminated by the tympanic membrane which vibrates in sympathy with the incident sound. Sound can also be transmitted to the inner ear by a process called 'bone conduction', where sound is propagated through the temporal bone.

Middle ear

The middle ear is a small air-filled cavity (epithelial lined). At one end of the middle ear is the tympanic membrane and at the other end are two openings known as the oval and the round windows. Motion of the tympanic membrane occurs when there are sound pressure variations in the ear canal. Finally the middle ear contains an auditory tube (eustachian tube) that connects with the nasopharynx of the throat.

The middle ear contains the three small auditory ossicles, known as the malleus, incus and stapes. The malleus is connected to the tympanic membrane and communicates vibrations to the incus, which in turn communicates with the stapes. Auditory vibrations are communicated by the stapes to the membrane covering the oval window (fenestra vestibuli).

Inner ear

The inner ear is composed of a complicated series of canals. The canals are divided into two main structures, an outer bony labyrinth and an inner membranous labyrinth. The bony labyrinth consists of a series of cavities, the vestibule, the cochlea and the semi-circular canals. The cochlea is a bony spiral that makes about $2^3/_4$ turns around a bony central core. The cochlea is itself partitioned into three separate canals, one of which (scala vestibuli) ends at the oval window.

The principle behind the operation of the tympanic membrane, auditory ossicles and oval window is straightforward. The tympanic membrane has a surface area approximately 22 times larger than that of the oval window.

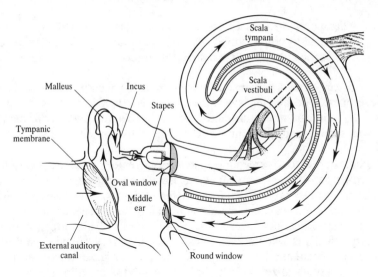

Figure 3.19 Schematic diagram of principles behind hearing.

The system acts rather like a small mechanical amplifier, increasing the auditory signals to a level where the oval window can couple the vibrations into the perilymph fluid of the inner ear. Figure 3.19 illustrates the process.

The vibrations in the perilymph cause the oval window to vibrate in sympathy with the auditory signal. This in turn causes the pressure to vary in the endolymph of the cochlea, causing the hairs of the basilar membrane to move against the tectorial membrane. The movement of hairs causes the generation of nerve impulses, which travel to the midbrain, to the thalamus and finally to the auditory region of the temporal lobe of the cerebral cortex.

3.3.2 Auditory localization

The pinnae are involved in the perception of sound outside the head. This can be demonstrated very easily by recording a sound source with two microphones and replaying this to a listener via a pair of head phones. The sound appears to originate from inside the head, whereas if the sound is recorded by a pair of microphones inserted into the ears of a dummy head (with artificial pinnae), the sound perceived by the listener appears to originate outside the head. Sound recorded in this way is known as binaural stereo. The shape of the pinnae are largely responsible for this, since they appear to interact with the audio signal.

Two mechanisms seem to be involved in our localization of sounds in azimuth, namely intensity differences, and temporal or phase differences between signals arriving at the ears.

- Intensity differences: Operate for audio tones whose frequency is above 1.5 kHz. The higher the frequency, the greater the effect of head masking (shadowing). Relative intensity levels can approach 20 dB attenuation in one ear compared to the other.

■   Temporal differences: An interaural delay as small as 10 μs can be detected by some individuals. An interaural delay in excess of 650 μs can be sufficient to localize a sound precisely.

The human ear can locate a sound source very precisely even in the presence of strong conflicting echoes. The hearing system exhibits an effect known as the precedence effect, by which it can reject unwanted sounds generated by a reverberant room. Provided two sounds appear within 1–5 ms, then the sound received first will be perceived.

The human auditory perception system is extremely complex. One of the most impressive of its capabilities is its ability to isolate a particular sound source from a collection of others, all originating from different places. The degree to which one sound masks another is called binaural unmasking, and depends upon the relative frequency, intensity and locations of the sound source. This effect, known as the 'cocktail party effect', is when a listener can stand in a very crowded and noisy room but still precisely locate and listen to any of a number of separate conversations. The human's ability to localize sounds has evolved to provide protection against environmental threats.

Audio localization is a function of:

1.   The difference in sound reaching the two ears.
2.   The differences in sound relative to the directions and range relative to the observer.
3.   Monaural cues derived from the pinna.
4.   Head movements.

Localization is affected by the presence of other sounds, and the direction these sounds originate from, especially if more than one sound source is involved.

Auditory localization is understood in the horizontal plane (left to right), but very little is known about auditory localization in the median plane, and front to back discrimination. The median plane is the intersection between front and back.

When a listener perceives a sound as originating from the right it usually means that the sound arrives earlier or is louder in the right ear compared to the left.

It is possible for sound to arrive 700 μs earlier in one ear than the other. Additionally, the sound in the ear furthest from the sound source can be attenuated by as much as 40 dB relative to the nearer ear. These interaural time and intensity differences provide the primary uses for sound localization. It is also known that the interaural differences have negligible effect at distances greater than 1 m from the head. In the real world sound arriving at a listener's ears from a single sound source will have arrived from multiple paths, derived from various reflections from other adjacent objects near the sound source.

At frequencies below 1 kHz the external ear can be approximated to a pressure detector on the surface of a hard spherical object (Rayleigh, 1945). This approximation is reasonably accurate for interaural time differences at all frequencies. At frequencies higher than 1 kHz the description is incomplete because the characteristics of the head become just as important as those of the external ear.

Figure 3.20 shows a spherical head of radius r, with the ears located at the ends of a diameter. If distant sound waves are incident on the head to the left of the line of symmetry XY at an angle θ, to reach the right ear the sound must travel further compared to the left by an amount given by the following expression:

$$d = r\sin\theta + r\theta$$

The interaural time difference t is given by:

$$t = \frac{d}{c} = \frac{r}{c}(\sin\theta + \theta)$$

where c is the velocity of sound in air.

Figure 3.21 shows the calculated interaural time difference for a hard diameter of 875 mm and a velocity of sound in air of 344 ms[-1].

Interaural time difference is independent of frequency and head shape. Interaural phase difference and pressure amplitude have been calculated for a spherical head by Hartley and Fry (1921). This data has been calculated for several frequencies and for various distances between the sound source and the head.

Experiments have shown that localization is more accurate for broadband spectra than for pure tones. For example, localization accuracy for a click is of the order of $8°$, while for a hiss the accuracy is approximately $5.6°$.

Head movement or movement of the sound source can be almost as effective in localization perception as binaural cues. The most dominant effect is a change in apparent loudness: displacement of $15°$ can result in a 2–3 dB change in loudness.

The head and shoulders modify the spectrum of the sound as it reaches the ears, and the pinna and ear canal further modify the sound on its way to the tympanic membrane (eardrum).

When a sound source exists directly in front of (or behind) the listener, the interaural differences are zero. Even when the vertical position is raised or lowered from the central position the interaural difference is still effectively zero. However, the listener is able to localize the sounds reasonably well. It seems reasonable to assume that by moving the head the sound is put outside the median plane, resulting in interaural differences. Familiar sounds can be distinguished because of the differential effects of the pinna. A sound is generally softer and different in timbre when originating from the back compared to the front.

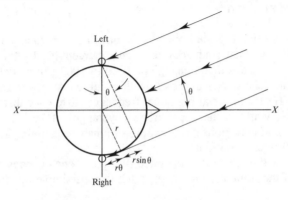

Figure 3.20 Interaural time difference.

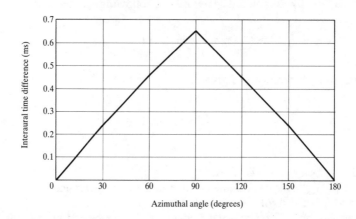

Figure 3.21 Calculated interaural time difference for a spherical head.

Timbre is the name given to that quality which distinguishes two auditory signals that have the same pitch and intensity (loudness). In a sense it refers to the spectral composition of the sound source. Terms such as brightness, mellowness and richness are often used. Timbre depends on the envelope of the sound signal and includes the rate of amplitude modulations.

3.3.3 Frequency analysis

In order to hear the individual components of a complex audio signal, the frequency components must be sufficiently separated from one another. When the component frequencies are too close, the signal is perceived as a single component. This is known as Ohm's acoustic law, and the ability to analyse audio signals into their constituent components is known as frequency selectivity. The ear can be said to act as a series of narrowly tuned filters. (Though this is an oversimplification of the auditory perception process.)

3.3.4 Pitch discrimination

The human ear is sensitive to sound pitch variations in the frequency range 1 kHz to 3 kHz. The minimal fractional frequency difference perceptible by the average human listener is 0.3%. This means that a change of 1000 to 1003 can be detected. Training, particularly with musicians, can improve on this figure. At lower frequencies in the range 32 Hz to 64 Hz the minimal fractional frequency difference that is perceivable is in the order of 1%, while in the upper frequency ranges of 16 kHz to 20 kHz pitch discrimination is extremely poor. The average human with unimpaired hearing can resolve about 2000 pitch variations.

A musician will confirm that the pitch of a pure tone depends on the frequency and the intensity of the stimulus. Moreover, pitch is not a simple function of frequency.

3.4 Physiology of haptic and kinaesthetic perception

3.4.1 Physiology of touch (cutaneous sensitivity)

Touch is the common word that is used to describe mechanical contact with the skin. A variety of other descriptive terms are used to specify mechanical contacts such as contact, vibration, sharp, pressure. Touch, or more accurately cutaneous sensitivity, is a complex subject because it considers other stimuli such as heat.

The skin is approximately 1–2 mm below the epidermis (outer layer). The skin in general causes a local disturbance to become distributed, thereby attenuating the sensation of touch. Certain regions of the skin are more sensitive to touch than others.

3.4.2 Anatomy of the skin

There are three mechanical stimuli that produce the sensation of touch:

- Step function. A displacement of the skin for an extended period of time, for example a small point resting on the surface of the skin.

- Impulse function. A transitory displacement of the skin that lasts for a few milliseconds.

- Periodic functions. A transitory displacement of the skin that is repeated regularly at a constant or variable frequency.

Experiments can be conducted to demonstrate that the skin has certain thresholds for touch (vibrotactile thresholds), the exact values being a function of the type and position of the mechanical stimuli. To complicate matters even further the skin's nervous system can perform spatial summation and is a function of position on the body. An equally important factor is temporal summation of mechanical stimuli events. Temporal summation increases as the stimuli frequency increases. Hill (1967) measured temporal summation thresholds as a function of the duration of a unidirectional mechanical impulse. He deduced a relationship between the duration and threshold that satisfies the following equation:

$$A_t = \frac{2}{1 - e^{-\left(\frac{t}{1.5}\right)}}$$

where A_t is the threshold amplitude (μm) and t is the pulse duration (ms). (The equation represents an integrator with a 1.5 ms time constant.) The equation is valid only for a finger-pad area, with a stimulation contactor of 0.6 mm diameter.

It is interesting that several researchers have considered using the skin to resolve different frequency components as a sensory aid for the hard of hearing. Unfortunately, so far the technique has not worked because of adaption to vibrotactile stimulation.

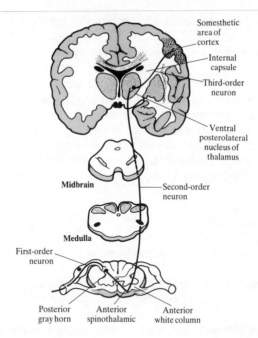

Somesthetic
area of
cortex

Internal
capsule

Third-order
neuron

Ventral
posterolateral
nucleus of
thalamus

Midbrain

Second-order
neuron

Medulla

First-order
neuron

Posterior
gray horn

Anterior
spinothalamic

Anterior
white column

Figure 3.22 Anterior (ventral) spinothalamic sensory pathway for touch, pressure and light.

This effect is a secondary characteristic of many sensations and amounts to a decrease in sensitivity to continued stimuli. Sometimes the sensation may disappear completely even though the stimulus is still being applied. Moreover, receptors vary in their ability to adapt. Rapidly adapting (phasic) receptors include pressure, touch, and smell. On the other hand slowly adapting (tonic) receptors are responsible for pain and body position.

It is also interesting that some sensations have after-images, which persist when the stimulus has been removed.

Cutaneous receptors are simple structures, consisting of dendrites of sensory neurons that can be enclosed in a capsule of epithelial or connective tissue. The nerve impulses generated by the cutaneous receptors are transmitted along somatic afferent neurons in spinal and cranial nerves, through the thalamus, to the general sensory area of the parietal lobe of the cortex. Figure 3.22 shows the neural pathway that conducts the impulse from a touch receptor to the posterior grey horn on the same side of the spinal cord. The neural pathway that conducts touch impulses (as well as light and pressure) is known as the anterior (ventral) spinothalamic pathway. Eventually the nerve impulse is passed to the ventral posterolateral nucleus of the thalamus. At the thalamic level there is some sensation of light touch and pressure. It is not fully localized until the nerve impulses reach the cerebral cortex.

The terms 'light touch' and 'discriminative touch' are used to refer to the ability to perceive that something has touched the skin, and to localize exactly the point of the body touched, respectively. Figure 3.23 shows the tactile receptors in the skin, which consist of hair root plexuses, free nerve endings, tactile discs, corpuscles of touch and type II cutaneous mechanoreceptors. Hair root plexuses mainly detect movements on the surface of the body – the hair acts as a simple lever. The free nerve endings are mainly concerned with the detection of pain but they also respond to objects in continuous contact with the skin. Tactile (Merkel's) cells are modified epidermal cells in the stratum basale of hairless skin. Their function is to assist in discriminative touch. Corpuscles of touch (Meissner's corpuscles) are found in the dermal papillae of the skin and are most numerous in the fingertips and palms of the hand. They are responsible for the perception of discriminative touch. The type II mechanoreceptors found deep within the dermis are primarily responsible for heavy and continuous touch sensations.

Cutaneous sensitive nerve fibres are categorized into four types: SA1, SA2, RA1 and RA2. SA1 and SA2 are slowly adapting nerve fibres and are responsive to an object that comes into contact with (and subsequently moves against) the skin. RA1 and RA2 are relatively fast adapting nerve fibres and they respond to movement on the skin. RA2 fibres are the fastest.

Experiments have been undertaken to determine the response thresholds amplitudes for different frequencies of stimulation (see Table 3.3).

Small features up to 2 μm high can be detected by the fast adapting nerve fibre endings called the Meissner corpuscles, and even smaller features (typically 0.06 μm high) can be detected by the faster adapting nerve fibre endings called the Pacinian corpuscles.

If a smooth glass or metal plate is processed so that a single 2 μm high point is present on its surface, and this is moved over the skin, it is possible to detect the presence of the dot.

There seems little doubt that the skin acts as a low pass filter, reducing the effect of local surface pressure variations and allowing surface profiles of objects to be classified in terms of surface curvature.

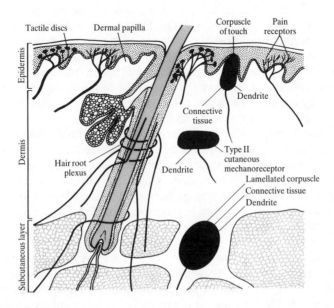

Figure 3.23 Shows the structure and location of touch receptors.

Table 3.3 Lowest response threshold amplitudes.

Nerve fibre type	Frequency of stimulation (Hz)
SA1	0–10
SA2	0–10
RA1	20–50
RA2	100–300

Other surface characteristics such as soft, hard, hairy and sticky all tend to cause local deformations of the skin. However, there is a distinction between rigid (hard) and compliant (soft) surfaces. For a hard surface to be felt after the initial contact, it is necessary to ensure that active pressure is maintained. Obviously, textured surfaces rely on some relative motion between the surface and the skin. Soft surfaces, on the other hand, are able to exert a slight positive reaction against the skin after the initial contact, which enables discrimination to take place between soft and hard surfaces.

Clearly, anyone wishing to construct a device to communicate the sensation of remote touch to a user must be fully aware of the dynamic range of the touch receptors, with particular emphasis on their adaption to certain stimuli. It is only too easy to disregard the fundamental characteristics of the human body.

3.4.3 Proprioception/kinaesthesia

Kinaesthesia is the term that covers our awareness of the movements and relative positions of the various parts of our body. Our kinaesthetic awareness takes into account the rate and direction of movement of our limbs and the static position when movement ceases. This allows us to estimate the weight supported by a limb or the force exerted by contraction of our muscles. The capability of a human to memorize a particular joint position is rather interesting. Not only is it possible to mimic the exact joint angle of one of our arms by the other (with one eye closed), it is also possible to remember this particular joint angle for more than 24 hours after the event.

Information from a variety of sources, including visual cues, is used to make kinaesthetic judgements. For example, a person might look at their limbs to discover their respective positions. Even though non-kinaesthetic cues are used to ascertain the positions of limbs, the kinaesthetic system is fundamental to determining the position and movement of the limbs due to tension signals originating from sensory receptors in the joints, skin and muscle. The muscle receptors provide an awareness of static limb position, while muscle receptors and vitaneous receptors together provide an awareness of limb dynamics.

It is interesting that we lack a sense of the static positions of some of the finger joints (inter-phalangeal joints). Our ability to sense finger position comes from cues including movement signals from the muscle/skin receptors and non-kinaesthetic cues.

Joints closer to the body are more insensitive to small angles compared to distal joints. Consequently, a small positional error in a joint near the body (such as the shoulder) with a long radius arm, can affect the positioning of a finger tip considerably greater than a single finger movement. This means that proximal joints are much more sensitive than distal joints. A secondary issue that must be considered is the velocity of individual joints. A small rate of movement might be too small for perception. Kinaesthesia is a complicated process because certain effects are not properly understood. For example, tensing one's muscles improves movement sense, probably because the responses of the receptors in the muscles are enhanced.

Humans can gauge the force produced by the contraction of certain muscles. Two separate mechanisms appear to be responsible for this:

1. Sensory inputs from tension receptors provide an awareness of muscle tension.
2. Command signals generated in the brain are monitored and provide a sense of effort.

Terms such as 'light' or 'heavy' describe our perception of the weight of an object, and depend on the actual weight of the object as well as on the condition of the muscles. For instance, consider a person holding a heavy object, supported by a fully extended arm. Over a period of time the person's muscles become tired and the object feels heavier. The muscle produces less force for a given level of excitation. Figure 3.24 shows the apparent increase in weight of an object as a function of time. An effect known as 'weight expectancy illusion' occurs when a heavy object is lifted prior to lifting a lighter object. Underestimation of the weight of the lighter object occurs. The opposite occurs when a light object is lifted before a heavier one. Humans can detect joint angles down to a fraction of a degree typically in the range 0.20°–6.10°, according to the joint being measured and the rate of movement. The order of sensitivity of the joints in decreasing sensitivity is: hip, shoulder, knee, ankles, elbow, knuckles, wrist, the last two metacarpophalangeal joints and finally the toes.

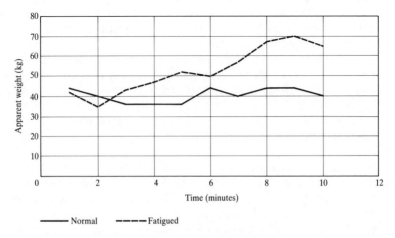

Figure 3.24 Apparent increase in weight of an object as a function of time.

It is interesting that we possess an internal mental image of the positions of our limbs/joints that does not depend on sensing information. This is coupled with a high degree of memory capability for limb position. However, it should be noted that this mental image can be fooled by the effect of the surroundings.

Cutaneous mechanoreceptors in the skin may be partly responsible for kinaesthesia because the skin covering our bodies stretches and contracts as we move. The effect of cutaneous mechanoreceptors is generally unclear although it is likely that they enhance kinaesthetic sensations derived from other means. There also appears to be some differentiation in cutaneous mechanoreceptors over different regions of the body. For example, cutaneous receptors in the hands, feet and face seem to play a part in kinaesthesia, whereas skin around the elbows contributes very little to kinaesthesia.

It seems clear that these receptors do not convey a sense of joint position. As discussed previously, the receptors in the skin have rapidly adapting responses that are unable to indicate static or slow displacements of the skin.

Joint mechanoreceptors are found in the ligaments and capsules of joints and adapt quite slowly to the stretching of ligaments and compression of capsules. Experiments can be performed to show that joint mechanoreceptors are unable to give information that corresponds to position or movement of the joint. The exception to this is when hyperextension of a joint occurs.

Muscle mechanoreceptors are probably the most dominant mechanism for kinaesthesia. Muscle spindles are sensitive to limb position and movement, while the Golgi tendon organs are responsible for detecting tension. The muscle spindles lie in parallel with the contractile elements of muscle tissue. The spindles can determine muscle stretch and rate of increase in muscle length. The Golgi tendon organs lie in series with the tension-producing muscle elements. They produce an indication of the tension developed in the muscle.

3.5 Virtual presence

Most people who have experienced different virtual environment systems state that they felt either 'part of a synthetic experience' or that they felt 'immersed in the experience'. It is important to realize that these two states are completely different and imply different degrees of presence. To be 'part of the synthetic experience' means that although one feels immersed to some extent in the experience, one is also aware of the outside world. Complete immersion does not take place. This is the case with some virtual environment games where one does not feel totally enveloped in the experience. (However, this does not affect the enjoyment and fun.) The overriding factor for this could be that one realizes the experience will last only as long as the money that was put into the machine! But poor graphics, presenting a cartoon type environment and a hand-held button that gears one's movements, restricts, or indeed prevents, complete immersion.

To be 'immersed in the experience' means that the person involved felt part of the actual environment. Immersion can take place slowly, such as when one watches a television thriller. The storyline needs some understanding until one becomes engrossed. Immersion can take place at a quicker pace when the television programme is of a greater immediate interest. For instance, for a viewer watching a nature programme of extreme beauty and realizing that he could never visit the actual area, his interest makes him feel part of the scene. He wishes he were there. A very fast rate of immersion occurs when a television camera has, for example, been placed at the front of a roller coaster ride. The viewer can actually experience the plunging effect as the ride dips.

Therefore, a visual cue that improves immersion is a powerful way of gaining a sense of presence in a virtual environment. The quicker the immersion, the more a person feels engrossed. In turn, extended immersion time leads to adaption and a sense of 'complete' presence.

A breakdown in the sensation of virtual presence occurs when the person feels tired or when the weight of the head-mounted display becomes uncomfortable. Unnatural movement or lags in the virtual environment can also lead to conflicts in the feeling of presence, but if the participant is stimulated with visual and auditory information of high fidelity and is allowed to interact with objects in the virtual environment, the feeling of presence can be very powerful.

Unfortunately, there is very little scientific literature that deals with this very important subject. This is further evidenced by the almost complete lack of objective measure. We are not very sure about what degree of virtual presence is required to train effectively in a virtual environment system. As we are dealing with systems that ultimately impact on operator performance we need to understand all aspects of virtual environment systems that have a possible bearing on the participant's performance.

We need to be aware of the way a human being interacts with a real world and the adaption that takes place when things change in the real or external environment. Ellis (1991) reports that our knowledge is constantly being updated by behavioral plasticity of visual–motor coordination and vestibular reflexes. Ellis goes on to say that 'a large part of our sense of physical reality is a consequence of internal processing rather than being something that is developed only from the immediate sensory information we receive'. Clearly, from this statement we can deduce that matching our virtual environment peripherals to the operator perceptual system is as important as how we present information to the operator. Research over the past twenty years has dealt with workload and how it relates to human performance. Perhaps with a virtual environment we must also take account of presence and its effects on operator performance. Sheridan (1992) states that 'Presence is a subjective sensation, much like mental workload and mental model – it is a mental manifestation, not so amenable to objective physiological definition and measurement'.

Ideally, we would like a set of repeatable objective measures for presence that indicates the degree of presence created by a particular system. However, as Sheridan points out, 'Presence is a subjective sensation and as such any subjective measures are likely to be multidimensional'. Engineers like to work with objective measures because these are usually much easier to obtain once they have been defined. In defining presence we are in a slight dilemma because we have not yet determined either subjective or objective measures. Several factors seem to stand out as essential in creating a strong feeling of presence. These are discussed in the following paragraphs.

Seeing parts of one's own body

There is no doubt that seeing parts of one's own body reinforces the feeling of presence. Attempts to produce on a screen computer graphic equivalents of, for instance, the hands, while helping to coordinate hand/eye movements, lowers the feeling of presence. A very strong feeling of presence can be achieved if the visual system allows actual parts of the operator to come into the field of view at the appropriate time.

High resolution and large field of view

If the framework of the display device is visible to the operator this can conflict with the operator's feeling of being in the virtual world. Therefore, the display device must present as large a field of view as possible. Ideally, the operator should be able to move his/her eyes to view objects just outside the region of peripheral vision. If a restrictive field of view is imposed the operator's head must be moved, which can lead to a reduction in the feeling of presence.

Familiarity of virtual environment or scene

If the virtual environment is one that relates to a real world then the time taken to adapt to it appears to be shorter. However, in certain environments a user's experience may prevent him from becoming fully immersed because of artefacts introduced by the virtual environment system.

One solution to the characterization of virtual environment systems is based on a model proposed by Zeltzer (1991, 1992), which assumes that any virtual environment has three components:

1. A set of models/objects or processes.
2. A means of modifying the states of these models.
3. A range of sensory modalities to allow the participant to experience the virtual environment.

Zeltzer represents these components on a unit cube with vectors relating to autonomy, interaction and presence (see Figure 3.25).

- Autonomy: This refers to a qualitative measure of the virtual object's ability to react to events and stimuli. Where no reaction occurs then the autonomy is 0, whereas for maximum autonomy a value of 1 is assigned. Scaling between 0 and 1 in this context is purely qualitative.

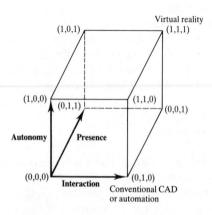

Figure 3.25 Zeltzer's autonomy, interaction and presence cube.

- Interaction: This refers to the degree of access to the parameters or variables of an object. A rating of 0 applies to non-real-time control of the variables, for example variables initialized during compilation or at the beginning of execution. A value of 1 is assigned for variables that can be manipulated in real time during program execution. Modern graphics systems allow a very high degree of interaction. However, it is necessary to consider the complexity of the application. A very complex application program may not be able to run in real time.

- Presence: The degree of presence provides a crude measure of the fidelity of the sensory input and output channels. The degree of presence has a high dependency on the task requirements – hence the application has a bearing.

The very early graphics systems that were programmed in non-real-time batch mode are represented by the point (0,0,0) on Zeltzer's cube. These early systems exhibited no interactivity. Examples include graph plotters and chart recorders. Diagonally opposite this point (1,1,1) is our target where we would have maximum autonomy, interactivity and presence. This is virtual reality. The sensory simulation would be so complete that we would not be able to distinguish the virtual environment from the real world. The point (0,1,0) can be achieved today, where the user can control essentially all the variables of an object or model during program execution. This can be achieved in real time. A point approaching (0,1,1) probably represents the status of virtual environments, where we can experience a high degree of interactivity with a reasonable degree of presence. Unfortunately, the degree of automation of the objects in the virtual environment is relatively low. The point (1,0,1) represents the situation where there is a high degree of presence and autonomy but low interactivity. An example of this would be a fully autonomous virtual environment where the human becomes a passive observer but is fully immersed in the virtual environment. The only freedom the observer would have is the ability to control their viewpoint. Any change of viewpoint would be oblivious to the objects in the virtual environment.

When I first attended one of Zeltzer's presentations I was not convinced that his abstract representation of a virtual environment would serve any purpose. However, as time has gone by I am finding his conceptual tool more and more useful in explaining the different categories of virtual environments.

Determinants of presence

Sheridan (1992) proposed three principal determinants for the sense of presence, but these determinants do not appear to take account of the dynamics of either the user or object. Perhaps Sheridan was only considering real-world interaction. However, when we are dealing with a virtual environment there will almost certainly be some form of inherent delay caused by lags in the tracking or the computer graphics systems. These lags and delays will reduce the feeling of presence. Therefore, the author added a fourth determinant that is concerned with the perceived dynamic behaviour of both objects in the virtual environment and responses due to operator-induced motor movements. The motion of objects in a virtual environment is very important in maintaining a sense of realism. (Refer again to Ellis' statement.) This implies that we have built up a mental model of how certain objects should behave in a dynamic sense. No matter how well an object is drawn and rendered it will look unreal if it moves in an unnatural manner. The motion of certain objects can even be more important than the way they are drawn or displayed. The four possible determinants of presence are:

1. Extent of sensory information.
2. Ability of the observer to modify their viewpoint for visual parallax or visual field. This also includes the ability to reposition the head to maintain binaural hearing.
3. The ability to modify the spatial relationships of objects in a virtual environment.
4. The closed loop performance due to an operator-induced motor movement. This also includes the dynamic behaviour of movable objects in the virtual environment.

The degree to which the operator or participant must be involved in or feel part of the virtual environment will depend upon the task to be performed. There is a temptation to concentrate on simulating as close as possible the real world by providing a rich 3-D photorealistic display with sound, tactile and force feedback. Matching virtual environment peripheral devices to the performance of the human sensory system is a difficult task. For now we must accept that technological limitations prevent us from achieving a complete match with all aspects of the human perception system. Therefore, it is necessary to consider various trade-offs. A virtual environment allows us to present information in an unnatural way or even to exaggerate a particular effect. In these instances it is difficult to predict what the merits are. In designing virtual environments we must look to human performance metrics and the subjective experience of presence to provide a measure of the effectiveness of a design.

The subject of virtual presence is addressed further in Chapters 6 and 8. It is worth noting here that the subject of presence and degree of immersion will play a very important role in future virtual environment systems because it could provide the means of assessing the performance benefits of these systems.

3.6 Summary

This chapter has concentrated on some of the important underlying human factors principles associated with virtual environments. The author intends that the material presented here will form a framework for other chapters. The major message from this chapter is that there is still a great deal to be learnt about the integration of a human into a virtual environment. A key requirement in the future will be the development of a series of metrics to measure human performance. With suitable metrics it will be possible to determine where limitations exist in our understanding of the human factors or the enabling technology. To quantify the benefits that a virtual environment system offers over alternative approaches it will be necessary to provide objective evidence of the gains. It has not been possible to go into great detail on the subject of human perception because this is a vast area and easily warrants a book in its own right. It is tempting to try to trivialize some perceptual issues but the reader should be warned against doing this because the subject is indeed very complex. Despite the vast amount of literature that is available today we are still learning a great deal about the interaction of our senses. The section on virtual presence probably holds many clues for the development of metrics in the field of virtual environment systems.

Recommended further reading

Boff K.R., Kaufman, L. and Thomas J.P. (1986). *Handbook of Perception and Human Performance* Vols 1 and 2. Chichester:Wiley-Interscience

Ellis S.R., ed. (1991). *Pictorial Communication in Virtual and Real Environments.* London: Taylor and Francis

Rock I. (1990). *The Perceptual World: Readings from* Scientific American *Magazine.* New York: W.H. Freeman and Co.

Thimbleby H. (1990). *User Interface Design.* Reading MA:Addison-Wesley/ACM Press

4 Virtual Environment Systems: Enabling Technology

Objectives

The objective of this chapter is to introduce the enabling technology behind virtual environment systems. Not all the available virtual environment equipments are reviewed because the field is constantly changing, with new developments taking place all the time. A range of different technologies spanning visual, auditory and haptic/kinaesthetic systems are given in terms of theory of operation, physics and implementation details. Several host computer platforms are discussed to highlight the required performance that has to be delivered by these systems.

4.1 Introduction

This chapter has been structured along the same lines as Chapter 3 so that the reader can readily find information about systems of direct interest. Care has been taken not to imply any preference for a particular supplier's equipment. It is difficult to give specific recommendations without first considering the requirements of a particular application. Some equipments are more suitable than others for certain tasks. However, by covering a range of equipments and highlighting some of their inherent characteristics the potential user can form a judgement as to their suitability.

4.2 Visual environment systems

The human visual channel is the most powerful sensory input system. Consequently, visual cues can be extremely compelling to the user. It is possible to confuse and disorientate a human observer even if other non-visible cues are present. For example, a cinema projection show where one stands in front of a very large or curved screen allows experience of a wide field of view projection. A film of a roller coaster ride in such circumstances gives viewers an apparent sensation of movement. The same confusion and disorientation occurs when one is sitting on a stationary train and the train on the next track pulls away very slowly.

This section reviews the whole range of display technologies that could be incorporated in a virtual display system. Head tracking systems are also reviewed because of their close integration with the display system that is required to produce a visually coupled system.

4.2.1 Helmet-mounted displays

Display technologies

Today there is a wide range of display technologies, each operating on a different principle and offering several unique characteristics. It is important to understand the different technologies when considering what display type to employ for a particular application. It depends on the type of application. Figure 4.1 shows the range of display technologies that could conceivably find application in helmet-mounted or virtual displays. The following section provides an overview of the relevant display technologies, giving typical specifications of the various performance characteristics. Display devices are characterized either as projection or direct view devices.

Direct view devices

Cathode luminescence

A range of display devices are based on a principle known as cathode luminescence. Such devices are essentially vacuum fluorescent tubes, where light is emitted from the phosphor-coated anodes when these are subjected to electron bombardment. The electron energies involved are considerably lower in comparison to cathode ray tubes.

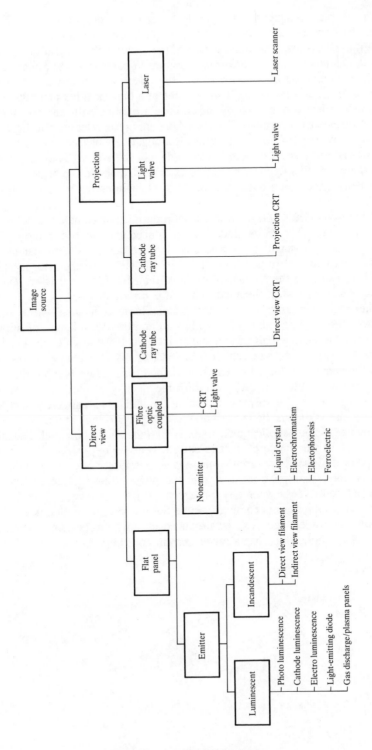

Figure 4.1 Display technologies.

The display image is made when a series of discrete anode elements are energized, as opposed to a focused beam of electrons striking a continuous anode surface. Figure 4.2 shows the construction of the vacuum fluorescent tube. The cathode is a thin filament that runs at a lower temperature in comparison to a thermionic value. The anode is composed of a series of discrete electrode elements with a coating of phosphor. In operation the anode is maintained at a high positive potential with respect to the cathode. Electrons emitted by the cathode are attracted to the positively charged anode. As the electrons bombard the phosphor, energy is released and light is emitted. To achieve some form of brightness control, a negatively charged grid (with respect to the cathode) is interposed between the cathode and the anode. The grid is made from a very fine mesh so that light from the phosphor-coated anode can be seen. The discrete anode elements can be laid out as segments of alphanumerics or as a rectilinear array of elements.

Television style displays with a resolution of approximately 241 × 246 pixels for a picture size of 23 × 23 mm have been produced using this technology. To address the display matrix a small microprocessor is used to drive a p-channel MOSFET transistor for each discrete pixel. To reduce current demands a capacitor is built between each pixel element and the silicon substrate of the MOSFET transistor. The phosphor voltage decays slowly when the anode voltage is turned off.

The phosphor used for most vacuum fluorescent displays is based on a combination of zinc oxide and zinc that has an emitting wavelength of approximately 500 nm. The bandwidth at half peak intensity is about 100 nm which means that colours from blue through to orange can be obtained by using suitable filters. Unfiltered maximum luminance of 700 cdm^{-2} can be obtained; this figure is more than halved for filtered operation. Unfortunately, operating the display at elevated brightness levels reveals the structure of the display, including the individual anode conducting wires.

Particular care must be taken with these displays if they are to be considered for helmet-mounted display applications. Even though the anode potential is relatively high (about 50–100 V) the anode current is extremely low (1–10 μA). The power supply circuit must be designed to ensure that there is no possibility of coming into contact with the anode supply. It is possible to design the power supply stage so that the anode voltage is reduced to zero when any more than 10 μA is drawn.

Colour displays are becoming feasible but the total resolution is extremely low. The vacuum fluorescent tube can be produced cheaply but is being displaced by the liquid crystal display, which has a lower current consumption.

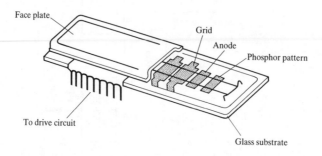

Figure 4.2 Vacuum fluorescent display.

Electroluminescence

Electroluminescence is generated as a result of light produced by a phosphor under the influence of an electric field. Light can be generated by an alternating or continuous electric field.

The thin film electroluminescent display is made from a layer combination of conductors and dielectrics with a luminescent phosphor at the centre. An indium–tin oxide transparent conductor is deposited on a glass substrate followed by a dielectric of high electrical breakdown strength. This is followed by a manganese doped zinc sulphide phosphor, a second dielectric and a near conductor (see Figure 4.3).

When a high electric field (1–2×10^5 Vcm^{-1}) is applied between the two conducting electrodes the ZnS layer breaks down into avalanche conduction, and current flows through to the dielectric interface. Charge builds up on the dielectric, the internal field in the ZnS layer is reduced and eventually conduction ceases. The electric field must be reversed to get an avalanche condition again. At the high fields involved, the electrons cause magnesium atoms to become excited and protons are given off. Display devices of this type of construction give off a yellow–orange glow (585 nm). For some time the effect was thought to be caused by ionization. However, it is now believed that the light is caused by emission from the ZnS layer due to electron impact excitation of the manganese activator.

The electroluminescent display can be matrix addressed by a simple crossed grid arrangement. Successful graphic and video displays have been produced in this manner (see Table 4.1).

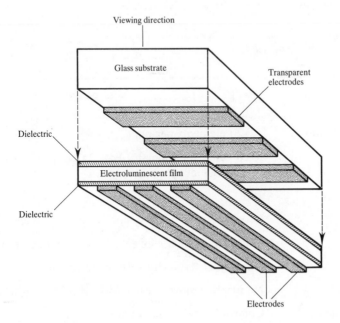

Figure 4.3 Electroluminescent display.

Table 4.1 Characteristics of electroluminescent displays.

Specification parameter	Electroluminescent display parameter
Spatial resolution	8–20 elements per cm; 197 elements per cm devices are currently being researched
Brightness	102 cdm^{-2} typical; 514 – 685 cdm^{-2} devices can be produced with a reduction in life expectancy
Contrast	10:1 typical; full video capability can be achieved with some devices
Colour	Full range, depends on phosphor selected; full colour may be possible in the future
Display size	152.4 mm 240 × 320 pixels; smaller devices have been made for HMD applications 25.4 × 25.4 mm with a resolution of 485 × 645 pixels
Aspect	4:3 viewing angle similar to conventional CRT
Storage/refresh	Operates with an inherent memory
Time constants	Compatible with video rate refresh
Temperature range	-20°C to 55°C
Power requirements	100–300 V, 10 W typical

Table 4.2 Characteristics of LED displays.

Specification parameter	LED parameter
Spatial resolution	12–20 elements per cm
Brightness	3426 cdm^{-2} for a single LED, 342.6 cdm^{-2} for an average area may be achieved
Contrast	100:1
Colour	Red, green and yellow; poor efficiency blue may be obtained
Display size	6 inches 200–300 elements; limited by power dissipation
Aspect	Directional, typically 150° viewing angle
Storage/refresh	No inherent storage capability, 100 Hz refresh achievable
Time constants	Compatible with video rates
Temperature range	-27°C to 55°C
Power requirements	1.5–2.0 V at 1 Acm^{-2} 400 W for a 127×127 mm device

Light emitting diodes

Light emitting diodes were one of the first display technologies to be incorporated in helmet–mounted display systems. They allowed reasonably bright, low weight solutions to be built. However, resolution was extremely limited due to the resolution of the LED matrix that was employed. Despite the low power consumption of LED technology, when high brightness was called for the LED drive current had to be increased. This meant that the device manufacturer had to devise ways of dissipating the excess heat to ensure a reasonable life span. Military applications demanded extremely high brightness levels to allow the LED symbology to overlay onto the real world (see Table 4.2).

Gas discharge/plasma panels

Plasma displays employ electric discharge in a gas to produce the light source. Two types of plasma display exist. These are an a.c. plasma and a d.c. plasma. In an a.c. plasma device an electric field is generated across the gas between two electrodes, just below the required potential to cause a discharge. To create a discharge the voltage is raised to the striking potential and a discharge occurs, resulting in light being generated. To switch the discharge off it is necessary to lower the voltage well below the striking potential. In the d.c. plasma device a mesh is incorporated between the row and column electrodes to restrict the migration of discharge from one pixel to another. Typical characteristics of gas plasma devices are shown in Table 4.3.

Table 4.3 Characteristics of a.c. and d.c. plasma displays.

Specification parameter	Gas discharge/plasma parameter
Spatial resolution	12-24 elements per cm for dot matrix
Brightness	103-171 cdm^{-2} typical, 1233 cdm^{-2} max
Contrast	20:1, grey scale not really possible
Colour	Neon orange, other monochrome and limited three colour versions are available
Display size	a.c. plasma: 430 × 430 mm 1024 × 1024 pixels d.c. plasma: limited to 200 columns
Aspect	Wide angle
Storage/refresh	a.c. plasma: inherent storage capability d.c. plasma: no storage capability; must be done digitally
Time constants	a.c. plasma writing speed: 10 ms for 512 pixels d.c. plasma writing speed: video rate
Temperature range	-20°C to 55°C
Power requirements	Drive voltage 200-300 V, 200-300 W

Incandescent

Incandescent displays are based on a heated filament that glows at a high temperature, thus producing light. These displays are not generally used to provide a virtual display by direct means. Instead they are used to provide either back lighting or the light source for a projected display. Unfortunately, they have the disadvantage of producing rather large amounts of waste heat. This can cause dissipation problems, particularly for small displays. Their major advantage lies with their ready availability and reasonable life expectancy.

Liquid crystal displays

Liquid crystal displays (LCDs) act rather like light valves because they effectively control the amount of reflected light that is incident on them. Since they do not emit light it is necessary to provide some means of external or back illumination. LCDs are found in a wide range of applications, a recent one being television type displays.

The operation of an LCD is based on the alignment of long organic molecules in the presence of an electric field. The fluid part of an LCD comprises long organic molecules (compared to width). When the molecules become aligned, the optical property of the material becomes birefringent. There are three types of arrangement for the molecules: nematic, cholesteric and smectic. The nematic arrangement is the most commonly used and consists of a parallel arrangement of molecules.

The basic construction of the nematic LCD is straightforward. Two glass plates with microscopic lines or grooves on the inner surface are brought together, almost in contact. The microscopic lines of each plate are at right angles to each other. When the nematic liquid crystal is introduced between the two glass plates the long molecules become aligned to the orientation of the microscopic grooves. Since the grooves are at right angles the molecules effectively twist to maintain alignment across the cell. A normal linear polarizer is then applied to each glass plate, orientated so that the transmission axis of the polarizer is in line with the orientation of the microscopic grooves. The twisting of the nematic molecules allows light to pass through the cell that would otherwise be operating in the crossed polarizer mode. In other words, there is no light transmission.

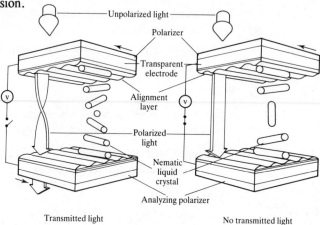

Figure 4.4 Liquid crystal display: operation.

To use the LCD as an addressable display it is necessary to deposit transparent electrodes on the inner surfaces of the two glass plates. When an electric field is maintained across the electrodes the molecules in the LCD become aligned. This causes a rotation of the molecules from their quiescent state, resulting in a change to the optical birefrigence. Light is rotated through the cell so that it does not pass through, and is absorbed in the linear polarizer. The magnitude of the electric field to achieve light modulation is of the order of a few volts. Operational reasons require that the mean d.c. level maintained across the LCD is zero. (The LCD fluid deteriorates in the presence of a d.c. electric field.) Other considerations require the LCD to be operated over a fairly narrow temperature range (see Figure 4.4).

Active matrix LCD

As the prime concern is with the presentation of video displays (where the display format is of a dynamic form) display resolutions approaching 1024 × 1024 are not uncommon requirements. This means that traditional pixel by pixel addressing is not practicable. To overcome this constraint the LCD array is electronically scanned in a sequential manner.

Timing constraints of this addressing technique means that each pixel is updated once every 'full frame refresh', resulting in a poor contrast image. This arises because each pixel acts as a small 'leaky' capacitor that cannot maintain its charge for very long. While the capacitance could be increased during the manufacturing process it ultimately limits the response time of the display. To overcome these problems LCD manufacturers have developed a technique of depositing an array of thin film transistors (TFTs) on the LCD – one per pixel. These transistors can be turned on to maintain the charge, thus ensuring that the display contrast is stable. The TFT arrangement has been perfected by the manufacturers to the extent that over a million individual transistors can be placed on a six-inch square LCD array.

A real challenge was realized when LCDs were required to display a full range of colours with a grey level capability. To achieve colour, each element on an LCD is assigned to a primary colour by a special filter deposited on the face plate of the LCD. The filter comprises small coloured sections arranged so that they lie over one of the LCD elements. It is then a simple matter to energize those LCD elements that lie under red filters to produce red light. This is an area where manufacturers of products needing colour LCDs must be very careful. LCD manufacturers quote display resolution in terms of LCD elements, whether they are red, green or blue elements. It is wrong to equate this resolution figure to a total colour display resolution. Indeed, most helmet-mounted display manufacturers who are using colour LCDs make this mistake.

The actual or true resolution is really a function of the manner in which the colour filter elements are deposited on the LCD face plate. There are five basic arrangements, as shown in Figure 4.5.

In this case it is perhaps unfortunate that the definition of 'pixel' is inappropriate. It is probably better to use the term 'element' for the smallest resolvable element on the LCD and reserve 'pixel' for the smallest resolvable colour group. In this way, it is easier and safer to make comparisons with other display technologies. To avoid confusion some researchers use the terms 'colour group' or 'colour triads'. (Imagine being offered an LCD with a resolution of 1024 × 1024 pixels only to discover that it has an actual resolution of 512 × 512 colour triads.)

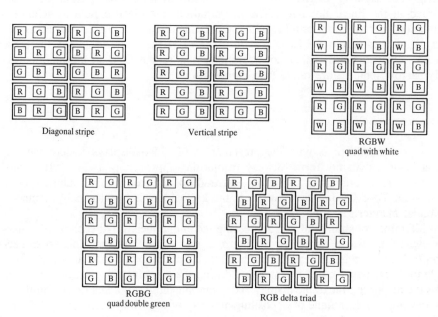

Figure 4.5 Typical arrangement of LCD pixels.

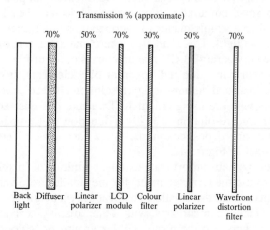

Figure 4.6 Transmissivity of a typical LCD.

Table 4.4 Characteristics of active matrix LCD displays.

Specification parameter	Active matrix LCD parameter
Spatial resolution	1024 × 1024 elements (512 × 512 colour pixel groups); take care when interpreting manufacturer's specifications (see Chapter 6)
Brightness	514 cdm^{-2}
Contrast	32:1, or 17:1 under 80,000 lumen m^{-2}
Colour	Yes, RGBG quad format or RGB delta triad
Display size	160 × 160 mm typical; maximum sizes currently are 300 × 300 mm; smaller devices are resolution limited. This is a feature of market demand rather than as a result of specific technical manufacturing difficulties
Aspect	±60° horizontal, ±45° vertical
Storage/refresh	Inherent storage capability
Time constants	Compatible with video rates
Temperature range	5°C to 55°C. Exposure to UV light can bleach some of the dyes over a period of time
Power requirements	50 W typical, the backlight consumes most of the power

The arrangement of colour elements is not arbitrary. The layout of colour elements can affect the appearance of the display. Indeed, the layout is generally governed by the end application. The delta triad configuration gives superior performance where grey scales are used in anti-aliased displays. This arises because the distance between identical adjacent colour elements is smaller than the other configurations. In some applications an excess of elements of a particular colour can lead to a predominance of that colour.

To produce a usable display active matrix LCDs must employ a fairly bright backlight. This is frequently provided by an arrangement of small fluorescent tubes mounted behind a diffuser screen. Even though the LCD cell may appear thin, it presents poor optical transmissivity, as shown in Figure 4.6 (see Table 4.4).

Image smearing

At one time LCD video displays were characterized by image smearing whenever anything moved in the scene. Modern LCD devices can achieve update rates in excess of 100 Hz, but there are still noticeable effects when LCDs show moving objects. Additional problems arise when using LCDs in helmet-mounted display applications. These problems are discussed in Chapter 6.

Cathode ray tube: Direct view CRT

Shadow mask CRT

The first practical colour cathode ray tube (CRT) to be used was based on a shadow mask arrangement. These colour CRTs are still used today. Three separate electron guns (red, green and blue) are used to provide three primary colour drives, each gun being aligned to activate the appropriate phosphor dot. The inner (front) surface of the CRT is coated with a three-colour phosphor arranged in triads of tiny dots. An alternative phosphor arrangement exists, based on a colour stripe arrangement. To ensure that the electrons from a particular gun only impinge on the correct phosphor dots, a metal screen (with an array of holes) is placed between the gun assembly and the phosphor. The resolution of the shadow mask CRT is governed by the size and spacing of the holes in the shadow mask as well as the granularity of the phosphor. As the size of holes is reduced, and the number increased, the brightness of the CRT falls. This is due to the beam current being lost in the shadow mask, leading to less energy being supplied to the phosphor. Figure 4.7 shows the basic arrangement of the shadow mask in a modern CRT (see Table 4.5).

Beam index CRT

Over recent years alternative CRT arrangements have been devised. One such technology is the beam index CRT, which employs a single electron gun to bombard the screen phosphor. The screen phosphor is arranged in slots (like one version of the shadow mask CRT). The key to the operation of this type of CRT lies in being able to determine exactly where the electron beam is at any point in time. The display is only used in a raster scan mode, which provides some measure of position determination but does not provide a precise spot position. To determine exact spot position a fourth phosphor is deposited on the face plate. This phosphor emits only ultraviolet light when energized by the electron beam, as it is scanned across the display. As the beam is scanned across the display a series of pulses is emitted by the ultraviolet phosphor. A small ultraviolet light detector is mounted on the side of the CRT to detect the pulses. These light pulses are converted into electrical signals that are used to multiplex the red, green and blue video information. Figure 4.8 shows a beam index CRT.

The beam index CRT is simpler to manufacture than a conventional shadow mask CRT but requires a higher level of electronics to control the complete display. The absence of a shadow mask means that the beam current is greater and leads to a much brighter display (see Table 4.5).

Penetrate CRT

Penetrate CRTs may find applications in helmet-mounted displays (primarily airborne) because of their high brightness capability. The screen phosphor is made up of two layers comprising red and 'usually' green phosphor. The two phosphor layers are separated by a non-light-emitting material.

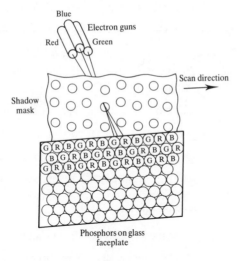

Figure 4.7 Shadow mask arrangement in a CRT.

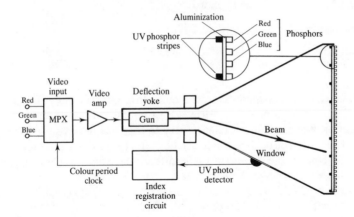

Figure 4.8 Beam index CRT arrangement.

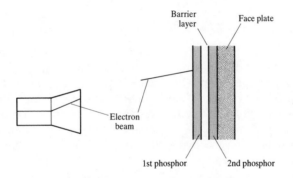

Figure 4.9 Penetrate CRT arrangement.

Table 4.5 Characteristics of direct view CRT displays.

Specification parameter	Parameter
Spatial resolution	20 line pairs per cm (colour CRT), 79 line pairs per cm (monochrome CRT)
Brightness	822 cdm^{-2} (Colour), 3426 cdm^{-2} (monochrome)
Contrast	3:1 (colour), 8:1 (monochrome)
Colour	Dependent upon choice of phosphor(s)
Display size	Almost unlimited but resolution is limited on the smaller sizes due to phosphor granularity and spot size considerations
Aspect	Unlimited, Lambertian emission
Storage/refresh	60 Hz typical, phosphor choice can extend or reduce performance
Time constants	Phosphor dependent
Temperature range	-20°C to 55°C
Power requirements	200 W (colour), 50 W (monochrome)

To bombard the phosphor nearest the electron gun assembly, the penetrate CRT is operated like a conventional one. However, to bombard the phosphor furthest away from the electron gun assembly it is necessary to increase the extra high tension (EHT) voltages so that the electron beam has greater energy and can therefore penetrate the outer layer. To control the colour of the emitted light from the CRT it is necessary to control the final EHT voltage. Unfortunately, it is not possible to produce a grey scale with this type of CRT, so the display should only be operated in cursive mode. Moreover, the total gamut of colours is limited to the range from red through to yellow–green. Nevertheless, this type of CRT technology may be the first to be used when realizing a colour airborne helmet-mounted display (see Figure 4.9).

Colour shutter CRT

An interesting display device results by combining two display technologies, CRT and LCD. The colour shutter display employs a conventional (white) monochrome CRT to produce the display image. The LCD device is placed after the CRT and is used to select, usually, one of two colours from the CRT emission, normally red or green. The LCD device is controlled by a very low voltage that is used to switch the state of the LCD. Images displayed on the CRT are produced twice in each frame, while the LCD shutter is switched between the two states. Any colour in the range red through to yellow–green can be produced.

In many instances the colour shutter CRT display is far superior to the penetrate CRT because the spatial resolution of the monochrome CRT is preserved. There is no line blurring caused by using two different EHT voltages, and the LCD can yield more highly saturated colours. Recent developments have led to three-colour LCD shutters that are capable of giving full colour displays.

LCD colour shutter

The problems of miniature display devices such as CRTs are reasonably well understood. Difficulty arises when colour operation is required because of the need to generate three primary colour images that are combined to produce a full colour image. Conventional fabrication techniques are unable to yield small area devices with a high resolution. This is because of several limiting factors such as phosphor granularity, display line width (governed by spot size), brightness and convergence (alignment of individual red, green and blue images).

Early attempts to overcome these limitations were based on a spinning colour filter wheel mounted in front of a monochrome CRT. Individual monochrome images corresponding to the red, green and blue components of a scene were sequentially displayed on the CRT. The filter wheel was rotated in front of it at a rate that was synchronized to the generation of primary colour images. The results of this system were particularly good because higher brightness could be achieved with no convergence errors. Unfortunately, because it was mechanically driven, system reliability proved to be a problem. Furthermore, the system did not lend itself to miniature displays. Consequently, the idea of full field switching was abandoned in favour of colour CRTs.

Tektronix has developed a modern approach to the colour filter wheel by employing large format liquid crystal shutter (LCS) technology. The LCS is an electronically switchable colour filter that comprises two separate LCS elements known as 'pi-cells'. The pi-cells also incorporate combinations of colour and neutral polarizers. Their arrangement is shown in Figure 4.10. The colour polarizer works by 'splitting' the red, green, and blue (RGB) components of the CRT emission into orthogonally polarized components. Light transmitted through the first polarizer near the CRT has blue light orientated exactly 90° with respect to the green and red components.

The CRT must be carefully selected to ensure that the spectral emission is compatible with the colour polarizers. In the Tektronix system, this is provided by a P45 phosphor. The next component in the LCS, after the first polarizer, is a pi-cell which is used either to pass incident light or rotate the light by 90°. Two additional colour polarizers and a pi-cell are used to produce separate red, green and blue displays. Table 4.6 shows the switching logic state for the two pi-cells.

Table 4.6 Switching logic state for the Tektronix liquid crystal shutter.

Colour	Front cell	Back cell
Red	Off	On
Green	On	Off
Blue	On	On
Black	Off	Off

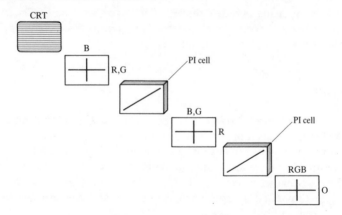

Figure 4.10 Tektronix liquid crystal colour shutter operation.

In order to produce a full colour display that is compatible with standard video systems, it is necessary to switch the colour shutter at 150 Hz for the European standard, and 180 Hz for the US standard. Each primary field is displayed at a 50 Hz or 60 Hz rate, respectively. To improve switching times the pi-cell is divided into horizontal segments that are parallel to the raster scan. A switching speed of 0.5 ms can be achieved to switch the pi-cell on; it takes 2.0 ms to turn it off. These figures will improve as the liquid crystal material improves.

A high resolution (1200 × 1024) 1-inch colour shutter CRT has been produced that looks set to revolutionize helmet-mounted display systems. The advantages of the LCD shutter are its zero convergence error, high resolution and maximum achievable contrast ratio. However, it has been noted that when the observer of shuttered display devices is vibrated with respect to the display, the image appears to break down into individual red, green and blue components. The severity of this effect will be dependent on the frequency and waveform of the vibration. For most applications, this will not present a problem, but further research is required to quantify the effect. It should be noted that all raster displays exhibit unusual visual effects when the observer viewing the display at a short distance is vibrated relative to the display. The phenomenon can be demonstrated readily by crunching a hard biscuit between one's teeth while viewing a raster display. This artificially introduces high velocity movement translations in the head that cannot be compensated by the vestibular ocular reflex.

Projection devices

Projection CRT

The projection CRT operates on the same principle as a standard CRT device except that it is constructed slightly differently. The projection CRT is required to project an image onto a wide field of view, typically a specially coated projection screen. Implicit in the name 'projection CRT' is the requirement for extremely high brightness and high resolution.

Increasing the beam current of a standard CRT to give increased brightness results in a short phosphor life: the phosphor may burn after only a few milliseconds. Too high a beam current can produce badly focused images because the electron beam width expands, giving a larger spot size. Projection CRTs are specially designed, employing higher brightness phosphors, and are usually more efficient at conducting heat away from the phosphor. To increase brightness, higher beam currents are called for, which demands an increase in EHT or accelerating voltages in the tube. This in turn requires the use of specialized circuitry in terms of EHT regulations, increased scanning currents, and of course phosphor protection in the event of scan failure or collapse during power off.

It is surprising how much of the light generated by a phosphor in a CRT never leaves the CRT glass envelope. To maximize the amount of light leaving the CRT, special optical techniques are used to transfer the light to the outside world.

Projection CRTs used in military helmet-mounted displays employ fibre optic plates to achieve a high coupling efficiency between the CRT face and the optical system. The fibre optic face plate also serves to produce a flat image for the optical system. In fact, such CRTs are extremely good examples of CRT design practices.

Light valve

Light valve display systems are generally characterized as being capable of extremely high brightness image projectors. The light valve technique is essentially based on a light control element whose light transmission or reflection characteristic is modified by either an optical or electrical signal. There are several light control elements that fulfil these requirements. One of the most popular techniques is that based on a specially designed liquid crystal cell (see Figure 4.11). A photoconductive layer is deposited onto one side of the liquid crystal cell and a dielectric mirror onto the other side. A light blocking layer and a photosensor area is integrated on the reverse side of the mirror. A voltage potential is maintained across the whole arrangement.

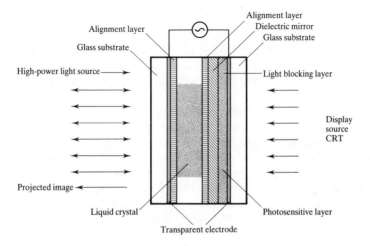

Figure 4.11 Liquid crystal light valve cell.

Table 4.7 Typical specifications of colour light valve projector.

Parameter	Specification
Resolution (50% MTF)	600 lines
Contrast	>30:1
Brightness	600 lm
Colour	Full colour
Response time	30–60 Hz
Grey scale	9 grey levels
Input sensitivity	100 μWcm^{-2}

Operation is fairly straightforward. An image source such as a CRT is used to form an image on the photosensor area. When the image source illuminates the photosensor area the photoconductor area drops in resistance in those areas corresponding to where the illumination is imaged. The voltage potential across the cell increases to the point where the liquid crystal is activated. The cell effectively becomes transparent, allowing a high brightness light source to pass through the liquid crystal cell and be reflected back off the dielectric mirror. Consequently, a low brightness light source can be used to switch a high brightness light source such as a xenon lamp (see Table 4.7).

Figure 4.12 shows how the light valve is used to control the high brightness light source to produce a projection display. Full colour light valve projectors, consisting of three separate drives into a dichroic beam splitter and lens arrangement, are available.

Other light valve techniques exist that rely on specially modified liquid crystal displays, rather like those used in small pocket LCD televisions.

Laser scanner

The laser scanner is a common device and is widely used. It relies on a small laser light source that provides a collimated beam for a scanning mirror assembly. Either rotating mirrors or nodding mirror assemblies are used to scan the laser light in cursive or raster fashion to create an image.

However, whether or not this technique will ever find an application in helmet-mounted displays remains to be seen. The laser light source will certainly provide the brightest and probably the highest resolution display, but the problems associated with shining coherent light sources into the eye will have to be resolved first. Furthermore, lasers are highly monochromatic and three will be required to produce a full colour display. Some applications will be able to use monochrome displays without any degradation of operator performance. Little can be reported on this display technology because most of the data is outside the public domain.

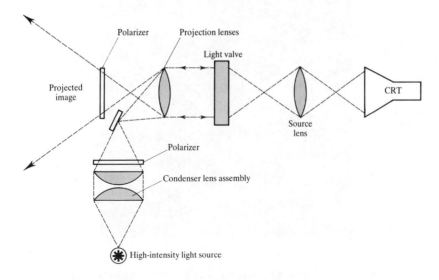

Figure 4.12 Light valve projection display.

Micromechanical silicon display devices

In the author's opinion one of the most important and promising technologies for future helmet-mounted display applications is based on an array of mirror elements, called a mirror matrix device (MMD). This section describes a display device based on micromechanical fabrication techniques used to produce an array of miniature mirrors on a silicon substrate, known as deformable mirror devices (DMD). Each mirror is electrically addressable by an underlying array of transistors. The device can be used to spatially modulate a beam of light and produce an image corresponding to the information represented by the mirror surfaces. By operating the device as a light valve with schlieren optics it is possible to produce large-screen as well as very small television type displays. The device may replace the conventional CRTs because of its ability to produce a brighter image with greater contrast. In miniature display applications it has the advantages of being extremely small, of low mass, and of small volume, in addition to having a low power requirement. The light valve mode also produces greater illuminance than conventional CRTs.

The display device is only achievable with the precision lithographic processes that have been developed for integrated circuit development (see Figure 4.13).

Device operation

A micromechanical device consists of a thin metal-coated (aluminized) SiO_2 membrane fabricated on a silicon wafer using normal integrated circuit processing techniques. DMDs are available that use a continuous metallized membrane placed over an underlying address chip, instead of the monolithically formed cantilever beams of the MMD.

Figure 4.13 Highly magnified view of an MMD mirror element.

The organization of an MMD is shown in Figure 4.14. The device is addressed electronically line by line. When a line of data has been loaded into a shift register it is serial-to-parallel shifted into line driver amplifier stage. The amplified signal is used to charge the capacitors of the individual mirror elements by turning on the pixel driver transistors for that row. The transistors are then turned off and the capacitors remain charged.

The other side of the capacitor is maintained at a fixed bias potential and the potential drop across each air gap capacitor causes the micro mirror to displace towards the silicon surface according to the absolute magnitude of the voltage drop. The addressing sequence is repeated for each line of information. By synchronizing the line shifting sequence to standard television sequences, it is possible to build up a charge representation in the individual air gap capacitors.

By flooding the surface of the array with collimated light the micro mirrors produce a phase modulation corresponding to the image signal. A schlieren optical system will convert the phase modulation into an intensity variation that can be viewed or projected as required. The display system shown in Figure 4.15 is typical of a schlieren optical arrangement.

The spatial light modulator (SLM) is driven by conventional circuitry to provide charges under the mirror elements. The reflective schlieren optic system uses a telecentric collimator lens. At the focal plane of the system is a small central stop and a small fixed mirror at 45° to the optic axis. The mirror directs light from an intense light source onto the SLM. In the non-active state the light incident onto the SLM is focused onto the back of the central stop, creating a dark field. When the SLM is activated light is reflected off the mirrors around the central stop to give an image that can be focused onto a screen or injected into the optical system. Each mirror element forms one pixel in the displayed image. The intensity of an individual pixel is a function of the reflectivity of the mirror element and light source intensity.

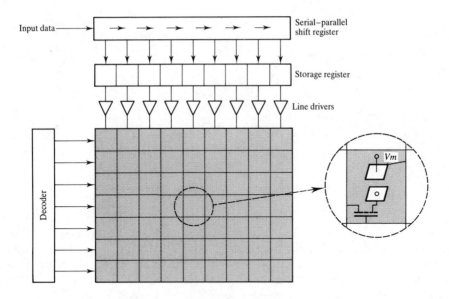

Figure 4.14 Organization of an MMD.

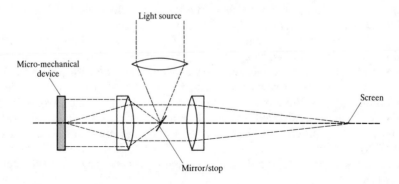

Figure 4.15 Basic configuration of a micromechanical silicon display device.

Helmet-mounted display optical systems

To specify, test and use helmet-mounted displays, it is necessary to understand the effects of optical design parameters such as focal length, exit pupil, eye relief and field of view. Only when these parameters are understood will it be possible to apply helmet-mounted displays in an effective manner. Helmet-mounted displays are becoming increasingly popular, being an integration between an image source and an optical system. It is very important to address the integration from an optical, electronic, mechanical and human factors viewpoint. Optical integration requires a complete understanding of these disciplines.

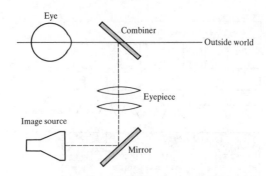

Figure 4.16 Simple helmet-mounted display.

Unfortunately, non-optical experts are frequently asked to specify, test and use helmet-mounted displays. Apart from lack of familiarity of the technical terminology, there is a danger that where trade-offs have to be made, wrong decisions can be taken that ultimately affect the user's performance in a virtual world. From a cost perspective, it is easy to specify an optical system so that the total cost is prohibitive or even unrealizable. Anyone with experience of optical systems is aware of the high cost of off-the-shelf optical components. Special 'to type' components are several orders of magnitude more expensive. A helmet-mounted display optical system is a complex design involving trade-offs between ocular focal length, objective focal length, system magnification, exit pupil diameter, field of view and so on.

The first point to note is that the design of helmet-mounted displays, particularly those with wide fields of view, is a complex undertaking. When binocular systems are required the design problem can become very challenging. Elementary physics text book considerations for optical systems can only be taken as an approximate guide. These simple formulae deal with paraxial light rays – rays that are infinitesimally close to the optic axis. Real light rays are anything but close to the optic axis. Modern optical design is undertaken with comprehensive computer optical design programs. Even so, it needs a highly skilled designer to interpret the results of the optical system. There have been many instances where the 'perfect' optical system has been designed on the computer, only to fail in practice.

To describe the importance of a helmet-mounted display optical system, a monocular 'see-through' helmet-mounted display will be considered. The monocular design represents an empirical design, all other helmet-mounted displays being a variation on this design.

To produce a non-see-through design, the combiner element is discarded or the combiner is replaced by a mirror. Figure 4.16 shows a monocular helmet-mounted display.

Image source

The image source for a helmet-mounted display is usually based on one of the display technologies described earlier in this chapter. It is selected according to spatial resolution, brightness, weight and type of display presentation requirements. Secondary issues such as safety (operating voltage) and robustness play an important role, and the resolution factor is also important. To obtain high resolutions from display devices that are limited in terms of pixel density it is necessary to increase their effective display area for a particular field of view. As display area increases, the weight of the display source also increases. To produce a small display the display resolution must effectively increase. Display resolution would not generally be a problem for small fields of view. However, when the field of view is increased beyond 20° or so, the consequential image magnification can make individual pixels so large that they can be seen easily. Unfortunately, it is not possible to increase the resolution of the display and decrease the display area because certain aspects such as phosphor granularity and pixel density become the limiting factors. The purpose of the optical system is twofold: firstly, to magnify the image from the display source to fill the required field of view; and secondly to combine the virtual image with the outside world. (The latter requirement does not apply to a non-see-through helmet-mounted display.)

Eyepieces

The simplest helmet-mounted display could contain an elementary eyepiece system comprising one or more lens elements, which act as a magnifier so that the image source appears larger. The purpose of the mirror source between the image source and the eyepiece is to bend the light path, so keeping the mechanical arrangement as compact as possible. A multi-element eye piece is generally used to reduce chromatic aberration effects. The half silvered mirror merely acts to reflect a certain percentage of the image source into the eye while allowing a proportion of the outside world scene into the eye. Hence, the half silvered mirror is often called a combiner.

To analyze the optical system, it is easier to unfold the system where it takes on the appearance of a simple magnifier (see Figure 4.17).

In paraxial optics terms, the relationship between object distance, image distance and focal length is given by the following equation:

$$\frac{1}{u} + \frac{1}{v} = \frac{1}{f}$$

where f = focal length, u = object distance (distance from image source to eyepiece), and v = image distance (the distance of the virtual image from the lens).

When the image source is placed at the focal point of the lens, $f = u$, v becomes infinite and the virtual image appears at optical infinity.

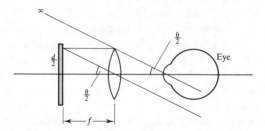

Figure 4.17 Straightened-out simplified helmet-mounted display.

The term 'collimated display' is often used to describe optical systems where the image appears at infinity. If the display source is placed nearer to the lens than the focal point, $u < f$, the virtual image distance v is displayed nearer than infinity. In fact, it is possible to place the virtual image at any position by adjusting the object distance u. (In practice only a small adjustment is possible because it can affect distortion correction.) In this arrangement, the eye must accommodate to the virtual image distance, rather than relax at the infinity position. One advantage of producing a collimated helmet-mounted display is that movement parallax is eliminated. This means that as the eye moves laterally with respect to the eyepiece, the resulting image does not move with respect to the viewer. Consequently, for a visually coupled system, head translation (x, y and z) relative to the optical system can be ignored. However, for the display image to be visible it is still necessary for the eye to remain within the exit pupil of the optical system.

For displays that are not collimated ($u > f$) head translation must be taken into account.

When a collimated display is used, the rays of light from the image source emerge from the eyepiece in a parallel fashion. The visual angle subtended at the user's eye is the same as that subtended by the display source at the optic axis of the eyepiece. The displayed image does not change in size as the observer's eye is moved along the optic axis of the helmet-mounted display. This can easily be verified by experiment. Light emerging from the eyepiece is contained in a diverging core.

A simple helmet-mounted display such as this does not have an exit pupil. The lens acts as a stop in the system so it behaves as its own pupil. The eye can be either side of the optical axis and still get a good image from the system. Some eyepieces contain curved or flat mirrors.

Combiners

The simplest (non-see-through) helmet-mounted displays arrange the eyepiece so that it is directly in front of the eye. For comfort (centre of gravity distribution) and safety, mirrors are often used to allow the image source to be positioned either side of the head.

To achieve a see-through capability, a partially reflecting mirror is placed in front of the eye, which allows the eyepiece and image source to be placed in more convenient positions around the head.

The partially reflecting mirror is called a combiner because it allows the image source to be reflected into the eye and the outside world scene to pass through. The optical properties of the combiner deserve special mention. The combiner can be designed to reflect all the visible wavelengths into the eye. This is known as an achromatic combiner. Furthermore, it is usually designed to reflect a certain percentage. For example, 50% of all visible wavelengths from the image source only transmit about 20% from the outside world. This allows the relative intensities of the image source and outside world to be balanced. Virtually any ratio can be designed by means of dielectric coatings. Earlier metallic coatings suffered from high absorption but modern coatings permit efficiency of almost 100%.

A problem with achromatic coatings is that a certain percentage of the light from the image source is reflected into the outside world rather than into the eye. Since the light output of some image sources is rather low compared to the outside world, it is necessary to obtain a higher reflection efficiency in the combiner. For monochrome image sources this can be achieved by using a trichroic mirror, which is tuned so that it reflects one wavelength in particular, with great efficiency, while the other wavelengths are transmitted with minimal absorption. This places demands on the image source because it must be compatible (from the point of view of wavelength) with the filter. Additionally, when the outside world is viewed through the filter, the selected frequency is removed from the outside world scene. This introduces a slight colour background or tinge to the image.

An important advantage of a three-colour combiner is that the reflected virtual imagery can be seen against very bright outside world images.

The combiner can be a flat plate (often used in aircraft head up displays) or may be curved to provide magnitudes of the reflected image. In this way the field of view of the helmet-mounted display can be made quite large. The design of combiners is a very involved process, and must be undertaken as part of the complete optical design. An important requirement of the combiner is to produce distortion-free images that can overlay objects in the outside world. Early combiner designs suffered from parallax distortions caused by the thickness of the combiner and had to be positioned very accurately with respect to the user's eye. Unfortunately, the human head comes in a variety of sizes, which makes setting up a very awkward process.

Relay lenses

The shape of the human head means that it is necessary to install the image sources in a position that may compromise the optical design. To achieve greater flexibility relay lenses are used to transfer the image from the display source to the eyepiece. The relay lens and the eyepiece together form a simple telescope, with the relay lens acting as an objective lens and the eyepiece as an ocular. In other words, the relay lens projects the image from the display so that it can be seen through the eyepiece. The positioning of the relay lens, relative to the display source, helps govern the total magnification of the system.

Light emerging from the eyepiece converges to an exit pupil, which is an image of the relay lens aperture. To obtain an acceptable image the user must place their eye into the exit pupil position. If the eye is moved sideways, outside this small region, the displayed image disappears from view rather abruptly. Even small amounts of helmet slip can cause the image to disappear in this way. The amount of helmet slip that can be tolerated depends on the size of the exit pupil. Maximum display brightness occurs when the eye is exactly in the exit pupil position. Other positions cause effective display brightness to fall off. For most applications the exit pupil must be greater than 10 mm, with 15 mm or more being preferred. However, simply increasing exit pupil diameter requires relatively large eyepieces. These can significantly increase both the total weight and the cost of the helmet-mounted display.

To analyse a helmet-mounted display comprising a relay lens system (such as that shown in Figure 4.17) it is convenient to unfold the optical system (see Figure 4.18). In this way it can be treated as an in-line series of lens components. Figure 4.19 shows the unfolded helmet-mounted display optical system.

Coherent fibre optic bundles can be used instead of relay lenses. In this case special design considerations must be followed because any optical mismatch not only leads to a reduction in brightness, but also causes a serious reduction in resolution or resolving power. A special form of fibre optic relay-based helmet-mounted display (known as a 'fibre coupled display') is described later in this chapter, and several examples are presented. Additionally, unlike relay lenses, the spatial resolution of the fibre optic bundle must be carefully considered. The fibre optic bundle can achieve limited magnification by tapering its output end. Unfortunately, coherent fibre optic bundles are built by hand and are therefore extremely expensive to buy from the manufacturer.

Field view

When the image source fills the total field of view of the eyepiece (or ocular), the apparent field of view θ and the angular subtense of the image source as seen by an observer are the same.

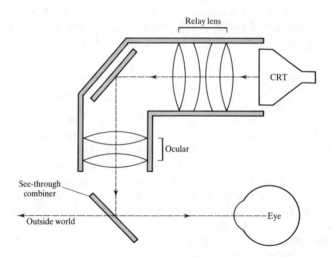

Figure 4.18 Basic folded relay helmet-mounted display.

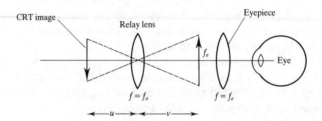

Figure 4.19 Unfolded helmet-mounted display optical system of Figure 4.18.

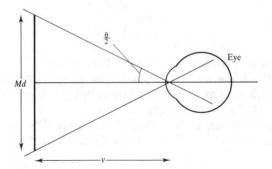

Figure 4.20 Field of view of helmet-mounted display.

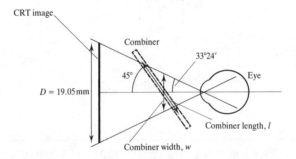

Figure 4.21 Combiner field of view requirements.

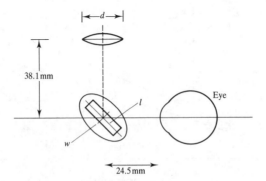

Figure 4.22 Example helmet-mounted display system.

$$\theta = 2\tan^{-1}\left[\frac{Md}{2V}\right]$$

where M is the image magnification, θ is the field of view, d is the display source diameter, and V is the distance of virtual image (see Figure 4.20). If a 19.05 mm CRT is used with a magnification of 8× and the virtual image distance is 32.6 mm then the field of view is 33°24′ (see Figure 4.21).

Supposing the combiner is inclined at 45° and placed 25.4 mm from the eye, and that the eyepiece or ocular is 63.5 mm from the eye (see Figure 4.22). From the previous equation:

$$\tan\theta/2 = \frac{d/2}{V}$$

$$\tan\left[\frac{33°24}{2}\right] = \frac{d/2}{63.5}$$

now $d = 38.1$ mm.

$$\tan\theta/2 = \frac{W/2}{25.4 \text{ mm}}$$

$W = 15.24$ mm.

$$L = 25.4 \text{ mm} \times \sqrt{2}\left[1/(1+\cot(16°42)) + 1/(1-\cot(16°42))\right]$$

$L = 23.6$ mm.

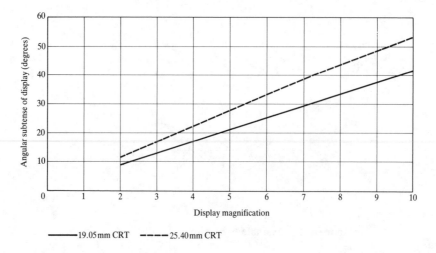

Figure 4.23 Display magnification: angular subtense.

From this example, it can be seen that the diameter of the lens in the eyepiece is 38.1mm. The combiner has a corresponding elliptical operating area of 23.6 × 15.24 mm. This example illustrates that the sizes of the eyepiece lens and the combiner are a function of their distance from the eye. Clearly, placing these components closer to the eye results in a smaller arrangement. However, care has to be taken not to touch the person's face with either the combiner or the eyepiece. Placing the eyepiece close to the eye can cause problems, with the eyepiece obscuring the outside world view. Therefore, final design must be a compromise between field of view, combiner size and eyepiece diameter. It is for this reason that curved combiners are often considered. Unfortunately, the design of distortion free curved combiners presents additional difficulties. Figure 4.23 shows a plot of display magnification against angular subtense for a 3/4-inch and 1-inch CRT.

Display quality

Display quality is an extremely difficult multidimensional parameter to define. This is compounded by the lack of agreement on what constitutes minimal acceptable display quality. Unfortunately, there is a subjective element to the definition. Generally, it addresses the following issues:

- resolving power
- spatial resolution
- display brightness and contrast
- distortion
- display dynamic range
- field of view – acceptability for task

The above list is not exhaustive because people have their own views on what constitutes a good display system.

Holographic optical systems for helmet-mounted displays

Development of holographic elements has reached the stage where several helmet-mounted displays have been fabricated. Primarily these have been designed for military application, but it is only a question of time before this technology becomes available to the wider community. There is no doubt that holographic elements will change our current understanding of helmet-mounted displays. The greatest benefit is perhaps better control over the optical design and weight.

Whereas conventional optical systems (refracture and reflective) rely on ray directions and the refractive index of the optical components, holographic elements rely on diffraction for determining ray directions and not surface shape. A simple comparison between conventional and holographic optical systems is shown in Table 4.8.

Table 4.8 Simple comparison of conventional and holographic optical elements.

Optical system	
Conventional	Holographic
Widely understood	Design procedures complex
Considerable amount of computer analysis techniques available	Very few computer analysis programs available
High efficiency	Potential for high efficiency
Relatively insensitive to operating wavelength	Very sensitive to wavelength
Very heavy and bulky	Lightweight and compact
Fabrication essentially normal	Difficult to reproduce
Not very rigid	Initial cost very high

Distortion correction considerations

Binocular disparity can be affected by the amount of distortion correction applied to a helmet-mounted display. For example, in a 120° optical system, as shown in Figure 4.24, a 1% distortion can lead to a horizontal disparity of 24′.

Binocular disparities arise from several defects in the optical design, including:

1. Magnification differences between the left-hand and right-hand channels.
2. Left-hand and right-hand channel images are rotated relative to each other.
3. The optic axis of the left-hand and right-hand channels are misaligned with respect to each other.
4. The focus adjustment is not consistent between channels.
5. Luminance differences between channels.

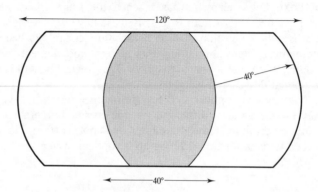

Figure 4.24 Wide field of view helmet-mounted display.

A key to the design of a helmet-mounted display is an understanding of which parameters a user is most sensitive to, and how these effects can be minimized by the design. Clearly, over-specifying a helmet-mounted display will have a knock-on effect of escalating costs. With the availability of high performance computer graphic systems it is feasible to consider applying certain distortion correction methods during display generation, rather than trying to accommodate them in the optical design. The 'trick' here is to minimize the optical distortion correction and employ corrections in the computer graphics system where appropriate. To a large extent, this depends on the capability and performance of the graphic system. It is possible to generate computational solutions for the distortion correction. Unfortunately, these can be so complex that it would take the highest performance graphics system several hours to compute the distortion corrected image. Obviously, this is not a good idea for real-time applications.

The type of image source can mean that a degree of electronic distortion can be considered. For instance, for CRT-based systems these special waveforms can be superimposed on the scan deflection signals applied to the deflection yoke. The resulting electronics assembly increases in complexity accordingly, and may require difficult calibration procedures.

Helmet-mounted display systems

The following section will examine several different helmet-mounted display systems and give some of the basic performance specifications that help illustrate the merits of each technology. The system designer will need to understand the relative merits of a particular technology to select a particular helmet-mounted display system for an application. Unfortunately, no one technology is likely to meet all requirements so the designer will need to undertake some form of trade-off analysis.

LCD-based helmet-mounted displays

Helmet-mounted displays based on small LCDs are relatively cheap and have become very popular in recent years. Unfortunately, the level of technology has not matched the users' requirements. Consequently lower resolution than that which is desirable has to be tolerated. However, for certain applications these devices are probably the best solution. The designer must give very careful consideration to the field of view and resolution of these systems. Specifying extremely wide fields of view will cause the overall display resolution to be very poor because of the limited resolution of the LCD. Provided one can work with a narrow field of view, then LCD-based helmet-mounted displays may be the best solution.

EyePhone helmet-mounted displays

The first non-see-through LCD-based HMD was built at the NASA Ames Research Center by McGreevy and Humphries in 1985 from monochrome LCD pocket television displays (see Plate 2). The display used the wide angle stereoscopic optics produced by Leep Systems. This development attracted considerable interest, but the resolution was very low and the display was monochrome. However, the idea of a low power, lightweight helmet-mounted display had been born. Many people commented that the concept would not become popular until colour LCDs were readily available. When VPL became involved with NASA, the term 'Eyephone' was coined. It would not be possible to describe all the Eyephone type helmet-mounted displays that are available because new devices are constantly being developed. However, since VPL was the first major producer of these devices, its product line will be described along with the LEEP Optics Cyberface 2 System. The latter device is interesting because it offers a wider field of view by rotating the two optic axes outwards. In the author's opinion considerable development is still required in the display field to give better resolution over the fields of view proposed. If smaller fields of view are required then the current limited resolution of the LCDs may be acceptable. (As will be discussed in Chapter 6, it is very important to understand the application.)

VPL Eyephone Model 2

The first Eyephone manufactured by VPL was the Model 2. It was based on miniature LCD modules mounted within a head-mounted display unit (see Table 4.9).

VPL Eyephone LX

The Eyephone Model LX is essentially the same device as the Model 2 except that the image is displayed through wide angle FMT Optics. The FMT Optics are based on Fresnel lenses, which are lighter in weight than the original LEEP optical system. They are claimed to have a field of view of about 108° with less geometrical distortion than the LEEP optical system (see Table 4.10). In the author's opinion the original LEEP optical system gave superior image quality. However, this view is purely subjective. The original head mount has also been replaced. Again in the author's opinion, the new version is extremely uncomfortable compared to the original. (It is probably fair to comment that all other helmet-mounted displays for virtual environment applications are equally uncomfortable.) This point will be dealt with in Chapter 6.

VPL Eyephone HRX

The Eyephone HRX is a colour stereo display system based on the Eyephone Model LX. Instead of the original 105,000 colour elements, the LCD used in the HRX has about 350,000 colour elements thus giving a higher resolution image (see Table 4.11).

In common with all display manufacturers who use LCD modules the actual resolution quoted is not strictly correct. The LCDs used in the HRX are based on a 720 × 480 matrix of individual red, green and blue elements. When these are converted to colour pixels (the usual method of specifying display resolution) the effective resolution is about 416 × 277 pixels. However, there is no doubt that the resolution and quality of display offered by the LCDs used in the HRX are far superior to those used in any other virtual environment type LCD-based helmet-mounted display. The author had the opportunity to evaluate the original prototype HRX helmet-mounted display. This device used the high resolution LCDs with the LEEP optical system.

Table 4.9 Specifications for VPL EyePhone Model 2.

VPL Model 2 parameters	Specification
Display source	LCD
Mode	Binocular
Field of view (binocular)	90°
Field of view (single eye)	75.3°h × 58.4°v
Binocular overlap	60.6°
Display resolution	185 × 139 RGB pixels
Eye to virtual image distance	398.2 mm
Object plane distance	16.4 mm
Object field radius (max)	28.1 mm
Virtual image field radius (max)	271.55 mm
Eye relief (normal user)	29.4 mm nominal
Angle between optic axes	0°
IPD	Variable
Distance between optic axes	64 mm
Transversal magnification	9.66
Offset of screen centre from optic axis	6.4 mm, 1.6 mm
Virtual image of right-hand edge	45.0°
Virtual image of left-hand edge	30.3°
Virtual image of top edge	31.8°
Virtual image of bottom edge	26.6°
Optical distortion coefficient D	0.32
Optical distortion coefficient D^{-1}	-0.18
Weight	2.5 lb
Video input	NTSC

Table 4.10 Specifications for VPL Eyephone LX.

VPL LX parameter	Specification
Display source	LCD
Mode	Binocular
Field of view (binocular)	108°
Field of view (single eye)	86°h × 76°v
Binocular overlap	60.6°
Display resolution	185 × 139 RGB pixels
Eye to virtual image distance	398.2 mm
Object plane distance	16.4 mm
Object field radius (max)	28.1 mm
Virtual image field radius (max)	271.55 mm
Eye relief (normal user)	29.4 mm nominal
Angle between optic axes	0°
IPD	Variable
Distance between optic axes	64 mm
Transversal magnification	9.66
Offset of screen centre from optic axis	6.4 mm, 1.6 mm
Virtual image of right-hand edge	45.0°
Virtual image of left-hand edge	30.3°
Virtual image of top edge	31.8°
Virtual image of bottom edge	26.6°
Optical distortion coefficient D	0.32
Optical distortion coefficient D^{-1}	-0.18
Weight	2.5 lb
Video input	NTSC

Table 4.11 Specifications for VPL Eyephone HRX.

VPL HRX parameter	Specification
Display source	LCD
Mode	Binocular
Field of view (binocular)	106°
Field of view (single eye)	86°h × 75°v
Binocular overlap	Not specified
Display resolution	416 × 277 RGB pixels
Weight	2.5 lb
Video input	RGB and Sync (NTSC timing)

LEEP Optics Cyberface 2

LEEP Optics have produced their own head-mounted display system called the Cyberface 2 (see Figure 4.25), which is a stereoscopic helmet-mounted display that uses two 4-inch diagonal colour LCDs with the LEEP Plus 25 wide angle optics. The Cyberface 2 is different from other LCD-based helmet-mounted displays in several respects.

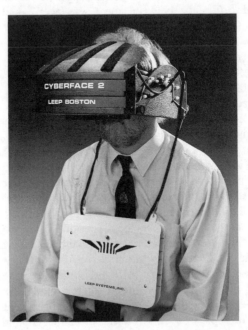

Figure 4.25 Cyberface 2, the latest helmet-mounted display from LEEP Systems Inc.

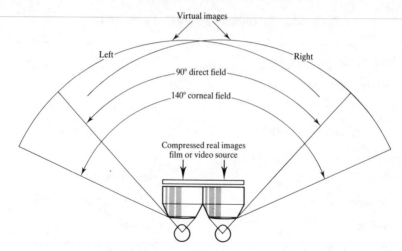

Figure 4.26 LEEP Optics Cyberface 2: field of view.

The most obvious difference is that the user wears a counterpoise around their neck. This is connected to the helmet-mounted display via fine steel cable and serves two purposes: to counterbalance the head-supported components, and to remove the dragging effect caused by bulky cables connecting the LCD units to the user graphic system. The helmet-mounted display is attached to a special head suspension system, a hat, via a quick-release mechanism. In the author's opinion, this mechanism can be more of a nuisance than an aid. Closer inspection of the system, including the counterpoise, reveals that the head still has to support the total weight.

The second difference between the Cyberface 2 and other helmet-mounted displays is that the Cyberface 2 provides a wider field of view for each eye as well as a 25° increase in horizontal field of view.

This has been achieved by using large LCD units and by arranging for the optic axes between the left and right eyes to be increased from 0° to 25°. (Refer to Chapters 3 and 6 for an explanation of the effect this can cause.)

The Cyberface 2 system LCD unit accepts either NTSC or 625 line CCIR video standard signals in RGB format. This greatly improves the image quality compared to NTSC or PAL composite video signals. The author found that it was necessary to add 75 ohm termination resistors in his Cyberface 2 system. Even though the specification indicated that the video was terminated, there was no evidence of this on the printed circuit board in the counterpoise. Users of the Cyberface 2 system are advised to install three 75 ohm resistors in their system to avoid problems with video overload and ringing effects on the video signal.

The LCD modules installed in the Cyberface 2 are essentially low resolution devices. To prevent the user from seeing individual pixel elements LEEP Systems Inc. have positioned the LCD image 4 dioptres beyond infinity. This means that the individual LCD elements are slightly defocused, which causes them to merge. The author believes that this can cause eye strain for some individuals after prolonged use, as a result of the eyes continually trying to produce a sharp image, which does not exist in the first place. The topic of spatial filtering of helmet-mounted displays is discussed in more detail in Chapter 6. The field of view of the Cyberface 2 is shown in Figure 4.26 (see Table 4.12).

Table 4.12 Specifications for LEEP Cyberface 2 helmet-mounted display.

LEEP Cyberface 2 parameter	Specification
Display source	LCD
Mode	Binocular
Field of view (binocular)	140°
Field of view (single eye)	°h × °v
Binocular overlap	90°
Display resolution	319 × 117 RGB pixels
Eye to virtual image distance	4 dioptres beyond infinity
Object plane distance	10 mm from field lens
Object field radius (max)	37 m at 70°
Virtual image field radius (max)	70°
Eye relief (normal user)	13 mm (non-spectacle wearers)
Angle between optic axes	25° divergence
IPD	64 mm nominal
Distance between optic axes	Axes crossed 144 mm on line intersecting eyeball centres
Transversal magnification	6× on axis
Focal length	42 mm
Eye lens radius	30 mm
LCD Size	2.4" × 3.2"
Offset of screen centre from optic axis	None
Optical distortion correction	Distance to any point on LCD display = 42 mm (focal length) × $(\theta - 0.18\theta^3)$ θ = angle of corresponding point in object space (radians)
Weight	68 oz
Video input	RGB and Sync (NTSC timing) RGB and Sync (PAL timing)

Virtual Research Flight Helmet

To meet the rising demand for helmet-mounted displays other companies have begun manufacturing their own products. One display that is gaining popularity is the Flight Helmet manufactured by Virtual Research. From a technical specification point of view there is very little difference between the quality of the display and VPL Eyephones (low resolution). This is governed by the type of LCD module that is used and the optical system. Incidentally, the Flight Helmet employs the wide angle LEEP system. However, the Flight Helmet is better engineered in terms of helmet form and fit. Its overall comfort is better than that of most other LCD-based helmet-mounted displays, because of its relatively low weight and careful balancing. Perhaps one of the more significant contributors to the improved comfort is the lack of an uncomfortable 'diving mask'-like structure around the optical system. While this reduces helmet stability, it makes the whole arrangement less claustrophobic.

CRT-based helmet-mounted displays

CRT-based helmet-mounted displays probably form the largest group within display technology-based systems. This development has largely been in the military field, where a wide range of different helmet-mounted display configurations have been built. The CRT has the advantage of being reasonably low cost, small in size and of high resolution capability. For most applications, the 1-inch CRT offers a good compromise between cost, resolution, weight and luminance performance. However, at the time of writing small colour CRTs with a high resolution cannot be obtained.

Fibre coupled helmet-mounted displays

Helmet-mounted displays employing LCDs possess a relatively poor spatial resolution. This can restrict the application, because LCDs cannot be manufactured to the required resolution. Furthermore, the true spatial resolution of a colour liquid crystal display is sometimes misquoted by manufacturers.

For certain applications a low spatial resolution can be totally unacceptable. This situation can be compounded if wide fields of view are required. A wide field of view optical system simply stretches the pixels out and effectively reduces their density per visual angle. CRT devices are capable of a higher resolution than LCDs but tend to be bulkier. The CRT is resolution limited because of electron beam diameter, spot focusing and phosphor granularity. Colour CRTs small enough to be installed into a helmet-mounted display do not exist with the required resolution.

A clever solution to this problem relies on using a large format, very high resolution CRT as the image source and coupling the image onto the helmet-mounted display. Flexible coherent fibre optic bundles are used to relay the image from the remote CRT to the optical system on the helmet.

The main advantage of the fibre coupled display lies with the ability to employ very high resolution display sources without incurring a weight penalty on the head. However, this does not come without problems. The design of a wide field of view fibre coupled display is an extremely complex task and can only be undertaken with a computer based optical design programme.

The basic principle of the fibre coupled display is shown in Figure 4.27. The image to be displayed is generated on a large format CRT (or light valve projector) and imaged into a coherent fibre optic bundle by a collimating lens.

The coherent fibre optic bundle operates exactly like a medical endoscope. (It may even have considerably more fibres than an endoscope.)

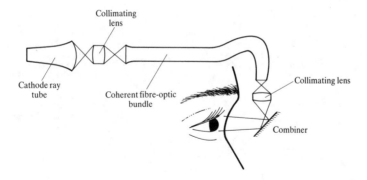

Figure 4.27 Principle of operation of a fibre coupled display.

Several characteristics are important when selecting a fibre optic bundle. The first requirement is a high transmission efficiency to visible light. The number of fibres in the bundle must be at least twice the required resolution. Typical fibre diameters are of the order of 5–10 μm. Constant flexing of the fibre optic bundle can lead to fibre breakage. When this occurs, either dark or coloured spots appear in the visual field. The easiest way of breaking the fibre is to bend the bundle around a tight radius. Fibre breakage can be reduced or almost eliminated by careful handling of the bundles.

The coherent fibre optic bundle 'relays' the image to a collimating lens on the helmet-mounted display. The collimating lens projects the image into the wearer's eyes by means of a combiner plate.

Even though the concept of operation of the fibre coupled display is relatively straightforward, many researchers have underestimated the level of optical design involved. Examples exist where standard photographic lenses have been used. Unfortunately, these systems do not work very well and suffer from excessive distortions for all except narrow fields of view.

CAE fibre optic helmet-mounted display

The CAE fibre optic helmet-mounted display (FOHMD) is an area of interest display based on flexible fibre optic bundles. Plate 20 shows the CAE system installed in a helicopter simulator. The fibre optic bundles transfer images from light valve projectors onto the helmet-mounted display. The system provides an instantaneous field of view of 127° × 66° (see Figure 4.28).

Each eye is presented with a low resolution background image with a field of view of 88° horizontally by 66° vertically. A binocular overlap of 38° is used to present a binocular image. The resolution of the background image is 5 arc minutes per pixel.

To produce a high resolution area of interest display image insert, an eye tracker system has been incorporated. The high resolution insert image is approximately 24° × 19° with a resolution of 1.5 arc minutes per pixel. The eye slaved insert image follows the direction of regard of the user's eye. Figure 4.28 shows the field of view of the system and the corresponding eye slaved insert (see Table 4.13). Details of the CAE optical system are given in Shenker (1987).

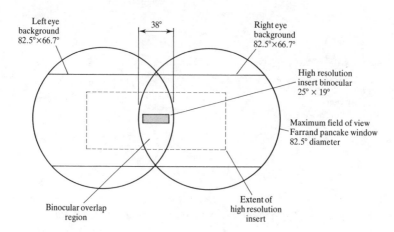

Figure 4.28 CAE fibre optic helmet-mounted display: field of view.

Table 4.13 Characteristics of the CAE FOHMD.

CAE FOHMD parameter	Specification
Display source	GE light valve
Mode	Binocular
Field of view background (instantaneous)	127°h × 66°v
Field of view insert (instantaneous)	25°h × 18.9°v
Binocular overlap	38°
Display resolution	5 arc minutes background
	1.5 arc minutes insert
Operating mode	Pancake™ window
Image distance	Infinity
Brightness	2570 cdm^{-2}
Contrast	50:1

British Aerospace/MBMT fibre coupled high resolution helmet-mounted display

Prior to the formation of the British Aerospace Advanced Cockpit Research Programme, the author worked on alternative solutions to the head up display (HUD). The HUD was evolving into a substantial piece of equipment, occupying considerable space in the aircraft. Integration of fixed forward looking infrared sensors to provide an improved night flying capability pushed the field of view of the HUD to figures of around 40° × 30°. Whether or not these large HUD fields of view improved pilot performance was, at that time, questionable. To achieve these large fields of view, the display manufacturers had to consider switching from conventional refractive optic design techniques to holographic techniques. These techniques allowed the large field of view to be achieved with lower mass than if a refractive optical design had been used. Unfortunately, the cost of the holographic technique was greater than traditional optical methods. Even so, the quality of holographic HUDs developed mainly by companies such as GEC Avionics was very high. From various trials that were conducted with these new HUDs, evidence began to emerge demonstrating that wider fields of view improved the pilot's performance. Unfortunately, there is a limit to how big the HUD's field of view can be because it is governed by the space envelope of the cockpit. Early helmet-mounted sights were too immature to be seriously considered as replacements for HUDs. The resolution of the display device (128 × 128 pixels) and head tracker (± 1°) were considered too low.

During the early 1980s, the author evaluated an interesting concept that had the potential to replace the HUD. The concept was based on employing a conventional HUD electronics unit and CRT, with a collimating lens. The collimating lens produced HUD symbology at infinity. The whole assembly was placed in or behind the pilot's seat, and the pilot was required to wear a special helmet with a simple combiner and a coherent fibre optic bundle, interfaced to a small lens assembly. These components were integrated into the helmet. The lens was situated at the rear of the helmet, the fibre optic bundle being used to relay the image to the optical assembly at the front of the helmet. To use the system the pilot had to sit in the specially modified ejector seat and arrange the helmet in such a manner that the rear lens on the helmet was positioned within the exit pupil of the CRT's collimating lens. A rear mounted HUD was achieved with this approach and it proved to be an interesting solution to the traditional HUD. Everything worked well, until the pilot rotated his head. At this point the image through the combiner became very distorted. The distortion was attributed to the helmet-mounted collimating lens moving away from the optical axis of the seat-mounted collimating lens. Consequently, the idea was abandoned. However, this trial demonstrated that high resolution, full colour imagery could be integrated on to a pilot's helmet without incurring a significant weight penalty. The next step was obvious: by extending the fibre optic bundle off the head and arranging for the CRT collimating lens to be fixed relative to the bundle, a high resolution image could be achieved with a helmet-mounted display. British Aerospace, Brough funded a small UK company to part-build a fibre coupled helmet-mounted display, with British Aerospace engineers completing the remaining part of the system and undertaking the integration into the cockpit facility. A high level of interaction between the two companies was essential so that an optimum design could be realized. In this way certain design corrections could more easily be achieved in the graphics system rather than in the optical system.

The fibre coupled helmet-mounted display is perfectly capable of producing high resolution full colour imagery (1280 × 1024) produced by a Silicon Graphics computer. Plate 6 shows a pilot wearing the British Aerospace, Brough fibre coupled high resolution helmet-mounted display, while Plates 4 and 9 show examples of the imagery that can be resolved by the system.

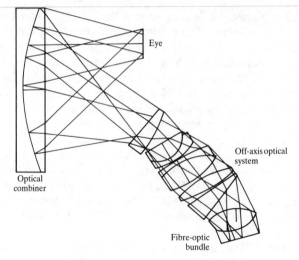

Figure 4.29 Schematic diagram of British Aerospace, Brough's fibre coupled helmet-mounted display.

The weight of the helmet-mounted display is not as high as it might appear because the fibre optic bundles are more or less self-supporting when they are arranged to pass under the arms. Obviously, the system is not designed for flight use in an aircraft. It would be unwise to attempt to eject with the fibre optic bundles still attached to the helmet. Each bundle is sheathed in silicon rubber for protection, which also ensures that the bundles are extremely flexible. The image source for the system was derived from very high resolution large format CRTs. These are special devices that have computer controlled convergence correction.

Another feature of the fibre coupled helmet-mounted display is that it is a see-through system. In other words, the user can still see real-world objects through the optical system and the computer generated imagery can be overlaid onto the real world. The technique to achieve this see-through capability is based on the combiner glass principle used in head up displays, with a few differences. To achieve a wide field of view, a special combiner glass was required that exhibited optical power in the reflection mode and a magnification of 1:1 in the transmission mode. In this way an outside world scene would pass through the combiner without magnification, while imagery from the helmet-mounted optical system would be magnified. This means that the combiner becomes part of the helmet-mounted display optical system.

Figure 4.29 shows a schematic layout of the combiner assembly. Unfortunately, for commercial reasons, it is not possible to reproduce the full optical system.

The development of the British Aerospace, Brough's fibre coupled helmet-mounted display has been a long and painful process, involving the solution of many problems. Some of these were solved by changes to the optical design while others were incorporated into the graphic transformations that were applied to the computer generated image, prior to display. Many lessons were learnt on how to measure the optical performance of the helmet-mounted display system during the development programme.

Table 4.14 Characteristics of the British Aerospace, Brough fibre coupled helmet-mounted display.

BAe fibre coupled helmet-mounted display parameter	Actual specification
Display source	Large format high resolution full colour CRT
Mode	Binocular
Field of view per ocular (instantaneous)	60°h × 40°v
Exit pupil (instantaneous)	10 mm
Binocular overlap	29°
Display resolution	2.8 arc min over full field of view
Fibre diameter	10 μm diameter
Image distance	1 m to infinity
Brightness	95 cdm^{-2}
Contrast	50:1

The fibre coupled helmet-mounted display is used to support both advanced cockpit research and virtual environment research programmes.

Although the complete system did not meet all British Aerospace, Brough's tight specifications, it has nevertheless proved to be a very important tool for high resolution, full colour, helmet-mounted display research. From a cockpit research point of view the system can emulate current and future helmet-mounted displays. By taking the specifications of these systems, it is possible to programme the fibre optic helmet-mounted display facility to emulate optical characteristics such as field of view, display resolution, and amount of overlap, and present the display symbology in a representative manner (see Table 4.14).

Polhemus Laboratories fibre optic helmet-mounted display system

Bill Polhemus, one of the original pioneers behind the first a.c. magnetic tracking system, formed a small company called Polhemus Laboratories Inc. to develop a fibre optic helmet-mounted display. Polhemus has developed a prototype system using sub-micron diameter fibres to produce a lightweight device. Simple optics have been used at the ends of the fibre bundles. Resolution of the bundle is quoted at 1000 × 1000 over a 1/4-inch square. The final display resolution is approximately equivalent to a 500-line CRT (see Figure 4.30). Polhemus' ambition is to produce a helmet-mounted display that is no bigger than a pair of spectacles. This is a real challenge !

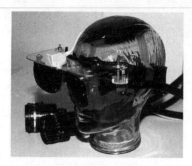

Figure 4.30 Polhemus Laboratories Inc. fibre optic helmet-mounted display.

Reflection Technology's Private Eye

A low cost, easy to use monocular virtual display has been developed by a company called Reflection Technology. The Private Eye display produces a 720 × 280 pixel image on a 1-inch virtual image in front of the user's eye. The image source is based on a light emitting diode (LED) line array, which comprises 280 individual LEDs driven by a computer signal. The device incorporates a one-axis scanning mirror driven by a ramp (saw-tooth) signal. The LED line array forms one axis of the scanner image while the oscillating mirror forms the other axis. The scanning mirror has been made extremely lightweight and is driven electromagnetically via a small coil assembly. The mirror moves through an arc of approximately 15°. The scanning mirror incorporates a simple method of feedback by interrupting a small optical switch at each point of maximum deflection. This signal is used by the scanner oscillator unit to maintain a constant scanning frequency of 50 Hz. The host computer transmits bitmapped image data to the scanner assembly in serial form to internal memory. A new line of data is transferred to the LED line array every 5 ms. Figure 4.31 illustrates the concept behind the Private Eye. Despite the constant oscillating of the mirror's pivot, it has proven to be extremely reliable in practice. Current technology restricts the Private Eye display to monochrome (red LED source). Nevertheless, the display is extremely good and provides a finely focused image. Although it may not be particularly suited to full virtual environment applications, because of its resolution and monochrome display, it is a very cost-effective virtual display. At the time of writing it is the cheapest virtual environment display available and could be applied to many important applications if it were coupled with a simple head position sensor. A distinct advantage of the display is its compactness and low weight.

The voice coil pushes against a spring-mounted magnetic counterweight that is set opposite the mirror. The resonant frequency of the counterweight system is the same as that of the mirror, so the entire mirror/counterweight coil mechanism acts like a tuning fork. Since the mirror and counterweight have the same effective inertia and always move in opposite directions, most of the vibration is cancelled out. The springs that support the mirror and counterweight act as virtually frictionless pivots for the mechanism and minimize energy loss in the mechanical system. Using springs instead of bearings also eliminates wear points, which can affect the alignment of the optical path. The springs are carefully designed thin metal flexures. Because the mirror travels through only a 15° arc, the springs are stressed to only a small fraction of their fatigue limit and are therefore very reliable over a long lifetime (see Figure 4.32).

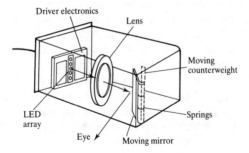

Figure 4.31 Principle of operation behind Private Eye.

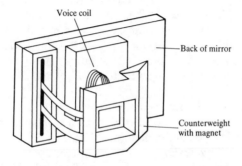

Figure 4.32 Private Eye: scanning mirror arrangement.

To synchronize the LED's output with the mirror's position, a stationary light source and photosensor are mounted behind the mirror. A tab on the back of the mirror allows the light to reach the photosensor as the mirror approaches its maximum deflection, thus generating a synchronizing pulse. Timing the movement of the mirror also permits energy to be applied at just the right moment to maintain the amplitude of the motion with minimum power consumption.

Additionally, the photosensor signal determines the proper timing for the display of each screen. This permits excellent alignment between the mirror's position and the display of the corresponding LED column, as the mirror scans a full screen image. The variations in column spacing due to the mirror's sinusoidal motion are easily corrected by adjusting the timing of the individual columns. Each pixel is located within 0.35° of the mirror arc, with an imperceptible frame-to-frame variation. This results in a stable image.

The 280 LED column is staggered left and right into a zigzag array, with the bottom of each pixel evenly aligned with the top of the pixel beneath it. Each side of the staggered LED column is illuminated at a slightly different time to allow the mirror's movement to combine left and right sides of the column, making the pixels appear to touch each other, top to bottom. This creates the appearance of a single, solid column, even though the display elements have a slight horizontal separation. It is thus possible to display solid vertical lines and solid areas without any of the blank intervening lines that are normally seen on CRTs between each scanned line. This feature is especially important in graphics applications.

The image is presented to the viewer through a magnifying lens assembly that sits between the mirror and the LED array. The lens assembly slides on a track and can be adjusted by the user so that the image appears to be anywhere between 9 inches and infinity from the user's eye. Therefore, the image can be placed at the same distance as physical objects in the user's field of view, thus avoiding the eye strain caused by shifting focus between a traditional display and other objects.

Other features

Traditional displays must cope with ambient illumination. The specific problems and solutions vary with the technology, but designers often find themselves sacrificing brightness to obtain higher contrast, and then pumping more power into the display to restore the brightness. The Private Eye has the distinct advantage of locating its display in a light-tight enclosure. The images appear as vibrant red characters or graphics on a black background with a contrast ratio of 70:1, though only ⅓ W of power is consumed. The Private Eye's very high contrast ratio, many times that of a typical LCD display, explains why the image appears to be so bright and sharp, despite the very low power consumption.

Red was chosen as the display colour because red LEDs are readily available and are the most power efficient. Additional colours or a combination of colour LEDs will be used in future models to create multicoloured images.

Electrically, the Private Eye runs asynchronously from the host device. The display has an internal control chip and screen buffer memory. The control chip takes serially transmitted bitmap data and sends it to the display's internal memory. The Private Eye then takes the bitmap and places it in shift registers adjacent to the LED array. The display is automatically and continuously refreshed with this image until the host device sends new data. The control chip also allows the Private Eye to go into a standby mode, conserving power during periods when the user doesn't need to see an image.

The complete Private Eye display is shown in Figure 4.33, which illustrates the extreme compactness of the system. While it has not been designed to compete with the much larger helmet-mounted displays it has the advantages of low cost and ease of use. The Private Eye display could potentially be a very important display device for low cost virtual environment systems. Without doubt, its portability will be a key factor when considering its application.

Meanwhile, over the coming years new enhancements and features will appear. The first improvement to be addressed will be the addition of grey scale or, in the case of the Private Eye, 'red scale'. Multiple levels of scale can be obtained by redesigning the controller to vary the LED's light cycles in accordance with the desired brightness. This can be done with no loss of resolution, allowing for 64 levels of grey scale. Up to 256 levels will require some additional development. The major impact of adding grey scale is that it will require a substantially bigger frame buffer, and higher speed interface electronics to transfer the additional data up to the cable (6 bits per pixel at 64 levels of grey scale, versus 1 bit per pixel at present).

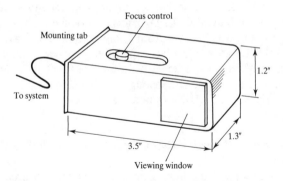

Figure 4.33 Private Eye: overall dimensions.

Table 4.15 Specifications for Reflection Technology's Private Eye display.

Private Eye parameter	Specification
Display source	LED line array
Mode	Monocular
Field of view	21.8° h × 14.2° v
Display resolution	720 × 280 pixels
Aspect ratio	25 lines, 80 characters/line
Operating mode	Non-see-through
Adjustments	Image position
Image distance	18 inches to infinity
Brightness	6.85 cdm^{-2} (nominal)
Contrast	70:1
Image type	Mirror scanner
Colour	660 ± 20 mm 16 grey levels
Refresh rate	50 Hz
Size	1.2" × 1.3" × 3.5" (2.25 oz)

Resolution will increase from model to model. The next model of the Private Eye will feature moderately increased resolution (perhaps 640 × 480) using the existing packaging technology. More substantial increases depend on the availability of denser packaging techniques. Replacing wire bonding with conductive paths between the chips laid onto the substrate should permit the development of megapixel resolution displays.

Colour will be possible when green and blue LEDs become available in arrays similar to today's red LEDs. The scanning mirror will visually superimpose the red, green and blue pixels from individual LED arrays to produce multiple colours. Blue and green LED arrays are still a few years from being commercially available.

Reflection Technology's five-year target is to produce a 1K × 1K (megapixel) full-colour display, in a smaller package. It is intended that this version will include fully animated graphics, at a price low enough for consumer electronic applications – essentially a high-definition TV (HDTV) in a matchbox.

Fake Space Laboratories Binocular Omni-Orientation Monitor (BOOM)

The BOOM display produced by Fake Space Laboratories overcomes many of the problems of current helmet-mounted display systems. Parameters such as weight and visual lag are kept to a minimum. Low cost commercial helmet-mounted displays employ low to medium resolution LCDs as the display source to keep overall head-supported mass to a minimum. However, for some applications low resolution helmet-mounted displays may be inadequate. The BOOM system overcomes these problems by employing higher resolution CRT-based displays and by offsetting the weight by means of a carefully designed counterbalance. The articulating counterbalance is instrumental in sensing the position of the display unit with precision optical shaft encoders.

Table 4.16 Fake Space Laboratories BOOM display performance.

BOOM display parameter	Specification
Display source	CRT
Mode	Binocular
Field of view (instantaneous)	140° × 90°
Binocular overlap	Not specified
Display resolution	1280 × 1024
Colour	Single or pseudo (not full RGB)

Table 4.17 Fake Space Laboratories BOOM tracker performance.

BOOM tracker parameter	Specification
Translation range	2.5′ high, 5′ diameter
Translation accuracy	0.16″
Angular resolution	0.1°
Phase lag	≈0
Interface	RS232

The output from the shaft encoder is virtually free of noise and offers least lag. The conversion from shaft encoder position to display position and orientation is considerably easier than with other space tracking systems.

To use the BOOM system, the subject merely pulls the display unit to the face so that he/she can then move around freely within the constraints of the articulating counterbalance (see Tables 4.16 and 4.17).

4.2.2 Position and orientation tracking systems

This section is primarily concerned with position and orientation tracking systems (including head tracking systems) where it is necessary to sense the position and orientation of an object in three-dimensional space. For example, hand position sensing is normally performed with the same type of tracker system that is used for the head.

There are four basic approaches to sensing the position and orientation of an object in three-dimensional space, based on electromechanical, electromagnetic, acoustic and optical technologies. In each case there are general variations in actual implementation. Each approach has its own merits and disadvantages, and the user must understand these to make the most appropriate choice for a given application. The principle behind many of these systems is often regarded as a 'black art', and very little is published. Purchasers of systems are not normally given technical details describing how the system works. Instead, they are given manuals that describe the configuration options available, with an example of how to use the data. When one is attempting to put together a real-time system for a virtual environment it is essential that precise details of operation are understood. This will ensure that the integration of the tracker into the virtual environment system is undertaken effectively without introducing unnecessary delays, which inevitably show up as a lag in the image. For example, most tracking systems incorporate some form of noise filter to remove the effect of 50 Hz mains hum. Although these filters, particularly the adaptive filters, are efficient at removing noise components they have a bearing on the effective update rate of the tracker. It is also important to know how the tracker works because the environment in which it is expected to work may have a detrimental effect on the performance of the system.

Electromechanical tracking systems will not be discussed in this chapter because they were covered in Chapter 2 (see Section 2.4). However, electromechanical tracker systems (and that includes measuring position with optical shaft encoders) will generally offer the highest resolution and the least phase lag. Phase lag is the time it takes to generate an electrical signal that corresponds to a given input. This feature could be very important for some applications.

A full description of the terms used to characterize the orientation and tracking system is given in Chapter 6. Examination of the literature of various manufacturers will reveal that different names are often used to describe the same parameter. Wherever specifications are given in this book, the standard definitions given in Chapter 6 are used, to enable comparison to be made.

A.c. electromagnetic tracking systems

Low frequency magnetic fields have been used in a range of position and orientation measurement applications. Most systems rely on free space geometry, although a few have been based on the effects of a nearby conducting medium. An extremely popular tracking system has been based on an a.c. electromagnetic concept. Figure 4.34 shows the basic system block diagram.

The a.c. electromagnetic system uses a three-axis magnetic dipole source and three-axis magnetic sensors. The source excitation signal and the resulting sensor signal output are represented as vectors. The excitation of the source comprises three excitation states, resulting in three vectors that are linearly independent of each other. The three sensor vectors contain sufficient information to allow the position and orientation of the sensor to be calculated. The system operates by tracking the position and orientation of the sensor and calculating the changes from the previous position.

This is achieved by using the previous computation to calculate linear transformations that are the inverses of the true source-to-sensor coupling. The transformations are applied to the source excitations and the sensor output vectors. The resulting function approximates to an aligned source and sensor. The processed output vectors differ from the excitation vectors (prior to transformation) by values that are linearly proportional to position and orientation. Individual coordinate changes are calculated from linear combinations of the elements of the processed output vectors, and these are finally transformed to the required coordinate frame.

The excitation source signals for the transmitter are generated in the drive circuit unit. Their amplitude is again controlled by a 12–bit multiplying analogue-to-digital converter. Automatic gain control was incorporated to ensure that an adequate signal to noise ratio was maintained for different source-to-sensor ranges. A carrier frequency 7–14 kHz was used to host the excitation pattern. The carrier frequency was chosen to provide the best compromise between design complexity, sensitivity, noise and source inductance. The excitation pattern is repeated between 30 and 120 Hz, being governed by computational performance, response time, noise and allowable source movement.

As the complete mathematical derivation is rather complex and involved, the interested reader should consult the excellent account given by Raab *et al.* (1979).

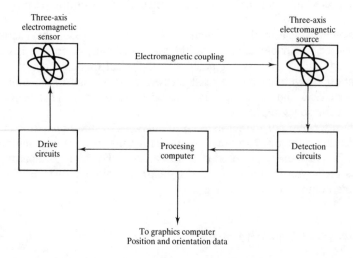

Figure 4.34 A.c. electromagnetic tracking system: block diagram.

A key requirement for the sensor is for it to be small and lightweight. The sensor and source coils are wound on ferrite cores to increase their effective sensitivity by a factor of 2–3.5. The early sensors measured 19×26 mm, while the source is slightly larger, typically 25 mm square. When driven by a peak current of 200 mA the magnetic moment of the source is approximately 0.086 Atm^2. The sensor correspondingly produces an output that is 0.12 V/(Atm^{-1}).

The sensor is connected to an associated electronics unit where the signal is amplified and synchronously demodulated prior to being digitized by a 12–bit analog-to-digital converter.

There are undoubtedly imperfections in the source and sensor arrangements due to rotation, gain and skew (cross-coupling between axes). These imperfections can be described by means of 3×3 fixed value matrices. Prior calibration of the source is performed by exciting its three axes and measuring the response in a Helmholtz coil. The sensor is similarly calibrated by exciting the Helmholtz coil and measuring the resulting responses in each axis of the sensor. The resulting data can be inserted in a pair of matrices as an inverse of the original measured data. By incorporating this data as part of the computation, the imperfections can be removed.

It is advantageous to be able to use different sources or sensors in an application, because in some installations the source has to be permanently attached to the user's helmet. By incorporating a programmable read only memory (PROM) that contains the sensor's unique characterization data in the connection plug, it is possible to avoid having to calibrate the tracker each time a sensor is replaced.

Environmental effects

As the a.c. magnetic tracker operates on a magnetic field, it seems reasonable to assume that metallic or other ferrous materials in the tracker's environment may induce a distortion. The a.c. magnetic fields produced by the tracker cause circulating (eddy) currents in nearby conducting materials, which in turn introduce a secondary a.c. magnetic field, causing further distortion. Unfortunately, analytical production of the distorted field is very difficult. Polhemus worked on the assumption that an infinite conducting plane produces 'as much as, or more' field distortion than another metallic object placed at the same distance from the source and sensor arrangement.

Electromagnetic theory allows the conducting plane to be replaced with an image source. The ratio of the free space and scattered fields can be estimated as the ratio of the inverse cubes of the distances from the sensor and source to its image. In other words, an object whose distance from the source is at least twice the distance separating the source and sensor produces a scattered magnetic field whose magnitude is less than that of the desired field.

In any tracking system it is very important to define a coordinate frame and a matrix to relate sensor output to source excitation. The relationship between the source and the sensor is shown in Figure 4.35.

The source coordinate frame X, Y, Z is used as the reference for the final measurements. The source axis can be aligned with any desired coordinate frame by modifying the excitation. The sensor position is specified in either rectangular cartesian coordinates (x, y, z) or spherical coordinates (α, β, γ) relative to the source coordinate frame. The orientation of the sensor is specified by a sequence of three rotations: an azimuthal rotation, an elevation rotation and a roll rotation.

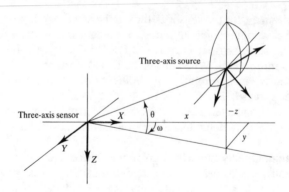

Figure 4.35 Relationship between source and sensor.

- Azimuthal rotation by ω about the Z axis from $+X$, $+Y$

- Elevation rotation by θ about the axis from $+X$ to $-Z$

- Roll rotation by ϕ about its X axis from $+Y$ to $+Z$

Source sensor coils have small diameters in comparison to the distances between them so they can be regarded as point sources. This approximation leads to only very small errors. The wavelength of the excitation source is made long enough ($\gamma \ll \lambda/2\pi$) so that only the near field component, the term varying as the inverse cube of distance, is significant.

Assuming that the coil is supplied with a current $i_{(t)} = I \cos \omega t$, the resulting magnetic field at a distance and off-axis angle is given by:

$$H_\varrho = \left[\frac{M}{2\pi\gamma^3} \right] \cos\phi$$

$$H_t = \left[\frac{M}{4\pi\gamma^3} \right] \sin\phi$$

The magnetic moment of the coil is given by:

$$M = NIA$$

where A is the coil area and N is the number of turns.

A time variation of $e^{i\omega t}$ is implied. In practice, the above components are valid for any coil shape if the distance between source and sensor is at least four times greater than the coil diameter.

To determine the relationship between sensor and source, vector notation should be used. (Assume that the number of turns and diameter of source coils are the same). The excitation of the source is represented by:

$$f_1 = [f_{1x}, f_{1y}, f_{1z}]$$

where f_{1x}, f_{1y} and f_{1z} represent the amplitudes of the currents exciting the loops in the X, Y and Z axes respectively.

The a.c. magnetic tracking system was originally developed by Polhemus Navigation Systems Inc. under the name of SPASYN (Space Syncro). SPASYN is a tracking system for determining the orientation between two independent rigid body coordinate frames. It is a five degree of freedom space tracker that measures three relative orientation angles and two angles in three relative polar coordinates of translation. The development of the tracker was in response to an application proposed by the Aerospace Medical Research Laboratory at Wright Patterson Airforce Base (WPAFB). The WPAFB requirement was for a system to measure the translation of a pilot's head relative to a reference frame fixed to the aircraft axis. The first application for SPASYN was in a visually coupled control system.

The SPASYN system comprises three units: a transmitter, a receiver and an electronics unit. The transmitter and receiver units are almost identical, consisting of three identical orthogonal windings on a core structure that has isotropic radiating or receiving properties.

The transmitter radiates a nutating magnetic vector field. When the receiver is near the radiated field, the magnetic field is loosely coupled into the receiver coils. By processing the appropriate signals in the electronics unit the direction of the line of sight containing the points representing the transmitter and the sensor can be calculated. The orientation of the sensor is represented by the three Euler angles ψ, θ and ϕ. The azimuth and elevation angles are relative to the x, y, z reference frame.

The nutating reference vector is defined by the following relationship :

$$f = col(E, N\cos\omega t, N\sin\omega t)$$

where E is the amplitude of the continuous wave component, N is the amplitude of the nutation component and ω is the frequency of the nutation (radians).

The transmitter operates at a nominal carrier frequency and each coil is modulated to achieve the properly pointed nutating field. The signal that is applied to the three coils is given by the respective component of the transmitter modulation vector e_m, where:

$$e_m = T_p^{-1} f$$

$$T_p^{-1} = \begin{bmatrix} \cos\alpha & -\sin\alpha & 0 \\ \sin\alpha & \cos\alpha & 0 \\ 0 & 0 & 1 \end{bmatrix} \begin{bmatrix} \cos\beta & 0 & \sin\beta \\ 0 & 1 & 0 \\ -\sin\beta & 0 & \cos\beta \end{bmatrix}$$

The angles α and β are determined by integrating the off-axis pointing error detected against the logic of the quadrature components of the nutation.

Polhemus tracker performance

Polhemus Inc. manufactures three orientation and position tracker models, the Isotrak, the 3Space Tracker and the Fastrak. The Isotrak supports one sensor, while the 3Space Tracker and the Fastrak support up to four sensors. When used with multiple sensors, the update rate of the 3Space is divided by the number of active sensors. With one sensor, the 3Space updates at a rate of 60 per second. The data rate for a single measurement is 12 ms. Computation requires an additional 5 ms and data transfer requires 6 ms (Rodgers, 1991). With four sensors, the 3Space updates at a rate of 15 updates per second (Polhemus, 1991). Several researchers report results that contradict the responsiveness described by Polhemus. Wang *et al.* (1990a) report 20 updates per second with 160–170 ms lag. Similarly, Wang *et al.* (1990b) report lags of 120 ms. Pausch (1991) reports lags between 150 ms and 250 ms, and Wenzel (1992) reports a latency of at least 50 ms. In a systematic study of noise and lag in the Isotrak, Liang *et al.* (1991) find lags of 110 ms at 20 Hz and 85 ms at 60 Hz. A better dynamic test is described in Adelstein *et al.* (1992). The accuracy of the Polhemus tracker systems decreases as the distance between sensor and emitter increases. This is characteristic of magnetic fields, which diminish geometrically over distance. Polhemus (1991) rates their system with the sensor at a distance of 762 mm (30 in) from the emitter as follows: resolution 6.35 mm (0.25 in); 0.1°; accuracy: 6.35 mm (0.25 in); 0.85°. Polhemus Inc. is currently working to improve orientational resolution (Rodgers, 1991).

Ferromagnetic materials alter the radiated magnetic field. The emitter generates an a.c. magnetic field that produces eddy currents in nearby computer cabinets and video displays. These currents then generate secondary a.c. magnetic fields that distort the emitter field pattern. The effects of the secondary magnetic fields can be compensated by software calibrated to the peculiar magnetic shape of a specific working volume. The computation required to undertake this mapping should not be underestimated.

Polhemus 3Space and Fastrak

Because of limited capability of early processing systems, early space tracking systems offered limited performance with respect to update rate, phase lag, and so on. Today, virtual environment system requirements are placing greater demands on space tracker technology, with the bias being towards faster, low lag systems. To this end a new generation of tracking systems is emerging based on digital signal processor (DSP) technology. Previous Polhemus tracking systems operated in the analogue/digital (A/D) domain. Signals from the sensor are amplified, bandpass filtered, gain control adjusted, synchronously demodulated and low pass filtered, before being digitized for calculation by a microprocessor (see Table 4.18). The Fastrak system employs a different approach, involving signal generation, signal detection and signal processing to calculate the position and orientation. The transmitter signals induced in the sensor coils are amplified by special ultra low noise differential input amplifiers. The output from these amplifiers is mixed with internal calibration signals before being digitized by a fast A/D. Each of the three axes is sampled by a dedicated A/D to improve throughput. Modern oversampling techniques have been employed at a rate much higher than the carrier frequency, because this reduces anti-aliasing and improves the signal to noise ratio. The resulting digitized data is then passed to the DSP for processing.

Table 4.18 Specification of Fastrak performance.

Fastrak parameter	Specification
Translation range	10′ max
Translation accuracy	0.03" RMS
Translation resolution	0.0002"
Angular range (azimuth)	±180°
Angular range (elevation)	±90°
Angular range (roll)	±180°
Angular accuracy	0.15°RMS
Angular resolution	0.05°
Update rate	120 Hz
Phase lag	4 ms; care should be taken when interpreting this value
Data supplied	x, y, z, azimuth, elevation, roll
Interfaces	RS232 (115.2 kBaud max), IEEE488 (100 kbytes s^{-1})
Synchronization	Yes, CRT

Performance is indicated for a source–receiver separation of 30 inches.

The following operations are undertaken:

- multiply/accumulate
- synchronous demodulation
- gain control
- filtering

The DSP also generates the drive waveforms for the transmitter unit. Figure 4.36 shows a generalized architecture for the Fastrak system.

Polhemus Fastrak performance

The Polhemus Fastrak has been designed from conception to be extremely fast, with a minimal lag. This has been achieved by means of the DSP as well as paralleling the A/D converter stage. Polhemus claims a phase lag response of 4 ms without any form of signal filtering. Any filtering to remove susceptibility to these effects would certainly increase the phase lag. It would also be very interesting to measure the dynamic performance of the Fastrak and compare it with other space tracking systems.

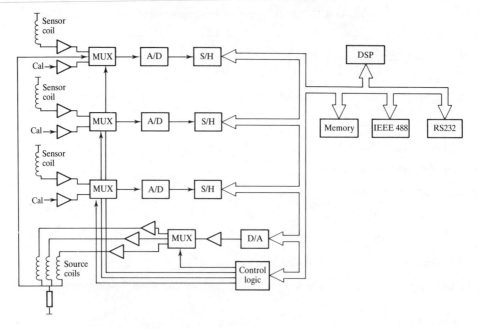

Figure 4.36 Generalized architecture of the Fastrak space tracker.

D.c. electromagnetic tracking system

The a.c. electromagnetic tracking system is particularly susceptible to the presence of electrical conductors (especially ferromagnetic material) near the source and sensor system. The nutating a.c. magnetic field generates eddy currents in the ferromagnetic material, which lead to the creation of secondary magnetic fields. Unfortunately, these fields distort the field pattern created by the a.c. electromagnetic tracker's source. The distorted field causes errors in the position/orientation data calculated by the tracker.

To reduce the effect of distorting eddy currents a company called Ascension Technology have developed a d.c. electromagnetic tracking system that only generates eddy currents at the beginning of a measurement cycle. Therefore, a steady state is reached where eddy currents decay to zero.

The d.c. electromagnetic tracking system transmitter comprises three coils mounted orthogonally about a cubic core, as shown in Figure 4.37. The transmitter is mounted rigidly to a reference structure. The cubic core is constructed from magnetically permeable material, which concentrates the lines of magnetic flux produced when a current is passed through any of the three orthogonal coils. If the coils are not mounted orthogonally with respect to each other it is possible to calibrate the tracker system and store correction data in a 'look-up table'.

The transmitter circuitry sends a small amount of d.c. to be driven through each of the three transmitter coils in turn. This causes a pulsed d.c. electromagnetic field to be generated sequentially by each of the three transmitter coils. One complete measurement period is 10 ms, divided into four intervals of 2.5 ms. In three successive intervals, current pulses are applied in turn to the three transmitter coils. In the fourth interval the transmitter is quiescent and no d.c. pulse is applied. Each pulse has a carefully controlled rise time; and the power level is controlled in accordance with the transmitter to receiver range, determined from the tracker's position output. This ensures that the system sensitivity is maintained over a wide transmitter-to-receiver operating range.

The receiver also comprises three separate coils wound orthogonally on a cubic core. At the centre of the cube is a cylindrical shell around which is an additional coil called the energizing coil. The receiver is operated as a three-axis magnetometer and the three sense coils measure, almost simultaneously, the resolved components of the magnetic field within which the receiver unit is placed.

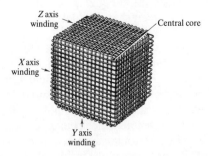

Figure 4.37 D.c. electromagnetic tracker system : transmitter unit.

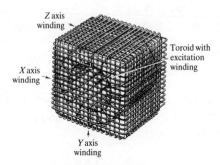

Figure 4.38 D.c. electromagnetic tracker system: receiver unit.

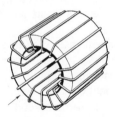

Figure 4.39 D.c. electromagnetic tracker: energizing coil.

A low-power a.c. current is passed through the energizing coil to make the cylindrical shell become magnetically saturated on a cyclic basis. This causes the d.c. magnetic field to pass undisturbed past the receiver or causes it to be attracted into it. The cyclic change in direction of the local d.c. magnetic field causes alternating currents to be generated in the three sense coils. The strengths of these currents is proportional to the resolved component of the local d.c. magnetic field. The complete receiver is shown in Figures 4.38 and 4.39.

Any non-orthogonalities in the three windings are calibrated out during manufacture and are stored in a look up table (EEPROM), which is integrated with the receiver. This allows the tracker to work with any receiver unit without undertaking calibration.

The electronics unit provides the energizing signals for the transmitter unit and in turn processes the data from the receiver unit to determine its position and orientation relative to the transmitter.

The ambient electromagnetic field, which includes the earth's magnetic field, is measured during the interval when the transmitter is inactive, and the three coils measure the component of the ambient magnetic field. In practice the ambient electromagnetic field may be different when it is measured in the next interval. The electronics unit interpolates the value of the ambient electromagnetic field at intermediate times. In particular, the ambient electromagnetic field is calculated for each of the measurement intervals. The electromagnetic field is measured in three successive periods. At the beginning of the first period the x-coil of the transmitter is energized. After this period the three receiver coils measure almost simultaneously their component parts of the electromagnetic field. Due to the ambient field, these measurements also contain a component that must be subtracted. The x-coil is then de-energized and the process is repeated for the other two coils.

Each measurement period gives nine data values. These are the electromagnetic fields transmitted by the three transmitter coils which are sensed by the three receiver coils. A further correction must be made because the transmitter is of finite size. Other corrections include:

- Residual eddy currents. Data measured during the mapping process is stored in a look up table and addressed by the eddy current correction algorithm.

- Permeable metal effects caused by metallic structures within the electromagnetic field.

- Noise filtering caused by local power supply electromagnetic fields. Some systems employ an adaptive filter algorithm that can respond to small variations in the ambient electromagnetic field.

The nine-element measurement matrix is then manipulated to give the position and orientation of the receiver relative to the transmitter. Major processing functions performed by the processing electronics unit include calculation of the x, y and z receiver measurements of the ambient electromagnetic field alone and the ambient field in the presence of the x, y and z transmitter coil fields. Interpolation is performed between successive intervals and determination of x, y and z transmitter fields by themselves.

To yield results with a high update rate and low phase lag the above computations require a fair degree of computational power.

Ascension Technology manufacture three basic tracker systems that employ the d.c. electromagnetic technique. These are called the Bird, the Flock of Birds and the Extended Range Transmitter (ERT) (previously known as the Big Bird). Each system is essentially the same, except the Flock of Birds unit is specially configured so that multiple units can be daisy-chained together to extend operational range or work together in the same environment. The ERT unit is a higher power version of the Flock of Birds unit. The transmitter unit is considerably larger than that used for other electromagnetic tracking systems. Its dimensions are almost 1 cubic foot, and it is extremely heavy. The higher power enables extended ranges of a radius of 8 feet to be achieved (see Table 4.19).

GEC-Marconi Aerospace (formerly GEC Avionics) in the UK have adopted the design for military applications. This has resulted in an extremely rugged unit that will operate in a wide range of harsh environments. GEC are able to undertake detailed mapping of the environment and provide an EEPROM that is installed in the electronics unit. This has the advantage of taking out nonlinearities caused by ambient electromagnetic fields, resulting in increased accuracy. Because of commercial constraints, specifications of the GEC d.c. tracker cannot be presented in this book.

Table 4.19 Comparison between d.c. electromagnetic trackers available from Ascension Technology Corp.

Parameter	Bird	ERT
Translation range	$\pm 24"$ x, y, z	$\pm 8'$ x, y, z
Translation accuracy	0.1" (RMS)	0.1" (RMS)
Translation resolution	0.03"	Not specified
Angular range	$\pm 180°$ azimuth	$\pm 180°$ azimuth
	$\pm 90°$ elevation	$\pm 90°$ elevation
	$\pm 180°$ roll	$\pm 180°$ roll
Angular accuracy	0.5° (RMS)	Not specified
Angular resolution	0.1° (RMS at 8")	Not specified
Update rate	100 Hz	100 Hz
Throughput	Variable	Variable
Data supplied	x, y, z, azimuth, elevation, roll	x, y, z, azimuth, elevation, roll
Weight transmitter	1 lb	1 lb
Weight receiver	1 oz	1 oz
Interface	RS232	RS232, RS422/485
Synchronization	Yes	Yes

D.c. electromagnetic tracker phase lag response

The phase lag of a tracker is the time difference between the start of a physical rotation of the receiver and the start of the corresponding output from the tracker electronics unit. For real-time considerations this is perhaps the most important performance parameter of the tracker system. Unfortunately, few manufacturers readily give specifications for this parameter. Ascension Technology Corporation have provided the following phase lag response information for their Bird model 6DFOB with PROM software revision 3.31. The continuous stream output mode is selected with a baud rate of 19,200. Receiver distances of $x = 12$, 18 and 24 inches have been used, where $y = 0$ and $x, z = 0$.

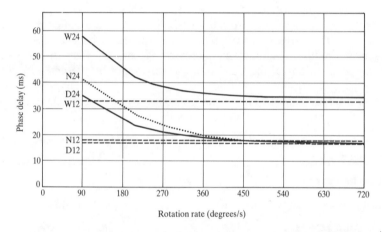

120 outputs per second; W, wide notch + d.c. filter; N, narrow notch + d.c. filters; D, d.c. filter only; 12, 24 receiver to transmitter separation (inches).

Figure 4.40 Bird tracker steady state phase lag delay.

The receiver was then given a step input rotation that corresponded to the following rotation profile:

Fast acceleration to a constant rotation followed by a deceleration to a stop. Due to servo stability the acceleration/deceleration rate varied as a function of the constant rotation rate in the following way: fast acceleration of 20,000 degrees sec^{-2} up to a constant rotation rate followed by a deceleration to a stop.

The actual delay is a function of the tracker filter characteristics, distance between transmitter and receiver, and the tracker model. To illustrate the phase delay, two different filter characteristics have been selected. Both filters are finite impulse response (FIR) notch filters that operate on signals of a sinusoidal characteristic. One is a narrow notch filter that eliminates a narrow band of noise, and the other is a wide notch filter that eliminates sinusoidal signals with a frequency of 30–70 Hz.

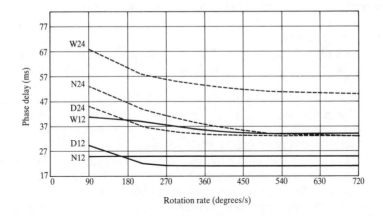

120 outputs per second; *W*, wide notch + d.c. filter; *N*, narrow notch + d.c. filters; *D*, d.c. filter only; 12, 24, receiver to transmitter separation (inches).

Figure 4.41   Bird tracker peak phase lag delay.

The tracker also incorporates an adaptive d.c. filter that is based on an infinite impulse response (IIR) low pass filter. The IIR filter is used to eliminate high frequency noise. Figure 4.40 shows the steady state phase lag characteristic, that is, the delay measured when the receiver unit reaches a constant rotation rate; in other words, when the acceleration is zero. Figure 4.41 shows the peak phase lag delay.

Ascension Bird tracker performance

In contrast to the continuous wave generated by the Polhemus 3Space tracker, the Ascension Bird tracker's emitter radiates a sequence of d.c. pulses which in effect switches the emitted field off and on. This design is intended to reduce the effect of distorting eddy currents induced by metallic objects, because such currents are created only when the magnetic field is changing. Since the Polhemus 3Space emitter radiates a continuously changing magnetic field, it is continuously producing eddy currents. The Bird emitter radiates magnetic pulses that generate eddy currents only at the beginning of the measurement cycle. Once the field reaches a steady state, no eddy currents are generated. The Bird avoids most eddy effects by waiting for the currents to decay before taking a measurement.

While the Bird minimizes the effect of conductive metals, it remains sensitive to the permeability of ferromagnetic metals. Ascension recommends that both emitter and receiver be at least 6 inches from ferrometallic objects to operate at rated levels of performance (Ascension, 1991a).

The Bird supports a single sensing unit. The ERT supports a single sensing unit over a larger volume of operation. The Flock of Birds supports one to thirty sensors and one to fourteen emitters in various configurations. The Bird is accurate to 2.54 mm at

609.6 mm and 0.1° at 203.2 mm from the emitter. ERT extends the working volume to a radius of 2.4384 m (8 feet) (Delaney, 1991). All Birds are rated by the manufacturer at 100 updates per second (Ascension, 1991a). Pausch (1991) reports that the Bird has a 24 ms lag, and Adelstein *et al.* (1992) give test results from their evaluation of the Ascension trackers.

The Flock of Birds links several Bird processing units with the Fast Bird bus. Depending on the configuration, the Flock can handle up to fourteen transmitters and thirty receivers.

The Flock is an upgrade of the Bird electronics unit. It radiates twice the emitter signal strength with half the noise at a given range. The Flock is reported to improve the Bird's range of operation to a 1.828 m (6 feet) diameter sphere (Ascension, 1991b). The Flock has three modes of operation: one transmitter–multiple receiver, walking Bird and time sharing. The one transmitter–multiple receiver configuration supports up to six Birds, each of which is connected to its own electronics unit. The electronics units are connected via the Fast Bird bus. In this case, the Flock signal strength is limited by the sensor closest to the emitter. This prevents the closest sensor from becoming oversaturated. However, if the sensors are widely separated, the emitted magnetic field may not be sufficient for the distant sensors to operate with usable accuracy.

The walking configuration supports the use of multiple emitters to extend the Bird's working volume. As the user walks from the working volume of one emitter to the next, the emitters are activated and deactivated to maintain continuous data collection.

The time sharing configuration supports several emitter–sensor pairs in the same working volume by time slicing. The electronic units for each emitter–sensor pair are connected with a Fast Bird bus (Ascension, 1991b).

Acoustic tracking systems

In 1968 Sutherland used an acoustic positioner designed by Seitz and Pezaris of Lincoln Laboratory, USA for a head-mounted display project. Since then, six degree of freedom acoustic position tracking technology has largely been ignored for virtual environment research because acoustic systems, unlike magnetic systems, have not been available 'off-the-shelf'. The major companies involved in producing head tracking systems have looked at increasing the algorithm accuracy of magnetic tracking systems.

In the early 1980s AEG (West Germany) introduced an ultrasonic system, which was marketed in the USA by WW Gaertner Research Inc. as an improvement over the magnetic system. However, this system was limited to an accuracy potential of 5 to 6 minutes. Therefore, it was not seen as the head tracker of the future. WW Gaertner Research Inc. initially believed that a vernier could be constructed to reduce the inaccuracies of the ultrasonic system.

WW Gaertner, under a contract from the Naval Training Systems Center (NTSC) in Orlando, Florida, showed that a vernier for the ultrasonic system was possible. However, the improvements in speed and accuracy were negligible in comparison with an alternate approach discovered by Gaertner.

Acoustic position trackers have been implemented using two basic approaches. These are time-of-flight measurement and phase-coherent measurement. Both systems are discussed here. Ultrasonic frequencies (above 20 kHz) are used so the emitters will not be heard. Consequently, acoustic systems are often referred to as ultrasonic systems. In principle, audible frequencies could be used.

Time-of-flight position trackers

A time-of-flight device determines distance by measuring the elapsed flight time of an acoustic wave. Multiple emitters and sensors are used to acquire a set of distances to calculate position and orientation.

The data rates for time-of-flight systems are limited by several factors. Acoustic waves travel at roughly 1 foot per millisecond, and the flight of an emitted wave must be completed before a measurement can be taken. Meaningful data is only available when a wave front arrives at the sensor. Additionally, these systems must allow for the emitters to 'ping' for several milliseconds after pulsing and wait for reflected pulses (echoes) to die out before new measurements can be taken. The time required is multiplied by the number of emitter–sensor combinations, because separate flight sequences are required for each combination. Because time-of-flight devices tend to have low data rates, they are especially vulnerable to ranging errors. The reliability of the measurements depends on a device's ability to detect the exact moment of arrival of an emitted acoustic wave. Detection of the arrival can be compromised by ambient noise from disk drives and CRT sweep frequencies. Air currents and sensor occlusion can also contribute to ranging errors. Increased filtering can compensate for errors, but the additional data requirement reduces the update rate and increases lag.

Lincoln Laboratory Wand

In 1966 at the Lincoln Laboratory, USA Roberts developed the Lincoln Wand (Roberts, 1966). This was a pen sized 3-D pointing device, intended to replace the light pen and Rand Tablet.

The Lincoln Wand was a time-of-flight device that used four transmitters and one receiver. The transmitters were pulsed in 10 ms intervals for a total cycle time of 40 ms (25 Hz). Roberts reported that the Lincoln Wand had respectable accuracy of 5.08 mm (0.2 in) and resolution of 5.08 mm (0.2 in). The device had a good tolerance for ranging errors from environmental sources. The receiver was tuned to 50 kHz to avoid room noise. Receiver occlusion could also cause gross errors. Smaller errors were reported from air currents and temperature gradients. To address these problems, the Lincoln Wand incorporated a gross error detector, damping filter and redundant data to ensure the use of accurate measurements. Roberts reported 'with damping of 0.1 second, the stability of the Lincoln Wand was 5.08 mm (0.2 inch) and the tracking of reasonable hand motions was excellent'.

Mattel Power Glove

The Mattel Power Glove uses a time-of-flight position tracker. Two ultrasonic transmitters are mounted on top of the glove at the back of the user's hand. Three receivers are mounted on an 'L' shaped bracket attached to a TV bezel. The glove must be pointed at the receivers for the system to track position. The Power Glove has a range of 3.048–4.572 m (10–15 feet) from the receivers and an effective working angle of 45° off the centre aids. The glove positioner has five degrees of freedom. Roll is reported as one of twelve possible positions. Since the glove must be orientated toward the receiver bezel, neither pitch nor yaw is reported. When the glove is within 0.3048 m of the receivers, the x, y, z coordinate information is accurate to 6.35 mm (Pausch, 1991).

Science Accessories Corporation Space Pen

The Space Pen generates an ultrasonic signal using a movable spark gap source and fixed ultrasonic linear microphones. System accuracy suffers from the environmental effects of air density and motion. The effective working volume is limited to 2 m^3 (Bishop, 1984).

Phase-coherent position trackers

Phase-coherent position trackers determine distance by comparing the phase of a reference signal to the phase of an emitted signal detected by sensors. A phase-coherent system can generate high data rates because phase can be measured continuously. The large data sets permit sufficient filtering to overcome the effects of environmental interference without detrimental effect on accuracy, responsiveness, or robustness.

Seitz–Pezaris head-mounted display position tracker

Sutherland used an acoustic position tracker as an alternative to the mechanical model he built for the head-mounted display in 1968. The goal was a new device constructed from readily available, inexpensive, narrow band transducers that would not be susceptible to pulsed noise sources.

The system used three transmitters attached to the head-mounted display. Each transmitter emitted a separate frequency in the 40 kHz range. A square array of four receivers was mounted on the ceiling to receive the signals. The phase shift for each emitter–sensor pair was stored as a 5-bit number, and the computer kept track of motions of more than one wavelength. However, the system could track changes within one wavelength, 7.62 mm (approximately 0.3 inch), but there was an ambiguity about which wave number the data represented. Sutherland called this 'initialization error'. Sutherland, Seitz and Pezaris attempted to solve this problem by using redundant data. In 1968 Sutherland reported that he had achieved promising results but had not finished his experiments.

Piltdown 3-D Compass

The Piltdown 3-D Compass is a six degree of freedom real-time orientation and position tracker (translation: x, y and z; orientation: azimuth, elevation and roll). Position tracking is achieved with ultrasonic technology. This is the first commercially available tracker to use phase-coherent techniques. Being an ultrasonic system it is immune to external magnetic fields and ferrous materials. Unlike time-of-flight ultrasonic systems, the Piltdown 3-D tracker is not affected by environmental noises such as jingling keys. The system consists of three components: a control unit, an emitter frame and a receiver frame. When activated, the 3-D Compass reports the position of the receiver frame to a host computer. Alternatively, a continuous position reporting mode is supported.

The Compass control unit controls the 3-D Compass operations and manages data collection and position calculation.

The emitter frame is a triangular structure that supports three ultrasonic transducers. Each transducer emits ultrasonic signals at a different frequency.

The receiver frame is a planar aluminium frame that supports four small data collection units, each of which houses a microphone and associated electronics for collecting the ultrasonic signals emitted from the emitter frame and transmitting them back to the control unit via cables. The control unit communicates with the host computer via an RS232 port.

The host computer initiates a command sequence which is transmitted over the RS232 interface and instructs the control unit to perform the following position tracking sequence:

- The control unit drives the three emitter frame transducers that produce the ultrasonic signals. Each of the three emitted signals is picked up by each of the four microphones on the receiver frame, giving a total of twelve received ultrasonic signals. The timing of the ultrasonic emissions is triggered by the control unit so that the phase of the emitters can be used as a reference. When signals are returned from the receiver frame, they are compared to this reference signal. The phase shift between the reference signal and the received signal is a measure of the receiver frame's distance from the emitter frame.

- The control unit performs calculations based on the phase shift data for each of the twelve signals. The results of these calculations are combined and reported to the host at a high rate. Several filtering techniques are used to compensate for a variety of ranging errors. The primary component of control unit is a DSP which controls and coordinates all the tracker's operations. The instructions for DSP operation reside in an EPROM. Included in the EPROM are the 3-D Compass operating system, the 3-D Compass internal command set, the position calculation algorithms, the position filtering algorithms, and the command set for host computer control.

- During the real-time position tracking operation, the DSP instructs the frequency generators to drive the three transducers on the emitter frame. These signals become a reference. The DSP then checks a buffer for data received from each of the four microphones on the receiver frame. The phase of each frequency in each signal is determined and compared to the reference signal. The result is a set of twelve phase differences. Because the receiver frame is rigid, and the relative position of the microphones remains constant, these phase differences can be used to determine the precise movement of the receiver since the last calculated position.

Table 4.20 Piltdown 3-D Compass ultrasonic position tracker specifications.

Piltdown 3-D Compass parameter	Specification
Translation range	4.572 m cube
Translation accuracy	< 2 mm
Translation resolution	0.1 mm
Angular range	Not specified
Angular accuracy	< 1.0°
Angular resolution	0.1°
Update rate	60 Hz
Phase lag	< 20 mS
Data supplied	x, y, z, azimuth, elevation, roll
Modes	Continuous, demand and incremental
Transmitter dimensions	457.2 mm equilateral frame
Receiver dimensions	76.2 mm triangular frame
Interface	RS232 (9600, 19200 and 38400 baud)

To correct for ranging errors that can be introduced by the environment, the DSP performs several filtering operations. The filtered data is reported to the host as an updated position. The more rapidly the unfiltered data is available, the more rapidly the filtering can proceed and the more frequently the position can be reported to the host computer. Owing to the high sampling rates possible with the phase reference measurement technique, receiver frame movements can be reported to the host without perceptible delay (see Table 4.20).

Evaluation of acoustic position trackers

Performance of time-of-flight and phase-coherent systems can differ dramatically because of the significantly higher data rates achieved with a phase-coherent device. In a small operating volume, time-of-flight systems can perform with good accuracy and responsiveness. As the range of operation increases, time-of–flight data rates decrease, making them less resilient to ranging errors. Also, time-of-flight systems are vulnerable to spurious acoustic pulses at any range. Jingling a set of keys will cause a time-of-flight system to generate gross ranging errors. Phase-coherent systems are intrinsically less vulnerable to noise. In general, because of their higher data rates, they offer improved accuracy, responsiveness, range and robustness. Phase-coherent systems are also less vulnerable to spurious pulses, and the excellent data rates permit abundant data for filtering without introducing lag. However, since phase-coherent systems do not directly measure distance, but only change in position, they are vulnerable to cumulative errors.

Time-of-flight systems are not prone to cumulative errors because every measure is an absolute reckoning of distance. Both types of acoustic systems are vulnerable to gross errors from sensor occlusion. Less significant ranging errors can result from disturbances in the air. Sociability of time-of-flight systems can be poor because the physical limitations of a small working volume provide less latitude to manoeuvre. However, the phase-coherent system can have excellent sociability because high data rates are available throughout a large range of operation. Both acoustic implementations allow multiple sensors to share the same emitter source.

Optical tracking systems

Optical trackers are more common than those based on any other technologies. Optical trackers were considered during the early 1970s but neither the processor technology nor the imaging sensors of the time were powerful enough to track a moving object. By the early 1980s processing power and the resolution of imaging systems had increased to the point where an optical tracker could be considered from a practical viewpoint. The first systems were essentially 2-D implementations.

Optical tracking systems have used a variety of detectors, from ordinary video cameras to $x-y$ area sensitive diodes. Either ambient light or light emitted under control of the position tracker was used. In the case of emitted light, infrared light is generally favoured so that the tracker does not interfere with the user's visual task. Optical tracking systems can be characterized as either fixed transducer or image processing.

Fixed transducer

Fixed transducer systems rely on there being a known distance between the emitters or sensors. Fixed transducer systems are the most common type of optical position tracker.

There are two approaches to fixed transducer architecture, known as 'outside-in' or 'inside-out' (Wang, 1990). For the 'outside in' approach, the sensors are fixed and the emitters are mobile. That means that the sensors 'look in' towards the mobile remote object. These systems require extremely expensive high resolution sensors. For the 'inside out' approach, the sensors are mobile and the emitters are fixed. That means that the sensors 'look out' from the mobile remote object.

This distinction addresses an important performance consideration for the design of an optical system. A long focal length lens resolves greater detail over a smaller area than a short focal length lens. However, a long lens subtends a smaller viewing area and reduces the range of operation. Conversely, a wide angle lens will have a larger working volume, with reduced accuracy. So, for a single set of emitters, as the working volume increases, the accuracy decreases.

For 'inside out' systems, both high accuracy and large range of operation can be achieved if multiple emitters are used in the working area. As the remote object moves about the working area, the sensors will always see the required number of emitters with sufficient resolution. The University of North Carolina is leading research into this type of optical tracker. An 'outside in' system does not benefit from a multiple emitter implementation because sensor resolution remains dependent on the proximity of the remote object.

SELSPOT

The SELSPOT tracker made by the Selective Electric Corporation of Sweden was probably the first commercially available optical tracker. It has been used by Mann (1981) for evaluating human movement via kinematic data acquisition experiments. The SELSPOT is an 'outside in' tracking system. A pair of special cameras are used to track a number of infrared light emitting diodes placed on the object to be tracked. The cameras employ lateral effect photodiodes that produce an x–y output corresponding to the 2-D location on the photo-diode surface. By using two cameras suitably placed it is possible to calculate a 3-D coordinate for each light emitting diode.

The SELSPOT tracker can track 30 light emitting diodes at 315 samples per second. Starks (1991) reports that the SELSPOT required controlled lighting but Mann (1981) reports that it was not adversely affected by ambient light. However, the SELSPOT is fairly sensitive to optical disturbances and can only be used indoors. Moreover, position data could not be obtained in real time (see Table 4.21).

Table 4.21 SELSPOT optical position tracker.

SELSPOT parameter	Specification
Translation range	1 m × 1 m × 1 m extendable with the addition of more cameras
Angular range	Not possible
Angular accuracy	N/A
Angular resolution	N/A
Update rate	315 samples per second
Data supplied	x, y, z

Honeywell Rotating Beam

The Honeywell Rotating Beam system is an 'inside out' implementation. Two small infrared sensors are attached to the helmet. Infrared sources mounted in the cockpit generate two thin fan-shaped beams that sweep across the cockpit. The helmet-mounted sensors detect the arrival time of the beams. The delay, from a horizontal beam reference position to detection by a helmet infrared sensor, is proportional to the displacement angle. Using the fixed distance between the sensor and the corresponding angle, the position can be calculated through triangulation (Ferrin, 1991).

Remote view optical tracking system

Most tracker systems have been developed specifically for use in confined spaces such as cockpits or simulators. They have a limited operating volume, typically 1–2 m. The exception is the Ascension Extended Range Transmitter tracker system which has an operating volume of 8 feet × 8 feet × 8 feet.

There are many virtual environment applications where it would be desirable to wander around the virtual world in a fairly natural manner. Several researchers have tried to overcome this deficiency with current trackers, either by adopting a means of 'flying' around the virtual world by gesture control or by employing a modified treadmill. What is really required is a tracker that allows the user to move freely around the virtual world. Such a system has been developed by the Department of Computer Science, University of North Carolina (Wang *et al.*, 1990c), based on an 'outside in' tracking scheme.

If the University of North Carolina tracking system is to be operated in a room that is 4 m square and assuming that it is necessary to track head rotation by 0.1° from one side of the room, a head rotation of 0.1° will move the light source by approximately 1 mm. This implies that the optical sensor must be able to resolve down to 1 part in 4000 (1 mm in 4 m). Wang *et al.* (1990c) have used an 'inside out' tracking system where the positions of the light sources and sensors are swapped over. The sensors are mounted on the helmet and the sources are mounted in a dense pattern on the ceiling. The example quoted by Wang *et al.* suggests that if the sensor uses a 50 mm lens with a 1 cm² detection area, the resulting field of view of the sensor 4 m away is 0.8 × 0.8 m². Therefore, a sensor that can resolve 1 part in 800 can easily detect the 1 mm displacement. CCD sensors could be used but they usually have a fairly limited spatial resolution and slower update rate. Wang and colleagues used lateral effect photodiodes, which have an inherently higher resolution. Figure 4.42 illustrates the arrangement of sensors and light sources.

The algorithms used to determine the position and orientation of the head are based on those originally proposed by Church (1945), who devised a means of working out where a camera was sited by taking a photograph, then making measurements of three known landmarks in the images.

Church defined two coordinate systems: a world coordinate system aligned to room coordinates, and a camera coordinate system. Church assumed that the camera could see three sources. Any two of the observed sources form an angle with the camera origin. The angle subtended by any two sensors is equal to the angle subtended at their corresponding image positions. The angles formed by the camera origin and the sensor positions in the image plane (points *P*, *Q* and *R*) can be calculated in the camera coordinate systems (see Figure 4.43). Unfortunately, the position of the camera origin is unknown in world coordinates. Church starts by guessing the position of the camera's origin in world coordinates, but usually the last known position of the camera is used. From this assumption it is possible to calculate the three angles in world coordinates.

An interactive search is undertaken to locate the correct 3-D camera position by minimizing the difference between the corresponding angles. System errors arise in this approach because of the measuring errors inherent while determining the positions of the angles, largely due to the resolution limitations of the sensor. Wang (1990) derived an expression for this error:

$$\varepsilon_\theta = \left[\frac{1}{a^2 + f^2} + \frac{1}{b^2 + f^2} \right] \frac{f D}{2r}$$

where *D* is the width of the sensor image area, *r* is the resolution of the sensor, and *p*, *q*, and *f* are as shown in Figure 4.44.

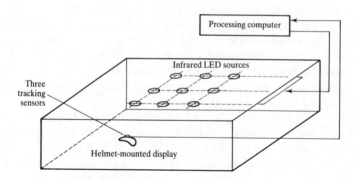

Figure 4.42 'Inside out' tracking system.

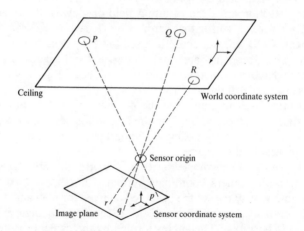

Figure 4.43 'Inside out' tracking system coordinate systems.

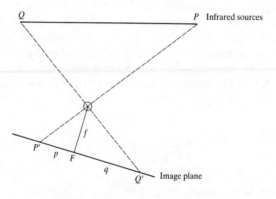

Figure 4.44 Calculation of errors in Church's tracking algorithm.

To keep the errors to a minimum, the sensor resolution should be maximized, a long focal length lens should be used, and the distance between sensors should be as large as possible.

In terms of the world coordinate set, the errors arise from the positions of the sources and can be expressed as:

$$\varepsilon_\theta = \left[\frac{x_a + y_a}{|OP|^2} + \frac{x_b + y_b}{|OQ|^2} \right] \varepsilon_p$$

where $P = (x_a, y_a)$ and $Q = (x_b, y_b)$

This equation suggests that using a smaller viewing error decreases the separation of the sources in the image plane. Unfortunately, this is in direct contradiction to the previous equation. Wang cleverly worked round this situation by employing several sensors.

The prototype system had an update rate of approximately 25 Hz and was limited by the host computer. A simulation was run on a higher performance computer and a faster update rate of approximately 200 Hz was achieved. The phase lag was estimated to be approximately 5 ms.

A drawback of Wang's system lies with the weight of the three sensor systems (including lenses) that must be supported by the user's head. The design of a full-scale system which will be based on a holographic lens assembly is currently being undertaken. Holographic lenses have the advantage of being very lightweight, but are also very expensive.

Overall, the optical 'inside out' tracking system has the potential for high speed, wide range and low phase lag compared to magnetic tracking systems.

WW Gaertner Research Inc./GEC–Marconi optical tracking system

WW Gaertner Research Inc. conducted experiments under the Phase 1 Naval Training Systems Center (NTSC), USA contract which showed that the use of position sensing diodes (PSD) with 1–micron resolution greatly improved the head tracker accuracy. Subsequently, the US Navy awarded WW Gaertner Research Inc. a Phase II contract to construct a prototype head tracker to be installed in the NTSC simulator. The advanced head tracking system developed by Gaertner was installed in May 1990. GEC-Marconi (formerly GEC–Ferranti) in Edinburgh acquired Gaertner Research Inc. to exploit the tracker systems for cockpit applications, and have undertaken a programme to re-engineer the Gaertner system in a more rugged format.

There have been many demonstrations showing that the system accuracy is greater than 30 seconds (6 seconds achievable) with an update rate greater than 250 Hz (2500 Hz achievable). This tracker system is not affected by any of the factors that adversely affect the accuracy of today's magnetic systems, whether they are a.c. or d.c. In addition, the Gaertner system has been designed to have a phase lag of less than 1 ms. This is a significant achievement, as will be discussed in Chapter 6.

The head tracking algorithm is based on a series of mathematical equations that are performed by a DSP (see Figure 4.45).

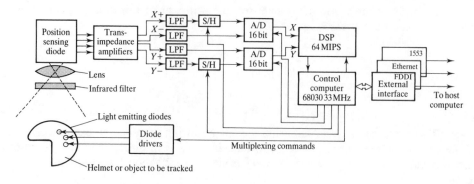

Figure 4.45 Gaertner Research Inc. GEC–Marconi optical tracking system.

The Gaertner system is very flexible with respect to different tracking situations. The single basic requirement for six degrees of freedom (x, y, z, roll, pitch and yaw) is a minimum of four emitters and receivers (there must be at least one of each) that are in sight of the others at all times. In other words, if there is one LED there must be three PSDs, and vice versa. In addition, the PSDs must have an uninterrupted view of the LEDs whenever positioning is taking place.

In the Gaertner head tracker, multiple LEDs are used to ensure constant coverage as the pilot turns his head. This could have been accomplished in other ways, such as mounting multiple PSDs or surrounding the PSD on the helmet with multiple LEDs in the cockpit. However, the specific application will dictate the optimum layout.

In applications where a full six degrees of freedom are not necessary, a single LED and PSD may be used. As the PSD can be two-dimensional, such as the one used in the Gaertner/GEC–Marconi head tracker, two degrees of freedom can still be attained. In all instances, the system operates in the following way. The LEDs are turned on in a known sequence. This multiplexing must occur because the PSDs can accurately position only one light source at a time. As the LED is switched on, the PSD records its X and Y position and sends the data forward. Obviously, if six degrees of freedom are not necessary or there are multiple PSDs, multiplexing may not be required. Once the PSD 'sees' the LED it outputs a current level that must be converted to a voltage level by trans-impedance amplifiers. The resulting analogue voltage is then converted into a digital signal with the A/D. The speed and resolution of the A/D are very important. In addition, the frequency response of the A/D must go down to d.c. (0 Hz) in order to detect no motion at all. This portion of the system must be matched to the update and resolution accuracy requirements. Ideally, the best solution, provided that the frequency response is acceptable, amounts to the fastest A/D with the highest resolution. Unfortunately, these two factors are difficult to achieve simultaneously. Once the digital signal is sent out of the A/D, it goes to the DSP, which uses the algorithm to compute the location of the sensed object. Many different algorithms can be used in this 'mathematical engine' and each has to be tailored for a specific application. The DSP outputs its data at the command of the control computer. The overall system functions are preprogrammed into the control computer so that even though it performs very few computations, it directs all information transfers. This includes sending data to other devices over a communications board such as Military Standard 1553, Ethernet or FDDI. The control computer also dictates the timing of the diode drivers.

The LEDs must be multiplexed so that the PSDs can locate them accurately. The diode drivers must be synchronized with the rest of the system to ensure that when an LED is on, the algorithm knows where it is in relation to the other LEDs it previously measured.

The emitters must be placed on the helmet, and care has to be taken in the design and manufacture of the custom helmet LEDs. Perhaps the areas of greatest importance are the lens, position sensing diode (to include support circuitry) and the LEDs. The IR LED sensing package is placed between 2 and 3 feet behind the operator's head. Distances greater or smaller than that will affect the spot size on the PSD and thus decrease its accuracy. Other operating ranges can be catered for but require a different lens system. If it is desired to have the receiver much closer than 2 feet then the field of view of the lens must be increased. With distances of 2–3 feet, WW Gaertner Research Inc. is now able to achieve accuracies greater than 30 arc seconds. Position sensing diodes take the centre point of the light from the emitter to calculate the overall position. However, it has been found that, in practical applications, the smaller the spot size on the face of the diode the more accurate the position reading given to the computer. When one is dealing with changes that are less than 1/10 of a micron, it is very important to be as focused as possible.

To meet specific requirements, such as very high accuracy, several versions of the system are available. These are accomplished by changing the lenses on the face of the PSD. One of the most attractive features of the Gaertner system is its adaptability to many different environments. The operator simply initiates the system by pressing a button. This eliminates the need for lengthy installations as well as mapping of the environment. The most important features of the installation are that the emitter is placed within 2–3 feet of the receiver and that the relative end positions of the six infrared LEDs, or the LEDs on the helmet, are known. Should the end user require that a different lens be used to accommodate a different layout, redesigning this portion can be performed by an optical lens designer.

The optical tracking system can be used interactively in multi-user situations. For this arrangement, additional detectors and emitters are required for the second operator. However, only one system drive unit is required. It should be noted that the system update rate will be shared between the two operators.

The PSD is a modified photodiode that produces currents proportional to the magnitude and position of an infrared spot on the PSD surface. The photocurrents from the PSD are in two pairs. One pair (the X pair) carries the information for the X position of the light spot. The Y pair carries the information for the Y position of the light spot. These photocurrents are in the micro-amp range and must be amplified and converted to a voltage to be read by an analogue to digital converter. This amplification should introduce as little noise as possible into the signal. The other requirement of the amplifier is that it keeps the PSD properly reverse biased.

The PSD amplifier comprises two stages. The first stage is the preamplifier stage, which is implemented with four operational amplifiers each in a standard trans-impedance configuration. The output of a given trans-impedance amplifier is a voltage equal to the product of the input current and the impedance of the feedback loop. For d.c. currents, the impedance of the feedback loop is equal to the feedback resistor value. Bias for the PSD is provided by the resistive divider network connected to the non-inverting terminal of the operational amplifier. This bias is removed from the output of the preamplifier by a second resistive divider network connected to the inverting terminals of each operational amplifier.

The second stage amplifier is comprised of four operational amplifiers, each of which amplifies one of the four PSD signals. The two operational amplifiers for the two X channel signals are configured for non-inverting gain. Two more operational amplifiers are configured as inverting amplifiers for the two Y channel signals. The output of the second stage amplifier from the PSD is adjustable from zero to full scale, so the full input voltage range of the A/D converter can be used.

Following the conversion of current to voltage by the trans–impedance amplifiers, the signals are sent to the next stage. The four outputs of the (PSD) sensor/amplifier section are fed to A/D convertors to allow a computer to perform the algorithm computations.

A person will probably not move his head faster than $1000°s^{-1}$, which can produce a signal of up to 10 Hz to be sampled. However, signals from 10 Hz to d.c. are very slow and, therefore, sometimes difficult to sample accurately and repeatably. To digitally reproduce a signal ranging up to 10 Hz, it must be sampled at a rate of at least 20 Hz. However, to stay within the real-time requirements of the system, the conversion rate must be significantly higher. Following the high speed conversion, the data must be passed at the same speed to the host computer digital signal processor.

The sample timing for the converters is generated in the timing section of the system. The timing section is the central control area overseeing diode multiplexing, A/D conversion, and system reset lines.

The converted digital data is sent serially to two ports on the digital signal processing (DSP with 64 MIPS performance) in the host computer. This DSP board receives the data, processes it and then uses it in an algorithm that computes yaw, pitch, roll, and x, y and z head orientation.

The purpose of the diode driver module is to provide noise-free, flat-top pulses of drive current to the infrared diodes. The output power of the infrared diodes is proportional to the current driving them. The pulses of current from the diode driver Module (DDM) produce pulses of infrared light from the diodes. The DDM accepts a six-line pulse trigger from the system clock, which defines the specific diode to be pulsed and the duration of that pulse.

A buffer circuit is implemented that accepts transistor transistor logic (TTL) pulses from a master clock and makes them capable of driving N channel MOSFET (NMOS) switches. First, the TTL signal is 'cleaned up' by sending it through a comparator that filters the noisy TTL signal into a clean square pulse signal. Next, the output current and voltage of the comparator is amplified by a high speed operational amplifier. The output is then used to drive the gate of the NMOS either high (on), or low (off).

Following the second state amplifier is one pole low pass filter, consisting of a resistor capacitor (RC) network. There is one filter for each of the four signal outputs. This filter provides a cutoff of 3.35 kHz. The output of this filter is then connected to the A/D converter.

Ambient light is filtered out by the following methods:

- Lens filters. These filters are chosen to eliminate most of the light outside the wavelength of interest.

- Dark samples. The PSD 'looks' at the set of four diodes seven times. Three of those samples are taken with all the diodes turned off. By repeatedly taking 'on' and 'off' measurements, the ambient light level is measured and compensated for. The level is subtracted every 150 μs.

- Digital signal processing. The processing unit is aware of which diode should be on and at what frequency it is pulsed. With this information it can filter out all non-compliant signals.

Though the focus of the image on the PSD is important, it is not nearly as critical as it is for a CCD-based system. The PSD looks at the centroid of the image and partially compensates for unfocused images. Lens design is an important feature of the system, and it offers great application flexibility. Therefore, unlike other head trackers a very large head box can be accommodated without loss of accuracy.

A thermo-electric cooler is used to maintain the temperature across the face of the detector.

Image processing optical system

Now that very high performance image processing systems are available one class of tracking system (based on image processing techniques) has just become feasible. This type of system involves monitoring a unique pattern on the user's head (usually drawn upon a helmet) and computing position and orientation as the pattern moves with head movement.

Two or more camera type sensors are employed to resolve the information in three dimensions. The technique is an extension of Church's method, described earlier. Advanced pattern recognition techniques are used to track head position. The more sensors the better, because it is possible for the pattern to become blocked from the camera's field of view. Additional sensors improve the redundancy of the system.

Unfortunately, pattern recognition systems are not yet available in the public domain because of the high cost of the specialized image processing hardware.

The image processing tracking system is not affected by the presence of magnetic fields or large amounts of metal in the immediate vicinity of the tracker. However, since the system relies on light being reflected off a unique pattern drawn on a helmet, lighting conditions must be carefully controlled.

Image processing tracking systems determine position by comparing known patterns to sensed patterns. Similar to fixed transducer systems, pattern recognition systems are inherently less accurate as the distance from sensor to remote object increases because the virtual image size of a remote object must diminish. In addition, pattern recognition systems suffer the disadvantage that they require complex algorithms to interpret the content of a scene. Incorrect interpretations can adversely affect accuracy. Six degree of freedom image processing pattern recognition systems have not been widely implemented.

Honeywell LED array

The Honeywell LED array system (Ferrin, 1991) was designed for cockpit use. Infrared LED sources are placed on the helmet in a prescribed pattern and are sequentially energized. The LED emitters are tracked by an externally-mounted infrared camera. The vector to each emitter is determined using camera focal length, focal plane, and the known image of each LED source. The helmet position is calculated using the four emitter vectors. Some applications require LED arrays on each side of the helmet and an externally mounted camera on each side of the cockpit.

Honeywell Videometric

The Honeywell Videometric system (Ferrin, 1991) uses a principle similar to that of the LED Array system, except that there is no need for active elements on the helmet.

The LED array is replaced by a unique pattern of symbols, which is sensed, regardless of position or orientation, by a cabin-mounted illuminator and camera. The vector from the camera to each emitter is determined using camera focal length, focal plane, and known image of each graphic pattern. The helmet position is calculated using the four emitter vectors. Some applications require patterns on each side of the helmet and an externally-mounted illuminator and camera on each side of the cockpit.

Evaluation of optical position trackers

Optical position tracking systems must allow for the inherent trade-off between accuracy and range of operation. To get around this problem, some manufacturers employ multiple emitters and multiple sensor arrangements, which can be complex to implement and expensive to build. An optical system with sufficient processing power can have very good response times because of available high data rates. Consequently, optical systems can be well suited for real-time applications, especially when compared with magnetic position trackers that have lower data rates.

Unfortunately, optical systems sometimes suffer from errors caused by spurious light, ambiguity of surface and occlusion. Perhaps a greater concern is the increase in ranging errors resulting from the decrease in accuracy caused by the shorter focal length lenses needed to view a suitable working area. Multiple emitter architectures offer a solution, but at the cost of added complexity. Systems designed for a small range of operation provide less latitude for maneouverability. For fixed transducer systems, 'inside out' implementations are better for tracking multiple remote objects than 'outside in' systems, because multiple sensors can be supported by a single set of emitters. 'Outside in' systems must differentiate between multiple sets of emitters with a single set of sensors. Pattern recognition systems tend to be less attractive because of computational complexity and lack of robust algorithms.

Miscellaneous space tracking systems

There have been other examples of space tracking systems. For instance in recent years, electromechanical goniometers (US Patent 4048653, JAP-63-121389, 147991, 63-

246094) have been considered, but have proved to be too cumbersome and not user-friendly. A simple pattern recognition system was developed by Pund (US Patent 4649425), and a research team from NTT (Japan) developed a pattern recognition technique that relied on a video system and an image processing algorithm operating on facial contrast.

4.2.3 Eye point of regard sensing systems

Eye tracking systems have been in existence for almost as long as head tracking systems. They range from simple systems mounted on spectacle frames to very elaborate systems based on electromyography. Rather than review every model, just a few are discussed here with references. Generally speaking, most existing eye trackers are unsuitable for virtual environment applications because they must be integrated with the helmet-mounted display system. This is certainly not a trivial task. Probably the only exception to this is the eye track system integrated in the CAE fibre optic helmet-mounted display, described in this chapter. Peters (1991) has described the eye tracker used on this helmet-mounted display.

A whole range of techniques have been used to determine a user's line of sight. Two types of system are available: those mounted on helmet-mounted displays (or eye glasses), and remote viewing systems. Many prototype or research systems have been employed. The head-mounted variants use sources and video cameras (infrared sensitive) to observe the subject's pupil.

One of the most recent eye tracker systems, produced by Biocontrol Systems (Palo Alto, CA), uses electromyography techniques, employing two electrodes that rest on the skin just below the eye.

Eye tracker systems designed for advertising research are usually based on remote viewing systems. The subject is generally confined to a chair and is only allowed to look in the forward direction. The line of sight is then determined from a television camera and video processing system. In operation, the user is presented with various visual stimuli, such as advertising posters, and the direction of gaze is computed as the subject fixates on various parts of the visual scene. Not all systems are capable of generating line of sight data in real time, although most are capable of capturing the data in real time.

Although the remote view eye track systems are interesting and bear some resemblance to head-mounted components, they are not really appropriate for virtual environment systems.

Head-mounted systems tend to be used for human performance and workload studies, where the direction of gaze of a subject helps to identify human resource allocation. Other applications have been devised that allow the user to designate objects in the visual field by fixating on them for a set period or by means of secondary commit sequences.

Perhaps the most demanding application for an eye track system is that used by CAE and others to display a high resolution insert around a wide visual field. These systems, known as area of interest (AOI) or centre of attention displays, make use of the fact that the visual actuity of the human visual system is highest in the fovea. This results in a dual resolution system: low resolution for the periphery and high resolution for the foveal region.

Such systems not only have to be lightweight but they must also sense the angle of regard of each eye and simultaneously compute position so that a high resolution inset can be positioned approximately in the field of view. It is also important to compensate accurately for helmet slip.

Miscellaneous eye tracking systems

Three companies stand out in terms of eye tracker technology: Applied Science Laboratories (Waltham, MA), ISCAN (Cambridge, MA) and NAC (Japan). They supply a range of eye tracker systems of varying performance. Unfortunately, these systems tend to be stand-alone and are probably unsuitable for integration with any helmet-mounted display without some form of major re-engineering.

An extremely good account of a range of eye tracker technologies is given by Young and Sheena (1975). Despite its age, it gives a good account of the various techniques, many of which are still applicable.

Integration of eye point of regard systems into a pilot's helmet-mounted display may one day enable the pilot to select virtual switches or control functions merely by looking at them. There seems to be some merit in using direct eye control to point to or designate targets, for reasons given by Calhorn *et al.* (1984). Under certain high 'g' manoeuvres, the pilot is unable to control some of the systems in the aircraft, such as making selections on the keyboard surrounding multi-function displays. The one system that appears not be affected by high 'g' loading is the human eye/oculomotor system. The American Super Cockpit and the British Aerospace Advanced Cockpit Research Programme are both addressing the integration of eye point of regard systems into the suite of cockpit systems. The speed and accuracy of an eye controlled system would appear to offer advantages in laboratory-based assessments. However, when the pilot is subjected to more representative task loadings, then eye point of regard systems may not be quite so good. A longer term research aim is to evaluate the performance of an eye point of regard system under representative task loading.

4.2.4 Virtual world generator systems

This section reviews the basic requirements of virtual world generator systems and in particular the graphics platforms that must be used to achieve the desired level of performance. The actual performance is a function of the task for which the virtual environment system will be used. However, the underlying principles are the same, whatever the end application. It is very important to consider how virtual world generator systems are integrated with the various peripheral devices. This aspect is very important for visual systems, including head tracking systems, where any system lag becomes very visible. The idea of close coupling between the head tracking system and the graphics computers that are used to render the scene will be discussed.

To complete this section, three graphics platforms are reviewed to highlight the level of performance that is required. Clearly, there is a wide range of graphics platforms, any of which could have been selected and would probably have met the early requirements. However, for illustrative purposes three very different platforms have been chosen: the top of the range Silicon Graphics SkyWriter and Reality Engine, and the Division ProVision system. There is a difference in cost of at least an order of magnitude between these systems.

Silicon Graphics platforms for virtual environment applications

Silicon Graphics produce a comprehensive range of high performance graphics platforms suitable for virtual environment applications. These platforms are all part of the same family and feature upward code compatibility. This means that development can be undertaken on cheaper, lower performance platforms, leaving the final choice of host platform until later in the development life cycle. One reason why Silicon Graphics platforms are a good choice for virtual environment applications is their good price to performance ratio.

It is possible to undertake development on a mid-range performance system with the knowledge that a higher or lower performance machine is available. Moreover, the progressive nature of the Silicon Graphics company means that the effective cost versus performance parameter is reducing all the time. The company's Graphics Library (GL) is becoming more and more widely adopted, and will probably soon become a standard.

Unfortunately, not all graphics computer manufacturers follow a code compatibility approach, which usually means that when higher performance is required the user has to switch to another vendor's product. Ideally, what is required in the future is a level of platform independence.

Rather than consider every Silicon Graphics product the author considered it more appropriate to describe their two highest performance machines, the SkyWriter and the Reality Engine. Unlike traditional image generators, these machines support high level image generation for 'out-the-window' displays, general purpose UNIX computation and high performance graphics to support a large variety of widely differing applications covering database development, mission planning, mission rehearsal, mapping and so on.

Both machines run GL, providing access to the embedded graphics hardware, and X-windows, the popular windowing system that provides a front end to IRIX, Silicon Graphics' version of the UNIX operating system. While the SkyWriter is a very complex system, it is also very flexible, and may be configured with varying numbers of CPUs, memory, and disks, and may drive between 1 and 8 output channels. This section provides an overview of the system architecture and its various components.

SkyWriter

A standard SkyWriter can be configured in various ways, depending upon how the system is to be used. The following sections detail the configurations and how they operate within the context of a virtual environment application. Other modes of operation are covered in the manufacturer's data sheets.

To utilize the two graphics pipelines in SkyWriter (to drive two high resolution (1280 × 1024) channels), the system can be configured for either dual pipeline or hyper pipeline development operation. When configured for dual pipeline mode, the output from pipeline 0 drives one display and the output from pipeline 1 drives the other.

The pipelines are completely independent, yet they can be genlocked together for frame synchronization. This means that each pipeline may display a different gazepoint, or eyepoint, or even a view of a completely different database or perhaps a completely different application.

To achieve the highest level of performance, an application must take advantage of the hyper pipeline configuration. A hyper pipeline takes advantage of the full performance of both pipelines to drive a single display. The outputs of the two pipelines are interleaved on a frame by frame basis by the built-in Pipeline Multiplexer (pMUX). Obviously, this configuration is unsuitable for binocular helmet-mounted display applications unless two SkyWriter systems are used, and even these would require synchronizing.

The graphics subsystem in the SkyWriter draws from the architecture of its predecessor, the PowerVision (VGX) line of graphics supercomputers. Like the VGX, the SkyWriter's graphics subsystem is pipelined, with several major subsystems being responsible for performing the entire task of generating the real-time 3-D imagery. However, unlike the VGX, the SkyWriter has two graphics pipelines in each system, enabling the display of two full resolution (1280 × 1024) screens running at full performance independently of one another, yet being driven by the same set of CPUs. An extremely important feature of the two graphics channels is that they can be synchronized together. This avoids the problem of presenting two out-of-step images to an observer, an effect that can prevent the two images from being fused binocularly.

The graphics subsystem has some other very significant differences, mostly pertaining to its ability to perform very fast, high quality texture mapping. The process of dealing with three-dimensional graphics data includes a series of steps progressing from geometric manipulations through to video display. The process begins with the graphics manager board, which transfers graphics commands and data from user memory across the MPlink bus to the graphics subsystem. This data is then fed into the appropriate graphics pipeline as determined by the display variable designator being used by the current process. The display variable designates which of the two pipelines is currently active, pipeline 0 or pipeline 1.

Once the appropriate graphics pipe has the data, it is fed into the Geometry Engine which distinguishes between graphics instructions and data and organizes the data for processing. Parallel processors then step in to perform the geometric transformations to translate, scale, and rotate 3-D objects and convert them from 3-D world space coordinates to 2-D screen space coordinates.

The 2-D screen space data is then fed into the next rank of parallel processors to perform the scan conversion from geometric to pixel data. The scan conversion subsystem walks along the top and bottom edges of each polygon, generating spans of pixels. A span is a match pair of pixels, where one resides on the top edge of the polygon and the other directly below it on the bottom edge.

The raster subsystem then takes the spans and iterates from top pixel to bottom pixel to find all the pixels between. The parameters for these pixels are also iterated so that textures, colours, and transparency can be smoothly changed from one pixel to the next. Pixel processors perform all the texture and colour interpolation functions, finally placing the finished pixel values into the frame buffer.

Reading the digital frame buffer data, the display subsystem converts the digital data to analog signals to drive display devices, sending out the component video as red, green, blue and alpha.

The first major section of the geometry pipeline is the geometry subsystem where vector and polygonal data is received from the application in world space coordinates and transformed geometrically. Standard object transforms include object scaling, rotating and translating, while later windowing and viewpoint transforms provide for perspective views into the model world with a particular field of view.

After all the viewing and other transformations are performed, the 3-D vertex coordinates are converted into 2-D screen coordinates for further processing in preparation for rendering the image into the digital frame buffer. Since all final imagery must reside in the frame buffer raster, the geometric data input into the system must be converted from vectors and polygonal surfaces to pixel data. The scan conversion subsystem takes 2-D vertex data as input from the geometry subsystem, then walks along the edges of the vectors and polygons, generating the intermediate pixels that lie along that edge. This is generally performed via a Bresenham algorithm.

The host side of the SkyWriter is supported by an advanced symmetric multiprocessing (SMP) based computational subsystem derived from the Silicon Graphics POWER series supercomputers. This subsystem combines parallel CPUs, memory, secondary storage and I/O to provide the SkyWriter with the ability to calculate real- time vehicle dynamics, communicate with A/D and D/A boards and devices, and access databases, as well as the ability to render realistic out-the-window scenes. All Silicon Graphics POWER series and SkyWriter systems are based upon the Mips R3000/R3010 RISC microprocessor and floating point processor. This means that any software developed for one machine will be inherently binary compatible with any other machine in the same product line.

Users can assign a process to one of the three priority bands that are above, equal to, or below normal UNIX processes. Within each band, processes can be assigned one of at least 32 vertical priority levels.

Users can also prevent the UNIX scheduler's ageing mechanism from decreasing the priority of a process as its run time accumulates. This freezes the process' priority at the assigned level. A process can also be locked into memory, ensuring that it will never be swapped out onto disk. On a multiprocessor system, a subset of the processors can be isolated from the non–determinism introduced by disk and network I/O processing. POWER Lock processor isolation, a feature of IRIX 4.0, goes beyond isolating a processor from non-determinism to allow a user to isolate a processor from certain memory management activities that extend interrupt latency. Communication among processors via shared memory is not affected by processor isolation. Processes running on isolated processors have full access to all UNIX services.

The SkyWriter has a standard I/O interface supporting Ethernet, an asynchronous SCSI controller, and VME bus interface. Data can be transferred between the host CPUs and the VME bus at 10 Mbit s^{-1}, while Ethernet speeds of 8–9 Mbit s^{-1} are supported. There is a single asynchronous SCSI channel capable of peak data transfers of 1.5 Mbyte s^{-1}. When there is a need for performance higher than that offered by the standard I/O interface, SkyWriter users can incorporate the POWER Channel option. POWER Channel is a replacement I/O interface board that offers the following benefits:

- Synchronous SCSI support
- Improved Ethernet performance
- Improved VME bandwidth
- Two SCSI channels per system

By supporting the synchronous rather than asynchronous SCSI interface, the bandwidth to the SCSI devices has been increased to 4 Mbyte s^{-1} with peak transfer rates of 2.4 Mbyte s^{-1}. Ethernet performance has been increased to 1.25 Mbyte s^{-1}, the absolute limit of the Ethernet specification. The VME bandwidth has been pushed from 10 Mbyte s^{-1} on the standard I/O board to 32 MByte s^{-1}, enabling much improved throughput between the CPU and add-on IPI2 disk controllers, third party I/O boards for A/D or D/A device communication, or add-on networking boards.

Reality Engine

Silicon Graphics recently launched a graphics platform called the Reality Engine, which is likely to set a new standard for virtual environment applications. However, the author has not had an opportunity to evaluate the Reality Engine in a demanding virtual environment.

Reality Engine architectural overview

The architecture of a dual pipeline version of the Reality Engine is shown in Figure 4.46. The first component of the system is a geometry engine, which handles the transfer of data from the MPlink bus and the processing of geometric data as it enters the pipeline. To maintain maximum throughput, a series of fast first in/first out (FIFO) memory devices are used to avoid queuing or bottlenecks in the pipeline.

The next component of the system is a raster manager that processes data from the geometry engine into scan converter pixel data prior to loading the data into frame buffer memory. The internal architecture of the raster manager ensures that image memory is interleaved between the parallel processors so that adjacent pixels are always processed by different processors.

The raster manager additionally incorporates the hardware to perform texture, colour allocation, sub-pixel anti-aliasing, fogging, lighting and hidden surface removal.

The final system is the display generator, which takes data from the frame buffers and processes it through the digital to analogue converters. Special custom circuitry has been incorporated to allow programmable pixel timings to be achieved so that resolution, refresh rate and interlace/non-interlace characteristics can be matched to a range of display devices.

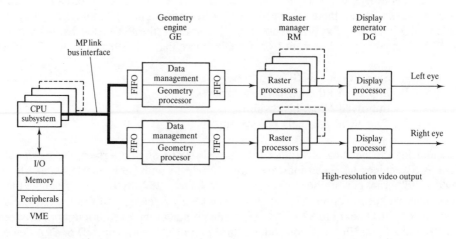

Figure 4.46 Simplified architecture of the Silicon Graphics Reality Engine.

A range of optional special purpose modules are available for the Reality Engine, but these will not be discussed here.

Overall System Performance

The Silicon Graphics Reality Engine has been tuned to address the needs of the visual simulation image generation market. Many of its features and capabilities are directly aimed at image generation. The primary areas of focus for performance tuning of the Reality Engine are:

- Textured polygon throughput: in excess of 210,000 textured anti-aliased polygons per second throughput capacity through the geometry engine section of the pipeline, enabling scenes of extreme complexity at high frame rates.

- Textured fill rates: up to 320 million pixels per second for anti-aliased, trilinear, MIPmapped, Z-buffered, lit, smooth, shaded polygons.

- Anti-aliasing performance and capabilities: incurring no performance penalty for anti-aliasing, Reality Engine is able to generate high quality imagery at high performance.

- Pipeline elasticity: FIFOs located before and after the geometry engine ensure that maximum concurrence is maintained throughout the pipeline. Thus, when the rendering subsystem is busy, the geometry subsystem is still able to operate in parallel. This results in a balanced load on the system and maximum throughput.

- Pixel output capabilities: a 2.6 Mpixel bandwidth bus at the back end of the display subsystem enables up to two high resolution (1280 × 1024) outputs driven from each pipeline. The display subsystem can be configured to generate custom line rate outputs.

- Texture memory access: 50 Mbytes per second texture download times from host into texture memory enable rapid paging of on-line textures, in turn enabling virtual memory capability for real-time loading of photorealistic texture maps.

Reality Engine texture

The Reality Engine has been purposely designed to be capable of displaying complex, texture mapped scenes at high (30–60 Hz) frame rates. Textures can be derived from actual photographs or generated synthetically. They may contain full or partial transparency at any point and support full R,G,B,A true colour. The following sections detail the various methodologies that have been utilized to achieve this high quality, realistic imagery.

Components

Reality Engine supports three levels of total texture depth: 16-, 32- and 64-bit. These are used to store texture information as full colour with transparency (RGBA), full colour (RGB), intensity with transparency (IA) or just intensity (I). Each of these types of texture is available with 12, 8 or 4 bits per component.

The 16-bit and 64-bit modes are new functions in the Reality Engine architecture. The 16-bit mode provides high levels of image quality using full colour, RGBA textures, but with reduced memory usage. Thus textures can be simply constructed by scanning images into the system from (for example) colour photographs, and then applied to polygons in the database scenario. The Reality Engine automatically converts the images to 16-bit textures. No special processing is required to achieve this photorealistic capability, just a good camera, a scanner and a Reality Engine.

The 64-bit mode is included to provide 12-bit per component capability for RGBA texture maps. Having 12 bits per component offers the advantage of enhanced image quality under low light conditions. On some systems, under such conditions, banding can sometimes appear because of the bits in the texture becoming 'oversampled': there are just not enough levels to handle the subtle light changes. With 12 bits per component, the number of light levels for each component is increased from 256 to 4096 (see Table 4.22).

Texture Memory Configuration

The Reality Engine provides an extensive 4 Mbytes of standard, on-line texture memory, stored as two banks of 2 Mbyte memory areas. This is approximately an order of magnitude greater than any prior Silicon Graphics architecture. With the 16-bit RGBA full-colour storage mode, this enables the display of database scenarios with a very high content of photorealistic texture imagery. Different texture types and modes can be mixed within the memory storage space. Efficient storage algorithms ensure that textures are stored sequentially within the memory area, which ensures that all the texture memory is used.

Minimum texture size is 2 × 2, and maximum is 1024 × 1024. The system is thus able to store two RGBA full-colour 1024 × 1024 textures. An example may be that a typical simulation scenario may need to use a larger number of 128 × 128 full-colour textures. In this scenario, Reality Engine can support 95 MIPmapped, full RGBA and 380 intensity-only 128 × 128 MIPmapped textures.

Intensity textures on Reality Engine can reference an 8-bit lookup table of 8-bit per component RGBA values to produce full coloured and translucent imagery from intensity textures. This further saves memory space and increases the overall texture capacity of the system. Table 4.23 explains some of the more commonly used sizes and capacities.

The Reality Engine supports a new function called 3-D texture. This function enables whole volumes to be stored in texture memory. The volumetric texels can have the same bit depths and functions as 2-D texels. Volume textures can also be MIPmapped, creating a series of volumes, each of which has one-eighth of the volume of the one above. Some example capacities are described in Table 4.24.

Table 4.22 Texture component options.

1 component (4/8/12 bit)	2 components (4/8/12 bit)	3 components (4/8/12 bit)	4 components (4/8/12 bit)
Intensity	Intensity	Red	Red
	Alpha	Green	Green
		Blue	Blue
			Alpha

Table 4.23 Texture map capacities.

Resolution size in pixels	Number of RGBA non-MIPmapped textures (16-bit)	Number of RGBA MIPmapped textures (16-bit)	Number of intensity-only non-MIPmapped textures	Number of intensity-only MIPmapped textures
1024 x 1024	2	0	8	0
512 x 512	8	5	32	20
256 x 256	32	23	512	92
128 x 128	128	95	2048	380
64 x 64	512	383	8192	1532
32 x 32	2048	1533	32768	6132

Table 4.24 3-D texture system capacity.

Resolution	Quantity	Texture type (16-bit)
64 × 64 × 64	64	Non-MIPmapped
64 × 64 × 64	55	MIPmapped
128 × 128 × 64	2	Non-MIPmapped
128 × 64 × 64	2	MIPmapped

Texture types and methods

The texture filtering methods on Reality Engine are extensive, providing the highest image quality. The system supports two modes of filtering:

- Non-MIPmapped

- MIPmapped

Non-MIPmapped texture functions

There are advantages and disadvantages to functions in both categories. The primary advantages of the non-MIPmapped textures are that they use one-third less memory. There are three mapping functions available: bilinear interpolated, point sampled and bicubic interpolated.

Bilinear interpolation mode looks at the S and T coordinates, finds the nearest four texels, and blends them together to generate the final colour value to be applied to the pixel being drawn.

Point sampling offers no real performance advantage over any of the higher quality modes. It is supported to provide backward compatibility with pre-Reality Engine architectures. When point sampling, the system takes the iterated texture coordinates for the current pixel being drawn and samples the specified texture to find the nearest texel to the current pixel's S and T coordinates.

Bicubic interpolation performs a weighted, two-dimensional blend of 16 texels in a 4 × 4 kernel around the texel sample location specified by the pixel's S and T co-ordinates. It is used in special circumstances to generate textured imagery of unparalleled quality without the use of MIPmapping.

MIPmapped texture functions

The primary texture mode of Reality Engine is trilinear MIPmapping, a technique that involves the generation of pre-filtered lower resolutions of each texture defined to enable system selection of the texture closest in size to the target polygon. This is the default and fastest texture mode on the system. Reality Engine supports all the modes used on previous systems (point sampled, linear and bilinear), but they are retained only for backwards compatibility. There is no performance advantage in using these other modes.

Trilinear interpolation is one of the highest quality texture functions available and is found on some of the more recent high end image generators. Trilinear interpolation performs two bilinear interpolations in the two MIPmap levels bordering the size of the polygon being textured, then blends the results of those interpolations for a total of nine blends per pixel textured. This produces images that are very stable under all circumstances yet look very sharp close up. There is no perceptible transition as the textures move relative to the eyepoint.

A further function that is available on the system is quadlinear 3-D MIPmapped texture mode. This is effectively trilinear interpolation of 3-D texture, automatically generating a series of 3-D volumes, each one-eighth smaller than the one above. The system interpolates between the eight adjacent pixels in the MIPmap two adjacent volume levels and then blends between the two results, thus achieving a four-way interpolation.

A number of additional advanced texturing techniques are provided on Reality Engine. Many of these can only be found on highend image generators. These are as follows:

- **Detail texture:** This function is a very powerful feature, increasing the effectiveness of speed, motion and position cues by providing extra detail automatically where it is needed. Detail texture blends in a second level of texture on the original as the eyepoint approaches the surface, and multiple pixels cover an area subtended by a single texel. This extra detail level is in fact a completely separate texture map, and is automatically and smoothly blended with the 'host' texture, gradually increasing the detail where the texels are oversampled. Thus, for example, on a road one texture would be used to depict the road at a distance, with line, skid marks, and so on, and 'close to the detail texture' would be used to depict the gravel and fine detail.

- **Sharp texture:** This is a useful function for depicting detail with the use of very few surfaces, such as for writing on signs. However, when the eyepoint gets very close to such areas, the appearance can become somewhat fuzzy and indistinct. Again, this is because the texels are being 'oversampled' and a single texel covers more than one pixel. Under these circumstances, sharp texture can add a substantial increase in definition to the overall scene without the use of additional texture memory.

- **3-D texture:** This advanced and highly flexible feature can be used to address a series of complex special effects. Texel values are defined in a 3-D coordinate system. Textures are then extracted from this volume by defining a 3-D plane that intersects this volume. The resulting texture, which is applied to the surface, is the intersection between the volume and the plane. The orientation of the plane is completely user definable. Sequential reads are blended with each other extremely rapidly. All normal texture attributes function with 3-D texture, including full-colour RGBA texture filtering functions and volumetric MIPmap capability. Thus, the displayable result from a 3-D texture is not a volume of pixels but a single 2-D texture map, extracted from a slice through a volume of texels and applied to a surface. However, it is possible to build up a volume of data by repeatedly slicing through the 3-D texture and applying that to a series of 'laminate' surfaces that represent the volume. For example, this could be used to simulate clouds or smoke.

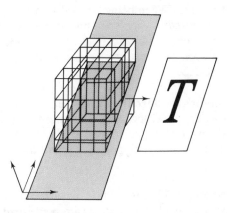

Figure 4.47 Accessing a texture from a 3-D texture map.

Some examples of ways that 3-D texture might be used are:

- Texture animations, such as moving people.

- Dynamically changing billboard textures. For instance, a tree billboard could actually change appearance as its angle to the eyepoint changes, even though it remains perpendicular to the viewer.

- Smoke, cloud and dust cloud simulation.

- Multiple levels of detail for textured surfaces. This would enable several images to be blended sequentially under user or simulation control.

■ **Projected texture:** A new capability on the Reality Engine enables non-orthographic texture mapping. This means that a full RGBA texture map can now be obliquely projected into arbitrary surfaces in a 3-D environment. When projecting texture onto texture, this involves a straightforward multipass technique. This is a powerful function enabling a whole series of unique special effects:

- Multiple steerable lights, which are defined by a texture that represents a cross-section through the light cone. Radial and axial attenuation are also supported.
- Aircraft shadow projection into 3-D objects such as terrain and buildings.
- Wind effects, such as helicopter rotor wash and wind wave surface effects for maritime applications.
- Support of true 3-D shadows.
- Moving ship's wake projected into moving waves.
- Projected reflections such as sun glint effects in space applications.

■ **Modulation and decals:** When being applied to a polygon each texture can be treated in two ways. Firstly, when operating as a decal, the colour of the texture replaces whatever colour is already inherent to the polygon. Secondly, when performing modulation, the texture colour is blended with the colour and properties of the surface.

■ **Texture transparency and contouring:** Textures may have full or partial transparency set as any texel location. This means that if the entire outer edge of the uniquely shaped texture (such as a tree) is set transparent, the texture may be placed upon a rectangular polygon, yet it will appear to have the outline of a tree.

■ **Perspective correction:** To ensure that no artefacts are introduced into the rendering process, per-pixel computations are performed in the raster subsystem to correct textures and fog for perspective distortions. These computations do not affect the system performance.

Texture performance

The texture fill rates on Reality Engine have been tuned to provide high levels of scene depth complexity at fast frame rates and high image quality.

The texture fill rate for Reality Engine is from 80 to 320 Mpixels per second for writing of trilinear MIPmap textured, sub-sample, anti-aliased, full-colour (RGBA), Gouraud shaded, lit, Z-buffered surfaces into the frame buffer.

Anti-aliasing

Anti-aliasing is a fundamental feature of any true image generation system. Artefacts caused by aliasing cause distraction in a simulation environment, minimizing the level of realism of the system and having the potential to cause negative training.

Reality Engine has been designed from the outset to provide high quality, high performance sub-sample anti-aliasing that is easy to use and tunable for different system configurations. The anti-aliasing is provided at no performance penalty. Moreover, anti-aliasing with Reality Engine requires no sorting of data and operates in conjunction with the Z-buffer for hidden surface removal. This is unique at this level of system.

Anti-aliasing is accomplished by retaining sub-pixel information for all vertices as they are transformed and processed through the pipeline (see Figure 4.48). Each vertex is computed with a sub-pixel accuracy in an 8×8 sub-pixel grid. Thus, there are 64 sub-pixel locations for each pixel rendered. When deciding how to colour a pixel, the system samples the sub-pixel grid with a certain number of samples per pixel, then determines the pixel coverage based upon the number of samples hit.

The following anti-aliasing functions are available in the Reality Engine:

- Point sampled: When performing point sampling, the system determines for each sample location within the pixel whether that sample is covered by the rendered polygon, vector or point.

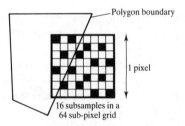

Figure 4.48 Example sub-sample and sub-pixel layout for a pixel.

- ▪ Area sampled: In area sampling, the system measures the percentage of the pixel covered by the primitive and translates that into the nearest covered point samples. In both cases, the colour and Z values are maintained for each sample, and performance should be the same. Area sampling is suitable for long, thin polygons, avoiding breakup.

Hidden surface removal

Hidden surface removal is performed by a high-resolution Z-buffer. The use of a Z-buffer avoids the need for database sorting and the use of binary separating planes, both of which increase the modelling effort and time required to generate a database and restrict the overall flexibility of the resulting simulation. The Z-buffer is particularly powerful for several moving models with articulated parts interacting with each other, such as an armoured vehicle training scenario. A Z-buffer-based system allows free movement of models without any need for concern about occultation. Another area where the Z-buffer is useful is when complex moving geometries intersect with each other, such as the hull of a ship interacting with moving waves.

Reality Engine handles Z-buffering and anti-aliasing simultaneously by storing Z-buffer values for each sub-sample. This ensures correctly anti-aliased polygon intersections. Resolution of the Z-buffer is configurable up to 32 bit, providing high Z-buffer accuracy for distant objects. Reality Engine supports correct occultation when combining translucency and Z-buffering through the use of alpha coverage masks.

Polygon capabilities

Colour

Colours may be specified in several different ways. For compatibility, a colour index mode is supported where an integer index value points into a fixed size table. More common is the use of fully specified RGB values for each colour as it is set. Each 24-bit RGB colour may be defined by three 8-bit RGB components. For low light intensity applications, each component of the RGB colour may be defined with 12 bits to achieve a 36-bit colour with a wider dynamic range.

Smooth shading

There is no penalty for performing smooth shading on objects rendered with Reality Engine. The Gouraud shading algorithm is used to smoothly shade the surface of each polygon using the current lighting model.

When performing Gouraud shading, the image engines interpolate between full RGB colour values for a given pixel within a polygon to enable smooth pixel to pixel colour transitions. Advanced lighting models enable the display of surface highlights and lighting features such as time of day or local light sources. This provides for clean, non-faceted rendering of complex objects in real time, and may be combined with transparency and texture for even more advanced effects.

Colour blending

When multiple occultation surfaces have partial transparency, the image engines also perform colour blending between each set of surfaces, depending upon the alpha values associated with each vertex, or even pixel, when texture mapping with alpha. These alpha values represent a degree of translucency from 0 to 1 and enable the simulation of windows, cockpit canopies, smoke, clouds, and other effects.

Lighting

Where the colour of the light as well as the intensity changes over time light sources may be coloured to allow for effects such as 'time of day' lighting. Light sources can be programmed with the following parameters:

- Specular, for highlights, direct effects.
- Diffuse, for broader, directional effects.
- Ambient, for environmental, non-directional effects.
- Emission, for self-luminous surfaces, vectors or points.
- Colour.
- Attenuation with distance.
- Local or infinite lights.

Surface properties

In order to handle different surface properties a 'shiny' component may be set for the current lighting model. This component may be changed from object to object to allow for a variety of surface types in the environment. Besides the light characteristics and the surface colour the property may be combined with texture mapping and transparency to provide the highest level of realism.

Atmospheric effects

A programmable fog/haze function in Reality Engine allows users to set arbitrary fog colour, which may then be blended in a depth dependent fashion with the colour of each pixel to be affected by the fog. This can be applied to the whole scene or controlled independently for different objects in the scene. For instance, light points may be less attenuated than surfaces in fog. This is sometimes known as per pixel fog. On the Reality Engine, it is fully corrected for perspective distortion. The fog is computed by means of a programmable function that the user can control by loading the requisite parameters into the system fog table. Alternatively, there are several standard exponential functions that can be used.

Polygon performance

The main focus of the Reality Engine for polygon performance is for polygons that are of high image quality, for example, textured, anti-aliased, lit, smooth, shaded. This is important for image generation applications, because the majority of the imagery that is being processed by the graphics subsystem is of a complex nature.

Reality Engine has been designed to address these requirements in two respects: the system can transform in excess of 210,000 textured, anti-aliased, Gouraud shaded, lit, Z-buffered polygons per second, which approaches an order of magnitude faster than previous Silicon Graphics systems; and the graphics subsystem has been designed with considerable elasticity. Two high capacity FIFO buffers are provided, one between the CPU subsystem and the geometry engine, and one between the geometry engine and the raster managers. These effectively allow the pipeline to exhibit considerable parallelism, enabling balanced throughput in the graphics pipeline.

Computational capabilities

A Reality Engine can support from one to eight CPUs in a parallel processing environment. Table 4.25 summarizes the CPU configurations and performance available.

Simulation applications lend themselves naturally to multiprocessing. Typically, multiple simulations operate concurrently. For example, flight dynamics, engine model, and landing model, the results from these calculations are required simultaneously for determination of the update of the vehicle position.

Silicon Graphics real-time operating system REACT

Silicon Graphics' IRIX operating system is based upon a POSIX compliant version of UNIX System V.3. However, it has required special modifications to support multiple processors, a concept not covered by standard UNIX. These special functions at the heart of IRIX have been combined under the banner of the real-time access technology kernel, REACT. REACT offers a set of system calls that enables real-time operation of systems running IRIX. Because real-time functionality is vital to the operation of simulators, REACT acts as the core of the system's host capability. REACT provides deterministic response to interrupts and deterministic process dispatch latency. Latencies for a multiprocessor system running IRIX 4.0 are shown in Table 4.26.

Table 4.25   Reality Engine: CPU configurations and performance.

Processor type	Number of processors	MIPS	MFlops
R3000 (33 MHz)	1	30	5.1
R4000	1	85	16
R3000 (40 MHz)	2–8	72–286	23–70

Table 4.26 Latencies for a multiprocessor system running IRIX 4.0.

Interval	Description	Minimum	Maximum
t_1-t_0	Interrupt latency	36 μs	51 μs
t_2-t_1	Interrupt handler	Application specific	–
t_3-t_2	Process dispatch	95 μs	138 μs

IRIX with REACT is true UNIX, so time-critical processes are identical to all other processes. This means that all UNIX software development tools are available to real–time developers. REACT is an integral part of IRIX, and interrupt latency, context switch time and process dispatch latency are clearly defined. A multiprocessor system can be configured to ensure that the appropriate user level process will begin execution within 200 μs after VME interrupt occurs.

Some of the key features of REACT are:

- Standard UNIX with deterministic response.
- Fast total interrupt response < 200 μs.
- Shared memory, symmetric multiprocessing with full user control over system resources.
- Highly productive software development environment.
- High performance networking.

By providing complete control over process priority as well as the assignment of processes and interrupts to processors, IRIX enables simplified system software implementations, minimal latency and maximal CPU utilization.

When running in kernel mode, IRIX periodically allows user level interrupts to be processed.

Deterministic response

UNIX was originally designed to distribute CPU time and other system resources equally among users of a time sharing system. As a result, predicting precisely when any event will occur in a generic UNIX system is impossible. IRIX with REACT includes the following extensions to generic UNIX that together result in a fully deterministic system suitable for real-time applications.

- Interruptible kernel
- Precise process priority control
- Non-degrading priority
- Locking memory pages
- Processor isolation

A key requirement of any graphics intensive activity is the level of support provided by development tools. The graphics programming language of the Silicon

Graphics platform is very powerful, but to create graphical objects and complex virtual environments requires a different type of programming environment. Fortunately, a wide range of development and modelling tools are available from third party vendors that go a considerable way towards reducing the effort of creating virtual environments. Several of these software tools are described in Chapter 5.

Silicon Graphics supplies a graphics performance profiling tool that allows application developers to investigate how graphics code loads the various stages of the graphics pipeline. An advantage of the profiling tool is that it allows the software to be fine tuned and highly optimized. An interesting feature of the profiler is that it allows the performance of other Silicon Graphics systems to be evaluated. This is very useful when deciding which graphics platform is suitable for a given task.

Division ProVision

Division Ltd (UK) have developed a fully integrated virtual environment system that supports the development of virtual environments and the interaction of a user with these environments. This latest generation parallel computer is called ProVision. It provides a cluster of processors that can be dedicated to a range of tasks. Separate autonomous processing systems can thus be dedicated to audio synthesis, image display generation, gesture recognition and so on. Division have a background in the development of parallel processing computers based on the Inmos transputer. The Chairman of Division is Dr Iann Barron, the designer of the first transputer. Not surprisingly Division's early systems were based exclusively around the transputer with an optional visual channel based on the Intel i860 graphics controller.

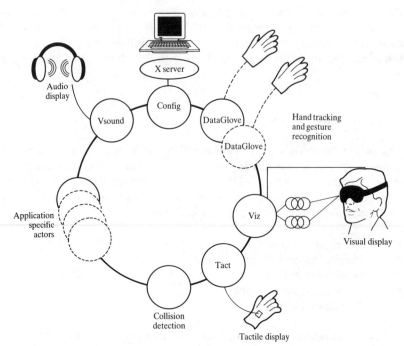

Figure 4.49 Division Vision range of platforms.

Division now has a whole range of integrated systems from the ProVision 100 at the bottom end to the SuperVision at the top. Figure 4.49 illustrates the integrated concept behind these Division products. This diagram illustrates how separate functions are performed in parallel by separate processing clusters.

SuperVision

SuperVision is a high performance parallel visualization system, which combines the flexibility of a multitransputer architecture with the performance of the Intel i860 to provide dedicated stereo visualization. The system is comprised of a control front end and a dedicated parallel graphics subsystem. The control front end is based upon the standard ProVision system, with multiple transputers providing data acquisition and control. The graphics subsystem employs multiple (1–32) i860s connected by a high performance scalable interconnect (200 Mbyte s^{-1}). Each i860 compute board has its own local memory and is connected to every other compute board via a dedicated point to point link. Each board can communicate concurrently, so that the bandwidth of the system scales linearly with the number of compute processors. Image generation is provided by the PAZ parallel renderer, running on multiple i860s. This means that a very flexible and expandable system can be constructed, with 1 to 32 i860s computing an image in parallel. The SuperVision system is software compatible with the lower cost ProVision system, running the dVS operating environment.

System overview

The SuperVision's control front end is a dedicated parallel virtual environment simulation system based predominantly on Inmos transputers. The basic architecture is outlined in Figure 4.50. Different transputers are dedicated to specific acquisition and display processing tasks. This provides distributed processing of 3-D position data, gesture data and so on, with guaranteed response times to local peripherals and localized 3-D transformation of this incoming data. Incoming hand and head positions and hand gesture can then be distributed to other processes which require this information. A separate transputer provides control of a dedicated digital audio system called Vsound. This provides independent stereo or quad audio display capability. Within the Vsound system a separate transputer with 4 Mbyte sample store drives two/four 16-bit DACs, and up to 8 independent samples can be replayed at 44.4 KHz, with localization in each of the four channels. This system can be further extended with a dedicated 3-D audio processor called the Convolvotron (see Wenzel, 1988). This takes up to 4 independent audio inputs from the Vsound system and localizes these inputs in space.

A message passing kernel called dNet provides a virtual routing system, which allows a process to communicate with any other, regardless of target processor. Intel i860s have been integrated into this system by providing each one with its own local I/O transputer. The dNet kernel running on the I/O transputer provides message passing services to any process running on the i860, so application code can be developed for either transputer or i860 with a common dNet message passing interface. In this way floating point intensive problems can be addressed by the addition of dedicated i860s.

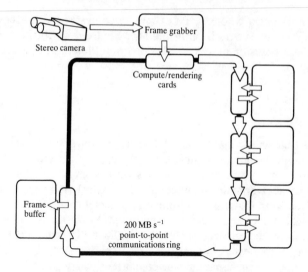

Figure 4.50 Division's SuperVision image generator.

For example collision detection performance can be increased by replacing the transputer with an i860. Application processes can also be developed for one or more i860s or transputers, as required.

While the underlying architecture of the SuperVision system is essentially a distributed memory message passing multiprocessor, a higher level of abstraction is provided by the dVS operating environment built upon this system. This enables sequential or parallel applications to gain access to the services provided by standard actors for visual processing, audio processing, collision detection and so forth, without recourse to direct communication.

The dVS library provides a general purpose data management system in which actors communicate implicitly by virtue of sharing instances of an element or data type. This greatly simplifies the task of application development, and ensures portability of application actors across a wide range of target machines.

A unique architecture for stereo visualization

The SuperVision image generator is based upon two high speed communication rings, each of which provides an interconnection between 1 and 16 compute cards. Each compute card combines a single 40 MHz Intel i860, with 4/8/16 Mbytes of local memory. Each of the compute cards operates in parallel to compute a fraction of the 2-D frame. The pixel data for a given frame is then combined for display in a remote frame store, which also sits on the communication ring. Other high performance acquisition systems, such as a 24–bit frame grabber, are supported so that live video images can be combined in real time with computer generated images to produce a composite image.

The communication system is a point to point link, which will route data packets from any processor on the ring to any other. This is a general-purpose communication system which has been designed to provide high bandwidth, low latency communication between large numbers of microprocessors, frame buffers and frame grabbers. Each processing cluster on the ring has a dedicated input and output port which run concurrently, so input and output transfers run in parallel. This communication system can be used for any data type, not exclusively pixel data. For example, live video from a frame grabber can be used as a dynamic texture within a computed frame, while object geometry updates are broadcast, and transformed polygon data is transferred between compute boards.

The PAZ renderer

PAZ is a high level PHIGS-like renderer, which runs on all of the current Division systems. It is a parallel renderer that has been developed to exploit the scalable performance of the SuperVision system. PAZ also provides direct support for multiple views, and so stereo images are easily generated and synchronized. PAZ has a high level object based application programming interface, under which the application manipulates object instances within one or more defined scenes.

The main aims of the PAZ design have been to maximize hardware utilization and multi processor scalability. For optimum performance PAZ has been designed to ensure minimal rendering latency and clipping operations. These factors have had to take account of generality and portability.

The underlying system support for the range of products is based on a distributed virtual environment system (dVS), which is described in more detail in Chapter 5.

4.3 Auditory environment systems

Auditory environment systems consist of technologies that provide aural communication with the user, such as speech recognition, 3-D auditory localization and synthetic speech output. Although the visual channel is the most powerful and compelling channel, the auditory channel can augment it in a way that can assist the user.

4.3.1 3-D audio localization systems

Since the development of stereo sound manufacturers have tried to improve the spatial awareness of sound. Attempts have been made to produce a quadraphonic system to create a 'surround sound'. However, early surround sound systems did not take into account free head movement and consequently the head remained in a fixed position. Dummy head recording systems have led to the introduction of reasonably effective surround sound effects. Today many films for cinema are recorded with a surround sound track. The advent of reasonably accurate head tracking systems along with digital signal processors allowed the concept of a true 3-D audio localization system to be realized. One of the first commercially available 3-D audio sound localizers was produced by Crystal River Engineering Inc., USA, in response to a requirement raised by the NASA Ames Research Center. Crystal River's 3-D localizer, known as the Convolvotron, is also marketed by VPL Inc. under the name Audiosphere. Other companies have tried unsuccessfully to produce a 3-D sound system. They may have failed because they did not fully understand the human process of auditory spatial localization.

Convolvotron

Spatial sound synthesis method

The spatial sound synthesis method chosen for the Convolvotron is discussed in Wenzel *et al.* (1988). The method involves direct convolution of audio signals with pairs of filters corresponding to measured pinnae impulse responses. These responses are measured for a variety of different directions of arrival at the left and right ear canals. Responses at finer resolutions than those measured are estimated using a linear interpolation technique.

The device operates on blocks of source data with typical durations of 5–20 ms. At the beginning of each block, directional data is provided by the host computer for each source in use. The directional data is in the form of four weights and four pointers to measure responses stored within the Convolvotron. These weights and pointers are used to compute an interpolated response for the desired direction. The result of the interpolation is a stereo pair of impulse responses known as the 'early response pair'.

At the end of the source block (beginning of the next block) another interpolated response pair is computed from externally provided directional data. This response pair is known as the 'late response pair' for this source input block. The Convolvotron effectively computes a time varying response pair that 'fades' from the early pair to the late pair, which it uses to filter the input block. For instance, let L be the number of coefficients in the measured responses and $W1$ to $W4$ be the weights that apply to measured responses left1 to left4 and right1 to right4. The early interpolated filters, for i equal to 1 to L, are:

$$\text{Earlyleft}(i) = W_1\text{left}_1(i) + W_2\text{left}_2(i) + W_3\text{left}_3(i) + W_4\text{left}_4(i)$$

$$\text{Earlyright}(i) = W_1\text{right}_1(i) + W_2\text{right}_2(i) + W_3\text{right}_3(i) + W_4\text{right}_4(i)$$

where W_1, W_2, W_3 and W_4 are the weights, and left_1, left_2, left_3, left_4, right_1, right_2, right_3 and right_4 are the measured responses.

Similarly, the late interpolated filters are computed from the late weights and pointers. The actual time varying responses can then be computed as a 'fade' from the early response pair to the late pair. That is, a decreasing linear ramp is applied to the early responses and an increasing linear ramp to the late responses. Let n be the sample index going from 1 to N, the number of samples in an input block. The time varying responses are:

$$\text{Left}(i,n) = (N-n)\frac{\text{Earlyleft}(i)}{N} + n\frac{\text{Lateleft}(i)}{N}$$

$$\text{Right}(i,n) = (N-n)\frac{\text{Earlyright}(i)}{N} + n\frac{\text{Lateright}(i)}{N}$$

The actual time varying convolutions can be calculated from :

$$\text{ouputleft}(n) = \sum_{i=1}^{L} [\text{left}(i,n) \times \text{input}(n-i)]$$

where L represents the number of coefficients in the measured responses.

$$\text{ouputright}(n) = \sum\nolimits_{i=1}^{L} [\text{right}(i,n) \times \text{input}(n-i)]$$

Note that the input index, $(n - i)$, can be zero or negative, corresponding to samples from the previous input block.

It is straightforward to show that the time varying convolutions described above can be rewritten as a fade between the outputs of convolutions of the input block with the early and late filters:

$$\text{outputleft}(n) = (N - n)\frac{\sum_{i=1}^{L} [\text{Earlyleft}(i) \times \text{input}(n-i)]}{N} + n\frac{\sum_{i=1}^{L} [\text{Lateleft}(i) \times \text{input}(n-i)]}{N}$$

$$\text{outputright}(n) = (N - n)\frac{\sum_{i=1}^{L} [\text{Earlyright}(i) \times \text{input}(n-i)]}{N} + n\frac{\sum_{i=1}^{L} [\text{Lateright}(i) \times \text{input}(n-i)]}{N}$$

Thus the Convolvotron is able to simulate the effect of a time varying convolution using two time invariant convolutions and a fade for each stereo channel.

The above computations are repeated for each additional source using early and late filter responses interpolated according to directional data for each source. The final left and right outputs are determined by summing the output results from each source in use. Figure 4.51 shows a simplified functional diagram of the signal processing for a typical case.

Processing architecture

The Convolvotron design consists of two main components and a host computer. The host computer must be an IBM PC or PC AT or equivalent. The computational heart of the device contains four INMOS A-100 cascadable digital signal processors. Each of these devices contains 32 parallel 16×16 multiply/accumulate cells along with a delay line and the necessary control lines for direct cascading. This processor chain is capable of computing a 128 tap finite impulse response (FIR) filter output every 400 ns for a peak processing rate in excess of 300 million multiply/accumulates per second.

The main controlling component in the Convolvotron is a Texas Instruments TMS320/C25 processor provided in a development system card built by Spectrum Signal Processing Inc. This card fits into the IBM card cage and provides some memory for the processor as well as an A/D converter, D/A converter, various timing circuits and a two-way port from the TMS320/C25 to the PC. In addition, this development system comes with an assembler/linker and monitor package to allow the system programmer to manage TMS320/C25 code on the IBM PC.

Figure 4.51 is a simplified block diagram of the system. The input data is provided by one to four A/D converters or may be supplied as digital input. Input data is buffered through TMS320/C25 external memory in a double buffer scheme. That is, data from each source is collected in one buffer while a previously collected block of data from that source is processed. As input timing for the system is provided by a hardware clock on the TMS320/C25 board, digital input sources must accept timing signals from the Convolvotron. At each sample interval an interrupt service routine on the TMS320/C25 reads the A/D samples into the buffers, writes the stereo output results to the D/A, and checks for a buffer full condition.

When an input buffer becomes full it is passed to a background process on the TMS320/C25 for convolution. The background process operates on complete buffers by pushing them through the A100 chain to form partial output results. These output buffers are 'faded' and mixed together to form stereo output buffers. The convolution and mixing/fading is considered to be a background process because it is interrupted approximately every 20 μs for A/D and D/A conversion. The details of this background process are discussed next. The first step in the convolution process is to load an input block into the A100 input FIFO. Next, the coefficients that correspond to the measured direction of this source at the beginning of the input block are loaded into the A100 coefficient memory. (These coefficients were calculated during processing of the previous block.) The starting address of a buffer in the dual-ported section of TMS320/C25 global memory must be set up at this time to receive the output from the A100 chain. The A100 chain is then enabled and the convolution occurs automatically under control of the FIFO circuitry.

After the block has been processed the output buffer will contain partial output data, specifically the output samples for the left (or right) ear for that source, for the early direction. This entire process (except for loading the input buffer) is then repeated for the other ear.

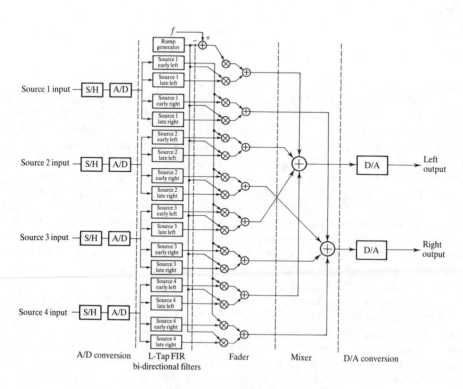

Figure 4.51 Crystal River Inc. Convolvotron functional diagram.

The TMS320/C25 now computes the coefficients corresponding to the late measured direction for this source, that is, the desired direction at the end of the input block. After computation these coefficients will be saved and used as the early coefficients during processing of the next input block. The coefficient computation takes as input four pointers to measured responses stored in the pinnae map as well as four weights associated with these impulse responses. The impulse response to be used in the convolution is computed as a linear combination of these responses using the weights provided. It is usually possible to complete this interpolation while the early convolution is running. In this case the TMS320/C25 must wait for the convolution to complete.

After loading the new coefficients into the A100s and running the convolution, the output data will reside in a buffer in dual-ported external memory similar to the partial output data from the early filter. The TMS320/C25 then repeats this processing for the other ear, convolution with early coefficients, interpolation of new (late) coefficients, and another convolution. The final result is that four partial output buffers have been computed for the source, namely early/left, early/right, late/left and late/right. All of the above, including the loading of the A100 input FIFO, are repeated for each additional audio source in use.

The final step in the background process is the mixer/fader, which combines the partial output buffers (sixteen of them for the four-source case) into a stereo output buffer. The left and right output samples are computed separately by combining the early partial output buffers weighted with a decreasing ramp with the late partial output buffers weighted with an increasing ramp (see Figure 4.51).

For this use of double buffered inputs and outputs to be successful, the above computations must take place in the time it takes to fill an input buffer from the A/Ds. This computation time is approximately proportional to the number of sources multiplied by the number of coefficients. Actually, the computation time is somewhat more than this due to the overhead activities of loading the input FIFO and starting the convolutions. The effect of these overhead activities can be made smaller by using larger block sizes. However, the total delay through the Convolvotron for audio and directional data is about twice the block interval. Thus, there is a trade-off between the maximum computational power the device can provide, namely the number of sources multiplied by the number of coefficients, and desired latency.

The computation time issues discussed above have to deal with the actual elapsed time during the background process. There is also a foreground (interrupt) process running which consumes a small portion of the cycles. This consumption is dependent upon the number of input sources being accommodated and ranges from about 10 to 15% of the available cycles.

4.4 Haptic/kinaesthetic environment systems

Haptic/kinaesthetic environment technologies allow the human operator to select and operate computer subsystems with a virtual hand controller that provides natural feedback via tactile stimulation and force feedback. The user's hand position and orientation is determined along with the position of the fingers. This data is input into the virtual world generator so that it can display an image of the user's hand (in the correct position and orientation) on the helmet-mounted display. By displaying virtual control panels it is possible to interact with the virtual controls. Moreover it is possible to grasp objects drawn in the virtual world and manipulate them. To provide the right 'feel' for the virtual world system it is necessary to provide tactile feedback so that the user feels resistance as an object is touched. Whether the user actually needs tactile feedback or not will depend upon the task.

4.4.1 Virtual hand controller systems

A number of devices are available that allow a user to interact with objects in a virtual environment. These devices have to provide spatial feedback so that a corresponding virtual object in the virtual environment can be displayed. This virtual object moves in a way that corresponds to the user's hand movements. The simplest devices, based on a standard computer mouse or joystick, are relatively accurate and robust despite their simplicity. Unfortunately, they do not allow the user to move in a natural manner within the virtual environment.

Other devices have emerged which track a user's hand movements in terms of orientation and absolute position in space. Some of these devices also incorporate sensors that enable the angles of the fingers to be measured. The accuracy and resolution of these virtual hand controllers depend on the method of sensing employed. The technology behind several virtual hand controllers is described in the following sections, along with a description of the principles involved.

At first it would seem that a virtual hand controller would allow natural interaction with objects in the virtual environment. Unfortunately, the lack of tactile and force feedback often results in unnatural movements of the hand. The principle behind a virtual hand controller is to determine the position of the hand and corresponding finger joints, and use this data to reconstruct a virtual representation of the user's hand on a display. As the user moves his/her hand, the corresponding virtual hand moves in the same manner. Assuming that there is no lag between the user's actual hand position and the computer generated image, the visual representation of the hand can take on a real appearance.

By sensing the position of the hand and fingers it is feasible to use this data not only to draw a computer graphics representation of a hand but also to determine whether or not a virtual object has been touched. When a virtual object has been touched the user should be given some form of feedback or indication. This can take the form of visual, auditory or tactile cues. Without tactile cues the user is often uncertain whether contact has been made with the virtual object, which can induce an unnatural response from the user as an attempt is made to grasp the object. Furthermore, any misalignment in the optical system can reduce the effect of stereopsis (depth perception), which results in difficulty in interpreting an object's exact position in space.

VPL DataGlove

The VPL DataGlove (see Figure 4.52) established itself as the most popular virtual hand controller because it was reasonably priced and offered a level of performance that was acceptable for experimental research. The DataGlove converts hand gestures into computer readable data. Optical fibre sensors are mounted on the back of a lycra glove to monitor finger flexions (see Figure 4.53 and a space tracking system mounted on the back of the hand monitors the position and orientation of the user's hand. A dedicated microprocessor controller unit interrogates the amount of light being transmitted through the optical fibre sensors and the data being returned from the space tracker. This data is analysed and transmitted to a host computer. The DataGlove Model 2+ measures ten joints: the metacarpophalangeal joints of the five fingers, the interphalangeal joint of the thumb and the proximal interphalangeal joints of the other four fingers. Optional sensors can be fitted to measure the abduction and minor joints. In order to accommodate different hand sizes three glove sizes are offered: small, medium and large. It is important to specify the correct size when ordering a DataGlove because an incorrectly fitted glove will require frequent re-calibration. Specifications for the VPL DataGlove are given in Table 4.27.

The DataGlove is controlled by the host computer via a set of 25 commands. Data records can be transmitted by the DataGlove controller at regular intervals from 30-60 Hz or on demand. The use of left- and right-handed gloves is permitted by means of a synchronization command. As will be explained in Chapter 6, whenever two electromagnetic tracking systems are used together it is necessary to multiplex the two respective transmitters.

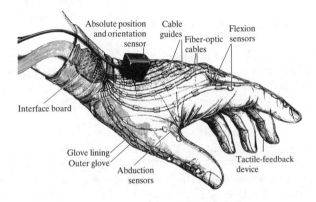

Figure 4.52 Schemmatic of the VPL DataGlove.

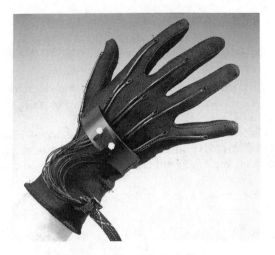

Figure 4.53 VPL DataGlove.

Table 4.27 Specification of the VPL DataGlove.

Parameter	Specification
Hand size	Small, medium or large
Resolution	1°
Joints	Metacarpophalangeal joints of five fingers Interphalangeal joint of the thumb Proximal interphalangeal joints of the other four fingers
Acquisition rate	60 Hz (30 Hz, 60 Hz or on demand)
Interface	RS232
Glove material	Lycra

Theory of operation behind VPL DataGlove

The use of a fibre optic cable as a means of measuring the angle of a finger is a clever idea. It is well known that if light is launched into a fibre optic cable that is bent, a certain amount is lost in the cladding, the exact value being a function of the bend radius (see Figure 4.53). The following section briefly describes the physics behind the process.

Fibre optics is the branch of science that deals with the transmission of light through a small glass or plastic fibre. The transmission of light through the fibre is based on the total internal reflection that occurs when light is incident at an oblique angle, which is greater than the critical angle (Brewster's angle) on an interface between two media of different refractive indexes. When light is incident at the interface between two dielectric media of different refractive indexes it will be reflected totally from the higher index side for all angles of incidence greater than the critical angle ϕ_2, given by:

$$\phi_c = \sin^{-1}\frac{n_2}{n_1}$$

where n_2 is the refractive index in medium 2 and n_1 is the refractive index in medium 1, assuming a perfectly cylindrical fibre with a refractive index n_1 clad with a medium of refractive index n_2, where $n_1 > n_2$.

Taking the case where the fibre is straight, let a ray of light pass through the fibre from a medium of refractive index n_o such that it is almost perpendicular to the end face of the fibre at an angle α. Furthermore, this angle should be greater than the critical angle ϕ_2.

Referring to Figure 4.54 and making use of Snell's law, the following relationship can be derived:

$$n_o\sin\alpha_m = n_1\sin\alpha'_m = n_1\cos\beta_c = n_1(1 - \sin^2\beta_c)^{1/2}$$

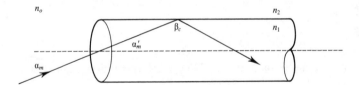

Figure 4.54 Theory of light propagation through a fibre optic cable.

now, $\sin \phi = n_2/n_1$

$$NA = n_o \sin \alpha_m = n_1 \left[1 - \left[\frac{n_2}{n_1} \right]^2 \right]^{\frac{1}{2}} = \sqrt{(n_1^2 - n_2^2)}$$

This relationship is often known as the numerical aperture, or NA, and is essentially a measure of the light gathering properties of an optical system. This parameter should really be called the nominal NA because it only applies to meridional rays. Skew rays almost always exist that are incident at angles greater than α.

Diffraction and surface irregularities between the glass fibre and the cladding cause the transmitted light to be de-collimated, hence reducing the NA. This de-collimation essentially causes the light to spread out.

An additional de-collimation effect is introduced if the fibre is bent. This causes a reduction in the effective NA.

A meridional ray transmitted through a straight fibre optic cable will remain in the same azimuthal plane throughout its passage through the fibre and emerge at the same angle α at which it entered. Any surface defects of non-perpendicular faces will cause the output angle to deviate slightly from this value. If the fibre optic cable is bent, the output angle will change according to the following relationship:

$$\Delta \cos \alpha_{out} = \frac{2dR \cos \alpha_{in}}{r^2 - (d/2)^2}$$

where d is the fibre diameter, R is the fibre bend radius, α_{in} is the half angle of incident cone and α_{out} is the half angle of emergent cone.

Now, $d \ll R$ and the relationship can be simplified to:

$$\Delta \cos \alpha_{out} = \frac{2d}{R} \cos \alpha_{in}$$

This relationship was defined by Potter (1961).

If a parallel beam of light is incident on a fibre of diameter 0.01 cm which has been bent over a radius of 2 cm:

$$\cos \alpha_{in} = 1$$

$$\Delta \cos \alpha_{out} = \frac{2 \times 0.01}{2} = 0.01$$

$$\Delta \alpha_{out} \simeq 8°$$

It can be seen that the de-collimation effects are quite significant for a bend ratio of 200:1.

It is thought that the fibre optic cable is treated at the joint by inscribing a tiny scratch on the cable. This increases the amount of light lost when the cable is bent.

The DataGlove's microprocessor is responsible for calibrating the DataGlove so that the angle of a given finger can be determined. Calibration of the DataGlove is a three–stage process. Firstly, the host computer specifies the voltage level that should be applied to the sensors in the glove. One of the sensors is used in a feedback loop to determine the best operating voltage for the sensors. The second stage of calibration relies on the fact that the raw output value of the DataGlove sensors is an exponential function compared to the bend radius of the fibre. As the response is an exponential curve only two points are required to produce a calibration function. Figure 4.55 shows a typical response curve for one of the fibre optic cables.

The calibration routine requires the user to make a flat hand gesture so that the fibre optic cables produce a 0° bend. This is achieved by placing the hand flat on a table. The user must now calibrate the system by holding the thumb so that the outer joint is at 90° and the inner joint is at 45°. Finally, the user must make a fist gesture so that the fibres are bent at 90°. Figure 4.56 shows the set of three gestures.

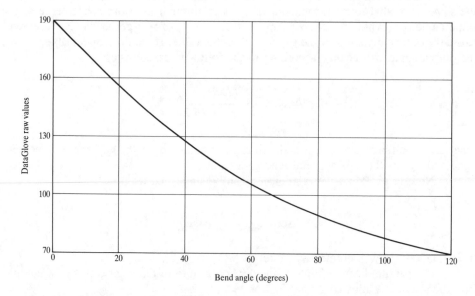

Figure 4.55 VPL DataGlove exponential calibration curve.

Figure 4.56 Gestures used to calibrate the VPL DataGlove.

The calibration routine then determines a 'best fit' exponential curve for each sensor and creates a look up table of angles that correspond to raw sensor values. Each user typically has their own look up table. It is also best to re-calibrate the glove every time it is fitted to the user.

Exos's Dexterous Hand Master

In 1988 Dr E. Marcus formed Exos Inc. in America, and began marketing the Dexterous Hand Master under licence from Arthur D. Little Inc. The Dexterous Hand Master is a high precision sensor system that accurately tracks the complex motions of the human hand. The system is based on an exoskeleton strapped to the dorsal surface of the user's hand. Each of the fingers of the exoskeleton attaches to a back plate, which holds the Dexterous Hand Master in place throughout the full range of motion of the hand. Attached to each finger joint is a Hall Effect Sensor. As the hand moves, these sensors measure three bending motions plus side to side motion for each finger. A total of 20 joint angle measurements are transmitted to a host computer. The device is designed to record flexion movements from a fully extended hand position, but not for hyperextension movements.

Calculation of Dexterous Hand Master output angles

Verification of Dexterous Hand Master output angles has been performed by Makowa (1986) by using a cadaver hand fitted with a Dexterous Hand Master. In order to measure joint angle accurately comparative goniometer measurements were taken from multiple X-rays. The cadaver hand was used principally to avoid the potential hazards of repeated X-ray exposure. Tension in the tendons was created by pulling the sutures, thus causing the finger to bend (see Figures 4.57 and 4.58).

Using Pythagoras theorem:

$$a^2 = L_1^2 + H_1^2$$

$$b^2 = L_2^2 + H_2^2$$

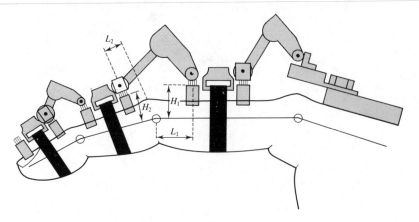

Figure 4.57 Exos's Dexterous Hand Master.

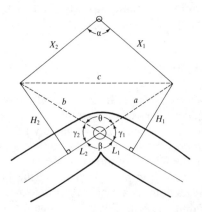

Figure 4.58 Exos's Dexterous Hand Master: calculation of joint angle.

Angles γ_1 and γ_2 can be deduced thus:

$$\gamma_1 = \tan^{-1} \frac{H_1}{L_1}$$

$$\gamma_2 = \tan^{-1} \frac{H_2}{L_2}$$

Now, α = Hall effect sensor measured angle, hence from the cosine law:

$$c^2 = x_1^2 + x_2^2 - 2x_1 x_2 \cos\alpha$$

$$\theta = \cos^{-1}\left[\frac{a^2 + b^2 - c^2}{2ab}\right]$$

Table 4.28 Specification of the Exos Inc. Dexterous Hand Master.

Parameter	Specification
Hand size	5th percentile female to 95th percentile male
Resolution	0.5°
Joints	20 joints angular position
Acquisition rate	100 Hz
Interface	RS422
Weight	11 oz

β can be found by substituting angles γ_1, γ_2 and θ.

$$\beta = 360° - \theta - \gamma_1 - \gamma_2$$

During calibration β is set to 180° for a straight finger, less than 180° for a flexed finger and greater than 180° for a hyperextended finger.

Mattel's Power Glove

Mattel designed a virtual hand controller called the Power Glove for the home video games market. The Power Glove, which is no longer manufactured, was used with Nintendo games machines. The Power Glove's performance was considerably lower than that of gloves manufactured for serious applications. The appearance of the glove was also very different, because Mattel wanted a 'futuristic' look.

The Power Glove used strain gauges (rather than optical fibres) based on flexible plastic with a constant resistive surface. A company called Amtec manufactured the resistive plastic material, which consisted of strips of polyester coated with 0.6 mm of a specially formulated ink.

A single sensor measured all the joints in the hand at once, which meant that it was not possible to determine the bend of a particular joint. Assumptions were made regarding the positions of the joints.

Hand orientation was determined by means of an ultrasonic transducer mounted on the back of the glove, which sent out ultrasonic clicks which were in turn sensed by three ultrasonic receivers. The time taken for the click to reach the receivers was measured. A maximum range of 1.524 m (5 feet) was permissible.

Unlike the other glove devices the Power Glove featured a control pad on the glove, incorporating start and select up/down/left/right cursor pads. These were surprisingly easy to use and could save the user from having to interact with a keyboard.

Although the Power Glove is no longer manufactured, keen interest is still shown in it. Despite its lower precision and limited sensing capability, the fact that it was inexpensive has attracted large numbers of experiments. Several articles have been written which give both hardware and software details for interfacing the Power Glove to an IBM compatible computer (Eglowstein, 1990).

Table 4.29 Specification of the Mattel Power Glove.

Parameter	Specification
Hand size	All sizes
Resolution	0.25"
Joints	1
Interface	Special Nintendo standard; can be interfaced to an IBM PC parallel printer port (refer to text)
Weight	Heavy
Glove material	Heavy plastic

Cyberspace virtual hand controller

Virtual Technologies (Virtex) have developed a precision virtual hand controller. The design award winning (*International Design Magazine*'s 1989 Annual Design Review) CyberGlove uses the latest in high precision joint sensing technology and represents the state of the art in instrumented gloves (see Plate 16). The CyberGlove will be one of the interfaces to Virtual Technologies CyberCAD virtual design environment, and will be used to create, exit and position 3-D virtual objects.

The CyberGlove employs up to 22 sensors: three bend sensors and one abduction sensor per finger, thumb and pinkie cross-over, wrist pitch and yaw. It is a high precision device, giving very accurate and repeatable output.

Repeatability is extremely important. Glove devices made by other manufacturers are prone to slip, necessitating frequent calibration. It is very annoying to have to stop using a glove and calibrate it. As the user's hand warms up the glove tends to slip very slightly, causing some of the trained gestures to become increasingly unreliable. The user generally tolerates this for a while because there is a tendency for him/her to adapt to the change in gesture, which can be verified by looking at a graphical representation on the computer display. When the user can no longer tolerate the change that is required, re-calibration of the glove must be undertaken. There is no doubt that the user's performance is affected by the need to adapt to a slipping glove. The design of the CyberGlove is such that the sensor output only depends on the true angle of finger joints and is independent of joint radius of curvature. Hence, sensor output is invariant with knuckle positioning so calibration remains constant each time the glove is worn. In addition, sensor output is linearly related to bend angle so resolution does not degrade at joint flexure extremes. The sensor outputs are decoupled and are highly independent of each other.

The fingertips and palm regions of the CyberGlove are removed to provide ventilation and permit the user to reliably use the fingers for typing, writing and grasping. The sensors are extremely thin and flexible and do not produce detectable resistance to bending. Glove material is an important parameter, and it must be chosen so that the glove 'flows' with finger movement.

Table 4.30 Specification of the Virtual Technologies CyberGlove.

Parameter	Specification
Hand size	Not specified
Resolution	Not specified
Joints	22 sensors: 3 bend sensors per finger, one abduction sensor per finger, thumb and pinkie cross-over
Acquisition rate	Not specified
Interface	RS232, up to 115.2 kBaud, selectable sample rate or polled I/O
Weight	Not specified
Glove material	80/20 Lycra/Nylon

When a CyberGlove is purchased Virtual Technologies provide the user with a range of software modules which enables the user to make use of the glove very quickly. At the time of writing the following modules are available:

- **Graphic hand model:** VirtualHand software to accurately display a graphic representation of the user's hand and finger motions on a computer screen.

- **Gesture recognition:** GestureGlove software, which uses the latest artificial neural network technology to recognize gestures. It allows the conversion of finger spelling to synthesized speech.

- **Force feedback (available soon):** CyberForce will provide computer programmable grip force feedback to the CyberGlove user.

Virtual hand controller interaction: gesture control

The idea of a virtual hand controller allowing a user to employ gestures to control a computer is not new. There have been many virtual environment demonstrations where gestures have been used to make a menu selection or reposition objects in the virtual environment.

The use of a DataGlove has perhaps been responsible for much of the media hype about virtual reality. The majority of photographs showing a virtual environment system also feature some form of glove device. Unfortunately, the incorporation of a virtual hand controller into a system is not as straightforward as might first be envisaged. The major issues behind virtual hand controller integration are dealt with in Chapter 6.

4.4.2 Tactile feedback

Touch is the common word used to describe mechanical contact with the skin. Other terms used to specify mechanical contacts are contact, vibration, sharp and pressure. Touch (or more accurately cutaneous sensitivity) is a complex subject because it considers other stimuli such as heat.

Anyone wishing to construct a device to communicate the sensation of remote touch to a user must be fully aware of the dynamic range of the touch receptors and particularly their adaption to certain stimuli. It is only too easy to disregard the fundamental characteristics of the human body.

ARRC Teletact Tactile Feedback Glove

The Advanced Robotic Research Centre, Salford, UK have developed a tactile feedback system for use with a virtual hand controller. This glove was designed in conjunction with Airmuscle Ltd, Cranfield, UK (see Figure 4.59).

The principle of the Teletact glove is straightforward. For the initial system two lycra gloves are used. The glove consists of 20 pressure sensitive resistive pads mounted on the underside of the glove. When the glove is worn the user feels the resistance of the pressure sensitive pads changing according to the force exerted. The output from the pressure pad is measured by an analogue to digital converter before being 'read' by a computer.

The second glove consists of 20 air pockets (or bags) which can be inflated by 20 pneumatic pumps, which in turn are controlled by the host computer. The pneumatic pump is connected to the air pockets by means of microcapillary tubing developed for the medical industry.

Figure 4.60 shows the configuration of one pressure sensitive resistive pad and its relationship to the air pocket.

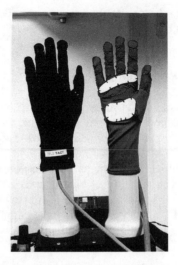

Figure 4.59 Teletact Glove system.

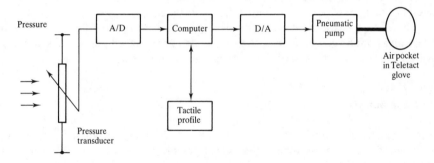

Figure 4.60 Teletact Tactile Feedback Glove principle of operation.

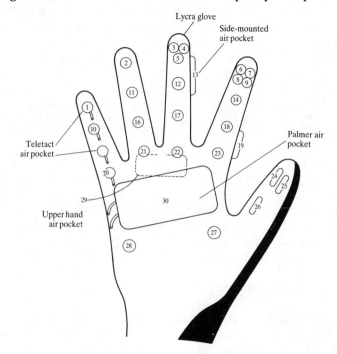

Figure 4.61 Teletact II arrangement of pressure pads giving improved feel.

The original Teletact glove is an extremely low resolution device: twenty tactile feedback points are inadequate to communicate an accurate 'feel' system.

An additional failing of the Teletact glove is its inability to communicate force feedback. If a virtual control push-button is displayed it is possible to push the Teletact glove right through it. This might not seem to be a particularly important issue, but it is probable that the unnatural interaction affects the performance of the operator.

However, a second generation Teletact II glove is being developed that will incorporate higher resolution fingertip air pockets, longer air pockets for the remainder of the hand and a system for providing palmar force feedback. The large palmar air pocket allows the user to exert grip forces and receive stimuli. It will be very similar in operation to Teletact I but will employ 30 pneumatic air pockets instead of 20. The arrangement of the air pockets is shown in Figure 4.61.

The design has a greater density of air pockets on the middle finger tip, index finger tip and thumb regions. Air pockets have also been placed on the back of the hand to give an impression of back of hand contact with an object.

Teletact commander

The use of current generation glove devices can cause operator problems because of slip and, sometimes, calibration difficulties. Until gestural languages are fully understood the use of a glove-like device to provide commands to a virtual environment will remain a problem. To overcome these difficulties a number of virtual pointing devices have emerged. These tend to be based on some form of joystick which embodies a space tracker system and an arrangement of push-buttons embedded in the joystick handle. These systems seem to be much more reliable and easier to use than glove–like devices.

The Advanced Robotics Research Centre, UK have refined virtual joysticks by incorporating simple tactile feedback into the joystick air pocket where technology similar to the Teletact glove has been employed. Depending upon the model, three to five air pockets have been incorporated into the joystick handle. Two types and locations of air pockets can be used. An air pocket 14 mm in diameter fits into the finger recesses while a lozenge shaped pocket (40 mm × 12 mm) lies on the back of the grip.

It is not necessary to employ both Teletact gloves in a given application. The first glove (the pressure sensitive glove) is used to collect tactile profiles of the virtual objects that are to be used, for example push-buttons. The 'pressure' data is then stored in the host computer for later retrieval. When the user reaches out for a virtual object the appropriate tactile profile is loaded into memory and used to drive the pneumatic pumps. Chapter 6 will discuss the realities and practical issues behind the actual implementation of a tactile feedback system.

4.4.3 Force feedback systems

Some applications of virtual environment technology require actual force feedback when a virtual object is grasped. Tactile feedback systems are limited in the sense that they cannot communicate the sensation of a solid object. When a virtual object is touched, visual, auditory and tactile stimulation effects are created.

Although the user gets an impression that a solid object has been touched, unfortunately it is possible to penetrate the virtual object and carry on through it. This effect is quite unnatural and can affect the user's performance if it is necessary to interact with objects in the virtual world.

The way to overcome this undesirable feature is to employ a positive force feedback system that prevents a virtual object from being penetrated. Feel systems have been routinely developed for flight simulations and robotic systems. These systems go a long way towards providing simulated feel, but are not able to create the same impression as real objects.

Force reflecting joystick

An interesting device known as a force reflecting joystick has been developed by Adelstein and Rosen (1992), primarily to study mechanical loading of pathological tremors (see Chapter 7), but it could also be relevant to a force reflecting manual interface to achieve kinaesthetic coupling in a virtual environment. Adelstein and Rosen's system is a two degree of freedom back–drivable manipulator, which couples the output of two d.c. motors to a handle operated by a human subject. The aim of the manipulator is to enable loads to be imposed on the arm of an operator, which can be controlled in real time based on measurements of kinematics and forces. The system is capable of being programmed to emulate a range of passive and active mechanical loads. The dynamic coupling implies that there is a bidirectional mechanical power exchange. The author has used Adelstein and Rodsen's system and was very impressed by the high fidelity of the force reflections that can be synthesized. Van Cott and Kinkade (1972) report that a 'physically fit adult male (upper percentile) can exert a volitional force in excess of 1000 N at the hand against a rigid surface', depending on hand position. These large forces rapidly deteriorate if the hand is moved, while exerting a force against a moving object. In order to determine the bandwidth and force requirements of their force reflective joystick, Adelstein and Rosen noted that repetitive volitional hand motion has a significant energy content at the first harmonic fundamental movement frequency as well as the fundamental movement frequency. Although their work was biased towards the study of tremors, their system has great relevance for kinaesthetic systems. Consequently, the force reflecting joystick was designed to achieve a sustained force capability of 120 N (40 N peak to peak) with an operational bandwidth of 0–12 Hz. Particular care was taken to ensure that the system phase lag (comprising mechanical linkages, sensors and processing electronics) was minimized. With a force reflecting device, inherent friction or compliance can affect the resolution of the dynamic mechanical load. A static friction level of 5% of the full dynamic force was selected.

The number of degrees of freedom obviously affects the perception of forces. In the human there are about 37 muscles in the shoulder, elbow and wrist joints. Six degrees of freedom devices have been designed by a number of other researchers, such as Ouh-Yough *et al.* (1989). Adelstein and Rosen's system was restricted to two degrees of freedom with an operating workspace of 15 cm^2. Nevertheless, some very useful work was conducted in experimental tremor research. This work will be developed to investigate psychophysical effects due to controller update rates and latencies. The temporal characteristics of the mechanical environment simulation must be understood to allow kinaesthetic interfaces to be produced.

4.4.4 Body suits

Full body instrumentation

The idea of monitoring the spatial relationships of the limbs of the human body is not a new idea. A system for precisely monitoring the position and orientation of multiple moving bodies has been described by Mann *et al.* (1981). The system they proposed was based on the SELSPOT Technology (described earlier in this chapter), and enabled high precision full 3-D kinematic data position and orientation relative to an absolute reference frame to be acquired at high acquisition rates. Studies have been conducted into the American Sign Language (ASL) using the SELSPOT system to monitor finger, hand and forearm movements. Other research has been conducted using the system to analyze activity covering animal, pathological and sport movement patterns.

The success of the VPL fibre optic DataGlove has led to the application of fibre optic sensing technology to a range of difficult instrumentation tasks. For example, VPL have developed a fully instrumented body suit that uses the same fibre optics system as the DataGlove. A large number of fibres are secured onto a body hugging suit. Measurements can be taken of limb position and used to control a computer graphics representation of the human body. Whether or not this type of system will find a real place in virtual environments remains to be seen. However, for research involving the positioning of the human being in a work area (for example, a vehicle cockpit or complex control station), such technology could be very important. One of the potential problems for manufacturers of a 'DataSuit' is the extremely wide variation in shape, form and profile of the human being. Experience with glove devices shows the need to use a correctly fitting glove, otherwise slippage causes the device to go out of calibration. Clearly, the problem would be much more difficult to solve with a full body suit. In order to instrument the body fully, it would be necessary not only to measure limb flexion but actual limb position/orientation in space. This implies that multiple space tracking sensors would have to be used. Depending on the technology used for these trackers, there may be consequences of using quite a few of these in the same operating volume, the most significant problem being update rate. The tracker system will either be a master/multiple slave configuration or a series of synchronized systems. Improving computation performance in order to achieve real-time performance for a single tracker is still rather challenging. Increasing the problem by tracking a multiple sensor will certainly be quite difficult. Optical tracking technologies, especially those based on remote viewing techniques, are probably going to be important in providing practical solutions to the problem of fully instrumenting the body.

4.5 Summary

This chapter has been very difficult to write because the technology is constantly evolving. However, I believe that it is important to establish benchmarks so that we can compare future systems against tried and tested approaches. This chapter has focused on the principles behind current technology, and has discussed possible limitations. In this way it is easier for the reader to get a basic understanding of the enabling technologies and then refer to scientific literature that will provide further information. For those interested in conducting research into new virtual environment peripherals it is very helpful to have an accurate account of the performance of past and existing equipment.

Recommended further reading

The development of technology for virtual environments is likely to be a changing field for some time. This will be driven by the need for higher fidelity systems and interfaces. It is not always possible to describe the latest technology in a text book. However, the interested reader is advised to consult one of the specialist virtual reality newsletters since these will generally contain an overview of the latest technology. The address for *VR News* is given below. The Patents office will often be able to provide more precise details of a given invention.

VR News, Cydata Ltd, PO Box 2515, London N4 4JW.

5 Virtual Environment Systems: Software

Objectives

The objective of this chapter is to examine the underlying software behind virtual environment systems. The complexity of future virtual environments will be extremely high, thus placing considerable demands on the software engineer. Resulting systems must be inherently flexible, and highly object orientated with a degree of parallelism. The software development environment is an area where some of the greatest innovations will take place over the next few years. Apart from providing translation from existing 3-D modelling systems a suite of world creation tools will be required. These tools will address model creation through to performance tuning of an application where real-time execution will be important.

5.1 Introduction

It is straightforward to integrate a single virtual environment type peripheral such as a DataGlove into a particular application, but it is another matter to integrate a more complex system involving several virtual environment peripherals in a way that does not require starting from scratch when mapping the system onto a different application. The idea of multi-user interactive application places further demands on the software.

Some form of framework must be developed on which to host new or future revisions of an existing virtual environment system because it is generally too expensive to engineer a new application from scratch.

It is unfortunate that to date there have been only a few examples of integrated virtual environment systems, and these are still in their infancy. While it is appreciated that not all applications will require a complex underlying software system the later generation interactive and fully immersive systems will require some form of virtual environment operating system. These will serve to buffer the user from the actual hardware. Several examples are already emerging. One common feature of virtual environment systems is the need for geometric databases for all the objects to be represented. There is a disadvantage that very few of the current virtual environment systems are able to use models created in another vendor's virtual environment system. The reasons for this are apparent when considering the large number of CAD packages available. The time necessary to generate complex 3-D objects with considerable numbers of polygons and other characteristics should not be underestimated. Ideally when a customer has developed a 3-D representation of his product the desire is to integrate this into whatever virtual environment system is appropriate without a major rewrite of the software. An interim solution seems to be the use of CAD translators to convert from one CAD standard to another. It is not uncommon for CAD translators to eliminate some of the object's attributes in the translation process.

A generic virtual environment standard is obviously needed, but whether future vendors of virtual environment systems agree remains to be seen.

Objects in the virtual environment must have a range of attributes such as:

- Static: position, orientation, visual characteristics (for example, material appearance)
- Dynamic: motion, behaviour, constraints (for example, collision), force

The software must take cognisance of these and other attributes and still deliver real-time performance. Several software tools that form the basis of today's virtual environment systems will be reviewed in this chapter. By examining these it is possible to formulate a view of what will be required in the future.

5.2 Integrated virtual world systems

Figure 5.1 shows the relationship between the real environment, the virtual environment and the user. This includes user interaction sensing and virtual environment display, where the user is presented with an interactive virtual environment covering visual, auditory and haptic displays. The technology to perform real environment sensing was described in Chapter 4.

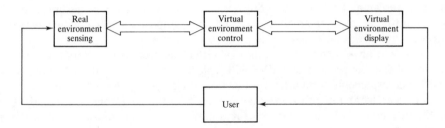

Figure 5.1 Integrated virtual environment system.

This chapter considers current examples and trends in integrated virtual environments. Requirements for future generation systems will be discussed.

High level object orientated techniques are ideally suited to the realization of an interactive virtual environment. Each object in the virtual environment will have its own set of attributes and may be part of another object, grouped into some form of hierarchy. Parent attributes may even be inherited by the lower level objects.

(As will be discussed in Chapter 7 one strength of a virtual environment system is its importance in rapid prototyping applications.) To achieve an optimal and cost-effective level of rapid prototyping, the use of appropriate software tools will be very important.

5.3 Desktop Virtual Reality: Superscape Virtual Reality Toolkit

In recent years there has been a steady development in desktop virtual environment systems. This has resulted in several products emerging based around the top of the range IBM PC compatibles incorporating a 486, 50 MHz processor. One such product is the Superscape Virtual Reality Toolkit (VRT) developed by Dimension International. It is more than a traditional CAD system because it permits a higher degree of interactivity and networking. VRT is easy to use and is a flexible programming environment. The Shape editor provided in the system allows objects to be created for the virtual environment, the World editor associates these objects with motion or behaviour in the environment and the Visualizer forms the runtime system for an application.

The low cost of a desktop system (including hardware and software) is extremely attractive. However, it must be emphasised that a desktop virtual reality system cannot handle the demanding requirements that are placed on a high performance, immersive virtual environment system. Extremely low latency graphic systems must be employed which rules out the current generation of PC–based products. For applications were a higher level of user interactivity is required, above that provided by standard CAD systems, VRT will be a useful asset.

5.4 Distributed Virtual Environment System (dVS)

Division Ltd (UK) have developed a software environment called Distributed Virtual

Environment (dVS) System (Grimsdale, 1991), for their range of parallel processing computers known as ProVision and SuperVision. The dVS has been designed to suit a range of different parallel architectures and will support loosely coupled networks, symmetric multiprocessors and single processor systems.

Division have developed the idea of virtual environment 'actors', which are a collection of discrete processes. A dVS will typically consist of a range of actors, where each actor is responsible for a different function of the system. An actor may be a single process or a collection of processes that interact with the environment database. Quite what the difference is between an actor and a process on a traditional multiprocessor parallel system is unclear.

An actor is created to simulate a component of the virtual environment or to act as an interface to the real environment. Each actor can be freely created or deleted to perform a specified task and may have a finite life span.

Actors cooperate in the virtual environment and share the same global data. Clearly, data used by other actors in the system must be consistent and it is the function of the dVS to synchronize global data among all other actors. Management of data consistency is removed from the user, thus easing the development task.

(The overhead of ensuring data consistency among actors must not be overlooked. This will be discussed in detail in Chapter 6.)

The object manipulated by an actor, the 'element', is an abstract data type; the element is just a data type and does not represent any actual data. An instance of a given element is called a 'parcel', and is essentially a package of data that is shared among several actors. Any actor can reference or hold a parcel, which means that it holds its own local copy of the parcel. Each actor can operate asynchronously from other actors, meaning that each parcel can be at a different state. An actor can initiate a request to change the global state of a parcel, which must be propagated to all other actors holding the parcel.

A consequence of non-deterministic transport mechanisms is that it is impossible to predict how long it can take to propagate a parcel update to every actor. Consequently each actor operates in its own time domain, unsynchronized with other actors. Where this mode of operation is detrimental to the task the parcel can be maintained in exclusive mode, by which updates to a parcel are reflected to all other copies of the parcel. Clearly this can have an effect on system loading and hence performance.

The actors are unaware of the presence, or location, of other actors attached to the environment database. Actors may be attached to the same physical environment database, where the database interface locally mediates the exclusive and general mode accesses to a parcel. A special actor called the 'agent' is provided by the dVS to mediate parcel updates between remote environment databases. It is the role of the agent to communicate with other agents to propagate parcel updates and accesses, using the database interface to propagate information to the remote actors from the receiving agent. A single agent is present at every environment database location, and within any database topology a single agent is nominated to be master and is termed a 'director'. The director operates as any other agent, but also provides a well-known connection point for other databases joining the existing database topology. The director retains global information about other database nodes and environments existing within the database.

The environment database consists of a collection of elements and parcels (created by the actors participating), which themselves may be partitioned by the use of environments. The elements are dynamic and are created at runtime by the actors. An Element pre-processor is used to prepare the element definitions and provide access routines to the data for use by the actors. An environment is very similar to a director tree, where each environment consists of a number of parcels and elements and other Environments, thereby providing information hiding.

Unlike some of the other virtual environment systems the user can program dVS applications at a low level (at the 'C' programming language level). However, a high level animation server (AMAZE) is also available, which allows virtual environment simulation without recourse to writing any code.

5.4.1 A dVS example: Bouncing ball

To illustrate dVS, a simple task of representing a bouncing ball with motion dynamics, collision detection and user interaction is given. Figure 5.2 shows the arrangement of actors.

- **Ball**: the actor that describes the motion of a ball and generates a ball trajectory. Accordingly, it generates an interest in collision elements and awaits events.

- **Dglove**: an actor that obtains the movement of the user's hand and monitors gesture.

- **Collision**: an actor that monitors the proximity of different colliding elements. When two objects collide it updates the collision instances, which in turn results in events that are propagated to the appropriate actors (in this case, Ball).

- **Viz**: an actor that creates a visible representation of the visual Elements.

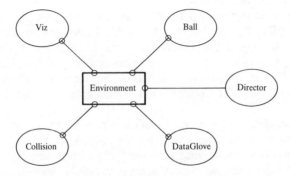

Figure 5.2 dVS bouncing ball example.

5.5 VPL RB2 system (Reality Built for Two)

VPL Research market a complete virtual environment prototyping system called RB2 which allows a user to construct virtual environments for evaluation purposes very quickly. The complete system consists of a suite of integrated software tools that can be executed on a range of Silicon Graphics computers.

In a sense, the RB2 system was the first complete virtual environment system to become available. Many peripherals used in the system formed the basis of the initial research that brought the whole subject of virtual reality alive throughout the world.

The RB2 software environment is described in some detail because it allows a user to construct a complete virtual environment quickly, without writing any software. Extensive use is made of visual programming techniques, unlike other virtual environment software toolkits where a competent 'C' programmer is required to construct virtual environments.

5.5.1 RB2 hardware configuration

The hardware configuration of the RB2 system is shown in Figure 5.3. It incorporates all the components required to place a user in an immersive and interactive visual and auditory virtual world. At the heart of the system is an Apple Macintosh, which acts as the virtual system processor. All the virtual environment peripherals except for the helmet-mounted display (EyePhones) are interfaced to the Macintosh. The space position and orientation tracking systems are linked to the serial interfaces of the Macintosh. This used to be limited to a Polhemus Isotrack system, but has now been updated to allow a wider range of tracking devices to be employed. The Macintosh is connected via an Ethernet interface to a Silicon Graphics workstation, which undertakes the display rendering operations. In a single Silicon Graphics workstation configuration, it is necessary to employ a video splitter to provide the left and right images. An increase in performance can be achieved by using separate Silicon Graphics workstations for each eye.

In the author's opinion (from a maximum performance point of view) it is essential to couple the data from the tracking system to the display generation system very closely. Transferring position and orientation data to the Macintosh for computation and then via the Ethernet to the rendering computers increases the delay, which shows up as a slight lag in the imagery.

Other virtual environment peripheral devices, such as a comprehensive digital audio synthesizer (EMAX), are interfaced to a Midi interface on the Macintosh. This system can capture or may be programmed to generate a whole range of complex audio signals. These range from special effects to compact disc quality sounds. The output of the audio synthesizer is connected to a 3-D audio localizer called a Convolvotron (described in Chapter 4). The Convolvotron is connected to a serial interface on the Macintosh.

The head sensor, DataSuit and DataGlove connect to the Macintosh via serial ports. An optional interface board is available, MacADIOS, which plugs into the Macintosh's NuBus. It can send and receive signals from many devices including the Alternate Input Device Interface, which accepts joysticks, foot-pedals and any other IBM compatible input device.

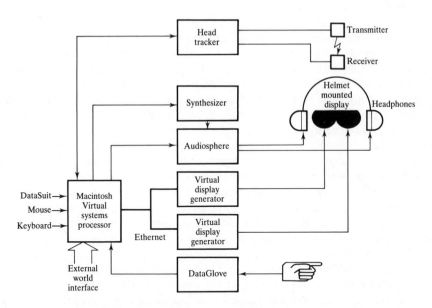

Figure 5.3 VPL RB2 hardware configuration.

The RB2 system provides a complete support environment for the creation, development and investigation of a virtual environment. The key to the success of the RB2 system has been the closely integrated nature of the software development toolset. It is possible to create rather complex virtual worlds with a high degree of integration without writing any software. The user merely creates the objects that exist in the virtual world using sophisticated CAD-like tools and links these objects together in a way that takes account of their interaction and behaviour.

In this way, it is possible for non-programmers to construct complex virtual worlds. However, the RB2 approach has a slight drawback that limits performance. This manifests itself as an increase in update time, which means that the objects move in the virtual world slightly slower than real time. For many development applications this is not a problem. The significant increase in productivity made possible by the toolset more than compensates for the slight non-real-time performance.

The main problem with the RB2 configuration lies with the performance. VPL have solved this by rehosting all the development tools on the Silicon Graphics computers and dispensing with the Macintosh. The virtual environment peripherals are interfaced via a dedicated interface.

The configuration shown in Figure 5.3 relates to a single-user system. RB2 allows two users to be brought together in a virtual environment, but this necessitates doubling the number of devices, such as the EyePhones, the rendering computers and the tracking systems.

5.5.2 Swivel 3-D Professional

Swivel 3-D Professional is a sophisticated 3-D modelling program that allows 3-D drawing, modelling and photorealistic rendering operations to be undertaken on an

Apple Macintosh. This program enables a designer to create objects for a virtual environment. All the features of a powerful CAD-like editor are present, such as the ability to link simple objects together to form complex ones. The rendering capabilities are rather powerful, with a range of render models (wire-frame, hidden time, outline shade, shade and smooth). A maximum of eight light sources are available with the ability to set individual lighting intensities and fill light (no shadow casting or specular highlighting). Additional features such as shadow effects complement the rendering capabilities. Facilities are provided that allow the designer to change the direct reflectance or specular reflectance of a material. Moreover, a whole range of materials can be simulated, including plastic, metal, wood, stone, marble and carpet. It is possible to manipulate a range of material characteristics. For instance, the following characteristics can be modified for wood: opacity, surface, grain and swirl.

Advanced features such as anti-aliasing of object intersections and edge effects are provided. Edge effects cover both object edges and depth edges where boundaries between different objects are outlined. The sense of space is intensified by drawing heavier or lighter outlines, depending on the steepness of the edge's depth.

Finally, a degree of animation is provided by the swivel 3-D program, which allows the virtual environment object designer to visualize moving objects. To some extent this feature is only really useful during the object creation stage.

Anyone interested in obtaining further details of Swivel 3-D Professional should consult Paracomp (1990).

5.5.3 Body Electric

Body Electric is the heart behind VPL's RB2 system because it links the objects of a virtual environment and allows behaviourial and interaction rules to be embedded in the system.

Body Electric is an open ended control system that controls the flow of data from a range of input devices to a series of output devices in a virtual environment. Users can create the data flow network that processes the data using Body Electric's features to produce the output required for a particular application.

Body Electric accepts input from a range of devices such as the VPL DataGlove, VPL DataSuit, Polhemus 3Space Trackers, digital inputs and analogue to digital converters. Later versions of Body Electric extend the number of peripherals that can be used. The input data can be processed using a variety of mathematical and logical operations to control the position and orientation of objects in the virtual environment. Both processed and unprocessed data can be saved to disk for later playback or post-processing. In addition, real-time data can be sent over Ethernet to host computers.

- Using Body Electric's data flow language, the user can define the behaviour of objects in virtual environments.

- With Body Electric's data recording and hierarchical data model, human motion can be captured and used to render sophisticated computer graphics animation.

- Using Body Electric's host communications, the user can teleoperate robots and other devices. It is possible to record action sequences for later playback instead of programming robots in traditional robot control languages.

- With Body Electric's MIDI capabilities, the user can play imaginary musical instruments or create algorithmic musical compositions.

Software configuration

Figure 5.4 shows the software configuration for VPL's RB2 system. A software CAD package called Swivel is used to create objects and models of the virtual environment. From the Swivel file of that world, Body Electric extracts a point for each object (along with its relationship to other objects) to form the hierarchical tree. Isaac, the software that renders the tree, must be run on a fast graphics computer. Isaac uses not only points and their links, but the actual shapes and colours of each object from Swivel. Body Electric reads (in real time) and modifies the positions and orientations of the points in the tree. The modifications are then sent to Isaac, which renders each object according to the update information received from Body Electric.

Inside Body Electric

Each input device (for example the mouse or DataGlove) feeds integer values to the raw data array (see Figure 5.5). This array holds the most recently acquired data values. The user can view these values by opening the raw window. Each of these values may be 'massaged' by reading into the data flow network, where the user can perform scaling, offsetting, filtering and many other operations by using data massage modules within the network.

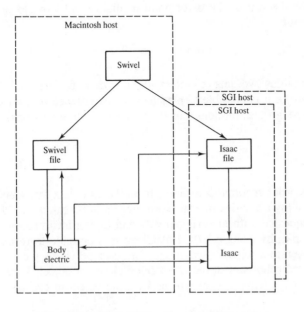

Figure 5.4 VPL RB2 software configuration.

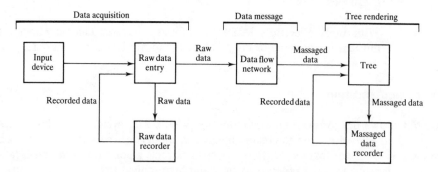

Figure 5.5 Inside VPL Body Electric.

The massaged values are then used to set positions and orientations of the points in the tree. The updated points can then be passed to Isaac for rendering into the EyePhone, or used by other programs on different computers. For example, to create a model of a clock, it is necessary to perform the following actions:

- Rotate the second hand.

- Get the raw value in seconds from the clock raw input.

- Massage its output into tenths of degrees of rotation using the times data massage module with a second input of 60.

- Set the roll of the pivot point of the second hand to this value.

Recording data

Body Electric provides two data recorders, the raw data recorder and the massage data recorder. They make it is possible to play back an experience in a virtual environment without going through the 'motions', or without a data flow network.

Raw data recorder

The raw data recorder records data direct from the raw data array before it has been processed. This allows a series of real-world events to be captured. Playback of these events can be requested with the original data and timing information simultaneously.

For example, by using a VPL DataGlove it is possible to record a sequence of movements to operate a teleoperated robot. The user performs the required 'motions' for the teleoperated robot so that the robot can pick up an object. Whenever the data is played back, the teleoperated robot will pick up the object in exactly the same way as the user.

When the raw data recorder is playing back recorded data, it temporarily stops acquiring new raw data. To other sections of Body Electric, the recorded data appears to be coming from the data acquisition devices in real time.

Massaged data recorder

Body Electric allows massaged data to be recorded in the same way as raw data. There is a requirement to repeat the response of the data flow network to raw data values received from external hardware. Body Electric does this by recording a series of tree renderings. When Body Electric records massaging data, the massaged data recorder obtains input from local tree coordinates. On playback, the data flow network is disconnected from the tree and the massaged data recorder's outputs are allowed to animate the tree.

User Requirements

Although Body Electric is a programming environment, one does not need to be a skilled programmer to use it. VPL have taken pains to ensure that the data flow networks and the syntax for editing are simple and intuitive. On-line help is also available.

Net editing

Nets are composed of data massage modules (DM) connected to each other by 'wires'. A data massage module takes several inputs, operates on them, then outputs one (or more) value so that it can be used as input to other data massage modules.

The names window

The process of creating a network is performed by dragging icons for data massage modules, raw inputs and points from the names window into a net window. As there are many icons, they are represented by their name, in the lower portion of the names window (see Figure 5.6).

The Net Window

It is easier to understand the data flow in a net. Data massage module icons are positioned to the right of the icons they get their input from (input pads are on the left and output pads are on the right of icons). This minimizes crossed wires, and makes it easier to follow the data as it moves from left to right (see Figure 5.7).

Raw data acquisition

Body Electric data flow networks can receive input from a variety of sources, including

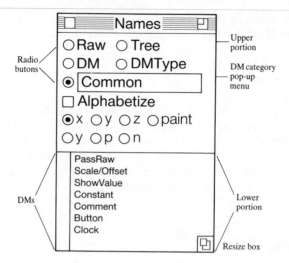

Figure 5.6 Body Electric names window.

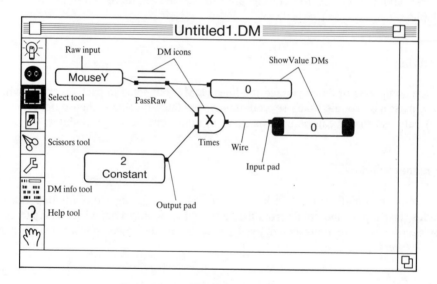

Figure 5.7 Body Electric net window.

the clocks (internal to the Macintosh) and other devices such as the mouse, the keyboard, and analogue and digital data from the external world.

Data acquisition is the process of getting data from the serial ports, the Nubus via cards like MacAIOS, and SCSI via STD bus interfaces. Data acquisition modules find and establish communications with input and output devices as required. Through these devices, Body Electric can communicate with hardware devices for a wide range of applications, such as animation, robot control and musical performance.

Raw data

Raw data is an integer data type into which all input values are converted. This arrangement allows Body Electric to access data from multiple sources. The range of raw data values depends on the type of input devices used and on the data acquisition modules supplied with the Body Electric application.

Instantaneous raw data values are held in a block of memory called the raw data array. This maintains no record of prior values (that is the purpose of the raw data recorder). Raw data is placed in the raw data array only for those input devices that have active data acquisition modules.

All versions of Body Electric are supplied configured for using sources of data internal to the Macintosh. Custom data acquisition modules are supplied by VPL Research on a special order basis.

The programmer can see what sources of raw data are available and the current values of the raw data by opening the raw window from the menu.

Data flow networks

Data flow networks are used to connect raw inputs to outputs (typically tree point attributes) with an arbitrary amount of processing or massaging of the data in between.

Networks are made up of raw inputs, data massage modules, points, and the wires that connect them. Raw inputs representing the mouse, clocks, and a potentially infinite variety of real-world data collectors are represented by small icons. The output of a raw input is always an integer.

Data massage modules can transform the data from raw inputs, points and other data massage modules with mathematical, logical and a large set of other flexible operators. They can process several different kinds of numbers as well as points and are represented as a two-line box.

Raw inputs are the source of data flowing into a network. Points are the major destination of data leaving the network and have many attributes. The position attributes (x, y, and z) and orientation attributes (yaw, pitch and roll) are maintained by a Body Electric network. Other attributes, such as constraints on the above six attributes and the point's name, can be seen and set by the user in the edit point dialogue box. Certain Swivel attributes, such as shape and colour, are not accessible to Body Electric. Point attributes are represented by icons that are the same size as raw input icons, but may have an input instead of an output, showing that they represent the setting of a point attribute.

Networks are viewed and edited as icons connected by lines. These lines connect outputs of raw inputs, data massage modules and point icons to the inputs of data massage modules and points. Figure 5.8 shows the constructs used in the network diagram.

Raw data fills up the raw data array asynchronously. Body Electric compiles a new internal net whenever a Body Electric net is edited. The compilation process works out the correct order to execute each module. This cycle is repeated as often as possible. Complex nets are cycled much slower than simple nets. If after each cycle Isaac has requested data, then information is sent from the net to Isaac. The overall cycle time is of the order of 30 Hz but is very dependent upon net complexity.

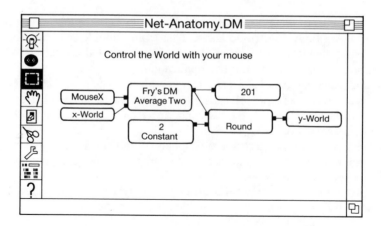

Figure 5.8 Net anatomy constructs.

Trees

Trees are hierarchical data structures of connected points that represent a 3-D model. The main values of points, x, y, z and yaw, pitch, roll, can be read and set by a Body Electric network. The major output of a net is the setting of these points.

The tree can be rendered in a tree window. By specifying that lines are drawn between certain points real-time stick figure animations can be created within Body Electric. The dynamic values in trees can also be sent to Isaac for real-time shaded polygon rendering. These are then displayed by the EyePhone or sent to other computers via the host communication protocol, for animation or robot control.

Trees can be created from within Body Electric, or by loading Swivel files. If the user starts by loading a Swivel file, modifications can be made to a tree and written back out into a Swivel file. These can then be viewed within Swivel as solid, shaded objects.

The dynamic behaviour of a tree can be recorded, played back and saved on disk in formats that can be read by both Body Electric and Swivel.

Points

Trees are made exclusively from hierarchically linked points. Each point has a parent; a point's children are 'down tree', and its siblings are 'left' or 'right' (although the positioning of points up, down, right or left of one another has nothing to do with their positions in the 3-D image). The placement of points in the hierarchy does influence how they move in the image when animated by the data flow network.

Local and global coordinates

The position and orientation attributes of a point are indicated in 'local' coordinates.

They are relative to their parent. A point with an x value of 13 is located 13 units from its parent along the x axis.

Each point's screen, or 'global' coordinates depend on the global coordinates of its parent, and so on, all the way to the top of the tree. The user can assess a point's global position by using a global position data module.

When the user moves a point, the point's coordinates are changed relative to its parent. Moving a point does not affect the parent. On the other hand, it does affect the global position of the point's children. The children move with the parent, maintaining the same relationship. Their global positions and the global positions of the 'grandchildren' are offset by the same amount as the point being moved. This linked behaviour makes animation of complex objects with moving parts very convenient.

The world

At the top of every tree is a point called the 'world'. The world is the eldest ancestor of all the other points in the tree. If you drag the world across the screen, the entire tree moves with it. Since it has no parent, its 'local' coordinates are the same as its 'global' coordinates in the tree image. You might think of the world as having coordinates that are relative to a 'universe' point whose position and orientation values are always zero.

In all other respects, the world behaves just like any other point. Its coordinates can be edited and its movements constrained. It is recommended that the name of the world point is not edited.

Point attributes

Points have many attributes, but only six of these are commonly used by a Body Electric network. They are the three attributes of orientation, yaw, pitch and roll. Some of the other attributes are viewable and editable within the edit tree dialogue, such as line drawing in the tree window. Isaac can display the shape attributes of an object associated with a point. Swivel can display as well as edit all attributes of a point's associated object except those pertaining exclusively to rendering in the tree window (line drawing between points).

Points not explicitly named by the user are named by Body Electric. Automatic names are generated by using the closest ancestor with a name and appending a unique suffix. As world is a named point, every point has at least one named ancestor. The suffix contains an integer for each generation, indicating the sibling order within that generation.

5.5.4 Isaac

Isaac is a computer program that resides on a Silicon Graphics host computer and is responsible for producing the rendered 3-D stereo images that are displayed on the user's helmet-mounted display. Isaac is initialized with a virtual environment model exported from Swivel 3-D and during execution it receives real-time changes from the environment behaviourial model of Body Electric. Isaac can be run on a single Silicon Graphics machine with a video splitter option to generate the left and right eye views.

Alternatively, for higher performance and reduced visual lags, two separate Silicon Graphic computers can be used. Several parameters are required by Isaac to correctly set up the visuals. These include inter–pupillary distance, eyeview and viewpoint.

The complete process for creating a virtual environment for use by Isaac is given below:

1.   RB2 Swivel: Creation of a static three–dimensional model of the environment.
     (a)   Create discrete 3-D objects.
     (b)   Link or associate models to form a hierarchy.
     (c)   Position and orientate each object in its initial state.
     (d)   Set bounds for object motions in terms of minimum/maximum values for position and orientation (x, y, z, yaw, pitch and roll).
     (e)   Uniquely name objects that will be manipulated by Body Electric.
     (f)   Save the static virtual environment in a regular Swivel file.

2.   Body Electric: Create the dynamic/behaviourial relationships between objects in the virtual environment.
     (a)   Load the Swivel virtual environment file.
     (b)   Create a network that points to dynamically changing values. This step is the key to creating a dynamic and interactive virtual environment.
     (c)   Save the net or tree file.

3.   Isaac
     (a)   Run Isaac on the host Silicon Graphics computers.
     (b)   Execute Auto Isaac command. This establishes communications between Body Electric and Isaac.

5.6 Virtual Environment Operating Shell (VEOS)

Virtual Environment Operating Shell (VEOS) is a software environment for prototyping distributed virtual world applications. It was developed by the Human Interface Technology Laboratory (HITL), Seattle, USA, for distributed virtual environment applications and has been in use for two years. However, VEOS is by no means limited to these types of applications. The VEOS project team consists of William Bricken, Geoff Coco, Dave Lion and Andy MacDonald.

The underlying design aim was to create a mechanism for specifying the tasks and assigning computational resources in a distributed design. A VEOS application can be broken down into distinct processes, which are as self-reliant as possible; the more self-reliant, the more efficient the whole system becomes. Each process can be coded separately, with provisions for communicating with the other processes in the system, and is implemented by a single VEOS entity on any network accessible UNIX workstation.

VEOS is an extendable environment for prototyping distributed applications for UNIX. The VEOS application programmer's interface is provided by XLISP 2.1. VEOS provides interprocess message passing and content addressable database access.

It is ideal for applications where hardware resources are not physically close or where machine dependent resources are isolated because of their platform, for example software packages and interface devices.

VEOS is also ideal for prototyping programs that employ coarse grain parallelism. It uses heavyweight sequential processes, corresponding roughly to UNIX processes. In this way, VEOS can be used to utilize a network of workstations as a virtual multiprocessor. 'C' programmers can build custom VEOS tools that are accessible from XLISP and thus are immediately compatible with other VEOS tools. LISP programmers can quickly design and run distributed programs, utilizing diverse hardware and software resources.

VEOS is not an operating system. It is a user level framework for prototyping distributed applications. Its main aim is flexibility and ease of use. This design comes somewhat at the expense of real–time performance. However, VEOS is claimed by HITL to be capable of good performance with proper application structuring and tuning.

Relying on only the most common UNIX interface, VEOS is platform independent. VEOS 2.0 has been extensively tested on DEC 5000, Sun 4, and Silicon Graphics VGX and Indigo platforms.

5.6.1 Fundamentals of VEOS

With VEOS, a programmer can specify how to accomplish the many computational tasks of a proposed virtual environment. VEOS allows a programmer to 'clump' these tasks into computational nodes of a distributed system. These clumps are known as 'entities'.

At present, each entity is implemented as a distinct UNIX process with the following native capabilities: interpretation of a coded task description (currently written in LISP), inter-entity communication, generalized data management (akin to tuple architecture) and generic pattern matching over local data space.

With VEOS, a designer can implement a virtual environment using a set of entities, each residing on the same or different UNIX-based machines (presuming network accessibility). Furthermore, because VEOS relies only on the most common UNIX interface, one virtual environment application may utilize multiple hardware platforms.

The best method for utilizing VEOS entities as nodes in a distributed application greatly depends on the parameters of the application; for example, the computational resources available, the topology of the network, and the location and compatibility of interface devices. Consequently, the VEOS design, wherever possible, foregoes making policy decisions so that the programmer enjoys maximum flexibility in designing a distributed application.

Entities

A VEOS entity is a stand-alone executable program that is equipped with VEOS native capabilities such as data management, process management and inter-entity communications.

The grouple

One of the aims of VEOS is to support a consistent and general format for program specification, inter-entity communication and database management.

Independently, these needs can be solved by some existing methods. For example, LISP provides generalized data abstraction (lists), and useful program control; Mathematica provides a generalized specification format and consistent treatment of data and function; 'Linda' provides generalized data management.

However, these tools do not share a common form. In addition, large components of these systems are extraneous for most situations. Thus, integrating such packages would prove costly and wasteful. Moreover, tying together such varied systems emphasizes the differences between their respective forms and expressions rather than their commonalities.

Consequently, an enhancement to the tuple was selected for the VEOS general format. This format is called the 'grouple'. Grouples can be seen as nettable tuples. Grouples are extraordinarily general for flexibility, yet the data they contain can be accessed specifically for debugging and performance efficiency. The sub-fields of a grouple are called 'elements'. As grouples can be nested, an element can be a grouple. 'Nancy', the VEOS data manager, uses the grouple for its standard data format.

VEOS now has a LISP interface. The LISP language was selected as the interface because there is a clear mapping from LISP lists to VEOS grouples. Furthermore, because LISP boasts program–data equivalence, programmers can store and pass fragments of entity specification using the VEOS kernel mechanisms.

Grouplespaces

Technically, a grouplespace is an ordinary grouple. There are two grouplespaces associated with an entity, which partition the entity's data. The grouplespaces are the work space, the programmer's run time database and the 'in space', where incoming inter-entity messages are placed. In VEOS 2.0, the 'in space' has been bypassed as an efficiency concern.

Pattern matching

The regime of pure algebraic reduction is well known to provide the ability to perform many kinds of computation. This scheme, also known as the match/substitute/execute paradigm (ex. in expert systems) can be implemented using a pattern matching mechanism. Nancy supports pattern matching over its grouplespaces. A pattern is a specific form that data can take. Patterns can contain specific data to match or wildcard symbols, which can be used to bind variables to values.

5.6.2 Components of the VEOS kernel

Nancy: The VEOS grouple manager

Nancy is a 'home-brew' database manager designed specifically for the VEOS project.

(As Linda systems manage data as tuples, Nancy manages data as grouples.)

Nancy performs all grouple manipulation within VEOS. This involves creation, destruction, insertion, copying, and so on. Since Nancy grouplespaces are merely named grouples, these are also an entity's fundamental database operations.

In addition, Nancy provides a powerful semantic for data searching, inserting and replacing within a grouplespace. This is the pattern matcher, a complete set of primitives to implement a match/substitute/execute engine as in an expert system.

From LISP, programmers have access to three Nancy operations: vput, vcopy and vget. These are sufficient for all grouplespace operations. As LISP expressions are passed to these Nancy primitives, they are converted to grouple format and then handled by Nancy's standard C interface.

Talk: The VEOS communications module

Talk is the only supported mechanism for entity communication. As VEOS entities provide coarse grain parallelism though UNIX processes, process (entity) synchronization and shared memory is not practical. Thus VEOS supports message passing as the only means of entity communication. Talk provides VEOS with two simple message passing primitives, vthrow and vcatch. From LISP, programmers can transmit a message asynchronously to another entity. The receiving entity is then at leisure to receive the message, also asynchronously.

Asynchronous message passing means that when an entity transmits a message, the operation succeeds reliably, whether the receiver is waiting for a message or not. Likewise, an entity can always check for incoming messages without waiting indefinitely for a message to arrive. This is also called non-blocking communication. Talk passes messages between entities with a flat linearized grouple format. The LISP/VEOS interface module performs this translation.

Shell: The VEOS kernel control module

The shell is the administrative workings of the VEOS kernel. It dispatches initializations, does interrupt handling, manages kernel memory, and so on.

5.6.3 Using VEOS from LISP

VEOS methodology

The VEOS kernel provides the following:

    1. Fast and powerful local database access.

        (a)   Built-in pattern matching.
        (b)   Internal grouple form converts to LISP lists.

    2. Clean and reliable message passing.

    (a)   Utilizes Berkeley sockets.

    (b)   Symbolic entity addressing.

3. Well-defined C interface.

    (a)   Can be retrofit to any high level language in the same way as LISP.

5.6.4 Writing software tools in C

Philosophy

Any software tool can be integrated with VEOS. However, certain features of software tools make them easier to integrate. The process of VEOSifying a software tool involves writing custom LISP primitives (usually in 'C') which decode LISP arguments and pass control to the software tool.

Given that all control will be passed to a tool via LISP primitives, the VEOSified tool will perform best if it is :

- Non-blocking: primitives should always return after a reasonable slice of time depending on application.

- Interrupt driven: as long as primitive entry points appear to accomplish their tasks quickly (use static caches, and so forth). In fact, for polling type software tools (input device drivers), interrupts are preferable to time-out reads in some situations, especially when data arrival is infrequent.

- Modular: the tool should perform distinct, well defined tasks. This assists the LISP programmer with task specification, and it makes writing custom primitives easy.

- Robust: able to handle lags in data flow and out-of-band data.

Legal restrictions are described in the file VEOS_LICENSE. To obtain VEOS software, register with HITL by sending your name, address, and proposed use to:

email: ftp 128.95.136.1 (milton.u.washington.edu)
             cd ~ ftp/public/veos
             binary
             get veos.tar.Z

postal: Veos Software Support
            Human Interface Technology Laboratory
            FJ-15, University of Washington
            Seattle, Washington   98195   USA
            e-mail: veos-support@hitl.washington.edu

5.7 Minimal Reality (MR): A toolkit for virtual environment applications

5.7.1 Introduction

Professor Mark Green and his team at the University of Alberta have developed a virtual environment toolkit, called MR Toolkit, for virtual environment applications. The complete toolkit is available free of charge from the University of Alberta to research institutions, but this excludes commercial exploitation. The MR Toolkit is extremely well written and is superbly documented and commented throughout. For academic institutions wishing to get involved in virtual environment research there is probably no better way of getting a head start than with the MR Toolkit.

The MR Toolkit is a subroutine library that supports the development of virtual environment and other forms of three–dimensional user interfaces. It provides support for various devices, such as the Polhemus space tracker, VPL DataGloves, VPL EyePhones and sound synthesis equipment, that are commonly used in virtual environment systems. In addition, the toolkit supports the distribution of the user interfaces over multiple workstations, data distributed over several workstations, numerous interaction techniques, and real-time performance analysis tools. The current version of the MR Toolkit may be called from 'C' programs on Silicon Graphics and DEC workstations. It presents an interesting alternative to the LISP-based VEOS toolkit.

The MR Toolkit reference manual (distributed with the toolkit) contains complete descriptions of all the routines in the MR library and their parameters.

It provides the basic services that are required by a programmer producing virtual environment user interfaces. However, it does not provide high level tools for the construction of virtual environment user interfaces, so the programmer must still write some code to perform special tasks. The code that must be written is tied to the particular application or specialized interaction technique.

5.7.2 MR Toolkit philosophy

The MR Toolkit is based on several years of experience at the University of Alberta in the construction of virtual environment user interfaces. It supports the functions that have been found to be important in a wide range of virtual environment user interfaces. Experience indicates that a toolkit for virtual environment applications must have the following characteristics:

- Efficiency: The quality of a virtual environment user interface depends on the real time required to reflect the user's actions in the images that are presented to him. The lag between action and image should be minimized for a smooth and satisfying interaction. The toolkit must be as efficient as possible to reduce lag.

- Flexibility: Virtual environments are a new interaction style, and thus the state of the art is changing very rapidly. A toolkit for virtual environments must be flexible enough to accommodate the changes in both hardware and software. That is, it must be easy to add support for new devices, and provide new types of interaction techniques.

■   Distributed applications support: Most of the virtual environment user interfaces that we have constructed require the cooperation of several workstations or computers. Typically, two workstations are used to produce the images for a helmet-mounted display, and a separate workstation or computer may be producing the information to be displayed. The programmer does not want to produce the program code required to handle the distributed aspects of the user interface in each application. Therefore, this should be handled by the toolkit.

■   Time management support: A virtual environment user interface must minimize the lag between user actions and their feedback on the head-mounted display.

The MR Toolkit is optimized for processing efficiency, but this is not sufficient for a number of applications. The application can control the amount of data presented to the user, and in this way control the lag between user actions and display. That is, the MR Toolkit can feed back display rates to the application to enable it to use this information to control the amount of detail that is displayed. The toolkit must provide this type of support so applications can adapt to the current display rate. The MR Toolkit assumes a hardware environment consisting of one or more graphics workstations, and 3-D input and output devices, such as the VPL DataGlove and EyePhone. A minimal configuration consists of a workstation plus a 3-D input device, such as the Polhemus Isotrak. For most work a head-mounted display with head tracker and a separate 3-D input device for entering positions and commands are recommended. The MR Toolkit was originally developed on Silicon Graphics workstations but can easily be ported to other compatible workstations, such as the IBM RS6000. The current version of MR (Version 1.0) runs on both SGI and DEC 5000 workstations. The MR Toolkit consists of three layers of software (see Figure 5.9). The bottom layer consists of a set of device support packages. Each package supports one device, and the package is viewed as a client/server pair. The client part of the pair is a set of library routines that interfaces with the server, while the server part consists of a process that continuously samples the device and performs low level operations such as filtering. As the server is continuously sampling the device, the client routines can quickly obtain the most recent value, without incurring the lag involved when requesting a sample from the device. The client/server model facilitates adding new devices to the system and distributing the processing load among the workstations.

The second level of the MR Toolkit consists of routines that process the data from the devices and convert them into a format that is more convenient for the user interface programmer. The routines at this level also provides standard services such as data transfer between workstations and work space mapping. In the case of the DataGlove, the routines at this level perform gesture recognition and provide visual feedback of the current glove state.

The routines at the top level provide a set of packaged services for the programmer. These services are based on the requirements of the average virtual environment user interface. For example, there is a single routine at this level that can be used to initialize all the devices required by the user interface. Therefore, the programmer does not need to remember the initialization routines for each device.

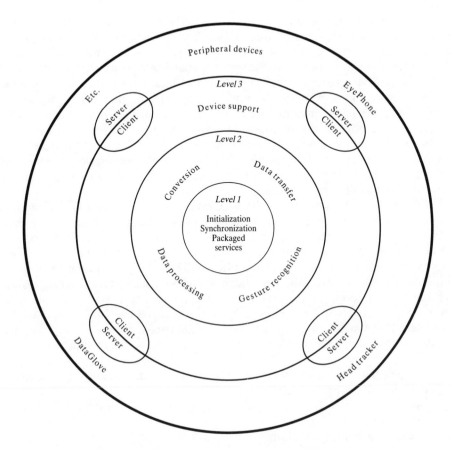

Figure 5.9 MR Toolkit software environment.

The routines at this level also handle synchronizing the data structures and display operations between the pair of workstations used to produce binocular displays.

The programmer can mix routines from all three levels of the MR Toolkit. However, care should be taken in doing this because some of the low level routines depend on the environment established by the higher level ones. The programmer should read the MR reference manual carefully to determine what the low level routines require. Mixing routines in the top two levels of the MR Toolkit is not a problem. This gives the programmer the flexibility to work at the level appropriate for the task in hand. It is assumed that most programmers will only use routines in the top two levels.

5.7.3 The MR Toolkit level

There are three roles that a user's program can perform in an MR Toolkit application. One program has to be in control of the application and is responsible for initiating the execution of the other programs. There will always be a master program in an application. However, there can be several slave programs in an MR Toolkit application. A slave program is used to produce graphical output. It is not involved with the other computations in the application. The typical use of a slave program is to produce one of the images required for a head-mounted display, but it could be used to produce other graphical output, such as status displays. A computation program performs some computation that is part of the application. This program typically runs on a compute server that is attached to the same local area network as the master program. Compute programs receive their input from the master program and periodically report their results to it.

An application that uses a helmet-mounted display will require two programs, with each program generating the images for one eye. The master program generates the images for the left eye and the slave program generates the images for the right eye. The decision as to which program generates the images for a particular eye was an arbitrary one made in the design of the MR Toolkit, but it is a standard that must be followed by all MR Toolkit programs. In an application, such as fluid dynamics, where one program is responsible for performing all the computations in the application, a third program is required. This program is used to compute the application data, which is then sent to the master program for display. Other slave programs could be used to provide a map of where the user is now located in a virtual space or to provide a control console.

A program that uses the MR Toolkit is divided into two sections, the configuration and compute sections.

MR Toolkit configuration section

The configuration section initializes the MR Toolkit and processes the configuration file for the application. This file allows the user to specify some of the configuration information, instead of hard coding it in the application.

MR Toolkit assumes a standard set of input and output devices when it is initialized, including the DataGlove, EyePhone, and sound synthesizer. These are the devices required by most MR applications.

In most applications there are data structures that must be shared among the programs in the application. These include the results of the computations, and the information that must be displayed to both eyes. The shared data structures can be identified in the configuration section of the program, and the MR Toolkit will handle the transfer of these data structures between the appropriate programs.

The MR Toolkit uses a simple model of data sharing. It is assumed that the master program has a copy of all the shared data structures. In addition, the MR Toolkit assumes that the data structure is only shared by two programs in the application. Thus, each shared data structure has one copy in the master program and another copy in a slave or computation program. The MR Toolkit assumes that one of these programs produces the data and the other one consumes it. Thus, there is a one-way transfer of data between the programs, but there are ways of getting around this restriction. This set of assumptions makes it easy to set up most of the data sharing that must occur in MR Toolkit applications, and it is still possible to produce more complicated process structures. For example, when using a head-mounted display, both the master and slave process must display the same information. The master program can generate this data, and then transfer it to the slave program before it is displayed. A shared data structure can be any 'C' data structure that does not contain pointers, since the value of a pointer in one program is not meaningful in another. Both programs that use the shared data structure must allocate storage for it.

MR Toolkit configuration file

A configuration file is a text file that contains some of the information that may be specified in the configuration section of an MR program. The use of configuration files allows for the customization of programs without the need to recompile the program. The most useful customizations are switching between stereo and regular mono viewing and changing the workstations on which the slave and computation programs run.

MR Toolkit compute section

The compute section performs the task assigned to the program in the MR Toolkit application. In the case of a slave program, the program waits for a packet of information to come from the master program and then produces the next image. For a computation program, the program produces the next set of results, transmits them to the master program, and waits for its next set of instructions (input for the computation). In this section, the program can call any of the non-configuration routines in the MR Toolkit that are appropriate for the role it is playing.

The compute section of the program is divided into two parts. The first sets up the environment used by the application, and the second handles interaction with the user. There are several details that must be dealt with before the application can start interacting with the user. The first of these is establishing the coordinate system used in the application. By default, MR Toolkit assumes a coordinate system that is based on the room where the equipment is located. The default unit of measurement is the metre, and the coordinate axis of the environment lines up with the walls of the room. The exact correspondence between room and environment geometry is determined when the MR Toolkit is installed at a particular site. The work space mapping package allows the programmer to define the coordinate system used within the application. When MR Toolkit is installed a room coordinate system is defined which will typically have an origin in one corner of the room. The reference point is specified in terms of this coordinate system. If a reference point is not specified then the origin of the room coordinate system is used.

Some of the devices used in MR Toolkit programs must be calibrated or otherwise initialized before user interaction starts. For example, if a helmet-mounted display is used it must be properly calibrated for the user's inter–pupillary distance. This can be done by calling an appropriate procedure. When gestures are used with the DataGlove, tables defining these gestures must be loaded into the master program prior to interaction with the user.

5.7.4 The package level

Packages provide a high level interface to some of the devices and services required by most virtual environment programs. Most of the packages attempt to provide a simple interface to the functionality that will be required by most applications. Thus, most do not provide the full functionality that is available from the device/service, just the functionality that is likely to be the most useful. Since these packages provide a limited functionality, they can be much simpler interfaces to the devices and services. This approach can drastically reduce the amount of code that must be written and the time required to learn how to use the package.

The Isotrak package

The Isotrak package supports the use of stand-alone Polhemus Isotrak digitizers. These digitizers report both the position and orientation of a sensor. The position and orientation information produced by this package is returned to the program.

The display packages

A wide range of display devices have been used in virtual environment applications, thus any package that supports this style of user interface must be capable of supporting more than one type of display device. The early versions of the MR Toolkit assumed that the only display device that would be used was the VPL EyePhone. The University of Alberta are now generalizing the display support in MR so an application program can be used with a wide range of display devices. If used correctly the display package takes care of the display device (masking most of the details of the particular display device from the user), thus making it easier to move an application from one display device to another.

The characteristics of the display device used in an application are specified in the configuration section of the application. At present, there are three broad classes of display devices: helmet-mounted, mono, and no display.

The helmet-mounted display device is modelled on the EyePhone. This device type assumes that there are two programs (master and slave) producing the two images required for a helmet-mounted display. A tracker is attached to the display, which gives the current position and viewing direction of the user. MR Toolkit handles setting up the viewing specification for both programs and synchronizes their presentations of the images on the helmet-mounted display. The mono device is modelled on one program producing the images seen by the user. The user's head position and viewing direction are also tracked in the same way as a head-mounted display. For this device type, MR Toolkit handles setting up the viewing transformations based on the current position and viewing direction of the user.

The DataGlove package

The DataGlove package is one of the more complicated packages in the MR Toolkit. It can be divided into two levels. The first supports basic interaction with the

DataGlove, including reading the current value of the DataGlove, sending this information to the slave process that is generating one of the images for the EyePhone and drawing the DataGlove in the environment. The second level supports gesture recognition, and is used in interaction techniques.

The Gesture data structures

One of the main functions of the DataGlove is to enter gestures that serve as commands or signals in most MR applications. A three-level data structure is used to represent gestures in the MR Toolkit.

Hand calibration and gesture editor

Programs are provided to calibrate the DataGlove so that its raw flex sensor readings can be converted into appropriate finger bend angles. During calibration, the user is taken through a four-step measuring process. Two steps measure only finger joints, and the other two measure only thumb joints. At each step, the user is asked to form the gloved hand into a simple posture, and then, when ready, to press the left mouse button. When the mouse button is pressed, the program reads the raw flex values of the DataGlove. These readings are then used to generate a calibration table for each finger and thumb joint. At each step, the program presents a picture of what the hand should look like.

Steps one and two calibrate the fingers. In step one, the user is required to keep the hand flat, so that the fingers are unbent, resulting in finger bend angles that are nominally 0°. Step two requires the user to hold the hand so that the fingers are bent 90° at the near and middle joints. The outer joint of each finger should be unbent. This step results in a hand that is roughly U-shaped, with the palm forming one side of the U and the fingertips forming the other side. The user should not make a fist, as this tends to overbend the fingers by about 20° at each joint.

Steps three and four calibrate the thumb. Step three requires that both thumb joints be approximately 0°, with the outer knuckle of the thumb touching the side of the palm of the hand. The user can achieve this shape by putting the hand palm down on a table and touching the thumb's outer knuckle to the side of the palm of the hand. Step four requires that the user bends the thumb's inner joint 45°, and the outer joint 90°. This can be done by making a loose fist with the index and middle fingers curled around the tip of the thumb.

When these steps are complete, the program generates calibration tables and loads them into the server.

Gesture editor

The gesture editor allows the user to create and edit MR Toolkit gesture files. Each gesture file has one or more gesture tables, each containing one or more gestures. Each gesture is a hand posture with or without an associated orientation. When the hand is in the associated posture, the gesture recognizer will respond with the value of the appropriate gesture. A posture is recognized by checking that each joint is within the active range for that posture. If all joints are within their respective active ranges, the posture is recognized. The gesture editor allows the user to create and edit new postures of this type.

The work space mapping package

Work space mapping is used to map device coordinates to environment coordinates in virtual environment user interfaces. In this type of interface three different coordinate systems are associated with the input and output devices.

The first is the device coordinate system. Most of the devices used in these interfaces have their own coordinate systems that depend upon their position within the room. For example, the DataGlove uses a Polhemus to sense the position of the user's hand. The Polhemus consists of two parts, a stationary source of electromagnetic radiation and a sensor mounted on the DataGlove. The hand position reported by the DataGlove is relative to the position and orientation of the source. Also, each device that uses a Polhemus will have its own coordinate system based on the position of its source. Thus, if a user interface uses both a DataGlove and an EyePhone, the coordinates reported by these two devices for the same physical position in space will be different.

The second coordinate system is the room coordinate system, based on the room that contains the devices and the user. All the device coordinates can be converted to room coordinates to give one consistent coordinate system. In room coordinates the DataGlove and EyePhone would report the same coordinates for each position in space. The use of room coordinates allows us to correlate the inputs from several devices and simplifies the mapping to the coordinate systems in the application.

The third system is the environment coordinate system, used within the user interface.

It is necessary to have mapping between the three coordinate systems above. The mapping from device coordinates to room coordinates depends upon the position of the devices within the room. Since the input devices (the Polhemus sources) are not moved very often this mapping can be viewed as constant. The mapping of device coordinates to room coordinates is stored in a work space file that can be accessed by any application. The mapping from room coordinates to environment coordinates depends upon the individual user interface, and each application will have its own coordinate system based on the application domain.

The work space file

The work space file records the current configuration of the input/output devices within the work space. This information includes the position and orientation of their coordinate systems, along with their unit of measurement. The position and orientation of all devices is then determined with respect to this coordinate system. The work space is a text file with an entry for each of the input devices.

Program interface

The majority of programmers will not need to use the facilities described in this section because the high level support libraries for the devices already make use of them.

The mapping from room coordinates to environment coordinates can be performed by a 4×4 matrix. Directly specifying this 4×4 matrix is quite difficult, so the specification of this transformation is divided into three parts. The first part of the specification is the units used in the environment. This provides the scaling part of the transformation. The second part is the orientation of the environment coordinate system with respect to the room coordinate system. This is a purely rotational transformation. The final part is the position of the origin of the room coordinate system within the environment coordinate system. The result of the complete specification is a 4×4 matrix that can be used to map between the two coordinate systems.

Specifying the position of the origin of the room coordinate system within the environment coordinate system is more complicated than the other parts of the transformation.

First of all, specifying the position of the origin is not usually the most convenient way of specifying this mapping. As the origin is in one corner of the room it is unlikely that the user will ever get close to the origin, and will normally be restricted to one octant of the room coordinate space. Instead, it is advisable to specify the position of some fixed point in the room coordinate system, known as the reference point. For example, if the user is sitting in front of a display screen using a DataGlove to manipulate a three-dimensional model, the reference point should be close to the resting position of the hand. Similarly, when using a helmet-mounted display, the reference point should be close to where the user normally stands. Once the reference point has been specified, the corresponding point in the environment coordinate system can be specified to complete the transformation. To navigate within the environment coordinate space it is advisable to change the mapping of the reference point into the environment coordinate space. This is done while the user is interacting with the environment.

One of the problems of using the DataGlove and a workstation is 'turning' the workstation to view the required area of interest. To do this, the user sets up the work space file with a transformation from screen coordinates to room coordinates.

The data sharing package

The data sharing package is used to transfer data between the programs that make up an MR Toolkit application. For example, the data structure that represents the result of a computation will be required by both the master program and the computation program producing it. The abstraction provided by the data sharing package is that both programs are sharing the same data structure. Each program has its own copy of the data, which can be manipulated without affecting the data in other programs. At key points in the programs data structures are synchronized, in the sense that one program sends the contents of its version of the data structure to the other program, which then copies the values. So in the previous example, at the end of each time step in the computation, the computation program would send the most recent version of its data to the master program. The mechanics of this data transmission are hidden by the data sharing package. The only information that the programmer must specify is the data asynchronous. In the case of synchronous data structures, the receiving program has control over when the data structure is updated. In asynchronous data structures, the receiving program does not have control over the updating of the shared data structure. This is not as bad as it sounds, because the data structure can only be updated when one of the procedures in the data sharing package, or another package that uses it, is called. Asynchronous shared data structures are the default, and they are more efficient. Synchronous data structures give the programmer more control over when the data structure is updated, but they could lead to deadlocks in the program.

The sound package

The sound package provides a simple device independent interface to sound creation. The main purpose of the sound package is to produce sound effects that serve as feedback to the user's actions. As a result, a simple model of sound production is used based on fixed sound samples produced by a sound editor (or the routines in the sound package). The sound package provides a limited mechanism for changing the properties of the sounds while the program is running. The sound package is divided into two parts; a server that interfaces with the sound generation hardware, and a set of client routines that are loaded with the user's program. At present, a server that drives the sound generation hardware in a Silicon Graphics 4D/20 or 4D/25 is available. In future, servers for other devices will be produced, including a MIDI server.

The sound editor

Program interface

The program interface to the sound package is divided into two parts. The first part deals with the connect to the sound server and playing pre-computed sounds, while the second part deals with the production of sound samples.

5.8 WorldToolKit (WTK) Sense8 Corporation

Sense8 Corporation have developed a toolkit called WorldToolKit (WTK) for virtual environment applications. At a basic level it can be considered a collection of over 400 functions written in 'C'. However, from a user's point of view WTK provides a complete application development environment for synthesizing virtual environments. An important aspect of this package is that it is hardware independent and will run on a range of graphics platforms from 486, 50 MHz personal computers using graphics accelerators to Silicon Graphics workstations. This means that development can be undertaken on lower cost platforms and the software later moved onto specific higher performance target machines. Application requirements will dictate the host platform to be used.

A typical WTK-based system will consist of the following components:

- Host computer
- WTK library

- Host computer
- WTK library
- 'C' compiler
- 3-D modelling package
- Image capture hardware/software
- Bitmap editing software such as Paint Box and, optionally, hardware accelerator graphics boards and memory management system

Although the user of WTK has to be a competent 'C' programmer, the package is an excellent system for those who want control over the creation of virtual environments at a detailed level and at a modest price.

5.8.1 Synthesis of the virtual environment

WTK is structured in an object–oriented naming manner. By applying an object–oriented naming convention, it is easier to maintain visibility at the programming level of what is taking place. The main classes are 'universe', 'object', 'polygon', 'vertex', 'path', 'sensor', 'viewpoint', 'light source', 'portal' and 'animation'. This means that WTK does not use inheritance or dynamic binding in the same way as object–oriented languages.

From a hierarchical point of view, the 'universe' is the uppermost class. Only one universe can be active within a WTK virtual environment. The universe is built from 'objects', including sensors, lights, animation sequences, portals, viewpoints, graphical objects, serial ports and others. In a sense, objects are the components of the virtual environment. However, a virtual environment can comprise several universes.

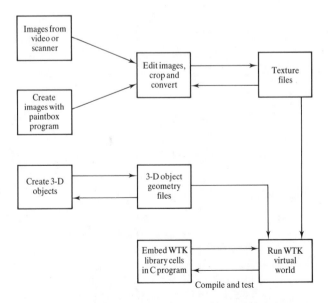

Figure 5.10 Creation of virtual environments with the WorldToolKit.

The universe contains all the objects of the virtual environment and is maintained by a 'simulation manager' within WTK. A function ('universe_new') is provided to create the universe. It performs an initialization operation on the graphics hardware, and sets up viewpoints and other internal processes within the WTK. Each WTK program must call the 'universe_delete' function prior to exiting the program in order to return the graphics hardware to its default state.

Figure 5.10 shows how the WTK is used to construct a typical virtual environment.

The universe is constructed from stationary and dynamic objects by the same CAD model. Each object is stored as a 'drawing interchange' (DXF) or WTK neutral file format (NFF) file. When the WTK application is executed, the individual object files are read in by two function calls. These are 'universe_load' for static objects and 'object_new' for dynamic objects. Dynamic objects are given behaviours through task assignments. Light objects are then added and the function call 'universe_go' is called to pass control to the real-time simulation manager.

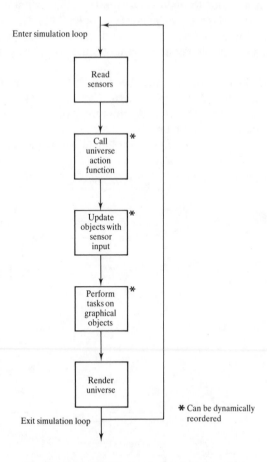

Figure 5.11 WTK simulation manager loop.

Simulation manager

The simulation manager is the most important part of WTK because it controls execution of the processes within the virtual environment. Figure 5.11 shows the flow through a simulation loop. The simulation loop can be executed once, or many times. The programmer can control events in the virtual environment by special action functions. During the simulation loop, individual objects can have task functions executed.

Objects in the universe

Geometric objects

Geometric objects are the basic elements of a universe. Some exist as stationary objects, while others exhibit dynamic behaviour. They can be organized in a hierarchical fashion, and can interact with each other. WTK allows a functional task to be assigned to control the behaviour of the object because objects can be dynamic.

Geometric objects are created using a CAD package that supports the Autocad DXF format or the WorldToolKit NFF. DXF is an interchange format that has been adopted by many CAD package manufacturers. All objects are created in the same manner as static objects. A library of objects can be maintained by saving individual DXF files, allowing easy addition or subtraction from a given virtual environment.

To improve the visual appearance of the object, it is possible to apply textures to the faces of an object. Textures can be derived from a variety of sources, including a video camera, a scanner or a 'paint box' program. WTK currently imposes a restriction on the texture resolution of 16×16 to 256×256 or any multiple. Any texture outside this can be converted by utilities supplied in the library. Higher resolution textures can be synthesized by using several texture patches, each texture pattern being between 16×16 to 256×256 pixels. The user will probably have to employ a paint box program at some stage to alter the texture pattern. This is a very simple process.

Textures can be displayed as ordinary, shaded or transparent. Ordinary texture appears at the same brightness irrespective of the shading value assigned to a polygon, while shaded textures are displayed at full brightness only when they are saturated with sufficient light. Transparent textures are applied when the source pixels are not black. The current version of WTK does not support textures that are both shaded and transparent.

A special type of object, known as a terrain object, can be created directly by WTK. Terrain objects can be defined from within WTK and can be used to create flat, random or data dependent terrains. These terrain options generate a flat 'checker-board' object, a random landscape terrain or a graphical terrain that is driven by user-supplied height information.

When an object is created in WTK, it is automatically loaded into the universe and becomes part of the simulation. In this context, if it is in view, then it is rendered, and it can perform a task. If it can perform a task, it can respond to inputs from sensor inputs, and can then interact with other objects.

During execution of the main simulation loop it is necessary to achieve as close to real-time performance as possible. When objects are too far in the distance for their detail to be seen, WTK uses a method of creating less complex objects from the detailed object. This process is called 'level of detail' and results in objects that are indistinguishable at an appropriate distance. By using the right combination of complex and simple objects, it is possible to improve display frame rate dramatically.

Geometric objects can have a behaviour associated with them, such as velocity. Once a behaviour has been associated it is called continuously throughout the simulation loop. The universe is a collection of ordered objects that must be operated on in a certain sequence, otherwise unexpected events can occur. Therefore, it is necessary to maintain an overview of how various objects are related to each other. This issue is very important when a compound geometric object is formed from simpler objects. The order in which the individual objects are updated will have an effect on the final position of the last object computed.

Sensor objects

In WTK the concept of a sensor is applied to any external device that can provide input into the computer, to control the position and orientation of objects. Sensory inputs can be used to modify the behaviour aspects of objects in the universe. Sensor objects can also be used to control the viewpoint of the observer. WTK supports a range of virtual environment peripheral devices, including:

- Advanced Gravis Mousestick (optical joystick)
- Ascension Bird tracker
- CiS Geometry Ball Junior
- Fake Space BOOM
- Logitech mouse
- Logitech 2D/6D head tracker
- Microsoft mouse
- Polhemus 3Space
- Spatial Systems Spaceball

Each of these input devices is supported by a special routine within the WTK library. The idea of writing an application program without having to worry too much about the specifics of a particular tracker device is very good for people who want to create virtual environments quickly. To link in a position tracking device it is only necessary to call the appropriate routine. Users who require more control over the interface performance will have to write their own dedicated code. As the WTK is 'C' based this will not present any integration difficulties.

During the development phase sensor objects can be interchanged. For example, a mouse could be switched for a head tracker. The user does not have to worry about whether the sensor works as an absolute positioning device, or as a relative or incremental positioning device. This makes it easier to debug applications.

WTK is designed so that it does not impose too great a time on real-time critical elements, such as those sensor devices that have to be directly coupled to a visual image. System lag will be a function of the type of sensor device used, interface standard, processing platform and efficiency of the sensor interface software. No performance parameters have been given. A series of functions have been provided to help programmers who require very fast update rates to construct custom sensor drivers.

Lights

WTK provides two forms of lighting models. One is an ambient light, where a background light is used to illuminate all polygons within the scene equally, despite their position or orientation. The second model is for any number of directed light sources that can be placed anywhere within the environment with a controlled position and orientation. Whenever new lights are added, or a directed light is moved, the shading of all graphical entities is computed. Polygons that get in the way of the light source (or in the way of another polygon) do not result in a shadow being created. This means that it is not possible to model shadows that occur in the real world.

A light can be attached to a sensor object so that it can be moved around within the scene. It is very easy to attach a geometric object to the same point as a sensor directed light source.

Viewpoint object

The viewpoint object allows the user to specify viewing geometries so that the virtual environment can be seen from any position, orientation and viewing angle. Several different viewpoints can be maintained within a universe but only one can be active at any one time. The user must specify the following parameters:

- Position: viewpoint position such as the left or right eye.
- Orientation: viewpoint direction.
- Direction: The user's viewpoint is a unit vector, which is an orientation composed of a viewpoint direction and a twist about this vector.
- Angle: Half angle of the display measured between the centre of the display screen and the left- or right-hand edge.
- Hither clipping plane: This is sometimes known as the near clipping plane. Drawing operations are clipped if they appear between the user and the hither clipping plane.
- Stereo: Defines whether the view is part of a stereo pair or to be displayed as a single display.
- Parallax: Defines the distance between positions from which the left and right eyes are drawn. This parameter is only used for stereoscopic applications.
- Convergence: This parameter defines the offset in screen pixel terms between the left and right eyes, and is only used for stereoscopic applications.

Viewpoints can be attached to sensor objects, so that the viewpoint can be dynamically changed in accordance with the movement of the sensor. For example, a viewpoint can be attached to a space tracker mounted on the head. This produces a visually coupled system. Several functions are available to manipulate the viewpoint as required by the application programmer.

Interaction with objects in the universe

The majority of virtual environment applications require objects in the universe to be able to interact with other objects. These objects may be under the control of the user or completely autonomous. When they collide with one another WTK has to perform tests to work out the intersection points. This feature can have an impact on the overall dynamic performance of the toolkit. If there are many polygons in a complex object, WTK must test for intersections with every polygon of the object.

A full range of mathematical functions are available within WTK to manage the dynamic behaviour of objects, and for dealing with 3-D manipulation tasks.

Entering another universe: Portals

The idea of a universe in WTK is essentially an abstract concept where all operations, and dynamic behaviour, are confined to a local environment. It is possible to 'join' adjacent universes together. Moving between different universes is achieved by 'portals', which are assigned to specific polygons. When the user's viewpoint crosses the designated polygon the adjacent universe is entered. Each universe can be considered as a separate entity and can have different rules or dynamic behaviour imposed on its objects. In many ways, the idea of a portal is rather like walking through a door into another room, except that the constants of one room can be very different from those of the other. It is possible to create several smaller universes together to make one large virtual environment.

Performance measures

When dealing with a real-time programming environment, it is very important to be able to determine iteration time of the whole (or parts) of the program. This allows the programmer to tune the application code to achieve maximum performance. WTK provides a series of utilities to time various stages of execution.

Other performance improvement features have been incorporated into WTK. One is an adaptive display resolution scheme which increases resolution when the scene does not change or move. (Obviously, for very fast head movements it may not be appropriate to draw and render an object at the highest resolution. During such movements it is likely that higher update rates will be more important.) In some applications it will be important to disable this feature. Therefore, library routines are available to provide an override.

5.9 Software Systems MultiGen

MultiGen produced by Software Systems is an interaction tool used for the creation and editing of visual system databases. Different versions of MultiGen are available to suit a range of platforms and applications. From a user's point of view, MultiGen is a very powerful 3-D modelling tool. Each implementation is based on a common user interface with a specific software subsystem to suit a particular platform. One of the advantages of the MultiGen product is that a user buys a basic 3-D modelling package and then buys specific extension tools to tailor the overall package to meet a particular application. MultiGen is probably one of the best 3-D modelling packages in the world and has become something of a standard in the field of flight simulation. Although it is quite expensive, the ease with which sophisticated models can be created more than repays the initial purchase cost. It is easy to overlook the time it takes to create complex models for use in a virtual environment. By employing well designed tools such as MultiGen for the creation of virtual environments and objects, it is possible to save both time and money.

The MultiGen modeller is not described in this book, because space limitations prevent a full examiniation of its many features. The interested reader is advised to contact Software Systems (or one of their distributors) and ask for a demonstration.

5.9.1 Digital Terrain Elevation Data (DTED) option

The terrain option allows a user to incorporate the Defense Mapping Agency (DMA) Digital Terrain Elevation Data (DTED) into a MultiGen file. DTED is a file that contains a grid of elevation spot height data set at fixed intervals to provide contour information for a given region. Each file represents a 1×1 degree area of the earth. The dimensions of the file depend on the longitude of the cell represented. From $0°$ to $50°$ North there are 1200 spot heights in both x and y. However, from $50°$ to $70°$ there are 600 spot heights in x and 1200 spot heights in y.

While considerable areas of the earth are available from a DTED database, it is not feasible to represent all the earth in the memory of a graphics platform. The sheer bulk of the data would overwhelm even the best available machines. Therefore, in order to keep the resulting polygon count down to an acceptable level, the user must select an area of interest.

The first object of the DTED is to convert DMA DTED from a standard format to the internal format of MultiGen. This means that the special tools available in Multigen can be used to process the data set. Once the elevation spot height data is converted to the MultiGen format, it is necessary to use either a polygon mesh (Polymesh) algorithm or a Delaunay algorithm to convert it into a polygonal data base. The Delaunay algorithm converts the spot data into triangles that fit the terrain efficiently. If the texture option is available, it is possible to texture the terrain automatically.

The Polymesh algorithm creates square terrain objects consisting of one, two or four polygons. The size of each object is a function of the post spacing. When the vertices of the polygon are coplanar, one polygon is created. If the vertices are not coplanar then the polygon is split into two. However, if the area contained by the mesh contains a peak, a fifth point is added and the area is split into four polygons. This process is used to convert the entire database into polygonal form.

The Delaunay algorithm works by converting the data into triangles by searching for areas of high curvature, edges of flat areas, ridges and valleys. It tends to be favoured because it produces a more accurate representation of the original data set than the Polymesh algorithm.

To ensure that maximum graphics throughput is maintained, it is possible to invoke up to three levels of detail switching. The converted polygonal data set can be projected onto either a flat earth, flat earth skewed, round earth, Lambert or a Universal Transverse Mercator (UTM) projection.

It must be appreciated that considerable amounts of data will be processed with this MultiGen option and it will take many minutes to process. Some versions of the DTED incorporate an area block batch processing mode, which fully automates the process. The tool is extremely powerful because it allows area blocks to be processed into several files. When the area blocks are processed together the batch mode ensures that one area will sit alongside another area without any holes appearing at any level of detail. Undertaking this task manually is extremely tedious and time consuming.

5.9.2 Digital Feature Analysis Data (DFAD) conversion option

MultiGen is configured to allow a DMA and Digital Feature Analysis Data (DFAD) to be imported into the modelling tool. This means that a designer can readily incorporate real-world data into a virtual environment.

DFAD is frequently referred to as cultural data because it comprises items such as roads, buildings, rivers and forests. By using the DFAD option it is possible to add cultural data to an outside world terrain display quickly. The coordinate system of the MultiGen modelling tool enables a user to correlate the latitude and longitude of cultural data to the corresponding latitude and longitude of the terrain display. A full range of tools is available to facilitate the process of laying cultural data onto the terrain. Many of the operations required in achieving the matching and the mapping of the two sets of data are fully automatic and are executed at the press of a key on the computer keyboard. For people wanting to create or populate their own terrain displays, it is a simple matter to use the manual editing features of the package.

5.9.3 Texture option

Many graphics platforms offer sophisticated real-time texturing hardware to improve the realism of computer generated displays. The performance of graphic systems is limited in terms of the number of polygons that can be drawn at any one time. Previously, the only way to produce a realistic computer generated display was to increase the number of polygons used to represent the object. Unfortunately, many thousands of polygons are required to produce a realistic image, and when real-time updates are needed, the graphics platform suddenly becomes very slow. Modern graphics platforms incorporate sophisticated texturing hardware that allows two-dimensional image data to be mapped over polygons. This means that a smaller number of polygons can be used and suitably textured to improve the realism of the object, while high throughput rates in the graphics systems are maintained.

The MultiGen texture option allows two-dimensional image data to be derived from a variety of sources and mapped onto the polygons in a visual database. Special editing tools are provided to modify textures or perform image processing operations on the two-dimensional image data sets. The texture option associates texture patterns with a given database by means of texture palettes. A maximum of 16 texture palettes can be assigned to a database file. Each palette contains 256×256 texels (one pixel is equivalent to a texel), and can hold a maximum of 64 texture patterns. A texel is the smallest unit of resolution used to define a texture pattern.

In order to impose a texture pattern onto a polygon, it is necessary to map a number of texels onto a number of pixels. The mapping of texels to pixels need not necessarily be one to one.

A useful feature of the texture option is the ability to make a texture pattern transparent. When this is coupled with the lighting and material models of the MultiGen modeller, it gives the designer considerable power to create extremely realistic looking objects. The designer can position, orientate, scale and shear a texture pattern onto any object. The texture pattern can be extended or replicated to fill user-selected faces of a range of polygons. Surface projection, spherical projection and radial projection tools are also available to map the texture onto a polygon. Other tools allow the designer to create or modify texture patterns. These tools are similar to 'Paint Box' type display editing programs, except that a range of image processing routines are available, such as warping, perspective corrections and histogram equalization.

In the opinion of the author, adding textures to a virtual environment image can transform the appearance of the virtual world dramatically, making it more readily acceptable to the user. As well as moving away from cartoon-like images, the correct use of texture can actually improve the update rate.

5.10 Gemini Technology Corporation Generic Visual System (GVS)

In order to produce an integrated virtual environment display it is necessary to take discrete 3-D objects and integrate them to form an interactive visual display. There are several ways of achieving this, the most laborious of which is to convert the 3-D data set into a display list and use this within a standard graphics environment. This approach is very time consuming because it relies on the manual creation of 3-D objects using low level graphics routines. Furthermore, it is often difficult or impractical to modify such objects after they have been created.

A more effective approach is to employ a 3-D modelling package to create the virtual objects and devise a means of integrating these into the virtual world. Gemini Technology Corporation have developed a product called a Generic Visual System (GVS). The aim of this tool is to produce a real-time visual simulated environment with minimal levels of coding. Their goal has been to ensure that minimal software is required to bring a visual database on line. The emphasis has been on employing high level tools to provide a visual system that is connected to a distributed computing environment. Although GVS was written for flight simulator applications, it has been used for virtual environment applications by the author and his team of researchers at British Aerospace, Brough, UK. The results have been very encouraging.

When GVS is coupled with a sophisticated 3-D modelling tool, it becomes one of the most powerful software environments for creating and interacting with a virtual environment.

In order to understand the GVS concept a number of definitions must be considered:

- Camera: A camera is a GVS resource which controls viewer position and orientation, as well as angle of view.

- Channel: A channel controls display geometry features such as display twist, display shear, viewpoint, near and far clipping planes and current viewing camera.

- Level of detail: This refers to automatic switching between levels of detail according to viewing distance.

Behind GVS lies a kernel model which undertakes most of the work in creating the virtual environment. The kernel is partitioned into a number of facilities that 'sit' on the host platform (see Figure 5.12).

A facility is essentially a piece of software which manages a GVS resource. It has the following elements:

- Database
- Initializing routines
- Manipulation routines
- Processing routine
- Shutdown routine

The facilities may be described as follows:

- GVS facility: The kernel facility provides high level execution control of a GVS application. Normally the user does not need to make a change to this part of the kernel. However, should some unusual applications require sophisticated operation, then this can be easily incorporated into the main routines.

Figure 5.12 GVS kernel manager.

- User facility: The programmer gains access to GVS via the user facility which allows specific initializing code to be inserted, followed by code for creating resources.

- Object facility: The object facility takes care of automated scene management object dynamics and articulated motion. Each object can have one or more levels of detail specified and, equally importantly, automatic object culling. This ensures that valuable machine resources are not wasted on drawing objects when they cannot be seen, or are too small to be resolved by the display. An important feature of this facility is the ability to assign equations of motion to each object. Therefore, it is possible to provide objects or parts of objects with motion behaviour. Provided one knows of a suitable motion equation for a particular movement, very realistic motions can be created, such as joint articulation around a pivot point or an object falling under the influence of gravity.

- Material facility: Objects imported into GVS from Multigen retain their material characteristics and it is possible to apply material definitions to the drawing primitives created through GVS. The following properties are provided: ambient colour, diffuse colour, emissive colour, specular colour, reflectivity coefficient and transparency effects.

- Texture facility: This facility is identical to the material facility except that imported objects retain texture components and GVS drawing primitives can be textured.

- Import facility: From a user's point of view, the import facility is probably one of the most important elements of the GVS kernel because it allows detailed models/objects and terrain models to be brought into a GVS environment.

- Scene facility: The scene facility creates scenes that are controlled by the user. Each scene is a collection of objects brought together in a user-specified manner. A virtual environment display is composed of a number of scenes. The scene facility is responsible for a number of low level tasks such as field of view culling, and restricting drawing operations to the displayed field of view.

- Light source facility: In order for the objects to become visible, light sources must be used with the scene created by GVS. The user has control over the colour of the light source, intensity, type (either local or infinite), position/orientation of light source and an ambient colour. It is easy to set up lighting conditions merely by creating the light source, and setting the position (if it is a local source) or defining a direction if it is an infinite source. The programmer then specifies the colour of the light source and ambient colour before adding the light to the scene or scenes.

- Camera facility: The camera facility in GVS is an interesting way of controlling what is displayed. Any number of cameras can be supported. Each camera controls the position and orientation of an eye point. For instance, two cameras could be set up to represent the left and right eye views, the camera position being controlled by the user's head position and orientation. A camera can track single or multiple objects as they move, or even be fixed to moving objects. The camera facility as implemented by GVS should not be underestimated. It is an extremely powerful, yet easy to grasp, concept for controlling viewing in a virtual environment. To give an idea of the flexibility of the camera system, consider a camera mounted on the end of a robot arm, consisting of an end effector, wrist joint, forearm, upper arm and shoulder joint. The user need not worry about the conversion of one axis set to another, from the end effector through to the shoulder joint. The camera facility takes care of this, converting the camera axis world coordinates.

- Channel facility: Close inspection of many software packages designed for so-called virtual environment applications reveal a lack of routines or facilities to tailor the displayed images to suit helmet-mounted displays. Other packages are fine for totally overlapping binocular viewing devices, but when partially overlapping displays are used, the programmer encounters problems. These problems become worse when the optic axis is not perpendicular with the projection plane. The GVS channel facility allows the programmer to assign a particular GVS camera to a channel and apply display twist angles or off axis projection connections to the image. In this way it is possible to accommodate different binocular overlaps and off axis projection systems. For stereo applications, the user merely specifies two GVS cameras, one for each eye. Even if the two channels are driven by different graphics platforms, as long as they are running GVS, the channel facility permits easy matching between the left and right eyes. Any number of channels can be created. For example, it is possible to create one channel which represents the sort of view that a rear-view mirror would generate. This could be called up in a forward view channel as a sub-channel, creating a real-time mirror view.

GVS was originally designed for visual simulation applications such as flight, ship bridge, tank and driving display simulators. As a tool for these applications, considerable development time can be saved because most of the features needed to construct complex simulation environments are included in the GVS kernel. If GVS is coupled to a sophisticated 3-D modelling package such as MultiGen, then one has an extremely powerful toolset to tackle the majority of visual simulation applications.

The author and his team at British Aerospace, Brough, use MultiGen and GVS together to create virtual environments with surprising ease. Therefore, considerable manpower and effort is saved, particularly in relation to previously manually coded versions.

Examples of such virtual environments are shown in Plates 8 and 9. Plate 9 shows that a person can sit in the virtual cockpit, which has been modelled to the nearest millimetre. In Plate 8 the virtual cockpit is shown situated in the aircraft. The person sitting in the virtual cockpit sees the virtual world in exactly the same way as if he or she were sitting in the cockpit of an ordinary aircraft.

5.11 Software considerations

This chapter has discussed a few examples of the software needed to create and maintain a virtual environment system. However, it is not just a matter of buying a range of virtual environment peripherals and then linking them together to form an interactive environment. Although it may be possible to construct very simple environments in this way, they will not serve any practical purpose.

The first requirement would be to define standards for the virtual environment so that there is a high level of consistency between the hardware, software and virtual environment. One only has to look at the proliferation of CAD standards to realize that there is an inconsistency. (Getting some CAD models into a particular CAD package can be extremely difficult or even impossible.) Generally, the most expensive component of a CAD system is the customer's database, because of the hours it takes to create the data. If the design information is to be used in a virtual environment, the user may not want to produce a new database or model, because of the cost. Therefore, the supplier of a virtual environment system must be able to import data from many different CAD systems. This may mean performing translation from one system to another.

It is not sufficient to have a mechanism to either import or create 3-D object data. It is necessary to link these 3-D objects together to form a dynamic environment, with each object possessing its own dynamic behaviour. This in turn may have an effect on the specification of other objects in the environment. Flight simulator manufacturers know only too well how detailed a flight simulator specification must be to describe accurately the system and the interacting elements. For the designer of a virtual environment, the problem is several orders of magnitude more complex because more variables have to be specified and controlled. As we are dealing with a human operator, who is very much part of the system, we must also bear in mind the performance requirements of the human interface. These must all be specified when defining the virtual environment. Regrettably, no standards currently exist and we must encourage each other to try to work to a set of common standards.

Probably one of the most difficult tasks in building a virtual environment is the definition of object/user interaction behaviour so that it can be captured and become part of the overall system. Conventional programming techniques do not lend themselves to this task, particularly if manual coding is required. There are probably too many complex interactions that have to be considered.

Visual programming tools such as VPL's Body Electric go a long way towards encapsulating the required behaviourial characteristics without the need for writing massive amounts of software. The idea of designing an interactive world with icons and using simple graphical constructs to link them together is very effective. The author's team constructed the interior of a virtual Rover 400 car using Swivel 3-D. Body Electric was used to define the behaviourial relationships between the individual objects, such as the steering wheel, gear stick and indicator stalks. (In fact, all the objects of the interior of a car.) It was possible to specify whether the user could move the objects as single elements or as groups. The fully interactive Rover 400 virtual car interior, shown in Plate 13, was constructed in a short space of time without writing any software.

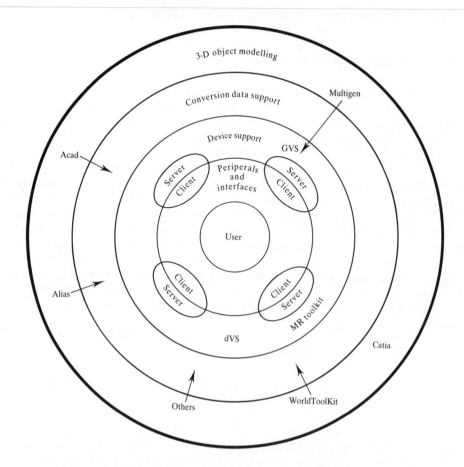

Figure 5.13 Suggested virtual environment toolkit configuration.

The power of modern visual programming tools must not be underestimated, both in terms of the amount of conventional programming effort that can be saved, and the consequential reduction in timescale. Moreover, a distinct advantage is that people who need to construct complex virtual environments can do so without necessarily having a very high degree of computer programming skill. In fact, computer programmers are probably the wrong type of people to construct virtual environments, because they are unlikely to appreciate the subtle features of a display that a vision scientist would consider important. Consequently, the efforts of the programmer should be directed towards producing the high level tools that a virtual environment scientist might need.

If the author were to propose a hybrid virtual environment development system, he would suggest using the following features 'extracted' from the packages described in this chapter. They would be enhanced and integrated.

- MultiGen: 3-D modelling objects with features such as terrain, lighting and texture models.

- Body Electric: Visual programming of the interaction/behaviourial environment.

- MR Toolkit: Low level peripheral device support.

- GVS: Visual scene management.

- dVS: Parallel processing communication environment.

Whether or not this suggestion represents an optimum configuration has yet to be determined. However, it is hoped that sufficient software companies will take up the challenge and produce a full integrated suite of tools. Figure 5.13 shows the proposed virtual environment toolkit.

5.12 Summary

Cost-effective development of virtual environments will require a suite of development and support tools, to allow the creation of components or objects within the environment as 3-D models. Standard CAD models may not be appropriate for applications where complex dynamics or behaviour rules are bound with the object. Dynamic objects will require some form of specification to describe their motion and behaviour within the virtual environment. When haptic/kinaesthetic interfaces become available it will be necessary to incorporate these attributes into the 3-D model database. If a realistic acoustic environment is to be modelled, then it may be necessary to model the acoustic properties of each object. A very interesting aspect of a virtual environment database is the way in which interactions should be specified. Very little work has been undertaken to develop a grammar or language to convey interaction. At present interaction is coded within the application program and will be difficult to move to another system. Until a universal (or standard) database format can be devised, there will be a requirement for translator programs to convert from one CAD system to another. Developments in spatial scanning systems (that can determine the profile of a real object and produce a database representation) will save considerable time and allow existing objects to be captured very quickly.

Modelling of objects in the virtual environment will probably remain the most time consuming task, hence, the most expensive. Modelling for other non-virtual environment applications certainly illustrates this point. There will be considerable overlap between the requirements of future CAD systems and those for a virtual environment. Provided that a standard database format can be agreed, these requirements will converge.

At the moment, modelling tools used for virtual environment applications are designed to be used outside the virtual environment. There may be considerable advantage in being able to design while in the virtual environment, and then update the product database accordingly. None of the available tools support this, although they do allow a designer to manipulate objects within the virtual environment. Nevertheless, this is a long way from interactive design.

Some virtual environments will support multiple users simultaneously, giving each person their own unique viewpoint. The virtual environment software must be able to support multiple viewpoints across different graphics platforms, and maintain a consistent database across them.

The creation of a virtual environment from separate objects is a logical approach but the process can be daunting. Most of the toolkits available to construct a virtual environment rely on associating 3-D objects with behavioural constraints. This is undertaken at a 'C' programming level. A more attractive approach is to employ a visual programming language, rather like Body Electric as used by the VPL RB2 system.

It will be important to achieve real-time or close to real-time performance. Tools will be required that allow the performance of the hardware and software to be measured. These tools will probably make use of special hardware within the graphics platform to give very accurate timing information. It may not be sufficient to rely on software timing loops to quantify performance.

Recommended further reading

Ellis S.R., ed. (1991). *Pictorial Communication in Virtual and Real Environments*. London: Taylor and Francis

Foley J.D., Van Dam A., Feiner S.K. and Hughes J.F. (1990). *Computer Graphics: Principles and Practice*. Wokingham: Addison-Wesley

6   The Realities of Virtual Reality

Objectives

The objective of this chapter is to develop an awareness of the current problem areas within the virtual environment field. Some problems are entirely due to the limitations of the technology, while others are caused by inherent features of the man–machine interface. By understanding where difficulties arise and how to take precautions against them, the quality and acceptability of virtual environment systems could be substantially improved. Several problems arise from the general lack of agreement on performance definitions and how a system should be measured. This leads to difficulty in comparing one system or component against another. If technology is to move forward then we need a series of common performance definitions so that task requirements can actually operate in these terms. Manufacturers will in turn be able to deliver the performance required rather than having to make their own estimates without considering the end application.

6.1 Introduction

Much has been written about virtual reality recently. In fact, the subject has received almost unprecedented press coverage, and quite outrageous claims have been made about the capabilities of systems. However, examination of some current virtual environment systems reveals that a number of fundamental issues need to be resolved. Quite apart from the obvious limitations in technology, the underlying human factors issues are little understood. It is tempting to separate the engineering issues from the human factors, but virtual environments involves a subtle blend of a range of disciplines. The freedom offered to the designer of virtual environment systems is almost unlimited in terms of how to represent the virtual environment.

To reproduce a real environment in every aspect would demand incredible computational and graphics performance. It is likely to be some time before this level of performance becomes available. For some applications it may be possible to employ a simpler environment that has been specifically tailored for the task. Through understanding of the human factors issues, it should be possible for the technology to be driven in a direction that leads to the hardware that satisfies a particular requirement. The total cost of a virtual environment system is likely to be the most significant factor for most customers.

6.1.1 Critical factors: Performance requirements

When specifying a virtual environment system many parameters are important, including:

- Image quality: jitter, jumping, blur.
- Display scene motion: vestibular/ocular conflict.
- Scene representation.
- Symbology artefacts: shape, size, opaque/transparent, update.
- Control mechanisms: zoom, declutter, cueing.
- Use of central and peripheral vision.
- 3-D and binocular disparity cues.
- Sensor fusion.
- Image stabilization.
- Head position sensor phase lag.

Ignoring these and other parameters will result in a system that does not fulfil the original objectives. Generally speaking, these parameters are task dependent, so a prior knowledge of the key task issues is of vital importance.

6.1.2 Critical factors: Human factors requirements

The key to the success of any virtual environment system is a detailed understanding of the complex human factors issues. Failure to take these issues into account will ultimately result in a system that is difficult and awkward to use. The following factors are but a few of the many that have an impact on the user interface. These are contrast, resolution, stability, registration, field of view, colour, collimation, eye relief, exit pupil, distortion and rendering. Moreover, these factors have a bearing on the technology used for the virtual world systems. Specialist human factors engineers readily acknowledge the psychological issues of the man–machine interface. Whereas traditional man–machine interfaces have relatively few variables, the virtual system offers an almost infinite number of choices to the designer. Hence, it is extremely important to understand the relationship between the desired psychological characteristics and psychological artefacts introduced as a result of limitations in technology.

Before a serious virtual environment application can be developed to a production standard, it is crucial that adequate prototyping is undertaken to understand where potential problems may occur. Another benefit from the prototyping stage is that the customer can see the virtual environment system. This will allow a better understanding of the customer's needs. It is not uncommon for a customer's conceptual visualization of a virtual environment application to be unclear. The prototyping stage is a cost effective way of deriving the specification for the final system.

6.1.3 Critical factors : Engineering requirements

While it is tempting to integrate all sorts of technologies onto the head coupled unit there are many major drawbacks. For example, if weight and centre of gravity distribution are not considered, problems will occur. The final head coupled unit must be lightweight (ideally less than 1 kg), comfortable to wear and a correct fit. Individual head sizes, shapes and inter–pupillary distances vary considerably. It is also desirable to engineer a system that does not require any form of adjustment.

An interesting point to note is that not everyone has the capacity for 3-D perception. Construction companies routinely screen workers with a stereopsis test to check whether potential staff will be able to control cranes. Depth perception is extremely important.

Examination of most helmet-mounted display systems reveals one of the fundamental limitations of current technology: small full colour, medium to high resolution display devices are not yet available. If a colour display is used for a helmet-mounted display the resolution will be quite low. Fibre coupled displays are an exception to this because they can 'relay' a high resolution full colour image from an 'off the helmet' image source to the helmet-mounted display. Furthermore, the weight that can be supported by the head limits the amount of equipment that can be integrated. If a very high resolution must be used, then current helmet-mounted displays must be ruled out unless fibre coupled displays can be used. Several new display technologies are starting to emerge but these must be developed further before they can be considered. A possible solution might be to use a counterbalanced CRT stereoscopic viewer such as that developed by Fake Space Laboratories for NASA Ames. This system retains the advantages of a visually coupled system while maintaining high resolution. For some applications it might be preferable to transfer from one task to another by moving a counterbalanced display into the user's field of view. (Obviously, with a helmet-mounted display it would be necessary to don and doff the helmet.)

6.2 Virtual environment displays

The human observer is very critical of a visual image. Even though there are few standards in determining factors such as acceptable image quality, almost everyone has their own interpretation of what is acceptable. It is unfortunate that we are unable to put a definitive standard forward because this would help display manufacturers to concentrate on the critical issues. Clearly, we must be able to relate measurable physical quantities to the subjective opinions of human subjects. This will require the development of a series of metrics to measure human performance. However, much can be gleaned from the television broadcast industry, where considerable work has been undertaken to develop metrics for issues such as display quality.

6.2.1 Display Resolution

The definition and measurement of display resolution has led to considerable confusion. Parameters such as modulation transfer function (MTF), optical line pairs, spot size and television lines are all in common usage.

Photographic or optical systems frequently use the optical line pair, which consists of one white and one dark line of equal width. Therefore, resolution is defined in terms of the number of line pairs per inch or millimetre. This relationship is only valid for lines of a rectangular luminance profile. Certain display devices, the CRT in particular, have a spot brightness that conforms to a Gaussian distribution luminance profile. In this case, it is necessary to specify the line width at a standard luminance level, usually taken as 50% peak luminance.

Not surprisingly, the number of lines differs from the value given by an optical line pair or by the television line resolution. The latter is simply based on the limiting resolution of minimum resolvable black and white line pairs derived from a standard television test chart or card. To illustrate the confusing situation, a system with a resolution of 416 optical line pairs will have 1000 TV limiting response lines.

Although there are some very high resolution virtual environment displays in existence, most helmet-mounted displays suffer from low resolution (see Chapter 4). For example, people who participate in virtual reality arcade games in the belief that they will experience the 'latest technology' are often very disappointed with the quality. What they do not realize is that the poor quality is due to low resolution in a cheap system.

Spatial filtering of LCD helmet-mounted displays

A number of manufacturers have developed a relatively low cost helmet-mounted display for virtual environment applications. LCD displays are used with a wide angle magnifier to present computer generated images to the user. For example, VPL quote a resolution of 360 × 240 for the Model 2 EyePhone. This figure is not the true resolution of the device: it represents the number of discrete red, green and blue colour element. In the television and computer graphics industry it is usual to specify resolution based on a colour pixel, each pixel comprising a red, green and blue primary colour element (see Figure 6.1). Calculated in this way, the resolution of the Model 2 EyePhone is approximately 208 × 139 pixels, considerably lower than the VPL quoted figures. VPL are not alone in making this mistake: all other helmet-mounted display manufacturers who employ LCDs have followed suit. The LCDs used in the EyePhone were originally designed for small television monitor applications. Normally the monitor user views the display about 18 inches from the eye. At this distance the visual angle subtended at the eye by an individual pixel is almost at the resolution limit of the eye.

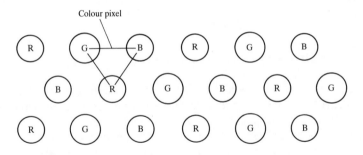

Figure 6.1 Arrangement of pixels in a typical LCD.

When a magnifying lens is placed in front of the LCD each colour pixel subtends an angle of about 0.25° at the eye. This explains why individual pixels can be seen very clearly. To prevent this, it is necessary to reduce the resolving power of the optical system. Teitel (1990) reports on the four approaches considered by VPL. These are:

- Defocusing.
- Scattering diffusers.
- Wavefront randomization.
- Wavefront randomizer with spatial frequency enhancer.

There are problems associated with all of these approaches. Defocusing of the helmet-mounted display results in considerable eyestrain because the eye will try extremely hard to bring the image into sharp focus. If each LCD element is assumed to emit light in a 90° cone then in order for the diffusing screen to work, the screen must be placed about 1 pixel diameter from the LCD. The active area of the LCD is followed by a colour mask, glass substrate and a polarizer. The dimensions of these components prevent the diffuser screen from being placed in the correct position. Placing a diffuser on top of the LCD also results in low contrast defined images.

A wavefront randomizer comprises a series of small prisms, which deflect light by a small amount. It can combine each individual colour element into a single colour pixel. It is necessary to match the characteristics of the wavefront randomizer to the distance from the LCD display. Using wavefront randomizer materials results in the highest spatial frequency passed by the optical system of 0.5. Unfortunately, the image suffers from lack of detail.

It is possible to introduce high spatial frequencies artificially in an image by employing a pattern of opaque areas in front of the wavefront randomizer. This technique does not add in more information to the image but it can give an impression of added sharpness. Whether or not it improves the subjective nature of the image is not fully understood.

A further consequence of overlaying a fixed pattern over the LCD (which itself is based on a pattern arrangement) is the possibility of moiré fringing or patterning. In a stereo display application any disparity between the moiré pattern across each eye can lead to strange visual effects.

A possible solution is to employ random pattern opaque overlay. This can help to eliminate the moiré fringes produced with fixed pattern overlays. In some applications it is better to remove the randomizer material because this results in higher contrast displays.

Display structure effects on perceived eye level

It has been reported by Stoper and Cohen (1989) and more recently by Nemine and Ellis (1991) that a matrix or discrete optical structured array can bias the perception of eye level in the direction of the pitched array. Moreover, there is evidence that a single pitched line is just as effective at biasing the apparent eye level as a grid structure. An extremely important study conducted by Nemine and Ellis (1991) investigated the influence of a pitched optic array on gravity referenced kinds and amounts of optic structure. They found definite evidence that a pitched optic array does bias perception of the gravity referenced eye level, such that there is a deviation of apparent eye level from true gravity referenced eye level. The consequences of this effect on certain tasks or applications using the helmet-mounted display have yet to be fully understood.

6.2.2 Display field of view

Figure 6.2 shows the field of view of the CAE fibre optic helmet-mounted display, one of the widest field of view devices ever built. The instantaneous field of view is 120° × 60°. However, this is considerably less than the human field of view, as shown by the bold lines.

It is tempting to try to make the helmet-mounted display field of view match that of the human. However, this is not possible because of increased weight and reduced image source performance. Severe constraints would be placed on the optical design. Additional parameters would also have to be considered, such as image source resolution and binocular overlap. All the parameters governing the design of a helmet-mounted display are interdependent. It is not usually possible to alter one parameter without affecting another. It is for this reason that helmet-mounted displays have been slow to develop. The design requires great skill on the part of the designer and manufacturer across several disciplines.

If one has to accept a smaller field of view for the helmet-mounted display (as is the case for current designs) then it is very important to understand the effect this has on parameters affecting user performance. User performance will also be a function of the task to be undertaken.

Launching into the design of a helmet-mounted display without first considering the application is likely to lead to disappointment later on in the project. Many factors are intimately related to each other in the design of a helmet-mounted display. Simply selecting an arbitrary field of view may seriously affect the user's performance and cause a knock-on effect with other parameters.

Selecting the field of view of a helmet-mounted display

Incorrect specification of a display's field of view probably has the most detrimental effect on the user's performance, particularly where the extent of the virtual environment is considerably greater than the field of view of the display.

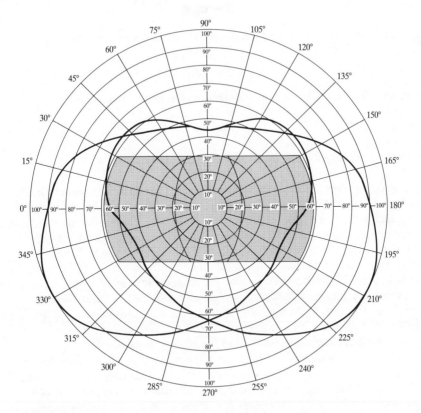

Figure 6.2 Human visual field of view with respect to helmet-mounted display.

To see and maintain a spatial awareness it is necessary for the operator to move his/her head. Selecting too small a field of view increases the amount and frequency of head movement. Selecting too large a field of view limits the effective resolution over the display area because of limited resolution displays. Therefore, field of view has a significant impact on the resulting specification of the other parameters of a helmet-mounted display. Wide fields of view place considerable demands on the image source, requiring an increase in luminance efficiency and resolution. Military cockpit applications generally demand the widest field of view, yet the priority is on weight reduction. Ground-based applications can usually tolerate an increase in weight. Irrespective of the environment the user's task and performance requirements dictate the actual field of view. (Figure 3.4 shows the field of view extent of the human visual system. The shaded area is the display's field of view.) It is not yet possible to manufacture a helmet-mounted display with this field of view that can be supported (unaided) by the head.

To achieve wide fields of view in helmet-mounted displays it is possible to produce partially overlapping display channels. Binocular vision is achieved in the central overlapping region whereas monocular vision is achieved in the periphery. Three common techniques are available to map the display system's pixels across the angular field of view. These are:

$$F - \tan\theta$$

where there is an excess of display elements at the edges of the field;

$$F - \sin\theta$$

where there is an excess of display elements at the edges of the field;

$$F - \theta$$

where the angular distribution of display elements is uniform.

$F - \tan\theta$ systems offer the best practical solution to the design of helmet display optics and can lead to simplifications in the optical design. This does not imply that the other mapping techniques are not appropriate. However, they will require additional transformation of the graphics image before it can be displayed on the helmet. While some graphics platforms can undertake the required transform in real time, using special hardware, other platforms have to undertake the transform with a software routine. This will obviously affect display update rate. Full binocular overlap systems can use other mappings to more closely match the user's eye resolution. In these systems the centre of the display offers the highest resolution. One word of caution, though; the operator's eyes tend to move within the visual field to points of interest. If these points of interest fall outside the high resolution patch then the display resolution will be very low. The operator will tend to look straight ahead so the benefit of using the eyes (in search type operations) will be lost. In many ways this effect is characteristic of limited field of view displays and the direction of gaze is constrained along the optic axis of the helmet-mounted display. Obviously, the operator's ability to do search and track operations will be affected. Perhaps a more difficult problem to address is the effect this will have on the operator's situation awareness.

Binocular display overlap

The human visual system has a region where images seen by one eye overlap those seen by the other eye. This is known as the binocular overlap region. To produce wide field of view displays some manufacturers produce a region of partial overlap.

Partial binocular overlap considerations

The design of binocular displays with a partial overlap has to take account of the visual requirements of the observer. There also needs to be an understanding of the potential sources of optical distortion, because this can lead to binocular disparity and binocular rivalry in the monocular/binocular regions.

A certain amount of binocular overlap is essential to stabilize the vestibular ocular reflex system, because without an overlap the eyes experience a muscular imbalance and the imagery may not fuse correctly. There is no evidence to indicate how much overlap is required for a particular task. Binocular overlaps in the range 50% to 100% are quite common. However, only a minimal amount of overlap is required to provide a fused image. Many experiments have been conducted to try to determine optimal values for partially overlapping systems; their results tend to disagree with each other. This is probably accounted for by other factors such as optical design effects, and alignment and image distortion variations between different helmet-mounted display systems.

A study by Knik (1984) investigated performance differences between helmet-mounted displays with partial overlaps of 25°–45°. No performance difference was noted for target tracking tasks. The partial overlap binocular helmet-mounted display can offer significant savings in mass while offering a wider field of view with no loss of resolution. However, the alignment, distortion compensation and binocular disparity effects of these systems require careful attention. As a general guide, whenever a moderately wide field of view is required it is probably better to employ a total overlap display system because then the binocular disparity effects are simplified. However, where very wide fields of view are required, a partial overlap solution is probably preferred, because overall mass is kept to a minimum.

Whenever partial overlap helmet-mounted display systems are being designed, it is very important to reduce disparities between the left and right eye. A particularly distracting phenomenon can occur with a raster-produced partially overlapping display. This is caused by the edge of the left eye overlaying the continuous image of the right eye and vice versa. One eye effectively sees the edge of the optical system against continuous imagery of the other eye. This situation gives rise to binocular rivalry and introduces dark bands on the outside edges of the overlap regions. After a period of time, these bands change in brightness and can become very prominent. Melzer (1991) refers to this effect as 'luning' and suggests that the crescent-shaped dark bands lie on the monocular sides of the binocular boundary. He suggests three possible solutions to the luning phenomenon, but the author can verify only the two given below.

Luminance roll off

The first potential solution is to reduce the contrast of the monocular/binocular edge. The luminance roll off can be achieved by placing suitable optical filters in the system or by applying electrical software compensations in the graphic system. Kaiser Electronics have found that a cosine taper of display luminance is optimal for minimizing luning effects. A secondary effect of luminance roll off is that a fuzzy image appears in the region of luning. However, this fuzziness is probably less objectionable than the crescent-shaped bands.

Contour lines

This method relies on drawing dark contour lines over the helmet-mounted display imagery, to separate the monocular imagery from the binocular imagery (see Figure 6.3). In the majority of cases, applying contour lines to the imagery completely eliminates luning effects. Considering the relative ease by which this method can be implemented, it should be given very serious thought.

Kaiser Electronics have conducted other trials to demonstrate that convergent partially overlapping binocular systems are less prone to luning effects than divergent systems.

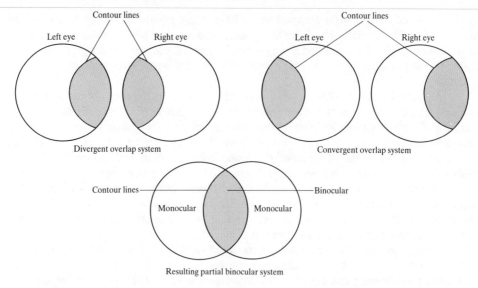

Figure 6.3 Illusionary contour lines present in a partial binocular overlap display.

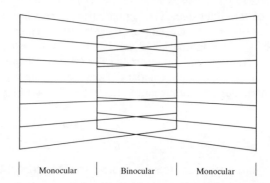

Figure 6.4 Trapezoidal distortion in helmet-mounted displays.

Trapezoidal distortion

Trapezoidal distortion is caused by tilting of the optical elements. To match imagery between the left and right channels, especially in the overlap region, some form of pre-distortion must be applied to the image prior to display (see Figure 6.4). A slight amount of trapezoidal distortion can be tolerated if the helmet-mounted display is a non-see-through system. If it is overlaid onto real-world objects, then misregistration effects become very annoying.

Effects of inter–pupillary distance (IPD)

The separation between a person's eyes, the inter–pupillary distance (IPD), has a wide variation. The average IPD is 63 mm, but it can range between 53 mm and 73 mm.

These variations mean that the exit pupil of the optical system must be large enough to be used by people within this range. If the exit pupil is not large enough, then some form of mechanical adjustment must be provided.

A person uses inter–pupillary separation as a basis to judge distances. Even though each person has a different IPD, the depth perception is the same.

If the images are at infinity and the optical system has a large exit pupil, a lateral change in eye position has no effect on the perception of images. However, if the image is not at infinity, then the varying IPD will mean that not all users will be able to fuse the left and right eye images correctly.

The solution is to take IPD into account and input the user's value before using the helmet-mounted display system.

Convergence correction

If a distant object is viewed by two eyes (unaided) the corresponding lines of sight to the left and right eyes are essentially parallel, whereas for near field objects the lines of sight converge. If a helmet-mounted display is taken where the optical axes are parallel for each eye then an image presented in the centre of each channel will be perceived at infinity. Few helmet-mounted displays are manufactured in this manner. They generally have their optical axes either divergent or convergent. Unless this is taken into account when the images are generated, the images will be perceived as coming from a near point or else will not be fusible in stereopsis terms. Divergence errors can also occur in vertical alignment. To correct for these effects the image must be transformed.

Field of view corrections

The user's eyes converge on near objects by swivelling inward while the lenses simultaneously accommodate to bring the objects into focus. However, in a helmet-mounted display the image appears at a fixed distance from the eye with respect to focus. In a real-world scene, objects appear at different positions. Whether this affects the user's performance still has to be determined.

It is uncommon for a helmet-mounted display to have a completely circular field of view because of the optical arrangement.

Due to necessary obscurations in the optical system caused by mounting components the virtual image may be truncated. These effects do not normally cause problems, except perhaps that displayed information invariably 'falls out' of the field of view, particularly when placed at the extreme edges of the display. However, very serious problems can arise when the display manufacturer takes steps to reduce the complexity of the optical system. To reduce complexity, weight and cost it is possible to undertake an optical design/graphics system trade-off exercise to make compromises in the optical design. Certain compensations can be performed by special graphics operations. An example is where specific optical geometric distortions (such as pincushion effects) are not corrected in the optical design. Not many high performance graphics systems are able to dynamically warp an image in real time without incurring a decrease in graphics performance. Obviously, by predistorting an image prior to presentation by the optical system it is possible to generate an undistorted image for the observer. If the graphics system can actually undertake this predistortion correction, the cost of the helmet-mounted display can be reduced. However, if the helmet-mounted display is used along with a graphics system that does not have this capability, real problems can arise.

Despite the excellent performance of the LEEP optical system, it does present a pincushion distortion effect. In the original application this was not important because the LEEP optics were used with predistorted photographs taken by a special camera. Many manufacturers of virtual environment helmet-mounted displays have simply used the LEEP optical assembly without any form of distortion correction. Users are generally unaware of the distorted images until a moving scene is observed, then some very strange peripheral effects can be seen. These distortions include severe barrel distortion effects at the edges of the display. Vertical structures in the image become curved at the edges of the display, then straighten out as the head is moved towards them, as they approach the centre of the display.

6.2.3 Distortion

Distortion correction considerations

Binocular disparity can be affected by the amount of distortion correction applied to a helmet-mounted display. For example in a 120° optical system as shown in Figure 6.5 a 1% distortion can lead to a horizontal disparity of 24'.

Binocular disparities arise from several defects in the optical design, such as:

1. Magnification differences between the left- and right-hand channels.
2. Left- and right-hand channel images are rotated relative to each other.
3. The optic axis of the left- and right-hand channels are misaligned with respect to each other.
4. The focus adjustment is not consistent between channels.
5. Luminance differences between channels.

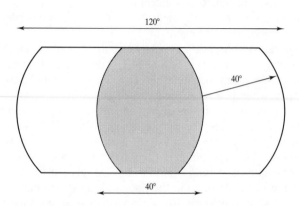

Figure 6.5 Distortion in a helmet-mounted display.

A key to the design of a helmet-mounted display is to understand what parameters a user is most sensitive to, and how the effects can be minimized by the design. Clearly, over- specifying a helmet-mounted display will have a knock-on effect on the cost. With the availability of high performance computer graphics systems it is feasible to consider applying certain distortion correction methods during display generation rather than trying to accommodate them in the optical design. The solution here is to minimize the optical distortion correction and employ corrections in the computer graphics system (where appropriate).

To a large extent this depends on the capability of the graphics system. It is possible to generate computational solutions for complex distortion corrections but the computation could take the most sophisticated graphics platforms several hours. This is obviously not appropriate for real-time applications.

Certain image sources enable a degree of electronic distortion to be considered. For instance, for CRT-based systems, special complex waveforms can be superimposed on the scan deflection signals. These require difficult calibration procedures.

Corrections to helmet-mounted displays based on LEEP optical systems

A number of helmet-mounted displays, particularly those employing the LEEP optical system (or its derivatives), present the user with a distorted field of view. The reason for this is that the actual optical system was designed for a specific wide field of view photographic camera where an inverse distortion transformation was applied to the viewing lens. For other applications, such as helmet-mounted displays, it is necessary to predistort the image presented to the viewing optics. Failure to do this can lead to a number of visual problems. Surprisingly, few users of the LEEP optical system actually take the distortion into account when designing their system. The distortion effect in the LEEP optical system has been published by Howlett, who designed the system (see Figure 6.6). At first, distortions may not be apparent and the user is completely unaware of their presence. There is also evidence that some users can become adapted to the distorted field. An example of this is when short-sighted people wear spectacles with a thick lens. Their spectacles cause quite severe distortion for peripheral objects. However, they usually adapt to the distortion effects after a few minutes. Occasionally, adaption can take several hours or days.

The mathematics described in the following section shows a technique that can be used to correct against the distortion effects caused by LEEP optical systems and their derivatives. The algorithms are a combination of separate correction algorithms calculated by Howlett, by Robinett (1992) and by the author. They also allow the user to set up the IPD by applying an offset in the X and Y axes of the display. However, it should be noted that although the algorithms appear reasonably straightforward, considerable computational performance is required from the graphics system if correction is to be employed in real time. In fact, very few graphics machines are able to undertake the polynomial transformation in real time. It is hoped that display system manufacturers will be encouraged to embody this transformation in dedicated hardware within their graphics platforms. The algorithms are intended to be of general purpose and appropriate for a range of helmet-mounted displays.

It is the responsibility of the system designer or programmer to obtain the necessary optical constants and display device specifications from manufacturers. However, the values appropriate for the VPL low resolution EyePhones are given by way of example in Table 4.9.

Referring to Figure 6.7, the case of a general-purpose magnifier placed in front of a display screen or image source is considered. Most image sources are of a rectangular format and a 4:3 aspect ratio is the most common.

In the magnifying situation, when the image source is placed between the lens and the focal point f, a point A in the image will be seen by an observer at O as a virtual image at point B. Given that the lens introduces a distortion, the task is broken down to one where the radial position of a pixel is related to its corresponding point in the virtual image by some functional relationship. This relationship is a feature of the magnification properties of the lens and its distortion characteristic.

The radial position P_{real} of a given pixel on the display source relative to the corresponding radial position of the pixel in the virtual image $P_{virtual}$ is shown in Figure 6.7. Because of the difference in aspect ratio it is generally more convenient to deal with normalized pixel positions.

The normalized position of the pixel P_{real} on the display source is given by P_{real_n} where:

$$P_{real\_n} = \frac{P_{real}}{\Delta_{real}}$$

where Δ_{real} is the object field width in the display source.

Similarly for the corresponding pixel in the virtual image plane:

$$P_{virtual\_n} = \frac{P_{virtual}}{\Delta_{virtual}}$$

where $\Delta_{virtual}$ is the object field width in the virtual image plane.

The nonlinear optical distortion normally associated with LEEP optical systems must be corrected by mapping all pixels on the LCD screen with a distortion correction function. The distortion correction function is the inverse of the image field distortion function; when it is applied the image appears correctly to the user.

The distortion correction that must be applied is dependent upon the optical distortions that are present. LEEP Optical Systems recommend that a third order polynomial approximation will suffice for most tasks.

The magnification of the optical system is:

$$M_{realvirtual} = \frac{\Delta_{virtual}}{\Delta_{real}}$$

(this is a paraxial relationship that strictly holds only for rays infinitesimally close to the optic axis.)

The distortion term (third order polynomial), the coefficient k_1, describes the amount of distortion present:

$$P_{virtual\_n} = P_{real\_n} + k_1 P_{real\_n}^3$$

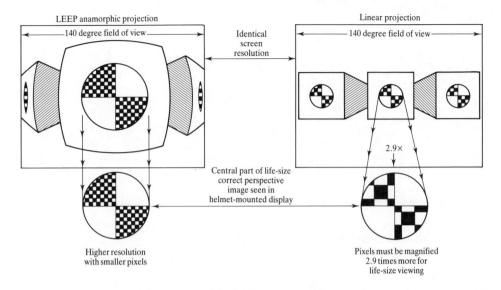

Figure 6.6 LEEP optical system anamorphic projection.

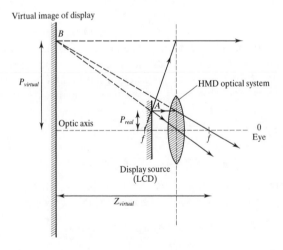

Figure 6.7 Relationship between display source and virtual image in a helmet-mounted display.

Expanding to rectangular coordinates (from Pythagoras theorem) gives:

$$P^2_{\text{real\_n}} = x^2_{\text{real\_n}} + y^2_{\text{real\_n}}$$

$$P^2_{\text{virtual\_n}} = x^2_{\text{virtual\_n}} + y^2_{\text{virtual\_n}}$$

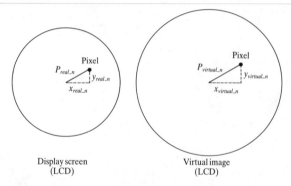

Figure 6.8 Relationship between pixel on image source and the virtual image.

Rewriting this expression gives:

$$P_{\text{virtual\_n}} = (1 + k_1 P^2_{\text{real\_n}})P_{\text{real\_n}}$$

The position of the virtual image of the pixel is given by (see Figure 6.8):

$$(x_{\text{virtual\_n}}, y_{\text{virtual\_n}}) = ((1 + k_1(x^2_{\text{real\_n}} + y^2_{\text{real\_n}}))x_{\text{real\_n}}, \; (1 + k_1(x^2_{\text{real\_n}} + y^2_{\text{real\_n}}))y_{\text{real\_n}})$$

from the position $(x_{\text{real\_n}}, y_{\text{real\_n}})$ of the pixel on the LCD screen.

The distance from the eye to the virtual image plane z_{virtual} is a constant. By combining the above equations it is possible to derive a function that gives the three-dimensional position of the virtual image pixel on the LCD screen $(x_{\text{virtual}}, y_{\text{virtual}}, z_{\text{virtual}})$ in terms of its screen coordinates $(x_{\text{real}}, y_{\text{real}})$. z_{real} is usually ignored since it is a constant.

Expressions for $x_{\text{virtual\_n}}$ and $y_{\text{virtual\_n}}$ can be considered as single valued functions of two variables.

$$(x_{\text{virtual\_n}}, y_{\text{virtual\_n}}) = D \, (x_{\text{real\_n}}, y_{\text{real\_n}})$$

The distortion correction function must be the inverse, that is D^{-1}. A polynomial approximation of the inverse is usually the most efficient to model on a computer.

$$r_{\text{real\_n}} = r_{\text{virtual\_n}} + k_2 \, r^3_{\text{virtual\_n}}$$

$$(x_{\text{real\_n}}, y_{\text{real\_n}}) = D^{-1} \, (x_{\text{virtual\_n}}, y_{\text{virtual\_n}})$$

$$(x_{\text{real\_n}}, y_{\text{real\_n}}) = ((1 + k_2(x^2_{\text{virtual\_n}} + y^2_{\text{virtual\_n}}))x_{\text{virtual\_n}}, \; (1 + k_2(x^2_{\text{virtual\_n}} + y^2_{\text{virtual\_n}}))y_{\text{virtual\_n}})$$

The two functions D and D^{-1} are not identical inverse third order polynomial approximations. The coefficients k_1 and k_2 have opposite signs.

If the graphics computer has spare memory capacity then a two-dimensional look up table for each of the output variables $x_{\text{real\_n}}$ and $y_{\text{real\_n}}$ can be used with interpolation between table entries.

This correction applies to a single eye system. However, the majority of helmet-mounted display systems are binocular devices. The user's eyes are displaced by a distance (IPD) that varies from user to user. Not all helmet-mounted display manufacturers overlap the left and right eye fields totally (that is, 100% overlap). Some manufacturers use partial overlap to give a wider field of view. To achieve the partial overlap manufacturers frequently rotate the optic axes of the left and right eye channels by a few degrees. Figure 6.9 shows the arrangement used by manufacturers who rotate outwards the two optical axes.

Since this arrangement is a partial overlap system it is important that pixels in the overlap region correspond exactly between the two channels. In other words a pixel A_1 in one channel and the corresponding pixel A_2 in the other channel must appear to the observer as though they exist at a single point C in the image. This implies that points B_1 and B_2 in the virtual image plane appear to be coincident.

To calculate the transformations for a binocular helmet-mounted display this procedure should be used. This procedure can be readily set up on a spreadsheet (see Table 6.1).

The distortion corrected images produced by the above technique are remarkable, but the computing power required to perform the correction in real time should not be underestimated. Howlett (1991) actually produces a much simpler algorithm that is a reasonably good first order approximation of the distortion. Moreover, it is computationally less intensive than the technique just presented.

Howlett's algorithm is:

$$R = F(A - 0.18A^3)$$

where R is the radial distance from the optic axis on the (nominal) focal plane of the observer, F is the axial focal length, and A is the angle of the collimated beam from the point being considered.

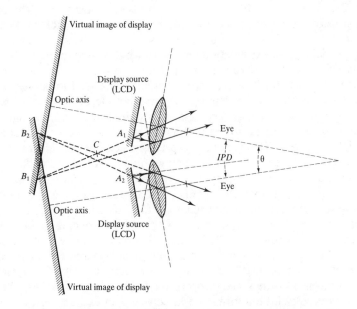

Figure 6.9 Helmet-mounted display with partially overlapping left and right eye fields.

This algorithm can be simply integrated into most graphic platforms with a minimal computational overhead. The user is advised to try to apply distortion corrections to their images; the results are well worth the effort providing unacceptable delays in the computation of the image are not introduced. It is not easy to give an indication of what is an unacceptable delay, because this depends on the task being undertaken.

6.2.4 Display contrast

The contrast of a display is a frequently overlooked parameter. For some applications, the ability of the display to correctly reproduce the grey scale information in a scene is a very important parameter. Failure to display all the necessary grey levels can lead to significant amounts of information being lost. To some extent, the display technology dictates the number of grey levels that can be resolved. Another important consideration is the nature of the background on which the virtual image is to be displayed. If, as in the case of the majority of virtual environment helmet-mounted displays, the image is displayed against a dark or black background, then display contrast (and brightness) can be considerably lower than that required for displays that work against full daylight ambient lighting conditions. This probably accounts for why LCDs are not normally used for viewing against full daylight scenes. Even so, LCDs tend to give lower contrast images than other display technologies even when used against a dark background. Some of the higher resolution LCDs give a lower display contrast than the lower resolution devices. Some people even prefer the lower resolution, higher contrast display to the high resolution, low contrast display. When the virtual imagery is viewed against a bright background it is important to use a display with a wide dynamic range in terms of its contrast and brightness capability.

On some CRT-based helmet-mounted displays the narrow spectral wavelength range of the CRT phosphor is filtered out of the outside world scene. The combiner is coated with a reflector tuned to the spectral emission of the CRT so that only that portion of the light is reflected into the eye of the user. This results in a very bright display that can be used in extremely high ambient lighting conditions. The technique is only really suited to monochromatic applications. However, several techniques do exist by which triple notch filters are used, although these tend to be very expensive.

One of the problems with displays that overlay the outside world scene is the wide dynamic control of brightness and contrast required to ensure that the display can still be seen. Automatic brightness/contrast control systems are not yet adequate for the majority of lighting levels. This is not so surprising when one considers the wide range of light levels that will be encountered in a helmet-mounted display's wide field of view.

When the user wants to display a video image on the helmet-mounted display it is important to match the gamma characteristics. Gamma is essentially a transformation function that describes the input/output relationship of the display device or the sensor. The designer of an ideal display system aims to produce an overall gamma of 1. In the case of a CRT-based system, the CRT gamma is approximately 2.2 and the camera gamma will have to be set at 0.4 to ensure a unity gamma. Failure to match the gamma will lead to a display system that does not operate linearly over the full dynamic range. In the worst case, most of the video information will be compressed into the black and white regions, with very little information in between. In extreme cases adjustment of the contrast and brightness controls will not provide any compensation.

Table 6.1 Corrections to helmet-mounted display: spreadsheet data.

Parameter	Symbol	Source of data
Display resolution (RGB pixels, not total number of RGB elements)	$H \times V$	Manufacturer's display specification
Optic axes angle	θ_{axes}	Manufacturer's display specification (or measure)
Eye relief	D_{er}	Manufacturer's display specification (or measure)
Field of view (maximum)	θ_{max}	Calculate from D_{er} and manufacturer's display Specification
Display image distance	$D_{display}$	Measure
Virtual image distance (from eye)	$D_{virtual}$	Calculate from $D_{display}$ and manufacturer's display specification
Magnification (transversal)	M	Calculate from $D_{display}$ and manufacturer's display specification
Optical distortion coefficient	k_1	Obtain from optical specification
Object field radius (maximum)	Δ_{real}	Obtain from optical specification
Virtual image field radius (maximum)	$\Delta_{virtual}$	$\Delta_{virtual} = M \times \Delta_{real}$
Inter–pupillary distance	IPD	Measure user
Display centre offset (from optic axis)	(D_{xreal}, D_{yreal})	Measure
Left-hand edge of display	(L_{xreal}, L_{yreal})	Measure
Right-hand edge of display	(R_{xreal}, R_{yreal})	Measure
Top edge of display	(T_{xreal}, T_{yreal})	Measure
Bottom edge of display	(B_{xreal}, B_{yreal})	Measure
Object height on display	P_{real}	$P_{real} = (x_{real}^2 + y_{real}^2)^{\frac{1}{2}}$
Normalized object height	P_{real_n}	$P_{real\_n} = P_{real}/\Delta_{real}$
Normalized virtual image height	P_{real_n}	$P_{virtual\_n} = P_{real\_n} + k_1 P_{real\_n}^3$
Angular position of point in virtual image	θ	$\theta = \tan^{-1}(P_{virtual}/D_{virtual})$
Angular position of display left-hand edge	θ_{left}	θ_{left} = from θ
Angular position of display right-hand edge	θ_{right}	θ_{right} = from θ
Angular position of display top	θ_{top}	θ_{top} = from θ
Angular position of display bottom	θ_{bottom}	θ_{bottom} = from θ
Vertical field of view of a single eye	$FOV_{vertical}$	$FOV_{vertical} = \theta_{top} + \theta_{bottom}$
Horizontal field of view of a single eye	$FOV_{horizontal}$	$FOV_{horizontal} = \theta_{left} + \theta_{right}$
Binocular overlap	$FOV_{overlap}$	$FOV_{overlap} = 2\theta_{left} - \theta_{axes}$
Binocular field of view	$FOV_{binocular}$	$FOV_{binocular} = 2\theta_{right} + \theta_{axes}$
Viewing transformation: translation	$M_{translation}$	$(\pm IPD/2, 0, 0)$
Viewing transformation: rotation	$M_{rotation}$	$(\pm\theta_{axes}/2)$ around y axis
Viewing transformation: perspective	$M_{perspective}$	Use $FOV_{vertical}$, $FOV_{horizontal}$ and offset $(\pm D_{xreal}/R_{xreal} - L_{xreal})$, $D_{yreal}/(T_{yreal} - B_{yreal}))$

Gamma mismatch accounts for many problems during the early stages of system integration. Care has to be taken when changing components in a system where the gamma has been matched. For example, changing over from a CCD video source to a vidicon-based camera can introduce gamma errors. Although most cameras can be adjusted, it is surprising how many people make this mistake.

6.2.5 Collimation

Helmet-mounted displays used in aircraft applications are collimated to optical infinity. This is to avoid parallax errors that make aiming impossible. It is necessary to make the display imagery overlay onto objects in the outside world. For most purposes objects in the outside world are assumed to be at optical infinity. If this is done properly, it is not necessary for the user to refocus to transfer from display imagery to objects in the outside world. Moreover, the objects appear to be at the same distance. To produce display imagery at infinity it is necessary to place the image source at the focal point of the helmet-mounted display optical system. Collimation can be checked by placing a 'reasonably' powerful telescope (previously set up to focus on infinity) in the exit pupil of the helmet-mounted display. If the image on the display appears to be sharp it is safe to assume that it is focused at infinity. If the focus ring on the telescope is graduated and marked in dioptres (this instrument is sometimes called a dioptrescope) it is possible to set the helmet-mounted display for other optical distances. It is not uncommon for a helmet-mounted display to produce a curved field, with the centre of the display at optical infinity and other parts several dioptres away. Operationally, this can cause problems for the user because the imagery appears to bow inwards.

If the display source is placed nearer to the collimating lens than one focal length, the resulting virtual image is displayed closer than infinity. The eye must now accommodate (focus) on to the image. If the eyes now move laterally with respect to the ocular axis, the information on the display source appears to move.

In a closed virtual environment display the 'collimation' is not quite so important because there are no outside world references. If an outside world scene is to be represented on a virtual environment display it may be necessary to consider displaying it at infinity.

6.2.6 Eye relief

It is interesting that the majority of commercial virtual environment type helmet-mounted displays do not accommodate for spectacle wearers, who therefore cannot work with many of these systems. The lenses designed for virtual environment use have been optimized to present a very wide field of view for a defined eye position. The closed display generally has some form of light shield or mask (like a scuba-diver's face mask) fitted to the helmet display. This is to prevent external light sources washing out the display. The presence of the mask and the precisely defined eye positions prevent spectacle wearers from seeing an acceptable image. Even though contact lenses are a solution they are not ideal for casual viewing of a virtual environment display. Therefore, the optical designer must take into account potential users who wear spectacles. There is no reason why the optical system should not be designed with this in mind. A simple redesign of the light-excluding mask would also be required.

Anyone who is involved in fitting helmets to aircrew, cycle riders, horse riders and so on will be only too aware of the enormous variation in human head sizes and the position of the eyes relative to the helmet. Obviously, designers must also take these variations into account. What is needed is a single size of helmet-mounted display. A partial solution to the problem is an enlarged exit pupil, so that whatever the dimension of the user's head, the eyes will always be within it.

6.2.7 Exit pupil

In practice the size of the exit pupil in a helmet-mounted display is an extremely important parameter. The exit pupil is the region where the eye must be located in order to see an image. It is essentially a single point in space where the eye can receive all the light that emerges from the system and the whole instantaneous field of view can be seen. Perhaps the biggest factor affecting the size of the exit pupil is the amount of movement that the helmet-mounted display is likely to experience on the user's head. All helmet-mounted displays generally slip or move on the wearer's head, and it is not uncommon for the eye to move outside the exit pupil. When this happens no image can be seen. The exit pupil diameter must be selected to take account of the expected helmet slip. However, it is not just a simple matter of providing a large exit pupil, because this impacts on the optical design and can add greatly to the overall weight and cost of the design. In specifying the range of movement of the helmet on the wearer's head the conditions under which the display is to be used must be considered. Operation in vibrating environments such as tanks or vehicles can subject the helmet to considerable displacement. Additionally, if the head is moved around in violent manoeuvres (as a combat pilot's head might) significant amounts of slip can occur. It is very difficult to eliminate slip altogether because the scalp moves relative to the skull.

6.2.8 Flicker

Provided that the display refresh frequency is maintained above a certain critical value (around 50–60 Hz), flicker cannot be perceived. The exact value depends upon several factors, including the external lighting around the display. In the case of a CRT display the phosphor persistence time can have a bearing on whether display flicker can be seen. If the persistence time is greater than a few milliseconds flicker can be eliminated. Unfortunately, too long a persistence time will cause the display image to smear, which introduces problems with fast graphics or moving images. Care should be taken when selecting the persistence time of a CRT. Increasing CRT brightness can also increase the persistence time of a fast phosphor to the point where dim after–images can be seen.

Particular care must be taken when using raster displays in a vibrating environment. At certain frequencies of vibration, the display raster can produce a visible aliasing effect because of the interaction between the display refresh frequency and the vibration frequency. Under extreme conditions of vibration the colour shutter display is known to break up into the primary colours. Similar effects can occur when raster driven displays are used in the presence of certain types of light, such as fluorescent strip lights. It is not possible to give specifics here because it is important to characterize the refresh frequency and the frequency of vibration. Any dampening or coupling effects into the helmet-mounted display must be considered.

6.2.9 Display/image registration

Registration between a virtual image and a real-world image is of paramount importance, particularly when the virtual image has to overlay the real world as it does in an aircraft helmet-mounted display. Any registration errors would not be tolerated. Similarly, if a virtual display has to overlay (for example, an unlabelled keyboard) a misregistration would be objectionable. The real problem arises when the data that is to be overlaid onto the real world is derived from other data sources, and errors are introduced when it is computed. In some circumstances very small misalignments in the imagery can be tolerated, but this becomes annoying with time as the user has to continually compensate for the error.

Registration errors arise from a whole series of situations including optical distortions and head tracker inaccuracies. The worst misregistration effects are those that are not immediately apparent. Instances have been known where the magnetic field around a tracker has changed, thus distorting the field radiated by an electromagnetic tracker. This field distortion can result from changes to a building or even new equipment being placed within a certain range of the tracker. The user may be totally unaware of the presence of this new equipment, but the field change or distortion can be noticed immediately.

Display alignment

It is very important to align the left and right eye images in a binocular helmet-mounted display. The user can tolerate slightly more misalignment in the horizontal axis than in the vertical axis. However, even slight amounts of misalignment can cause operator fatigue after a relatively short period of time. To overcome misalignment errors the manufacturer often incorporates some form of mechanical adjustment on the display. This has the disadvantage of increasing the head-supported mass, which can also become objectionable after a short period. It is usual to find minor adjustments such as height and inter–pupillary distance adjustment on the helmet-mounted display. It is possible to make other adjustments via electronic means such as shifting the image on the image source. This can be done either by injecting small amounts of d.c. bias into the deflection circuitry or by adding a small offset into the graphics computation process. It might seem straightforward to display a crosshatch grid on each display channel and arrange for a small shift (usually under user control) so that the two grids overlay each other, but this approach can lead to errors because of improper convergence on the display. Some very complex patterns have been used to help align the two channels, but this can be quite confusing for the inexperienced user. It is possible to employ quite simple display structures to help the alignment. Some researchers use a pair of boxes as shown in Figure 6.10. When the left and right eye channels are properly aligned they take the form of a single square partitioned into four smaller squares. This pattern can be used in the centre of the display and simply enlarged to cover a wider field of view. However, it can still cause errors because identical structures are presented to both eyes, which sometimes try to converge to produce identical retinal correspondence points. Researchers at Wright Patterson Airforce Base have suggested using patterns that provide exact end point correspondence between each eye, yet different images for each eye. A suitable pattern is shown in Figure 6.10. Wright Patterson researchers have also found it necessary to flash these patterns to prevent convergence errors.

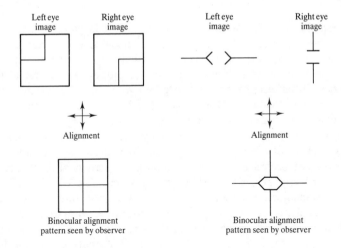

Figure 6.10 Alignment patterns to set up a binocular helmet-mounted display.

Therefore, the patterns should be flashed repetitively, with the image being on for about 75 ms and off for a period of between 100 and 125 ms.

If a see-through helmet-mounted display is used the imagery must be collimated at the distance of the real imagery otherwise serious alignment errors will be introduced as a result of accommodation errors. It is a straightforward matter to arrange for the display software to allow the user to align the pattern manually and store this data in a data file for future reference. Occasionally it will be necessary to re-align the helmet-mounted display because of changes in component tolerances, temperature shifts or general settling down of the mechanical components.

Display/image stability

In order to achieve good visual acuity a stable image must be presented on the retina. It has been reported by Guedry *et al.* (1978) that retinal image motion between $15°s^{-1}$ and $25°s^{-1}$ can reduce visual acuity five times. If the head is moved through $90°$, the eye movements that compensate for such a movement can exceed $100°s^{-1}$, thereby reducing visual acuity. Two mechanisms are responsible for generating compensatory eye movements in response to a head movement. These are the vestibular ocular reflex and the visual tracking mechanism (pursuit and optikinetic). Head acceleration is detected by the vestibular system of the inner ear, which generates the vestibular ocular reflex signal to control the eye movement. The vestibular ocular reflex is an open loop control system which operates for short duration movements. Obviously, there are positional errors. The visual tracking mechanism operates to correct this error on slow movements, but with considerably more precision than the vestibular ocular reflex. The combined operation of these two mechanisms is called 'the visual vestibular ocular reflex' and it provides an extremely stable image on the retina.

Display jitter

Depending upon the stability of the display circuits it is possible that jitter may be introduced into the displayed image. This manifests itself as a small but noticable motion in the image. Not surprisingly, it is related to visual acuity and resolution and will be detected when the motion exceeds the minimum resolution by the eye at the specified viewing distance. Jitter effects can be observed as a blurring of the image, which reduces the perceived resolution. Obviously, jitter in a display that has a long delay or persistence time can be extremely detrimental. If the jitter frequency is higher than the critical fusion frequency, then two or more images may be seen. This can result in fine lines drawn on the display being seen as broad lines at frequencies above the critical fusion frequency. The presence of jitter can reduce the perceived resolution to an extent where it can affect user performance, especially where fine detail must be resolved. Jitter is sometimes subjectively specified as 'no observable jitter' or 'no visible jitter'. To specify jitter levels, it is better to quote the maximum motion of a displayed element. This should ideally be less than one half of the spacing between adjacent pixels.

Jitter or oscillations in the virtual world may strongly contribute to simulation sickness. Nettinger *et al.* (1990) report on several studies suggesting that visual or physical oscillations in the range of 0.2–0.25 Hz are maximally conducive to motion sickness. While position tracker error is a significant contributor to visual proprioceptive conflict, the eradication of errors will probably not end reports of simulator sickness in virtual environment systems, because simulation sickness is polygenic (Kennedy and Fowlkes, 1990). Other variables such as image motion in a user's visual field may still lead to simulation sickness. This is especially true for those subjects who are prone to feelings of vection (illusory sensations of self motion) (Nettinger *et al.* 1990).

Display field of view, resolution and weight trade-off

There is a relationship between display field of view, display resolution and weight. If either field of view or resolution is increased, then head-supported mass also increases and a trade-off must be undertaken. Additionally, as field of view is increased, resolution must be proportionally increased, otherwise individual pixels will become visible and interfere with the user's performance. It would be unwise to assume that for all applications the widest possible field of view or resolution must be used. The author has found that a lower spatial resolution display becomes more acceptable (subjectively) when texture is incorporated into the scene, rather than just Gouraud shaded polygons. The exact reasons for this are currently being studied. Nevertheless, there is a cost associated with an increase in either field of view or resolution. The cost of the optical system increases dramatically as field of view increases. A similar pattern emerges for an increase in resolution because this tends to push up the computational requirements, and more graphics processing has to be undertaken per frame. Dual resolution display systems that take advantage of the small region of high visual acuity (peripheral region) are extremely expensive. Indeed, these displays are only appropriate for applications where extremely wide fields of view (approaching that of the human visual system) are required.

Centre of gravity

The helmet-mounted display is generally located in front of the head, but this causes a shift in the centre of gravity and can result in asymmetrical loading of the head and neck. The resulting 'offset' centre of gravity forms a 'moment', causing a torque on the operator's head and neck muscles. Excessive weight can make the operator feel tired. Increases in head weight and a shift in the centre of gravity increases the torque, or bending stress, in the neck due to movement of the head. Clearly, the design must be undertaken in such a way that the centre of gravity of the helmet-mounted display is as close as possible to that of the head and neck.

6.2.10 Specifying binocular helmet-mounted or head coupled displays

It is possible to buy an 'off-the-shelf' helmet-mounted display which will provide the purchaser with a simple display. However, it will have been designed around a basic requirement, and it is unlikely to have been optimized for a particular task. When a helmet-mounted display is required for a serious application (where performance is important), it will be necessary to specify parameters that have a direct bearing on the user's performance. For example, resolution and field of view can affect task performance. However, extreme caution should be exercised when dealing with the parameters of a helmet-mounted display because they are inter-dependent.

Although a few binocular mounted displays have appeared on the market there is very little scientific literature describing optical tolerance limits for image differences and optical alignment requirements. Examination of some manufacturers' products suggests that they are unaware of the importance of these parameters. One or two helmet-mounted displays appear to be nothing more than a simple arrangement of a set of wide angle optics placed in front of a pair of liquid crystal displays with an uncomfortable head mount. Clever use of plastic extrusions gives a 'futuristic' appearance to the helmet but the cosmetic camouflage does not improve the poor quality of the design.

The primary requirement of all binocular mounted displays is to present an image to each eye. The images may be slightly different (left and right eye scenes). Most helmet-mounted displays exhibit a slight horizontal and vertical misalignment error of the optical axes. A user should be wary of a manufacturer's claim that there is a zero misalignment error, because it is very difficult and expensive to make such a system.

For most applications perfect alignment is not necessary (in fact, in practice it is impossible to achieve). However, it is important to know what is an acceptable tolerance for a user. Provided one can meet the requirement, the two images will fuse into one and the user becomes unaware that he is viewing two separate images.

When misalignments are present, the user's eyes are affected by severe eyestrain and performance is seriously reduced. The onset of eyestrain is also time-dependent. Short exposure to misaligned systems may be acceptable, but can become completely intolerable after a few minutes. Some individuals can accept higher degrees of misalignment than others.

Table 6.2 gives the list of parameters that must be specified when purchasing a helmet-mounted display. Table 6.3 gives the definitions for the most important alignment errors of a binocular mounted display.

Table 6.2 Specification of helmet-mounted display.

Specification parameter	Value	Tolerance
Field of view		
Binocular overlap (where relevant)		
Virtual image distance		
Exit pupil		
Eye relief		
Optic axis angle		
Viewing transformations		
Display resolution		
Display image source		
Combiner transmission		
Distortion correction requirements		
Raster size		
Raster video standard		
Cursive video input		
Brightness		
Contrast		
Gamma		
Video bandwidth		
Interocular adjustment		
Inter–pupillary distance (where appropriate)		
Helmet weight		
Audio communications interface		
Power supply requirements		
Miscellaneous requirements		

Extreme care should be taken when either interpreting of specifying helmet-mounted display parameters. Underspecifying a helmet-mounted display will inevitably lead to a system that does not work, while overspecifying will increase the cost. The latter also increases the risk that the manufacturer may not be able to develop such an item. However tempting it is to blindly quote specifications and performance figures for helmet-mounted displays, it is sheer folly to do so without first considering the task/application.

Table 6.3 Critical alignment parameters of a helmet-mounted display.

Optical alignment tolerances	Definition
Collimation difference	The difference between the image plane distance.
Collimation error	The distance error in an infinity collimated display when the image is not at infinity.
Horizontal misalignment	The horizontal alignment error between the two optical axes.
Magnification difference	The difference in image size between each channel.
Rotation difference	The rotation about the optical axes of one channel relative to the other. This is sometimes referred to as twisting.
Contrast difference	The difference in contrast between the two channels.
Luminance difference	The difference in luminance (brightness) between the two channels.

A paper by Self (1986) at first sight seems to give a system designer all that is needed regarding helmet-mounted displays, but the figures were derived as a result of trials with a handful of subjects and a head up display, and they should be treated with great caution. (The paper does contain an appropriate warning that the figures quoted should only be used as a guide.)

6.3 Virtual environments: Position and orientation tracking

This section examines the key requirements of the position and orientation tracking systems used to determine (for instance) the user's head line of sight and the position of the hands. The most important of these is the head line of sight or head position tracking system: it performs an extremely important role in an immersive virtual environment system. The required performance of the head tracking system is frequently underestimated. Employing a head position tracker with inadequate performance will generally lead to a visually coupled system that suffers from all sorts of problems, including simulation sickness. It is important to analyse the task requirements of a given application to derive the performance requirements of the individual components. To make matters worse, several manufacturers of position/orientation tracking systems use different and often conflicting names when they specify the performance of their systems. The unwary user can easily make the mistake of misreading an ambiguous specification. The following section will elaborate on the parameters that must be considered when applying a tracking system to a particular application.

Position tracking systems are frequently taken for granted and little attention is given to the parameters that affect system performance. For example, unless the head tracker is carefully integrated with the visually coupled system, unacceptable lags will become evident in the images presented to the user. While the head tracker is not the only source of lags within a visually coupled system, it is important to understand its contribution to the overall lag.

At one time some users thought that update rate was the only critical parameter of a space tracking system. However, designers concerned with 'man in the loop' tasks were conscious of other timing-related issues. More recently another term has been introduced: 'phase lag'. While lag parameters provide an indication of tracker performance there are other interrelated parameters that must also be considered. These include static accuracy, dynamic accuracy, latency, phase lag and update rate.

When designing a visually coupled system it is important to understand the consequence of each of these parameters, their interdependencies and how one parameter may be offset against another in order to achieve optimum performance.

6.3.1 Definition of terms

Examination of manufacturer's literature and technical publications covering space tracking/orientation systems reveals that there is disagreement on the basic definitions regarding system performance. Anyone involved with the purchase of a tracking system will be faced with comparing inconsistent performance figures. For instance, the important parameters of a tracker's performance, latency and phase lag, are regularly interchanged, even though they mean different things. The matter is made considerably worse when manufacturers interchange these values. In this way, one tracker can appear to be better than another. One also wonders if manufacturers use consistent measurement techniques when determining actual performance.

Complementary research is being undertaken at British Aerospace, Brough, UK, the University of Hull, UK, NASA Ames Research Center, USA, the University of North Carolina, USA and the University of Alberta, Canada to provide an independent assessment of tracker performance.

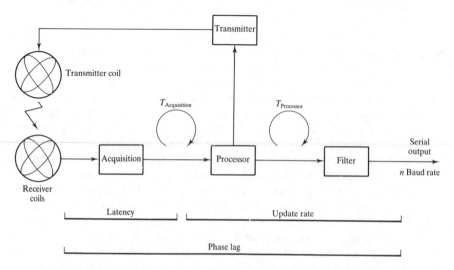

Figure 6.11 Generic architecture for a head tracker system.

Several performance criteria will now be defined to avoid misinterpretation of performance specifications:

- Static accuracy
- Dynamic accuracy
- Latency
- Phase lag
- Update rate
- Registration
- Signal to noise ratio

To assist with these definitions, Figure 6.11 shows where the main timing delays occur in a generic tracking system.

Static accuracy

Static accuracy is the ability of a tracker to determine the coordinates of a position in space. This figure is the maximum deviation from a reference value on a single sample with no averaging or deviation applied. It is the most empirical measurement (raw data value), and is therefore objective. When quoting accuracy it is essential to state how the accuracy was measured and what type of confidence window was applied.

The factors contributing to the static accuracy include:

- Receiver sensitivity
- Transmitter signal to noise ratio
- Analogue to digital converter resolution
- Analogue component noise tolerance levels
- Rounding error during algorithm computation
- Environmental effects
- Algorithm errors
- Installation errors
- Operator error during measurement process

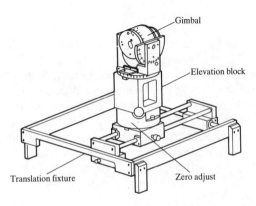

Figure 6.12 Precision position/orientation calibration table.

These factors contribute differently to the error of the overall system; some parameters have a greater effect on static accuracy than others. It is not possible to sum the individual errors for an overall system error, neither is it possible to look at the maximum error and attribute overall system performance to that single component.

In order to measure static accuracy it is necessary to use a metallic-free calibration table such as the one shown in Figure 6.12.

Dynamic accuracy

Dynamic accuracy relates to the system accuracy as the tracker's sensor is moved. Dynamic accuracy is an additional attribute to the static accuracy.

The following factors contribute to the system's dynamic accuracy:

- Processor type
- System architecture
- Time dependent system components

Dynamic accuracy is extremely dependent on static accuracy. If a long integration period is used the trade-off between static and dynamic accuracy is reasonably straightforward. For a large number of acquisitions, over a long integration period, the dynamic accuracy can be quite good. If a time limit is imposed, as it will be for fast tracking systems, then dynamic accuracy suffers. The less time there is to acquire data and solve the coordinate position, the fewer acquisitions can take place.

Measurement of the dynamic performance of a position/orientation tracking system is a complex engineering task. At first it might seem a simple matter to displace a tracker's sensor by a known amount and collect the resulting data. When one examines the actual implementation of a tracker, it soon becomes apparent that simply measuring the output of a tracker in conjunction with the motion input applied to the sensor leads to an error. This arises because the tracker incorporates some form of output buffer that is updated at a user specified rate. An inappropriately set update rate will lead to system problems.

Latency

There are several definitions of latency. Some manufacturers use ambiguous definitions, and others interchange latency and phase lag.

Latency is the rate at which the acquisition portion of the system can acquire new data. As such, it deals with signals in the analogue domain and is an evaluation of the ability of the receiver to perform in real time. There are two aspects to this. The first aspect is the accuracy of the receiver assembly, and the second is how quickly the receiver can sense a change in the transmitter position. Summing update rate with latency results in the phase lag response.

Phase lag

Many people in the virtual environment field make the mistake of assuming that the update rate of the head position sensing device (or hand position tracker) is the parameter that governs the effective update of the virtual environment system. They mistakenly believe that merely by increasing update rate, the update of the visuals can be improved. If one works on the assumption that the computer graphics system can keep up with the increased data rate from the tracking device, one has also inferred that the tracker is keeping in track with the movement of the head (or hand). Most tracking devices incorporate some form of high speed computer to produce an output corresponding to a precise position or angular displacement of a sensor. In the static sense, or with a very slow–varying sensor position, the output from this computer tracks the absolute position of the sensor in space within the accuracy limits and resolution of the technique or computer used. When the sensor is more dynamic the output from the computer can lag the actual position of the sensor by an appreciable amount. This is generally known as the phase lag. Phase lag response is a very important parameter, second only to the accuracy of measurement, in the specification of a space tracking device. Unfortunately, few manufacturers quote such a figure. Those who do employ different methods and definitions to determine the amount of phase lag. It has also been found in practice that the phase lag response is a function of the rate of change in position or orientation of the tracker's sensor.

The effect of a high phase lag is often mistakenly taken to be an update problem with the graphics system. The visible characteristic of any form of lag in a visually coupled system manifests itself as a time delay before new scene information is computed. Depending upon the manner in which the tracker data is integrated with the graphics system, the image presented to the user can either appear to freeze for a fraction of a second, or not keep track with the head position. If a totally closed helmet-mounted display is used, the effect of this can be almost intolerable after a few minutes of use. If the user is required to search over large visual fields, the effect is very detrimental to their performance. Extreme effects can induce nausea.

To reduce the overall phase lag the virtual environment system designer must not only ensure that the head tracking system has the minimally acceptable phase lag response for the desired task, but also take care that the system configuration does not exaggerate the effect.

If one has a free hand in the design of a virtual environment system then utmost priority must be given to the integration of the visual systems, ensuring that they run as quickly as possible. Interfaces that rely on waiting until an interrupt has been serviced are not advisable because waiting time can be detrimental to the visuals. The designer must appreciate that the human being is very good at detecting even the smallest amount of lag in a visual system.

Major contributors to phase lag include:

- Architecture
- Processor type
- Algorithm

System architecture is very important and all elements must be chosen for real-time performance. This is especially true in the acquisition stage where real-time data collection is critical. The processor must be able to calculate position and orientation data quickly enough to keep the overall phase lag figure low.

Clearly, the type of algorithm used is important because an iterative solution will mean that the processor has to calculate position and orientation many times. If the algorithm is properly designed each iteration will yield a more accurate solution. Unfortunately, each iteration increases the amount of phase delay. A second approach is to use a deterministic solution. In this case orientation is calculated for each iteration, and position is calculated less frequently.

All time-dependent components affect phase lag performance. If any of the components are improved then phase lag will be reduced. However, there is a trade-off between static and dynamic accuracy and phase lag. In applying a tracker to a visually coupled device it is important to understand the requirements of the end application and how these relate.

To measure phase lag, very special care has to be taken to ensure that the measurement process does not introduce additional phase lag effects. Adelstein *et al.* (1992) report and improve on several techniques tried by Bryson and Fisher (1990), Liang *et al.* (1991) and Hirose *et al.* (1990) to determine phase lag. Unfortunately, these latter investigators did not actually measure the performance of the space tracker alone. The swinging pendulum used by several of these researchers was not an acceptable method of inducing controlled motion in a tracker system because the cable attached to the tracker's sensor would have an effect on the time period of the pendulum: the timing period of the pendulum could not be adjusted without changing the position and path of the sensor. Adelstein *et al.* (1992) have compiled a series of requirements for a test facility that can measure phase lag. The most important of these are:

1. The test facility must be capable of applying precisely controlled inputs to the tracker system.
2. The test facility must be able to measure the input displacement of the tracker's sensor accurately.
3. Time stamping must be applied to the input displacement data and to the output of the tracker system. A common clock must be used to avoid timer synchronization effects.
4. The test facility must allow a range of dynamic inputs to be applied to the tracker's sensor in a way that covers the bandwidth of volitional human limb and head motion.
5. The test facility must not introduce noise or other effects into the tracker's sensor output data.

Update rate

Update rate is the tracker's ability to output position and orientation data to the output port. Many users place high update rate at the top of their requirements list. Unfortunately, they do not fully understand the relationship between this parameter and the others.

To some extent update rate is dependent upon the factors that contribute to phase lag. Update rate is not a function of the acquisition process and consequently it does not reflect overall system performance. The system processor can have a significant bearing on the update performance, in the sense that it must manipulate the algorithm and calculate the position and orientation value before outputting the data to the output port. Because of slow internal processing systems, some tracker systems use old data when new information is not available. Some tracker systems store recently acquired position/orientation data into a buffer array that is then read by a processor to provide output data. A consequence of taking output data faster than it is being input into the buffer is that update rate and static accuracy can be high. However, phase lag and dynamic accuracy performance are generally very poor.

Registration

Registration is the correspondence between actual position and orientation and reported position/orientation. A system with good registration accurately maps the remote object's movement throughout the working volume. Good resolution and accuracy alone do not imply good registration, because poor registration can result from accumulated errors that cause the reported position to drift from the physical position.

In some cases misregistration may not be significant. This is the case with a conventional 2-D mouse. Mice frequently lose their registration, yet users are able to mentally re-adjust the position and operate the mouse without further complication. Likewise, in some virtual environment applications, users of six degree of freedom position trackers can mentally adjust the translational position as long as they do not encounter a physical barrier such as a wall. However, unlike a 2-D mouse, a six degree of freedom position tracker must report orientation. Registration must be precise, because the tracker reports the orientation (as well as the position) of the user's head. Errors in orientation appear to be especially important.

Registration is vitally important if the application combines the physical and virtual worlds. The importance of good registration is amplified when tracking multiple moving objects. This is the case with goggles and gloves, where the reported distance between head and hand must correspond to the position indicated by proprioceptive senses. Another example might be that of two virtual environment users shaking hands simultaneously in both the physical and virtual worlds. Misregistration would mean that they would not be able to do this. The effect of misregistration is discussed later in this chapter.

Mechanical position trackers have good accuracy, responsiveness, registration, and robustness. However, they also tend to have a limited range of operation. Moreover, mechanical linkages do not allow multiple users to work in the same working volume. One clear advantage of mechanical position trackers is that they can more easily accommodate an integrated mechanism for force feedback. Consequently, they may be well suited for telerobotic or constrained virtual environment applications. Several techniques exist for optical position trackers such as fixed transducer, pattern recognition, and so on. The fixed transducer technique is the one that is most frequently implemented. Optical systems must be applied carefully because there is an inherent trade-off between accuracy and range of operation. For applications where an extended range of operation is required, it will be necessary to reduce accuracy. Conversely, increased accuracy requirements will mean that range of operation must be sacrificed. The accuracy for an image processing system employing pattern recognition will be affected by faulty scene recognition. In addition all optical systems are affected by objects or by the user obscuring the line of sight between the light source and the image sensor. The solution to this is to build in a level of redundancy, so that multiple light sources and sensors are used.

To date, magnetic tracking systems have been widely used for visually coupled systems. Unlike other position tracking technologies, magnetic systems are relatively inexpensive and readily available. Unfortunately, magnetic tracking systems are less suited to real-time open room applications compared to optical or acoustic systems. As working volume increases, magnetic tracking systems lose accuracy and registration due to impaired resistance to noise. To compensate, significant filtering must be added. This in turn degrades the system's responsiveness. Nevertheless, magnetic position trackers have proven very effective at short range. The successful use of the magnetic tracking systems in cockpit and flight simulator applications accounts for 'off-the-shelf' availability and consequently for widespread use in early virtual environment applications.

Acoustic position trackers have been implemented using time-of-flight and phase-coherent measurement techniques. Performance for the two techniques can vary significantly for open room applications. Phase-coherent systems offer better performance because of their higher data rates. If a small operating range is required, both implementations offer good accuracy, responsiveness, robustness, and registration. Time-of-flight systems are more vulnerable to acoustic noise. Phase-coherent systems offer good accuracy, responsiveness, range, and robustness but are vulnerable to cumulative errors. Both systems can suffer gross errors from occluded sensors. Because of the larger working volume, the phase-coherent system offers better sociability than the time-of-flight system.

Signal to noise ratio (S/N)

The signal to noise ratio of a position/orientation tracking system gives a simple indication of the signal component relative to the noise component expressed in dB ($20 \log_{10} S/N$), or as a unitless number. The S/N is obtained by taking a statistically significant number of position/orientation samples in known positions and calculating the mean vector sum(s) for each position and orientation. The mean vector sum of the one sigma (standard deviation) deviations yields the noise component.

6.3.2 Coexistence with other position sensing devices

If there is a requirement to track more than one object in a virtual environment (for example, head and hand) then it is very important to consider which method should be used to perform the tracking operation. By far the most common tracking system used today is based on the electromagnetic system such as the Polhemus or Ascension. It is not possible to use two separate tracking systems within the same operating area unless they are synchronized, because the electromagnetic fields will interfere with one another. It is difficult to synchronize two separate trackers, especially if they are of different types; the interleaving or synchronization operation leads to the update rate being halved. In most visually coupled systems, head tracker performance is already a limiting factor. Therefore, halving the update rate to track the hand can introduce very serious lags in the usual scene generation.

A more effective solution is to use a different technology, one that does not cause interference to other systems. For this purpose, given today's technology, an optical tracker is the most suitable.

6.3.3 Tracking at extended ranges

There are several ways of achieving position and orientation tracking at extended ranges:

- Large extended-range electromagnetic devices
- Multiple, daisy-chained devices
- Networked optical system

Each method has its merits, but the choice will depend on task and budget constraints. Probably the simplest to implement is the extended range electromagnetic device such as the Ascension Extended Range Transmitter. Even though this system can operate in an 8-foot radius sphere, a number of operational considerations have to be met. For example, even though the d.c. electromagnetic technique is relatively insensitive to the presence of metallic structures in the vicinity of the transmitter and sensor, the extended transmitter range increases the liklihood of encountering metallic structures.

The second method is probably the most effective because it employs a series of small range electromagnetic trackers that have been daisy-chained together. One tracker is nominated as the master unit and all others synchronize to it. Unfortunately, the cost of this method can be quite high because it requires one complete tracker system per daisy-chain element.

The third method relies on employing a unique pattern of light sources mounted on the ceiling of a room (see the section on remote view optical tracking systems in Chapter 4). A drawback of this method is that it requires a room to be dedicated to the task, although the overall cost can be quite low in terms of peripheral support equipment.

6.3.4 Effects of inaccurate position tracking

Errors in the position tracking systems can create serious problems for the user. In virtual environment applications, the user's hand, head or other body part are tracked to create the experience of being in the virtual world. When errors occur, coordinates of the body in real space do not correspond to the coordinates in simulated space. When this misalignment of the virtual and real world involves the represented body of the user, the illusion of simulated space tends to break down. There have been persistent reports that some users experience simulation sickness, an illness resembling motion sickness (Chung et al. 1989; Fisher, 1989; McCauley, 1984). The symptoms include dizziness, nausea, oculomotor disorders, and lack of concentration (Kennedy and Fowlkes, 1990; Walker et al. 1970). Whether this syndrome is a permanent feature or can be overcome by training (or better use of visual cues) has still to be investigated. As the technology develops the apparent realism is continually being improved. Virtual environments share this problem with other simulators. According to Kennedy and Fowlkes (1990) 60% of subjects exhibit some mild symptoms associated with simulation sickness, though less than 0.1% will be affected so strongly as to vomit. More disturbing is the report that 10% of pilots in flight simulators experience after–effects that can persist for several hours (Baltzley et al., 1989). This is a potentially serious problem for the virtual environment industry. If the unpleasant and disruptive experience of simulation sickness continues to afflict a sizeable percentage of users, the widespread use of virtual environment systems may be impeded (Biocca, 1992).

Position tracking plays an important part in the illusion of self-motion through a simulated space. The strength of the illusion is dependent on the ability to fool our perceptual system. The perceptual system has evolved over millennia to make use of the affordances (Gibson, 1966; 1979) or cues provided by the physical world that we see, move around in and touch. A significant part of perceptual processing is dedicated to creating a mental model of the space that surrounds us (Johnson-Laird, 1983). Correct mental calculation of the parameters of either physical or virtual space is required to guide hand–eye coordination, eye movement, and body stabilization in space. The perfect registration of the visual and physical experience of a space can help the body accomplish difficult tasks such as keeping the eyes on a visual target when the head and body are in motion.

When a position tracker reports inaccurate data, the user is faced with the problem of constructing a mental model of the surrounding space from incompatible (if not contradictory) physical cues. In general, the user experiences a conflict between the perceived visual space and the perceived proprioceptive space. (The proprioceptive system is the perceptual system that informs the user of the position of body and limbs in space.) Information from the visual system tends to dominate in such conflicts, and conflict may cause the user to experience the symptoms of motion sickness (Reason and Brand, 1975). Position tracker error contributes to three kinds of visual proprioceptive conflict. These are:

- Contention between the observed and felt positions of a hand or limb.
- Lag in reported body position, especially when the head has moved and the view of the represented visual world lags perceptibly.
- Jitter or oscillation of the represented body part.

Simple lack of registration between the perceived and observed position of a limb is the least critical source of error. For example, a similar error occurs when an individual first wears a new pair of glasses. The perceptual system is highly plastic and can accommodate a stable error (Held, 1965; Welch, 1978). The errors of a position tracking system may be more complex than those from a pair of spectacles. Tracking error can vary throughout the working volume, causing variable distortions. Consequently, variable discrepancies between seen and perceived positions defeat the perceptual adaptation. For example, if a perceptual adjustment to a misregistration of X is required for one position and an adjustment of Y is required for another position, the user's adjustment is disrupted. The user is then forced to re-adapt continually.

Registration of orientation must be especially precise because the position tracker reports the orientation of the user's head. Error in head orientation will create an inter-sensory conflict between the information presented by the visual and vestibular systems, and in some cases, the proprioceptive system. (The vestibular system provides a sense of balance.) The vestibular system gets its cues from gravitational and inertial forces, and the proprioceptive system from the felt position of the body muscles, but the visual system is dominated by the computer generated image in the head-mounted display. Consequently, head orientation errors in position tracking will create mismatches between the computer generated image and the vestibular system. This will lead the user's perceptual system to recalibrate by adjusting input values from the less dominant sensory organs to match the information from the sensory organ receiving the most attention, usually the visual sense (Canon, 1970). Misregistration in head orientation may involve adjustments to independent perceptual programs (Redding, 1973a, b,

1975a, b). Interestingly, users may adapt more slowly to misregistration of the yaw axis than to errors in the roll axis (Redding, 1973a, b, 1975a, b). Also, the process of adaption to error can be significantly disrupted by delayed feedback (Hay, 1974; Hay and Goldsmith, 1973; Held et al., 1966). Finally, lag in orientation data accounts for most of the system delays experienced by the user (Liang et al., 1991).

The experience of perceptual lags between body movement and movement within the virtual world leads users to minimize rapid movements that accentuate the visual proprioceptive conflict. This inhibits natural movement in the virtual world and can interfere with those applications requiring naturalistic simulations.

6.3.5 Improving space tracking systems

The majority of space tracking systems generate noisy position and orientation data. If this is unfiltered it appears as a jittering image on the display. Modern tracking systems try to compensate for this by incorporating noise filters. Some of these employ adaptive filtering techniques that are extremely effective at adapting to changing noise environments, reducing the noise to almost imperceptible levels. A consequence of these and other filtering techniques is an increase in the phase lag of the tracker system, which leads to lags between head movement and visual feedback. Whenever a tracker is used in a new environment, it should first be operated without any filtering. This gives a first order assessment of the amount of noise present in the vicinity of the tracker. The reader should note that noise levels can change throughout the day. (The author can certainly vouch for that!) If at all possible, position and orientation data should be captured and analysed using one of the many statistical analysis packages. It is possible to get an idea of the sort of noises to which the tracking system is susceptible. This will be dependent on the tracker technology used.

It is better to try to locate the source of tracker noise and take steps to eliminate it rather than find solutions to mask it. Prevention is better than cure.

Predictive techniques for improving space tracking systems

Many virtual environment designers will be faced with technology that does not come up to specification. Provided that steps can be taken to eliminate or reduce noise in the tracking system, additional measures can be taken to compensate for certain lags in a visually coupled system. These methods rely on using prediction techniques to determine how the head is being moved, and the position it will be in when it stops moving. This means that it is necessary to track head position and orientation, and calculate trend information relating to parameters such as acceleration/deceleration. It should be possible to use standard control system theory to work out phase advance algorithms to compensate for the induced lag. However, it should be noted that lag compensation is a complex task, and when a human is in the loop it is not easy to undertake with deterministic techniques. A simple extrapolation technique investigated by the author and his team permitted several 'look ahead steps' to be calculated. For certain applications, this technique was reasonably successful.

The designer of a visually coupled system must pay particular attention to how the space tracker is integrated into the system. The tracker manufacturer provides a high degree of flexibility in the tracker interface so the output data can be transmitted either continuously or on command. The user should understand the significance of these two operating modes, because they will have an impact on total system performance.

There is little doubt that operating the tracker in continuous mode and at the highest baud rate will result in minimal lags between a head movement and the corresponding data appearing at the output of the tracker system. Unfortunately, this technique may have serious implications for the complete visually coupled system design. For example, there is a temptation to input tracker data into a standard RS232 interface on the host graphics platform. Unless this RS232 interface has been specially designed as a high speed interface, the host processor is likely to overload because of the excessive number of interrupts.

The alternative approach is to use point or polling mode, where the user requests data from the tracker at the appropriate time prior to the data being needed by the graphics system. The theory is that the user takes into account the intrinsic delay caused by the tracker, but in practice this is not easy to perform because the user must accurately time his/her software. If changes are made, it is necessary to re-time the software.

It is interesting to study the way humans move their heads. The movements are generally orientation based, with relatively infrequent or small translation displacements. When translational movements do occur they tend to be along the line of sight direction. A person's sensitivity to position and orientation jitter varies according to direction. For instance, we are more sensitive to image displacements (caused by jitter) that occur perpendicular to our line of sight. We are also more sensitive to lag effects along our line of sight rather than perpendicular to it. This suggests that whatever filtering technique is used, it must have an anisotropic characteristic.

Predicting head orientations: Kalman filter

A very powerful prediction algorithm has been developed by Liang et al. (1991) based on Kalman filtering. To apply a Kalman filter, Liang et al. suggest that the first stage is to convert the output from a tracker system into linear components, rather than the usual quaternion form. The magnitude of rotation θ can be extracted from a quaternion of the following form:

$$q = \left[\cos\frac{\theta}{2}, \ x\sin\frac{\theta}{2}, \ y\sin\frac{\theta}{2}, \ z\sin\frac{\theta}{2} \right]$$

to give a unit vector:

$$n = (x, \ y, \ z)$$

If one examines head movement, several characteristics are evident:

1. The orientation of the head changes by a very small amount between successive samples.
2. The user changes head position in short bursts followed by long periods of stable rest.
3. The angular velocities/accelerations are non-zero during changes in orientation.

These assumptions mean that it is possible to simplify the Kalman filter by filtering x, y and z and then normalizing back to a unit vector that is coupled with a filtered θ component to form the resulting quaternion. Liang *et al.* then model the orientation of the user's head as a random variable that changes orientation at random intervals and experiences a limited rate of change. Consequently, a Gauss–Markov process was used to describe head movement that has the following state equation:

$$\ddot{x} = -\beta \dot{x} + \sqrt{2\sigma^2 \beta}\, \omega(t)$$

where $\dot{x}$ and $\ddot{x}$ are the first and second derivatives of the filtered variable, repectively, $\omega(t)$ is the white noise sequence, β is the time factor and σ^2 is the variance factor.

The state equation implies the following:

1. $\dot{x}$ tends to be zero (due to the negative coefficient $-\beta$).
2. $\ddot{x}$ is driven by random noise caused by acceleration during rotational movements.
3. β is a relatively stable time constant as a result of the limited velocity and acceleration of head movements.

The smoothness of the prediction can by controlled by adjusting the time factor β and variance factor σ^2. An increase in β tends to increase the rate at which velocity is predicted to return to zero, but at the expense of overshoot. Liang *et al.* conducted tests and used a 20 Hz sample rate (the Nyquist limit of head motion is approximately 10 Hz) with the Kalman filter predicting one step ahead of its measured data. The reliability of prediction tends to decrease as the prediction period increases.

Despite the assumptions made by Liang *et al.*, especially with respect to their linearization step, the Kalman filter algorithm made a marked improvement to reducing lags. A full pseudo code description of the Kalman filter algorithm is given in their paper.

6.3.6 Specifying position and orientation tracking systems

In order to specify a position/orientation tracking system accurately, it is very important to understand how the tracker will be used and what it will be used for. Issues such as the operational environment can greatly influence the selection of a particular tracking technology. One of the most critical parameters to specify correctly is the required dynamic performance of the system. It is not just a matter of defining latency, phase lag and update rate, because the complete system must be taken into account. To achieve maximum data throughput, the dynamic performance of the host computer will influence the overall performance. With some graphics systems it is possible to saturate the host process completely, or by commanding the tracker interface, to send data far too quickly. It is tempting to try to increase the tracker's update rate by opting for a higher band rate. Unfortunately, too high a rate can cause the interface to generate an excessive number of interrupts on the host computer that effectively 'steals' time from the graphics operations. Obviously, this depends largely upon the system architecture behind the graphics platform but the message illustrates the point.

Table 6.4 Specification of space tracking systems.

Specification parameter	Required performance		Achieved performance	
	Value	Tolerance	Value	Tolerance
Position/translation				
Range x, y, z				
Accuracy				
Resolution				
Orientation/angular				
Range azimuth				
Range elevation				
Range roll				
Accuracy				
Resolution				
Dynamic performance				
Latency				
Phase lag				
Update rate				
Band rate (when required)				
Interface(s)				
Type (e.g. RS232, parallel)				
Data supplied				
Format(s)				
Synchronization				
Operating mode				
Single configuration				
Multiple configuration				
Other				
Filter characteristics				
Tracker technology preference				
Power supply				
Dimensions				
Transmitter				
Receiver				
Processor unit				
Weight				
Transmitter				
Receiver				
Processor unit				

Ideally, one should be able to characterize each component of a visually coupled system in the form of a transfer function. Each major system, such as the tracker, would be composed of a series of smaller transfer functions. This would make it relatively easy to construct a system diagram and analyse the end-to-end performance. Adjustment or fine tuning could be achieved to ensure that the overall system meets the necessary performance. The requirements of the head tracker should be drawn from this type of analysis, thus ensuring that the appropriate one is selected. Until the performance of several tracker systems and graphic platforms is determined in this way, the system integrator will have to rely on his/her judgement.

Examination of tracker manufacturers' specifications readily reveals ambiguities and inconsistent specification parameters. This makes comparison across a range of different tracking systems very difficult. Moreover, not many manufacturers seem willing to give details of how they arrived at their specified performance values. This quite often means that the end user buys a system that appears to be suitable, only to find that the actual system does not fully meet their requirement. In defence of the tracker manufacturers, it is not always their fault that a system does not come up to expectation. A visually coupled system is very complex, involving finely tuned hardware and software, and the tracker is only one part of the overall system.

There are two basic ways of buying equipment. One is simply to take a manufacturer's specification sheet and compare this against one's own requirement (assuming there is a specification sheet). The other is to issue a requirement to the manufacturer and ask them to declare compliance against this specification. The first approach is probably the most common but the purchaser has to rely on his own or the the end user's ability to interpret the manufacturer's specification. The second approach is generally used by larger procurement agencies because it allows the purchaser to define the specification parameters and indicate required performance. In this way, the purchaser can control how the manufacturer specifies performance. When an assessment is made against other manufacturers the process becomes much easier. There is another clear advantage of the second approach: the manufacturer provides exactly what the purchaser wants, rather than the end user having to be content with what the manufacturer believes is required.

For example, the majority of tracker manufacturers provide an RS232 serial interface to output data. (There are a few exceptions.) While the RS232 interface is convenient for IBM PC or compatible applications, it cannot be called a high performance interface. The most demanding virtual environment applications would greatly benefit from a high speed parallel interface. This may require a slightly more expensive interface in the host computer but the performance improvements will be more beneficial in the long term. It is quite surprising how much time is consumed in attempting to optimize an RS232 interface device driver, to no avail. Most manufacturers will respond to market demand, so by imposing requirements on tracker manufacturers, the purchaser is more likely to get the sort of performance and system functionality that is needed.

The first step in specifying a tracking system is to define an unambiguous series of specification parameters so that the manufacturer can relate performance in these terms. Table 6.4 shows a good way of indicating required performance and encouraging the manufacturer to think in these terms.

6.4 Virtual environments: Visually coupled system requirements

6.4.1 Visual cues: Symbology artefacts

Rather than wait until display and computer graphic technology has reached the point where real-time photorealistic displays are feasible (though this has to be established as a requirement), it is possible to use simplified displays by taking into account limitations in the technology. This approach is much more sensible because it obviously keeps the cost down and simplifies the software. However, unless the virtual environment system is very carefully designed it is possible to introduce undesirable visual artefacts into the display. These can confuse the human operator and, depending upon the application, can become extremely dangerous in safety critical situations. There is no doubt that visuals are extremely compelling and simply generating displays without an understanding of the complex human factors is fraught with problems.

6.4.2 Performance requirements for virtual environment illusion

So far the quantitative performance required to create the virtual environment illusion has not been specified. Many researchers have discussed aspects of performance: Wenzel points out the necessity of rapid response for the creation of real-time audio images (Wenzel, 1992); Pausch suggests that latency is more important than visual resolution or stereoscopy (Pausch, 1991); Chung and colleagues speculate that 100 ms latency is acceptable (Chung *et al.*, 1989). In a study of the effects of lag on perceptual adoption, Held and Durlach (1991) conclude that adaption is reduced with delays of 60 ms, is clearly impaired at 120 ms, and that presence starts to break down at delays beyond 200 ms. Liang *et al.* (1991) make several notable observations:

- Data rate is the most important factor.
- Perceived lag is caused by delayed orientation data.
- Perceived image jitter is caused by noise (ranging errors).
- The effects of lag can contribute significantly to software engineering costs because the problems associated with managing the position input queue in real time.

The performance of visually coupled systems should be studied in terms of perceptual data and motion dynamics. There is not yet a sufficient understanding to simulate the stimulus structure of the perceptual environment. Optimization of the visually coupled system illusion can only be achieved if the performance of the technology is matched to the perceptual system, a system that has evolved to perceive the natural environment. Failure to match the requirements of the perceptual system may appear as flaws in the illusion of a virtual environment. The available psychophysical research is a useful guide for current research. However, using these findings to determine the specific performance requirements of a visually coupled system is dubious because of over-generalization. Current research represents examples of the perceptual research necessary to quantify the performance required for a visually coupled system. Meanwhile, a gap exists between perceptual understanding and technical practice. The development of visually coupled systems technology in the absence of appropriate perceptual research is not surprising.

However, the gap of understanding is not a barrier to current development. The effects of inadequate performance are mitigated by the adaptability of the human perceptual system. For this reason, perceptual imperfections may be acceptable, because slight, and sometimes gross, distortions can cause the user to adjust the visual or proprioceptive processes unconsciously. This is the case with current virtual environment systems. Despite perceptual distortions they produce an adequate illusion for many users. However, sometimes mismatches are beyond the tolerances of the perceptual system, causing the virtual environment illusion to collapse. More seriously, perceptual conflicts may contribute to simulation sickness.

To create a perceptually rich virtual environment illusion, we must understand the performance requirements of the human perceptual system. Only then can rational trade-offs be made. This applies not only to discrete technologies such as position tracking, but to the visually coupled system as a whole.

Progressive refinement of the virtual environment illusion

There is no doubt that real-time, high quality images and detailed virtual environments place an extremely high demand on today's computer hardware. Our understanding of the complex human perception system is at best rather limited. While it is easy to say that the visual display should be matched to the performance of the perception system, it is another matter to undertake this task. Until we fully understand complex visual interactions we must be prepared to accept educated guesses of the actual requirement. If we had a series of reliable metrics for performance we might be able to determine the critical aspects of a visual system. Unfortunately, at the moment these metrics do not exist.

From work conducted to date, several observations have been made that seem to improve visual systems performance and acceptance by a user. These include the following:

- Objects in the virtual environment must move realistically even at the expense of other attributes. The user can quickly spot an object that behaves in an unnatural manner.
- As the user is moving around the scene the resolution or object detail can be reduced. There is little point in devoting computational effort to drawing detailed objects while the user is moving them.
- When the user stops moving, or objects have stopped moving in the virtual environment, then apply progressive refinement to the image quality.

The key to the above guidelines lies in knowing when to degrade the image when it is moving. Many of the better graphics toolkits employ discrete level of detail to improve drawing operations when the object is at a distant range. There is little point in generating a complex object comprising hundreds or thousands of polygons when it is only two pixels high on the display.

Any discontinuities or 'glitch' in the displayed image will be immediately noted by the observer. An occasional glitch can instantly destroy the virtual illusion. Any form of lag in the image presented to the user will also cause an adverse effect.

Level of detail

When constructing a virtual environment display it is important to draw only what can be seen. If one considered drawing an outside world display consisting of an undulating terrain, then it would make sense to draw only those parts of the image that were contained within the field of view of the helmet-mounted display. Modern computer graphics systems allows the programmer to specify a far clipping plane beyond which no drawings take place. By not drawing terrain features in the distance, which could not possibly be seen by the observer, time is saved. When clipping at an arbitrary distance, it is far better to relate this clipping plane to the resolution of the display so that unnecessary drawing does not take place beyond the resolution capability of the display.

Although this technique is adequate for most applications, particularly those that stretch out to infinity, problems do arise when extremely large features such as mountain ranges are in the distance. Obviously, the far clipping technique would prevent the distant mountains from being drawn, but this is not a satisfactory situation. However, there is a solution to this that works on the principle of 'level of detail switching'.

Sophisticated 3-D modelling tools such as Multigen allow the user to set up detailed models of the virtual objects and their environments. These modelling packages are able to remove detail from the model without changing the basic outline as a function of distance from the observer. In other words, as the observer gets closer to the object, then more and more detail is drawn in. Level of detail switching can substantially increase the update rate of certain displays without introducing visual effects such as false horizons or objects that suddenly come into view.

6.4.3 Display scene motion (vestibular/ocular conflict)

In order to produce a clear image it is necessary to present a stable image on the retina. During normal viewing two human perception mechanisms are responsible for ensuring that a stable image is maintained: the vestibular ocular reflex and the visual tracking mechanism. These mechanisms generate eye movements that compensate for head movement and movement of the target being observed.

When the head is moved signals are generated in the vestibular system of the inner ear. These signals have a short latency (Peli, 1990) and are controlled in an open loop mode. Residual errors are corrected by the visual tracking mechanism, which functions with a long delay and slow movement, but is extremely accurate. Together, these two mechanisms produce a stable retinal image. Guedry *et al.* (1978) report that retinal image motions between 15 and $25° \text{ s}^{-1}$ can reduce an observer's visual acuity by a factor of five or more.

Excessive disparity between the vestibular and visual input can lead to motion sickness or to sensations of loss of balance (ataxia).

There are other types of apparent image motion that occur when the eyes move within certain types of helmet-mounted displays. As the eyes move parts of the displayed image appear to jump or move as a result of the interaction between rapid eye movements (saccades). Further details are given by Peli (1990). Displays that exhibit persistence, such as a CRT, are less likely to suffer from this problem. However, with the move towards higher resolution displays, with increased frame rates, persistence time will be reduced.

Although the persistence of existing CRTs does not usually cause a problem with rapid eye movement, it might become a problem in the future.

6.4.4 Auditory localization considerations

The human's auditory channel is frequently overlooked as an effective means of communicating information from a complex user interface. Common uses are to present simple audio tones to indicate various warnings.

One of the distinct advantages of the auditory system is that it works in parallel with the visual system and can be used to augment visual information. In fact, the auditory system often draws our attention to a particular situation before the visual system, because of its 360° field of regard. In a sense, the information picked up by the ears directs our line of sight. However, it would be wrong to assume that the auditory system is infallible. In fact, when the human operator is under extreme workload or stressful conditions, it is possible for the auditory system to shut off. In this case the human operator fails to hear anything and tends to concentrate exclusively on the visual/manual task. Moreover, the auditory system, like most human perceptual systems, quickly adapts to the external environment and an operator can be unaware of a constant background noise. When a change occurs in the background auditory signal, the operator becomes aware of the change very quickly. For instance, a sudden loud noise can startle.

Most people who drive cars are very good at detecting slight changes in engine noise. The change in noise draws the driver's attention to the engine, and action can prevent the car breaking down.

Apart from the auditory system's ability to discriminate between acoustic characters such as intensity, pitch, timbre and rhythm, it is exceptionally good at acoustic segregation. The 'cocktail party' effect was discussed in Chapter 3. The auditory perception system allows us to focus on a single auditory signal that is surrounded spatially by other sound sources. Probably one of the reasons why the auditory system is not often used is that it cannot always be relied upon to provide indication of an event. However, by using an appropriate audio signal in conjunction with a visual cue, it is likely that the dual information presentation will lead to less ambiguity in interpreting an event. The visual/auditory cue will tend to reinforce or enhance the information content.

Many people assume that the only mechanisms involved in spatially locating a given sound source are interaural intensity differences and interaural time delays, but these assumptions do not take into account that most human subjects can localize on the vertical median where interaural cues are minimal. It is now well known that the pinnae are partly responsible for sound localization. Under certain circumstances sounds placed in the front hemisphere, and close to the median plane, can sometimes be perceived as emanating from the near hemisphere. The reason for this reversal is not fully understood. If the listener is free to move the head around, the reversal effect is almost eliminated.

While humans can locate sounds to within 5° to 10° of the actual position, they are not so effective at resolving range information. Operating in a free space environment, one without reflection, improves range determination because echoes, which can confuse the listener, are eliminated.

Computer synthesized binaural sound localizers tend to operate by using head related transfer functions (HRTFs). Filtering in the frequency domain is achieved by means of point to point multiplication operations: in the time domain it is achieved by a process known as convolution (Brigham, 1974). By combining the HRTFs with a sound signal it is possible to spatialize the sound in any required direction.

6.4.5 Image/graphic generator issues

The design and implementation of the graphics system can have a critical bearing on the performance of a visually coupled system. There is no doubt that the problems of lag in an interactive computer graphics system are complex. Those associated with the tracker system have been discussed. However, the overall system lag can be a function of the way in which a computer graphics system has been constructed. Real-time interaction with a virtual environment places a high demand on the technologies involved. Unfortunately, few manufacturers are able, or willing, to quote transmission delays through their systems. It is relatively straightforward to quantify transmission delays through a single processor system but with multiprocessor architectures the matter becomes extremely complex. Sometimes it may not be possible to work out the exact transmission delay through a multiprocessor system. Instead, timings can only be calculated with a degree of uncertainty or tolerance.

From a complete system point of view, two types of lag can be defined: total system lag lag and position lag.

Total system lag

Total system lag is the time delay between a user interaction, for example, between head or hand position tracker and a corresponding movement on the display (see Figures 6.13 and 6.14).

Noise or uncertainty in the computation process within the tracker or graphics generator will cause a jitter in the output response.

Position lag

Position lag is induced by velocity and is defined in two parts (see Figure 6.15):

- The distance moved from a known position (at a given velocity)
- The actual distance moved in the virtual image.

Position lag is also a function of the velocity of the tracker's sensor and any filtering applied to the output of the tracker. Unfortunately, total system lag and position lag are not completely independent of each other. An expression describing the overall effect of transmission lag and position lag on a virtual object as a function of real object position is given by:

Virtual object position = Real object position − Total system lag × Velocity.

In practice measurement and calculation of these parameters is extremely involved.

To reduce the system-dependent lags in a visually coupled system it is important to be able to measure the individual lags comprising the total system lag. Architectural design can have a significant bearing on the total system lag.

Figure 6.13 shows an idealized visually coupled system architecture. The tracker is assumed to be interfaced to a dedicated I/O processor whose task is to convert tracker data into data appropriate for a graphics rendering computer.

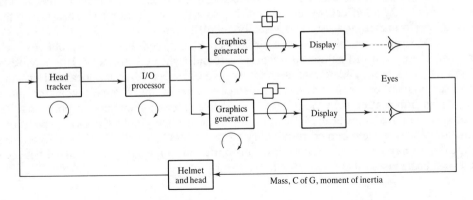

Figure 6.13 Simplified visually coupled system architecture.

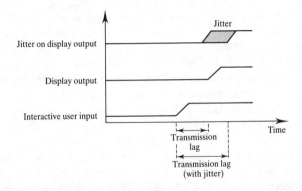

Figure 6.14 Total system lag within a visually coupled system.

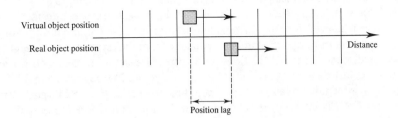

Figure 6.15 Position lag within a visually coupled system.

Two identical graphics channels are used – one per eye. Information generated by the I/O processor is supplied simultaneously to the graphics generators. In theory, this approach removes the synchronization problems between the left and right eye channels. The individual timing delays through this architectural arrangement are given in the figure. A visually coupled system is a closed loop system involving a helmet-mounted display mounted on the user's head. Parameters such as mass, moment of inertia and centre of gravity all affect the feedback path response. This in turn has a bearing on the overall performance of a user in a visually coupled system.

Departure from the idealized visually coupled system can cause problems such as synchronization difficulties between the left and right eye channels. This manifests itself as an apparent update rate between the two channels. Even the idealized visually coupled system can suffer from this defect if one of the channels contains more displayed information than the other, for example, a greater number of polygons. To reduce or eliminate this effect it is necessary to ensure that graphics drawing operations are completely written into corresponding frame buffers before the buffers are swapped onto the display generation electronics. This buffer swap must be synchronized between the two channels so that it occurs simultaneously.

Very high performance graphic systems for virtual environments

One of the key components of a virtual environment system, apart from the display device and tracking system, is the graphics platform. The displays produced in a virtual environment need not necessarily be mimics of the real world, but when they are, an extremely capable graphics platform is required. This platform must be capable of producing high resolution displays with real-time performance, while achieving the necessary level of photorealistic realism in conjunction with a variety of lighting effects. A more detailed examination of the requirements reveals that there are additional considerations such as synchronization between the left and right eye channels. If drawing and display operations between the two channels cannot be synchronized, then the eyes of the observer will be presented with unusual disparity effects. Under extreme situations caused by differential loading of the two graphics channels, it is possible for the image presented to appear as two separate images that cannot be fused, or at best, can only be fused for part of the time. Unfortunately, few graphics system manufacturers can accommodate true left and right eye synchronization. Indeed, some stereo graphics systems make no attempt at display synchronization.

A separate area of concern is the way in which time–critical data is input into the graphics system. For instance, most head tracking systems employ a serial RS232 interface. This can hardly be called a real-time high performance interface, and it is surprising that it is used for time-critical applications. At first sight, it might appear to ease the integration of peripherals into a virtual environment system, but careful analysis will reveal that most of the RS232 lines on a graphics system are designed for terminal I/O and not for fast data transmission. Consequently, the low level terminal I/O drives are frequently interrupt driven, which means that the faster the RS232 part is run, the more the host CPU is interrupted. This leads to the situation where the graphics system CPU is spending more time in servicing the interrupt than on the critical graphics operations. Obviously, graphics performance is compromised and the virtual environment illusion suffers.

To produce convincing systems in the future, it will be necessary for the graphics platform vendors to re-think their system architectures in line with the unique requirements of virtual environments. Equally, manufacturers need to reconsider their tracker designs and how these designs should be integrated. These recommendations are not new. They have been in existence since visually coupled systems emerged, when a requirement was clearly identified for very tight/close coupling between the tracker system and the graphics generation system.

Space tracker filter considerations

Space tracking systems such as the Ascension Bird employ several user-selectable filters to remove the effects of noise caused by electromagnetic coupling into the sensor system. Unfortunately, these filters, in common with all other tracking systems, can introduce lags or delays into the position and orientation data. Where a user is attempting to get minimal lags in a visual system, it is very important to understand the effect that a particular filter has on the tracker's performance. An incorrectly applied filter can cause very serious and unacceptable visual lags. Moreover, attempts to remove all filters can result in noise-induced effects causing unacceptable jitter and instability in the visual image.

By way of an example, the Ascension Bird provides three basic filter types each exhibiting very different characteristics. The first two are finite impulse response (FIR) notch filters, and the third is an infinite impulse response (IIR) low pass filter. The FIR filters provide narrow and wide a.c. notch characteristics.

- a.c. narrow FIR: This filter is provided with two taps and is used to eliminate a narrow band of sinusoidal noise. If minimal phase lag is required, then this filter should be used in preference to the a.c. wide FIR because it has approximately one third of the throughput delay.

- a.c. wide FIR: This filter is provided with six taps and is used to remove sinusoidal noise signals in the range 30–70 Hz. This filter should only be used in conditions of high noise levels because it can have a detrimental effect on visual image lags.

- d.c. IIR: This filter is an adaptive low pass filter that is used to eliminate high frequency noise components. In most systems this filter should be 'on' unless the application incorporates its own filtering algorithm. The user can supply a constant that is used by the IIR filter to define the lower end of the adaptive range. This constant can vary from 0 (an infinite amount of filtering – outputs never change) to 0.99996 (no filtering will be applied). This value should not be decreased below 0.008, otherwise the noise level will increase because of the mathematical precision being reduced.

Although not connected with the filter characteristics of the Ascension tracker system, the update rate selected by the user can affect overall system performance. To reduce errors resulting from the presence of highly conducting metals such as aluminium, the update rate should be reduced. Unfortunately, this has a knock-on effect of increasing the phase lag. Changing the update rate to compensate for low conductive, highly permeable materials such as carbon steel or iron has negligible effect.

The user must be extremely careful not to select an update rate that is equal to the line frequency (50 or 60 Hz).

6.5 Virtual environments: Interaction with virtual objects

6.5.1 Interaction within a virtual environment using a gestural input device

The majority of virtual environment systems seen today almost always feature the VPL DataGlove. Photographs of the DataGlove show the user employing some form of strange gesture, and video recordings inevitably show the user making strange, if not unnatural, grabbing gestures, seemingly interacting with another world. The concept of operation of DataGlove type devices has been explained in Chapter 4. While there is nothing too difficult to understand in terms of the basic operation of a DataGlove the incorporation of a gestural input device in a virtual environment system is another matter. Early suggestions for glove devices included basic interactions such as 'grab' and repositioning operations, as well as 'navigation' manoeuvres within the virtual world. Many early researchers derived their own series of gestures, which were generally unrelated and not consistent from one researcher to another. As more people became exposed to the developing gestural languages it became apparent that using glove devices to 'fly' through a virtual world actually detracted from the performance of the user. This was largely due to the unnatural gestures being either difficult to achieve reliably or non-intuitive, hence, difficult to remember. A few researchers generated menu-like structures that appeared to 'hang' in space. The user was required to reach up to these menus with a DataGlove and employ some form of gesture to indicate a particular selection. In essence, early gestural devices were seen as rather strange. Once the initial 'hype' subsided, several researchers began to look at solving some of the issues associated with glove devices.

Other non-gestural-based applications also emerged that relied on connecting the output of the DataGlove to teleoperated robot arms. In this application, movements of the user's hand were interpreted by a computer to allow the robot arm to mimic them. This type of application has generally been more successful than the early attempts to employ gestures.

Other applications of the DataGlove allowed the user to interact with virtual objects and change parameters interactively, such as position, orientation and size. The use of the DataGlove within a computer aided design environment was obvious.

Since the realization that the *ad hoc* use of gestures causes particular difficulty for the operator, many research groups have begun to address the key issues. This section addresses teleoperation issues as well as discussing some interesting work where neural networks have been used to recognize specific gestures.

6.5.2 Control of a robotic manipulator using a gesture control language

Teleoperated control of robot gestures is especially important in hazardous environments. The simplest arrangement is where the user's hand gestures are communicated directly without interpretation to an appropriate robotic manipulator. Hand gestures are translated to the manipulator, allowing its greater power to be used, for example, to pick up heavy objects that are beyond the capabilities of the human operator. Other applications translate natural-like hand gestures into a series of operations or commands that a robot can understand. This type of arrangement can often overcome limitations of the human hand, such as the impossibility of continuous rotation about an axis, for example, unscrewing a screw. A manipulator operated in this way is intuitive to use because it behaves more or less like the human arm. An interesting system has been developed by Gigante and Papper (1992) at the Royal Melbourne Institute of Technology. Their system comprises a series of components:

- Interaction mechanism
- Coupling mechanisms
- Constraints (limitations on robot arm behaviour)
- Robot arm editor

During operation the user's hand movements are transferred directly to the robot arm, and minimal cognitive effort is required on the part of the user. To provide access to additional capabilities in the robot arm, a series of gestures have been developed (see Figure 6.16). These gestures cover the following actions:

- Clutch: Disengages from gesture control and can be used to prevent inadvertent hand gestures from being sent to the control system. A similar arrangement is often used in a speech recognition system where the command 'sleep' is used to isolate the speech recognizer.

- Lock: Fixes the robot arm in a certain position. This allows the arm to be precisely locked onto a particular axis or reference frame and is used, for example, to locate and screw a nut onto a bolt.

- Continuous wrist rotation: In this mode the robot arm rotates about the wrist axis, allowing a screwing action.

- Stretch: This gesture allows the arm length to be extended. This will usually be beyond the normal range of the human arm.

- Ambidextrous: In this mode the robot arm can be swapped from a right-handed arm to a left-handed arm.

These gestures have not been optimized in any way and many users will find it difficult to perform some of the gestures, particularly the ambidextrous ones. Nevertheless, Gigante and Papper attempted to classify gestures into a form of gesture language. Gestures were classified as hand, state or motion gestures.

Hand gestures involve relative flexure of the user's fingers, irrespective of hand orientation. State gestures are governed by the orientation of the hand and the flexure of the fingers. These gestures cover the traditional point and fly operations, and stop and start. Motion gestures are those that describe some path in space as the hand is moved.

One problem with the use of gestures lies with the precision to which the glove device can measure each finger's flexion. Moreover, large groups of gestures tend to be difficult to learn and remember. Unfortunately, little work has been done to assess user performance with a gestural control system. The precision of glove devices is continually being refined. The CyberGlove is probably the most precise of today's glove devices. However, modern computer technology can go a long way to assist the user of gestural input devices.

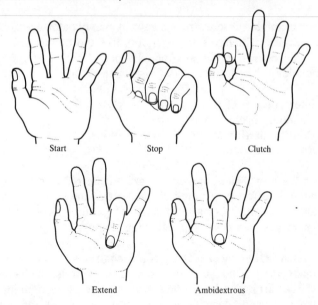

Figure 6.16 A range of gestures used to control a robot manipulator.

A technique is required that will allow a user to train the computer with the necessary gestures, in a way that matches the gestures that are comfortable to the user. Traditional DataGlove systems require the user to calibrate the glove by measuring the angles of each joint, and storing the information so that when the user makes a similar gesture, each finger angle is compared against the stored data. When a series of finger angles corresponds to a stored gesture, a signal is generated that represents the specified gesture. Unfortunately, there is very little tolerance on these gestures and a slight angular variation usually results in a failure to recognize the gesture or, worst still, the wrong gesture being identified. Angular variations can be caused by the glove slipping on the hand, which can occur easily if the glove does not fit very well. There are a range of techniques for classifying data, such as maximum likelihood estimation, which may be used to recognize gestures. Unfortunately, these techniques tend to involve considerable amounts of data preprocessing, which does not lend itself to real-time gesture recognition. Moreover, some of these techniques require very detailed understanding of the nature of the input data.

Several researchers, including Väänänen and Böhm (1992), have examined the use of neural networks for the recognition of gestures. Neural networks can be trained with static and dynamic inputs without having to define transfer characteristics in an analytic way. They can also be trained very easily in a fast and interactive manner. Their application to gesture recognition problems is obvious. Väänänen and Böhm have used back propagation networks because of their ease of use and powerful nature. The neural networks were designed to cope with both static and dynamic gestures. Static gesture recognition is much easier than dynamic gesture recognition, which relies on taking hand movement into account. For static gesture recognition it is only necessary to obtain information about the angles of the fingers.

Static gesture recognition

For the purposes of illustration, assume that a VPL DataGlove is used. This produces two outputs per finger, one for each joint. The outputs must be preprocessed so that they range from 0 to 90°. These outputs are then scaled to give an output in the range of 0 to 1, because neural networks work more efficiently with this range. Back propagation neural networks are used to recognize the gesture. These neural networks have three layers: an input neuron layer, an intermediate (hidden) neuron layer and an output neuron layer. The input neuron layer must have as many input neurons as there are inputs. In the case of the DataGlove this is 10 neurons. The number of intermediate and output layer neurons depends upon the number of actual gestures that must be recognized. If only eight gestures are required then the intermediate and output neuron layers will generally employ eight neurons each. Figure 6.17 illustrates the principle.

Dynamic gesture recognition

Dynamic gestures involve the movement of the hand in conjunction with finger gestures. There is obviously a time element that must be encapsulated by the recognition process. The neural network must take into account information from the hand position and orientation tracker over several samples. The neural network will be more complex because there will now be a further six inputs (hand translation x, y, z and hand orientation azimuth, elevation and roll). To allow the time element to be taken into account a pair of shift registers are used to store a sequence of gesture samples over a period of time. New data is clocked into the shift register and then into the neural network. Figure 6.18 shows a neural network gesture recognition system that employs both static and dynamic gesture recognition.

It will be noted from Figure 6.18 that an additional processing stage is required for position and orientation recognition. This is the derivative stage where it is necessary to determine the relative movement of the hand. Two neural networks are required. The first recognizes finger gestures and has 50 inputs (5 inputs per 10 joint angles). The number of outputs depends on the number of dynamic gestures used. The second neural network uses position and orientation data (6 inputs) to recognize a specific hand gesture. An additional output is made available from the second neural network that corresponds to a static hand position. One of the disadvantages of neural networks is the rate at which the required number of neurons increases. In this example, with a five sample time window, 50 input neurons are required. As the number of actual gestures increases the number of intermediate and output neurons also increases. Dynamic gestures are probably more natural and intuitive than static gestures but are more difficult to recognize. In real-world situations a user will employ gestures to augment or amplify a spoken opinion or command.

Ideally, a simpler approach is required for gesture recognition, to avoid the need for detailed analytic approaches to gestures. This is particularly important because the sizes of different users' hands will vary, so a given gesture will generally be slightly different. Clues to a suitable solution come from modern speech recognition technology. Adaptive neural networks have been applied to speech recognition (Lippman, 1989). A neural network can be trained with a complicated mapping from input to output. Once trained, it can readily generate new situations and can be retrained very simply.

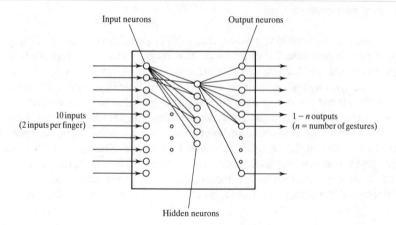

Figure 6.17 Back propagation neural network for static gesture recognition.

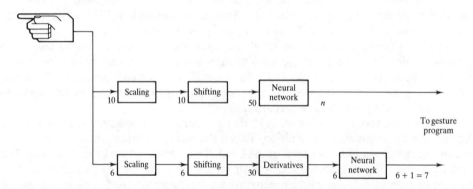

Figure 6.18 Dynamic gesture neural network recognition system.

The key characteristics of a neural network include:

- Neural networks can be trained with almost any input to output mapping.
- To teach a neural network, only the input function and output mapping are required.
- Neural networks can be retrained simply by being presented with a new input–output mapping.
- Neural networks can be tailored to suit an individual's needs.

An extensive neural network system has been developed by Fels and Hinton (1990) to convert gestures made with a VPL DataGlove into suitable commands for a speech synthesis system. Hand gestures derived from the American Sign Language (ASL) have been trained into a neural network (Wilbur, 1979), resulting in a system capability of approximately 203 gestures. By making appropriate ASL gestures it was possible to generate corresponding speech from the speech synthesizer. A neural network comprises layers of simple neurons (like processing elements). Individual neurons connect to one another by weighted connections and each neuron has a state that is governed by a previous layer. The complete input x_j received by a neuron j is defined by:

$$x_j = \sum_i y_i w_{ji} - b_j$$

where y_i is the state of the ith neuron, w_{ji} is the weight on connection between the ith and jth neurons, and b_j is the bias on the jth neuron.

Biases are really the weights on extra input lines whose activity is always 1. The neural network is trained by applying the external input vector to the input neurons of the network, and the states of the other neurons are determined by the activation function. The network's knowledge about the function it has learned is encapsulated by the connections and weights between neuron layers. The input vector is propagated through the network and the output is compared to the desired output vector. The weights are then adjusted until the error function is minimized. The simplest way of adjusting the weight is to calculate the gradient of the error function with respect to the weights, a process known as back propagation (Rumelhart *et al.*, 1986).

6.5.3 Haptic display technologies

Haptic displays are an augmentation to visual displays that can improve perception in virtual environments through the use of force fields and objects with impenetrable surfaces. There is some evidence that haptic augmented virtual environment systems can offer an almost twofold improvement in performance, compared to 'visual only' systems.

Outstanding unknowns with haptic display representations

The following questions remain unanswered with respect to haptic systems:

- Do haptic displays aid perception in a virtual environment?
- What level of improvement in performance can haptic displays offer to a user in virtual environments?
- What should haptic technology be used for?
- How good should the haptic representation be to aid perception in a virtual environment?
- What is the effect of lag on performance with haptic displays?
- What is the effect of 'mechanical backlash' in a haptic display system?

Safety aspects of force reflecting devices: Kinaesthetic displays

It is worth drawing attention to the safety issues of kinaesthetic display systems, because under certain error conditions they are capable of causing serious injury. Adelstein and

Rosen (1992) state (in relation to kinaesthetic display systems), 'The human subject who volunteers to participate in experiments with the apparatus is, in effect, being asked to shake hands with a device that has force, velocity and acceleration capabilities similar to those of an industrial robot!' Imagine holding a device if it were capable of entering an error state where maximum displacement amplitude was suddenly achieved at the maximum frequency of oscillation! Clearly, if force reflecting joysticks are to gain acceptance, then the health and safety issues must be addressed. Safety systems must be incorporated (at least to aircraft safety standards), ensuring operator safety. Even with low force exerting systems it will be necessary to demonstrate a high level of safety. This will require a different and more rigorous approach to the design of the hardware and software inherent in such a system. Integration of one of these devices will mean that the virtual environment system becomes safety critical. Aircraft designers know only too well what this entails in their design process.

Scaling in an interactive virtual environment

Scaling, or more correctly 'the maintenance of correct geometrical or spatial relationships between virtual objects', is an important perception consideration. Scaling effects can occur in several ways. Two common causes include nonlinear mapping of the environment, and exaggerated scaling/magnification/minification.

If a virtual environment is overlaid or mixed with the real world, then any non-correspondence between the two worlds will be immediately apparent and may even lead to rejection of the virtual system. In many respects, the overlaying of a virtual environment onto the real world presents a challenge for the designer, and it can be used to test such systems.

Nonlinear mapping

A virtual environment can be scaled 1:1 with the real world, so that a movement of 1 m in the virtual environment corresponds to a 1 m movement in the real world. Errors in the position and orientation tracking systems can lead to a nonlinear correspondence between the virtual and real environments. Whether or not this nonlinearity affects user performance depends upon the task being undertaken. Consider a virtual control station, such as a vehicle cockpit, where the spatial relationships of the displays and control interfaces have been carefully designed. After a period of training the user instinctively knows where to find control interfaces, due to an internal sense of body position (kinaesthesia). When the interface to the operator is purely visual, such as a vehicle instrument, a degree of nonlinear positioning can be tolerated provided that only small head movements are made. Nonlinear mapping appears as unnatural movement of the virtual objects as the head is moved.

A user required to fixate on one of these virtual objects as the head is moved can quickly become fatigued. Tracking nonlinearities tends to increase as the head or hand tracking system is moved away from the boresight or initial calibration position. This means that objects that have to be fixated, or objects that are normally positioned in the peripheral field, will demand unnatural head/eye movement.

When the user is required to interact through some form of virtual hand controller with a virtual environment, nonlinearities between the tracked hand and the virtual object can cause very annoying compensatory movements of the hand. Although the human kinaesthetic feedback system can slowly adapt to certain nonlinearities, this does not seem to apply to virtual interaction tasks. There is a tendency to overcompensate when interacting with the virtual object.

The visual geometry of the virtual environment remains consistent with the equivalent real-world situation, and this interferes with the human kinaesthetic feedback system. The user can tolerate these effects by interacting much more slowly with the virtual environment than would be the case in the real world. Obviously, this can affect the user's performance, particularly if a tracking type task is to be performed. To some extent these effects are similar to delayed feedback, where the user makes a movement and a corresponding movement in the virtual environment occurs after a certain time delay. Anyone experiencing a lower performance virtual environment system for the first time will be acutely aware of these deficiencies. The required compensatory actions can often lead to a certain amount of 'thrashing around' in the environment.

Magnetic-based tracking systems are probably more susceptible to additional non-linearities being introduced into the virtual environment. Depending on whether the tracking system is of an a.c. or d.c. type, the presence of certain conductive materials in the real environment, within the operating envelope of the tracker, can lead to shifts or offsets in the tracked position/orientation, as well as the nonlinearities described above.

It is rather interesting that the human operator can actually adapt to these shifts over a relatively short period of time, provided that the virtual environment is completely immersive, and no direct visual contact is made with the user's hands. It is possible to slowly introduce a position shift in the system such that the user slowly shifts hand position to compensate for the displacement (the user remaining completely unaware that their hands are in an unnatural position). Obviously, there is a maximum position shift that can be tolerated, where the user becomes incapable of compensating for the effect. Usually, the first sign that the user gets that an unacceptable shift has occurred is when an object that is within the visual field is unreachable. This can come as quite a surprise if the helmet-mounted display is removed while the user's hand is retained in the extended position. Fortunately, it is possible to characterize the real-world environment and map out any position/orientation shifts and nonlinear effects that exist. This imposes additional complexity in either the tracking system or graphics system. The task of mapping the working volume of an environment should not be underestimated. Not only does it take a long time to make measurements, but a vast amount of data is collected that must be reduced into a look up table or some form of polynomial or algorithmic solution.

Exaggerated scaling/magnification

One of the unique advantages of a virtual environment is the ability to place a person in an otherwise impossible environment. For example, users could be placed in microscopic worlds at a molecular level, or in macroscopic worlds such as a virtual planetarium. Movement within these environments would not be scaled 1:1 with the real world (for obvious reasons). However, situations can be envisaged where a user normally operating in a 1:1 virtual environment is presented with a magnified view of an object. For example, consider a virtual city. It is possible to move around this city viewing its components at various ranges. It may be desirable to zoom into a part of the visual image to inspect some fine detail. In this mode it is very important to apply some suitable scaling to any interactive virtual peripherals. This may seem very obvious, but the author has seen some examples where this has been neglected.

However, of great importance is the need to develop a reliable and intuitive method for moving (navigating, commonly called 'flying') within the virtual environment. Using a specific gesture with a glove-like device may not be the best approach. It will be important to address whether or not the operator's spatial awareness is suppressed by staying stationary (with feet effectively on the ground), while flying around the virtual world. Unfortunately, we do not know nearly enough about situation awareness in the real world, let alone in a virtual world.

6.6 A cautionary remark

There is evidence suggesting that under certain circumstances virtual displays can cause problems. Roscoe (1984, 1985) reported operational problems involving aircraft head up displays (HUDs). He refers to Newman (1980), and states that the HUD can cause disorientation when flying in and out of clouds.

Pilots have also reported a tendency to focus on the HUD combiner, rather than on the outside world scene. Added to this information is experimental evidence indicating that human eyes do not accommodate at optical infinity when observing collimated images. Instead, the eyes tend to accommodate to the resting accommodation distance about 1 m away (Hull *et al.*, 1982). The effect of this is that the visual scene appears to reduce in size. Aircraft pilots tend to judge a target to be further away and the dive angle shallower than it actually is. Roscoe suggests that the displayed image should be magnified by an appropriate amount to offset the reduction in size caused by the misaccommodation. In doing this, the magnification would have to be variable to suit individual perceptual bias. In a sense, Roscoe's remarks may only apply to see-through virtual environment applications, and only in situations where the pilot is unaware of his/her actual relationship to the real world. However, Roscoe does state that a reduction in resolution of a displayed image of a real world may lead to a suppression of very important visual cues. For instance, one's inability to judge acceleration or speed is a function of the texture gradients that flow into our visual perception system. The reduced resolution display may remove or modify the optical flow in such a way that we misinterpret what is happening.

The interested reader should consult Roscoe (1961, 1976, 1981, 1984, 1985). The author considered it prudent to draw the reader's attention to the incomplete understanding of the human perceptual system. Even if we fully understood our perceptual mechanism, it would be difficult enough to determine the effect that technology would create. In fact, in many respects, the technology is probably the limiting factor. As far as the designer is concerned, inappropriate technology may well introduce additional artefacts that our perceptual system responds to in unexpected ways.

Some researchers refuse to come to terms with Roscoe's statements (even though experimental evidence does support his claims), while others are in complete agreement with him. It is far better to accept that we do not yet fully understand the human perception system. Researchers must take every precaution to ensure that problems do not occur.

6.7 Summary

This chapter has addressed the areas of virtual environments where further research is required to establish better definitions and where our understanding is weakest. As our knowledge increases we will be able to define more precisely the requirements of the man–machine interface and the performance expectations of the enabling technology. The overall aim is to produce an interface that matches the human to the task in a natural, intuitive manner without incurring additional cognitive workload.

To achieve these goals we must be able to extract the key performance features of the virtual environment and use these to drive the manufacturers of such technology to produce equipment matched to the task.

7 Applications of Virtual Environments

Objectives

This chapter describes existing applications for virtual environment technologies. While some of these are based on research investigations, or concept demonstrations, they suffice to illustrate that the virtual environment field will influence the way that we interact with computer-based systems. A virtual environment system can be regarded as the next generation computer interface. With careful introduction of the technology we will be able to take advantage of the remarkable performance of modern computer systems in a more natural and intuitive manner.

7.1 Introduction

The previous chapters have concentrated on the underlying science and engineering of virtual environments. Whether one describes this branch of technology as virtual environments, virtual reality, artificial reality, cyberspace or another name does not really matter, because what is important is the fact that the basic principles behind the technology must first be acknowledged, addressed and mastered.

As with all new technologies, it is tempting to believe statements that this new concept is the solution to all computer problems. If we do believe it, there is a danger that less sophisticated and more cost-effective solutions will be overlooked in the desire to forge ahead too quickly.

In a field such as virtual environments where an increase in system performance is desired beyond that which is available today, it is important to quantify the benefits that the technology will give before forging ahead.

Will further expense and further research be cost effective, or is it best to direct funds into developing the less sophisticated technology already available? Careful consideration will mean that funds are directed at developing the most appropriate technology.

While still developing available techniques, the scientist should be given time to understand the human factors side of virtual environments. In many respects, the technology that allows a virtual environment to be assembled has arrived before we fully understand the human factors or the engineering implications of this type of man-machine interface. Nevertheless, the evidence available today indicates that a virtual environment system could revolutionize the way in which humans interact with complex computer-based systems. Many manufacturers already see this technology as a cost saver.

With so many potential applications, it is difficult to predict exactly where the greatest benefits will occur. It is unlikely that there will be just one standard of virtual environment interface to suit all needs and all applications. Technological and cost limitations will mean that the task or application will dictate the level and sophistication of technology employed. Many applications will drive the development of the technology in a specific direction and may very well lead to spin offs in other application areas.

7.2 Applications

In addition to highlighting possible virtual environment application areas, part of this chapter will review some applications that have already been tested in a virtual environment. It is not possible to describe each application in great detail, because some are covered by commercial confidentiality agreements. However, what is presented will give the reader an insight into the diverse range of fields that could benefit from the introduction of this technology.

For convenience, the examples described in the following sections have been grouped into a series of application areas. Many of them could be applicable to more than one area.

7.3 Scientific visualization

The whole field of scientific visualization has changed significantly over the last decade because of the tremendous advances in computer graphics technology. Almost all branches of science are of necessity dominated by a need to present complex multidimensional data sets to the researcher. Early visual representations were either simple animated sequences or a complex static representation of some event. More recent systems are capable of displaying massive, multidimensional data sets in a dynamic manner with significant levels of user interaction. Scientific visualization has advanced to the stage where simulations that once took hours, or even weeks, to compute are now condensed into a matter of milliseconds. This has allowed the scientist to explore all sorts of areas and boundaries of understanding that would otherwise have been impractical or too expensive simply because of the computation time.

There is little doubt that dynamic visual displays help one to understand how various parameters interact with each other, especially over a period or through certain conditions. The nature of modern visualization systems allows the scientist to interact with the multidimensional data set in the hope that new or otherwise hidden phenomena will be revealed. The scientist has to represent the multidimensional data in a clear and effective manner. The relative ease of computing very dynamic visualization tempts one to rush ahead without examining the nature of the resulting data and how it should be used. Given the enormity of multidimensional data sets, there is a real problem in deciding how to present the data to the user. It is easy to generate very complex displays that are perceptually ambiguous and impossible to interpret. At first only 2-D displays were available, but this rapidly evolved to 3-D displays, whereby perspective displays could be used for data representations. More recently these have been extended to stereoscopic displays where the data set appears in front of the user's display screen.

Virtual environment technology has now emerged where the user can actually become immersed in the multidimensional data set. Couple this with the interactivity offered by virtual environment systems, and we have a recipe for the ultimate visualization system *or* a complete disaster. Ellis (1989) warns that 'the subjective spatial impressions provided by a visualization system are particularly important if the display is to be a basis for immediate interaction with the actual environment that it depicts'.

Ellis suggests that adjusting the field of view so that the image correctly reproduces the object's lines of sight for an observer does not necessarily guarantee that the most accurate spatial perception will be achieved. Observers sometimes demonstrate systematic errors in exocentric judgements under viewing conditions that are 'telephoto' or 'zoom' representations. To correct errors in egocentric orientations it may be necessary to introduce some form of compensation. Scientific visualization involving virtual environments is currently being considered for a wide range of subjects.

7.3.1 Visualization of planetary surfaces

NASA scientists have overlaid sequences of images taken from NASA spacecraft onto planet surface altitude data. The sample database was from Mars. This has meant that it is possible to synthesize flights over the planetary surface, even though it is not yet possible to reach the planet by manned spacecraft. 'NASA scientists are particularly excited by virtual environment planetary explorations' (McGreevy, 1991).

7.3.2 NASA Ames virtual wind tunnel

NASA Ames Research Center is the home of the world's largest full-scale wind tunnel, large enough to hold full sized jet fighters. NASA researchers are engaged in a Numerical Aerodynamic Simulation (NAS) project that one day may render conventional wind tunnels obsolete. They are working on a virtual environment project called the 'Virtual Wind Tunnel'. The project is an attempt to exploit the technology developed in the NASA Ames VIEW Laboratory. The research group is looking at visualization and user interfaces especially for exploring and understanding the output of Computational Fluid Dynamics (CFD) codes. The flows are very complicated and the data sets large. Many visualization tools started off as metaphors for the exploration of flows in the wind tunnels. NASA Ames scientists chose an aircraft around which to simulate the flow of a fluid. 'The goal of the Virtual Wind Tunnel Project is to produce a system that will permit a flow scientist to interact with 3-D time varying flow calculation results' (Beard, 1992). The computational facilities to support the NAS facility are very powerful and include a Cray-YMP/8, a Cray-2, a Thinking Machines Corporation CM-2 Connection Machine with 32,000 processors and DataVault, and an Intel 128 processor iPSC/860 computer where each processor is a 40 MFLOPS double precision i860. Visualization is handled by Silicon Graphics platforms. Plate 21 shows the NASA Ames Research Center Virtual Wind Tunnel.

An early prototype of the Virtual Wind Tunnel was demonstrated at Visualization 90. The hardware was based around a boom mounted, head tracking, stereo viewer and a VPL DataGlove. The whole system was driven by an SGI 320/VGX workstation. The demonstration allowed the operator to see the surface of the aircraft in the flow, rendered as outlined polygons (with hidden lines removed), and to use the Polhemus space tracker on the glove to start a particle trace. This demonstration worked in much the same way as smoke emitted in a wind tunnel, with it being viewed from any location to see which way it would go. Gestures allowed a user to freeze a trace, start a new one and grab the model, allowing it to be repositioned and orientated.

NASA chose the boom mounted display because they wanted better resolution and brightness than was obtainable over the lower cost helmet-mounted display. Current high resolution CRTs are too heavy for integration into a helmet-mounted display. The boom has built-in tracking, therefore a person using a boom in an office could look away to answer the phone, or look to see who was entering the room. He could call someone else to see exactly what he was looking at. The boom was made for NASA by Fake Space Systems and it was shown at Cyberthon.

There are other virtual environment projects being undertaken at NASA Ames, mainly in the Human Factors Directorate, the parent organization of Advanced Display and Spatial Perception Group. This includes a synthesized locality specific acoustics laboratory and a planetary exploration system based on reconnaissance photographs.

7.3.3 Molecular synthesis

Interest in using virtual environments to undertake complex molecular synthesis experiments has been generated largely as a result of the pioneering work at the University of North Carolina where chemists can manipulate molecular models of drugs in a virtual environment. The key to this activity is the use of force feedback to test for optimal orientations for binding sites on other molecules. This is called molecular docking. Special force-reflecting joysticks have been created to provide high fidelity force feedback with bandwidths in excess of 30 Hz. The University of North Carolina have developed a full six degrees of freedom force feedback manipulator, shown in Plate 1, to present force and torque vectors in molecular docking investigations.

If the force feedback system is to be effective, it must possess a high mechanical bandwidth. A consequence of this is that it must be very carefully designed to protect an operator from harmful force reflections. In early generation systems serious injuries have resulted from the use of such systems.

7.4 Medical applications

Virtual environments have the potential to revolutionize medical imaging. Nearly all the enabling technology is already being used in the medical field, or is being used in various virtual environment laboratories. Developments in computer graphics technology are bringing the cost versus performance figure down to more affordable and acceptable levels. It is only a question of time before virtual environment technologies are coupled with medical imaging data to give massive improvements in diagnostic treatment.

To illustrate the potential of a virtual environment system to medical applications, several possible uses are suggested.

7.4.1 Virtual stereotactic surgery

An application to improve intraoperative localization systems has been developed to aid neurosurgeons. The system employs a position sensing articulating arm integrated with a 3-D image processing system. The image processing system reproduces a patient's preoperative computed tomography (CT) data set. The basic system allows the tip of the articulating arm to be correlated with the patient on the operating table.

Neurosurgeons have to integrate a whole series of CT slices to build up a mental 3-D image of the patient. Stereotactic frames can provide 3-D localization of an intracranial target for surgical planning before the operation is carried out. A whole range of free hand surgical navigation tools have been developed in recent years. One of the most successful is the 'Viewing Wand' developed by ISG Technologies (Leggett *et al.*, 1991) (see Figure 7.1).

Small adhesive backed metallic beads about 2 mm in diameter are applied to a patient's scalp in six different positions before the preoperative CT scan. During the CT scan the patient's head is fully supported to ensure that it does not move. A whole series of slices are taken at approximately 3 mm increments. Slices at other increments can be taken if necessary. The CT scan data is transferred to an advanced 3-D image processing station where the 3-D objects such as skin surface, fiducial markers, skull and tumour sites are constructed as 3-D objects. The reformatted data is visualized with the articulating arm. While the patient is being anaesthetized the surgeon can preview the CT scan data. To maintain registration between the patient and the data set Mayfield pinions are used to immobilize the head. The articulating arm, which has a six degree of freedom sensing system, is used for spatial localization. The surgeon initiates a registration and calibration procedure by touching the six marker positions on the patient with the articulating arm. After registration, the articulating arm gives the surgeon interactive control over the display of the 3-D objects.

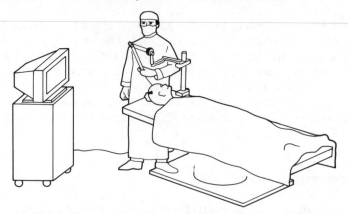

Figure 7.1 Articulating arm used for spatial location in neurosurgery.

Features such as image rotation, zoom and degree of translucency permit examination of deep structures, in connection with overlying structures.

The registration is valid as long as the patient's head does not move. The probe is moved around the area of interest while the surgeon observes the 3-D display and decisions are taken on the best entry point and trajectory, to minimize incision, the size of dural opening and gyral incision.

One clear disadvantage of this and other surgical techniques is the need to immobilize the head in a set position.

At times it would be useful to move the patient's head but this causes a loss of registration. Technologies used for virtual environments have the potential to allow free head movement and provide easy visualization of the 3-D CT scan data set. Either helmet-mounted displays or counterbalanced displays would be appropriate for this task.

The first and probably the most important technology that could be applied is the head tracking system. It should be possible to mount a tracking system to the patient's head and avoid the need to use Mayfield pinions to immobilize the head. It should also be possible to mount a tracking device on the end of a laser or other scalpel and accurately track the cutting tip. In this way the surgeon could be guided to the areas requiring surgery as identified on the CT scan data set. This concept is not entirely free from problems, because an operating theatre is full of metallic materials. These may preclude electromagnetic tracking systems. Moreover, the whole virtual environment system becomes potentially safety critical, which demands a very stringent approach to complete system design, software and eventual acceptance.

7.4.2 Magnetic resonance imaging systems: A virtual environment

The demand for the application of magnetic resonance imaging (MRI) systems to non-invasive examinations of patients is increasing. While this technique does not replace X-rays or other inspection methods, the relative ease with which it can be undertaken and the very high resolution imagery it can present to the surgeon make it an important medical tool. Many patients are routinely screened with MRI systems to detect changes in the body, so that a problem can then be treated in its primary stage.

7.4.3 Pathological tremor investigations

Neuromuscular output of the body tends to lead to involuntary oscillations called tremors being superimposed on the output. For able bodied, healthy people this tremor is very small and requires very sensitive equipment to detect it. However, in neurologically disabled people, these pathological tremors are quite obvious and can have sufficient amplitude to obscure concomitant voluntary muscular activity to a point where the voluntary action is useless. Frequency of oscillation ranges from 1.5 Hz for certain pathological conditions to 12 Hz for normal healthy tremor (Adelstein and Rosen, 1992). Several mechanisms are suggested for the source of these tremors, including:

- Autonomous pacemakers in the brain and spinal regions.
- Tuned resonance of limb biomechanics.
- Marginal stability due to conduction latencies in neuromuscular reflex loop pathways.

Non-invasive techniques to investigate tremogenic mechanisms rely on using some form of controlled mechanical loading until there is no tremor response. For instance, it has been found that an externally applied mechanical load can stop pathological tremors. The work reported by Adelstein and Rosen indicates that the tremor could be caused by autonomous pacemakers in the body. Apart from having important medical implications, this could have significant outcomes for kinaesthetic display systems, where the need for an effective kinaesthetic coupling for force reflecting manual interfaces is so important.

7.4.4 Ultrasonic imaging: A virtual environment perspective

Ultrasonic imaging is routinely used by doctors and physicians to examine structures in a patient in a non-invasive manner. Ultrasonic imaging relies on launching an ultrasonic wave into the body and then being able to detect the acoustic reflections as it passes through the body. The reflection intensity and scattering of the ultrasonic wave is a function of the composition of the body between the ultrasonic transmitter and receiver. Different structures in the body can be readily differentiated. The technique is frequently used to check on the development of a foetus in a pregnant woman. With appropriate training the physician can interpret the two-dimensional images and identify irregularities. The gender of the unborn child can also be identified.

Some extremely interesting work is being conducted at the University of North Carolina (Stix, 1992) in combining the ultrasonic imaging system with a virtual environment display system. The idea is to transform the image from a real-time ultrasound scanner to the viewpoint of a physician, wearing a helmet-mounted display. The physician will then have a view of the ultrasound image superimposed onto the body of the patient. The technique relies on the helmet-mounted display having a see-through capability. Figure 7.2 gives an artist's impression of the concept. Stix (1992) shows a photograph of Professor Henry Fuchs, one of the principal investigators, demonstrating the concept.

The physician could use the system to make accurate spatial judgements when placing probes inside the body, for example, when performing an amniocentesis test.

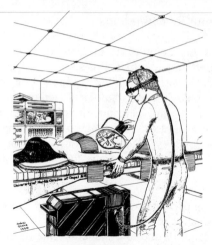

Figure 7.2 Ultrasound examination.

Currently, the physician has to interpret the ultrasound image and manipulate the needle of the syringe through the uterine cavity to the amniotic sack. Future enhancements to the system will include the integration of a 3-D ultrasound imaging system and wider field of view see-through helmet-mounted displays. With proper use of 3-D display techniques it will be possible to visualize images as though they are inside the patient, rather than mysteriously floating above.

7.4.5 Radiation treatment planning

Currently, planning of radiation treatment requires physicians to examine 2-D representations of a patient's anatomy. Their aim is to work out optimal radiation beam placement to deliver appropriate radiation doses to tumours, while minimizing exposure to healthy unaffected tissues. By manipulating a patient's CT data set, or MRI set, with a virtual representation of the radiation beam placements, it is possible for the physician's spatial awareness to be improved, with the benefit of reduced radiation exposure for the patient. Although it seems obvious to employ a helmet-mounted display for this task, it may be that a conventional computer graphics display, possibly with a stereoscopic capability, is adequate.

7.5 Teleoperations and hazardous environments

The prospect of distancing a user from a hazardous environment by a virtual environment system has particularly exciting possibilities. The use of teleoperated robots is not a new idea; indeed, they have been used routinely in many applications for a number of years. The current generation of teleoperated robots (or vehicles) do not convey a sense of real presence within the hazardous environment. A remote operator's actions in controlling a robot by remote control, even though he/she may be in a safe location, can still have disastrous consequences. For instance in the handling of radioactive products, a spillage can incur an expensive clean up operation. Even today a totally autonomous robot is still probably out of the question for many tasks. A robot that has a high degree of manual intervention is likely to be a requirement for the immediate future. One of the distinct advantages of a human operator is the person's ability to make decisions based on minimal information, or at best to refer to knowledge from a previous situation. Current robot systems are not normally able to communicate the necessary level of awareness to an operator, who is required to control manually or intervene in a current task. The idea of coupling an image from sensors mounted on a robot to an operator has been tried many times. One of the first documented teleoperated virtual environment system was reported in 1958 (Comeau, 1961). As described in Chapter 2, this system consisted of a video camera slewed to head position. Unfortunately, the resolution of the head tracker, head-mounted display and gimbal platform were too low to make the system useful.

Work by NASA has stimulated activities in teleoperation. Applications for space exploration are obvious, but not without unique problems. For instance, the communication delay between the remote operator and the robot vehicle system presents an interesting manual interaction problem. Teleoperation research is being undertaken by several institutions throughout the world.

7.5.1 Virtual Environment Remote Driving Experiment (VERDEX)

The Advanced Robotics Research Centre, Salford, UK, under the direction of Mr R. Stone, has developed an experimental test bed for human factors evaluation of telepresence technologies. The test bed is known as the Virtual Environment Remote Driving Experiment (VERDEX) (see Figure 7.3). VERDEX involves the integration of a remote head slaved stereo audio visual system coupled to a helmet-mounted display. The remote robot is based on a Cybermotion K2A Navmaster (Stone, 1991). Other man–machine interfaces such as speech recognition and a virtual hand controller (the VPL DataGlove) are integrated into the system.

The aim of the research project is to allow a virtual image reconstruction of a remote environment by using the geometric output of non-visual sensors and data fused with a computer aided design (CAD) representation of the environment. The user can control the robot through the real environment via a virtual interface. When the robot detects objects in the real environment that do not appear in the virtual environment, it will take appropriate collision avoidance. For certain tasks, the user is able to control a pair of head slaved cameras to interact with the real world.

A spin-off from the VERDEX project has been the development of the Teletact range of tactile feedback glove devices (described in Chapter 4).

Another significant development from the project has been the development of a special 3-D image analysis system. This imaging system is able to scan an area and determine the size, shape, position and orientation of objects in a real environment. The resulting data is further processed and incorporated into the virtual environment. The long term aim is to be able to use the system to map out the real environment, so that it can be used either by autonomous robots or along with a supervised robot system.

It is already possible to buy short range 3-D scanners from companies such as Cyberware. These systems can accurately scan an object's shape and colour to give a full colour image, which can then be displayed on a graphics workstation. This process allows a user to capture the shape and colour of any object for later use in a virtual environment. Example applications include clay models, human heads, reconstructive surgery and cosmetic surgery.

Figure 7.3 Virtual Environment Remote Driving Experiment (VERDEX).

7.5.2 European Space Agency (ESA): Man in Virtual Space (MVS)

The European Space Agency, European Space Research and Technology Centre, are reportedly working on virtual environment techniques to design spacecraft and to train astronauts (Davidson, 1991). The aim is to develop a generic virtual environment tool, named 'Man in Virtual Space' (MVS). The MVS tool is expected to simulate several space environments so that the operator believes that he/she is part of, or immersed in, the virtual space environment. Specific applications are obvious, and include the design validation of manned space systems and training of astronauts in a simulated micro-gravity environment. The initial ESA research activity is concentrating on the level of realism and interactivity necessary to allow the operator to fulfil these tasks. A variety of interfaces with the virtual environment are to be used with 3-D stereoscopic displays, virtual hand controllers (incorporating force feedback), speech recognition and voice synthesis. Later research will inevitably be conducted in multi-user applications where two or more astronauts are required to cooperate with each other in the same virtual environment. Possible applications include extra-vehicular activities. In many respects the ESA programme is very similar to other virtual environment research programmes being undertaken elsewhere in the world. However, one of the important features of the ESA is that they intend to achieve a certain level of standardization and interconnectivity with other simulation facilities. Despite the relatively long development record behind virtual environment systems, there seems to have been very little attempt to standardize on issues such as geometrical object creation, defining object motion and object interaction. This is an extremely important aspect of all virtual environment systems.

Very little has been published in the public domain about the exact ESA MVS configuration but it is known that the proposed system architecture followed the lines shown in Figure 7.10. ESA ran a competitive bid programme for interested parties to tender against the requirement. In due course more will be heard about this research programme.

It would be wrong to imply that ESA are the first to consider the application of virtual environments in space research. NASA have been leading this field for many years. Other companies have been active too. For instance, the Spacecraft Operations Simulation Facility at Martin Marietta have been using a system by which a trainee astronaut can 'fly' around in a virtual space station or orbiter. A multi-axis Manned Manoeuvring Unit (MMU) simulator is used and computer generated images are presented on a large screen projection system (Skidmore and Pulliam, 1986).

7.6 Virtual cockpits

Research establishments in the defence sector have been gaining experience with the next generation helmet-mounted display systems. Dr Tom Furness, formerly of Wright Patterson Airforce Base, and Dr Dean Kocian developed the Visually Coupled Airborne Systems Simulator (VCASS) in 1985. The VCASS system led to the USAF Super Cockpit Program and the birth of the Virtual Cockpit. Plate 22 shows the latest VCASS helmet-mounted display. Concurrently the author and his team at British Aerospace, Brough were developing a virtual cockpit facility. A wide range of virtual man–machine interfaces are being integrated to complete the virtual cockpit. These systems include helmet-mounted displays, head tracking systems, eye point of regard systems and virtual hand controllers. The virtual cockpit facility has been designed to research and evaluate future cockpit technologies within a mission context. It is recognized that cockpit design, and indeed any man–machine interface, is extremely task-dependent. Moreover, the optimum man–machine interface is a function of the level of technology available.

For many years the defence establishments have been applying state of the art displays and control technologies to the design of aircraft cockpits, but the rather rapid introduction of computer based technology in automated and more capable systems and multipurpose displays actually led to an increase in pilot workload. In the 1970s the increased functionality of the emerging avionic systems was reaching the point where the pilot was in danger of becoming saturated with information. Attempts were made during this time to quantify and develop metrics for pilot workload, but a secondary requirement began to emerge from the studies, which was labelled 'situation awareness'. This term has so far defied definition, because we have yet to develop suitable metrics. As technology was being developed at an ever increasing pace it was outstripping our understanding of the integration of technology. The man–machine interface of the emerging technologies was no longer a simple interface. Instead, it was becoming a subtle compromise between optimum human factors design and practical engineering. The realization that a top level design had to be adopted was dawning on the majority of researchers in the field. Operational requirements had to be decomposed into functional requirements before dealing with the allocation of the pilot cognitive resource.

From these studies it was possible to begin to derive features of the technology that could meet the operational requirement. In a sense, a fairly orderly approach was taken regarding the decomposition of operational requirements into the development of technology. Other developments in this area dictated that the pilot needed an indirect view of the outside world. The virtual cockpit was seen as a solution to this problem and development programmes were accelerated.

Figure 7.4 shows the schematic configuration of a virtual cockpit system. The virtual cockpit is a modular workstation that can communicate spherical and spatial awareness of the outside environment and tactical scene to a pilot. The USAF Super

Cockpit Programme postulated that 'in the future all the conventional cockpit instrumentation could be portrayed by a helmet-mounted display'. The developing virtual environment technologies, such as virtual hand controllers, were suggested as possible replacements for the usual pilot control interface with virtual switches.

The cockpit of the fast jet presents the greatest challenge for the designer of a virtual environment system. The designer has to deal with the limitations of technology and complex human factors as well as designing with safety at the forefront of the mind. Flight safety clearance places stringent demands on medical, mechanical, acoustic and life support requirements.

The virtual cockpit system presents a considerable challenge for the human factors engineer and cockpit designer alike.

British Aerospace, Brough, under the direction of the author, have established a Virtual Cockpit Research Facility to address the complex human factors and engineering issues behind the virtual cockpit. This facility has been designed to be flexible in terms of the type and nature of evaluations that can be undertaken. These range from stand-alone human factors and engineering evaluations of a specific technology, to dynamic 'pilot in the loop' evaluations involving the integration of a range of virtual environment technologies. Particular care has been taken to ensure that any of a range of different virtual cockpit technologies can be integrated and evaluated (see Figure 7.5). Facilities are being developed to measure the specifications of manufacturer's equipment. Examination of any virtual environment equipment reveals ambiguous definitions and hence specifications.

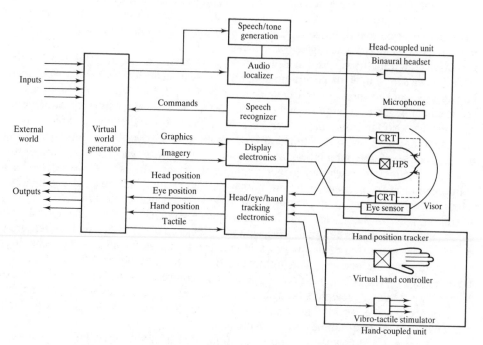

Figure 7.4 Generic virtual cockpit: functional architecture.

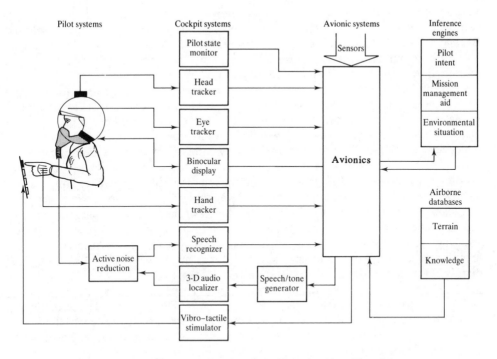

Figure 7.5 Virtual cockpit research facility: functional breakdown.

The development of the British Aerospace Virtual Cockpit Research Facility is at an advanced stage. Many virtual cockpit systems have already been evaluated. There have been many spin-off developments from this programme including the high resolution fibre coupled helmet-mounted display described in Chapter 4.

7.7 Virtual Environment Configurable Training Aids

7.7.1 Initial VECTA (Standard): 1991 Paris International Air Show

The British Aerospace VECTA System, with two concept demonstrators, evolved as a 'spin-off' from the virtual cockpit research programme, under the direction of the author, Prof. R. S. Kalawsky. Although these two systems are not products in their own right, they are key tools in the development of the next generation training products. Considerable knowledge has already been accumulated on the requirements of virtual environment technology applied to extremely serious applications. Three notable steps include:

1.   The development of the VECTA concept.
2.   Improving the resolution of helmet-mounted displays.
3.   RAVECTA (see Section 7.7.3).

The first was the development of a complete virtual cockpit using fairly standard components to highlight both the advantages and disadvantages of immersive virtual environment systems. Display resolution proved to be a major limiting factor, particularly with the helmet–mounted display that was used – a VPL low resolution EyePhone. British Aerospace worked with VPL Inc. and took delivery of the prototype VPL high resolution EyePhone. Overall resolution was almost double that of the low resolution version. It greatly improved display quality.

The initial VECTA concept demonstrator was integrated in time for the 1991 Paris International Air Show, where it was exhibited to the world. Despite the limited resolution at that time it commanded attention and created considerable interest. The majority of the 'feedback' was very beneficial to the programme and helped to identify the critical development areas. Figure 7.6 shows the initial configuration of the Paris version of VECTA. All software was produced 'in-house' and optimized to achieve maximum performance. In operation the pilot can sit inside a Hawk cockpit and fly against a computer generated outside world. Even though the EyePhones were incapable of generating the full 1280 × 1024 pixel resolution of the Silicon Graphics computers, this resolution was used to get an idea of the overall system performance. Clearly, reducing resolution of the drawing operations so they matched the resolution of the helmet-mounted display would have speeded things up. However, the likely required display resolution is about 1000 × 1000 pixels.

Despite the relatively high performance graphics machines being employed many deficiencies were highlighted in the VECTA system. These included lack of texture information, limited display resolution and poor representation of objects in the virtual environment. It certainly makes one wonder how other companies manage, using platforms of lesser capability.

The second step in the development of VECTA was focused on increasing the display resolution of the helmet-mounted display – improved phase lag response in the head tracking system, use of even higher performance visuals with the introduction of real-time texture and more detailed visual information.

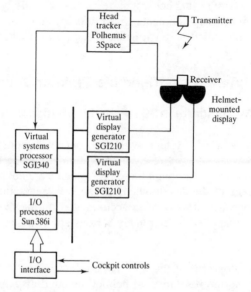

Figure 7.6 VECTA, 1991 Paris Air Show: initial configuration.

7.7.2 VECTA (Standard): 1992 Farnborough International Air Show

The standard VECTA requirements for the 1992 Farnborough Air Show were considerably more demanding than those presented at the 1991 Paris International Air Show in terms of visual fidelity. Greater emphasis was placed on more accurate representations of the outside world, more detailed cockpit layouts, reduced system lags and more representative aircraft performance, the latter being an extremely important point, because the virtual environment system must not only be able to reproduce the required visuals but also ensure that motions in the virtual environment are representative. To some extent, inaccurate motion effects can destroy the virtual environment illusion. This is especially true when a trained operator such as a pilot is expected to use the system. Obviously, embedding this additional level of realism into the simulation incurs an added processing demand. (This is the area where the manufacturers of virtual environment games fall short.)

The resulting system architecture for the next generation VECTA system is shown in Figure 7.7. A considerably higher performance graphics platform was used to obtain higher update rates and real-time texture. One of the problems of the initial VECTA system was that it was difficult to synchronize the operations of the two separate graphics processors both in terms of drawing operations and display raster generation. The distinct advantage of the later generation VECTA system is that both the left and right eye channels can be synchronized, to avoid the disturbing retinal disparity effects that otherwise occur.

To improve productivity in terms of software development, special software tools were used to create and integrate the virtual environment. Development time can be significantly reduced and productivity increased by using appropriate software tools. Although these tools may seem expensive they pay for themselves rapidly, simply because of the development time they save.

Creation of realistic looking virtual environment objects can be very time consuming. The greater the detail that is required, the more effort has to be put into the modelling stage. Using conventional programming techniques to construct accurate models is not the right way forward. By using a software modelling package it is possible to create very complex and realistic looking objects very quickly. Provided the right modelling package is used, object database organization becomes much easier. Techniques such as level of detail switching can reduce the computational effort on the part of the graphics computer.

An additional feature of the later generation VECTA system was that it could be networked to a remote pilot station, where another pilot could fly one of the targets in the outside world from a desktop console or from another networked VECTA system, which could be integrated together. This allowed simultaneous multi-user participation.

In operation, the user could sit in an accurately represented (to the nearest millimetre) aircraft cockpit and fly over a textured, sunlit, undulating terrain. Other environmental features such as fog/haze and cloud were incorporated. Initial reaction suggests that the display resolution can be reduced provided there is a high level of texture information present in the image. However, the reasons for this and the amount of texture versus resolution needed are not fully understood. This issue is currently being investigated.

Plate 8 shows the outline of the aircraft the pilot could sit in and the cockpit detail. Plate 9 shows the detail of the outside world and the aircraft. A cooperating aircraft is also shown.

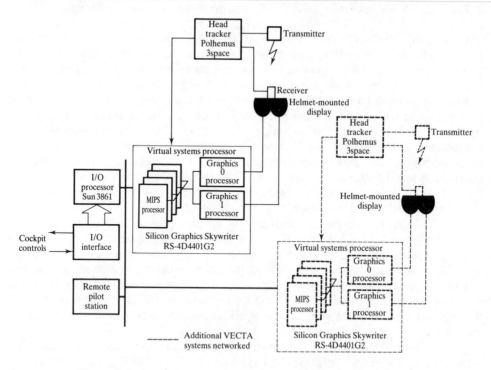

Figure 7.7 VECTA, 1992 Farnborough Air Show: configuration.

The current VECTA configuration, along with the initial version, is deficient in one respect: it could make certain training very difficult, because it is not possible to see any part of one's body. At best, a computer drawn hand could be used, but this is only a partial solution.

7.7.3 Real and Virtual Environment Configurable Training Aid (RAVECTA)

The RAVECTA concept was based on the requirement to integrate a virtual environment into a real world. The most obvious way of achieving this was to employ a see-through helmet-mounted display, such as the one described in Chapter 4, but to do this would have meant integrating the virtual image into the real world, which would necessite mapping the real world so that the computer generated image could be precisely located. However, with this approach any lags in the visual system or head tracking system would have caused the virtual image to 'swim' around the real world. This effect would have been quite disconcerting. (When tracking systems do become available with negligible lags it might be possible to use a see-through helmet-mounted display for such an application.) Another drawback of this technique is that the pilot could put his/her hand into the area where the virtual image was located; unless the hand and fingers could be tracked precisely, the virtual image would overlay the hand.

Clearly, an alternative solution was required. The author recalled his earlier work with television systems where he had used chroma keying systems for video effects and suggested that it might be possible to use such techniques to mix a virtual world with a real world. To test his idea appropriate equipment was borrowed from a photographic and television museum. The concept was to mount a colour television camera onto a helmet-mounted display and couple the resulting video into the helmet-mounted display via a chroma processing system. The chroma processing system was set up to 'gate' an externally supplied video signal whenever a unique colour was detected by the camera. Therefore, by painting an object in the real world with a unique colour, the author thought it could be possible to mix in virtual environment visuals in place of the special coloured areas. The resulting image proved the concept, but suffered from several problems. The chroma processing systems were not able to meet the stringent requirements of the application. Eventually, a special configured chroma processing system was used with additional video processing circuitry. This system was extremely good, in fact, much better than the author had expected. Figure 7.8 shows the general layout of the real and virtual environment configurable training architecture. The exact configuration of the chroma processing system is subject to commercial and confidence restrictions.

It is the author's view that the concept behind RAVECTA will have extensive applications for future virtual environments. Many ideas that were previously thought of as impossible or difficult to achieve have now become easy to implement.

Key characteristics of RAVECTA:

- No registration required between real and virtual worlds.
- No graphics processing overhead.
- User's hands not obscured by virtual imagery.
- Virtual imagery can be collimated to infinity, just like the real world if required.
- Flexible application.
- Employs real tactile feedback.

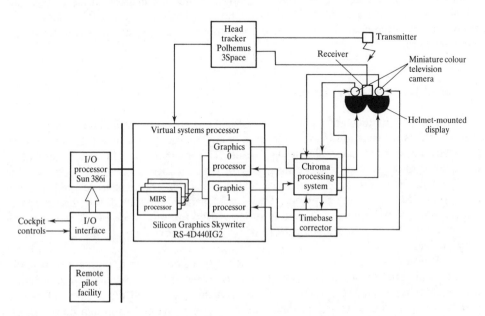

Figure 7.8 Functional architecture of the RAVECTA system.

To give an idea of the enormous range of applications, a few examples are given below.

Driving simulator

A driving school could use these devices by simply instrumenting the steering wheel, brake and accelerating pedals and gear lever. Outputs from these interfaces would be input into a graphics system. The graphic system would be programmed to display a typical road scenario that is controlled by the user's interactions. The learner driver would sit in the car and don a helmet-mounted display incorporating miniature television cameras. To get an appropriate view of the outside world it would be necessary to paint the car windows with a unique colour, such as blue.

The cameras would pick up an image of the car interior and the blue windows. The chroma processing system would then switch the computer generated outside world wherever there is blue in the camera image. The use of a head tracker would allow the learner driver to look all around and see door pillars, windscreen arches and so on in their correct positions.

The same system could be used without any modification for a lorry, tank, train, and so on.

Mission rehearsal system

Imagine a pilot sitting in his aircraft waiting to go out on a mission; he could simply wear a RAVECTA head set and link the virtual environment processor to his aircraft throttle and stick. A blue tarpaulin or other blue light source could be positioned over the cockpit canopy. The pilot would then get a full outside world display whenever he looked out of the cockpit. Therefore, he could rehearse his mission in his cockpit and maintain a constant state of readiness. When he is required to go out on his mission, he simply removes the helmet-mounted display, unplugs a cockpit interface connector, and away he goes.

7.8 Maintenance systems

Desktop publishing aids are routinely used for the preparation of detailed maintenance manuals. This information is available to the maintenance engineer in a highly detailed form but takes up considerable storage space. The maintenance engineer often has to carry large amounts of microfiche material, for which a special viewer is required. The maintenance data must be continually updated, which can be expensive, and it is not always carried out by the engineer. Faced with a fault situation the engineer has to search through vast amounts of data in order to find the tiny piece of information that he/she wants. If the microfiches get out of order, and they often do, the task becomes very difficult.

The storage capacity of computer based systems continues to increase, especially if an optical disk technology is used. It is easy to see the time when the maintenance engineer carries a small personal computer with integral optical disk system. It would then be a simple matter to encapsulate all the necessary maintenance data onto a single optical disk and employ sophisticated computer database search techniques to rapidly find the required maintenance information.

At the moment the maintenance engineer is still required to be very knowledgeable about the system he/she is responsible for. What if this knowledge could be encapsulated with the maintenance data? The engineer would not have to attend very expensive training courses and update programmes to familiarize himself/herself with the equipment. A virtual environment system has the potential to relate maintenance information to the actual piece of equipment. Appropriate head coupled 3-D views could be displayed on a small helmet-mounted display by the engineer's personal computer (see Figure 7.9). The image could be an accurate facsimile of the faulty equipment and dynamic instructions could be given on-screen as the work progresses. Prior to visiting the site the maintenance engineer could even preview the problem to familiarize himself/herself with the task in hand.

The virtual environment system need not be too complex and a real-time update may not be required.

An early generation system has been demonstrated by British Aerospace, Brough, employing an IBM PC compatible computer linked to a Reflection Technologies Private Eye system. The operator requests particular maintenance data by means of a speech recognition system.

Future generation virtual maintenance aids may involve a fully immersive virtual environment where the user is essentially linked to a full system database by means of a helmet-mounted display, virtual hand controller incorporating tactile and kinaesthetic feedback and head/hand tracking systems. The user would be able to completely visualize and 'feel' a simulated system, on which he/she could perform maintenance training. For more complex systems such as those in power stations, in aircraft or in ships, it may be possible to assess/verify that maintenance could be carried out on the system before it is actually built. This would allow the designer to ensure that particular components could be replaced without stripping half of the plant or aircraft down.

If virtual environment technology develops to the point where reliable tactile feedback is available then it is easy to conceive a situation where the complete product could be visualized in virtual environments and appropriate training given. This could take the form of a computer-based self-paced training programme.

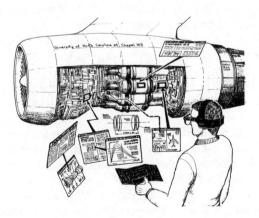

Figure 7.9 Portable maintenance training aid.

7.9 Computer aided design/computer aided manufacture

7.9.1 Rover 400 car interior design: A virtual environment computer aided design tool

The principle of interacting with a CAD database is an old idea. Designers have been routinely using sophisticated CAD workstations to visualize complex models. The designers can interact with the model via a simple interface such as a mouse or dial and button box, moving the image around to get different views of the CAD model. These techniques allow the designer to examine the design for human factors considerations, ease of assembly and even ease of maintenance.

Some CAD workstations use stereo graphic techniques to improve data visualization. One of the first applications considered by the author and his team for his virtual environment laboratory was to apply virtual environment techniques to the interactive design of car interiors. In fact this particular project began as a concept demonstrator to highlight the benefits and disadvantages of a virtual environment design tool to a current design process. Many people had spoken about the tremendous potential of being able to manipulate complex CAD data by means of a DataGlove-like device, while wearing a helmet-mounted display. A concept demonstration was developed in the British Aerospace, Brough Virtual Environment Laboratory. Specifications for the interior of a Rover 400 car were taken and a fully interactive virtual car interior was created using tools such as Swivel 3-D Professional and Body Electric. The potential car designer could sit inside the virtual car on a real car seat. The complete car interior could be designed by reaching out and 'grabbing at' objects, such as the steering wheel. In fact it was a simple matter to convert the car from right-hand drive to left-hand drive by grabbing the relevant parts and repositioning them from the left-hand seat. Other CAD-like features were embedded in the system, such as the ability to change the size of certain objects dynamically. The demonstration served to illustrate the benefits and disadvantages of current virtual environment technology, while acting as a design assessment tool.

Many people were extremely surprised to learn that the whole demonstration had been put together in a relatively short time without a single piece of software having been written. It was put together by constructing CAD-like objects and by using a visual programming language employing graphic icons to create the interactive and behaviourial links. Plate 12 shows the physical interface the designer uses, comprising a VPL HRX EyePhone, DataGlove, Convolvotron and car seat. The Silicon Graphics rendering computers are not shown. Plate 13 shows the view that was generated by the system with the user's hand in view. Many people, including car designers, engineers, scientists and stylists, were invited to try this system. Most people were surprised to realize that they could not 'take' to the DataGlove, finding it difficult to get used to, but in fact very little practice is needed before it does become very easy to manipulate. After careful questioning it became obvious that they were expecting some form of kinaesthetic feedback. However, they did realize and accept the DataGlove as an important design tool, because the designer of a car, for instance, would be able to sit inside his design and visualize the interior. In fact, a tool of this type would be invaluable for ergonomic layouts. When several car stylists tried the system it was obvious that they wanted something more than a simple demonstration. They wanted to be able to walk around the design of the car and look at specular reflections across the surface, feel the upholstery, grab hold of the steering wheel and feel its diameter. Obviously, this was only a subset of the things they do to get a 'feeling' for a design. The limited display resolution was clearly a problem for the stylist. Interestingly, they have themselves tried to use very high resolution CAD systems to give detailed computer graphic visuals of a car, but even these systems have been unable to replace full size mock-ups.

7.9.2 Virtual CAD

Large manufacturing organizations have been using CAD tools as a matter of routine for many years, totally encapsulating their designs in a computer database. The availability of lower cost CAD design tools means that most manufacturers now employ CAD throughout their design/manufacturing process.

Several 'CAD-like' software houses have jumped on the 'VR band-wagon' and can now offer 'Desktop VR systems'. These seem nothing more than traditional low cost CAD systems with the added advantage of some form of animation, so that CAD objects can be dynamically controlled via some predefined motion equation. The more sophisticated CAD tools have had this feature for many years and it does seem a little odd that the modern low cost tools should be labelled 'Desktop VR'.

To avoid possible confusion between 'Desktop VR' and virtual environments, the term 'immersive virtual environments' has now been introduced. In essence, this term refers to a virtual environment system that employs a helmet-mounted display or a BOOM-like display to present a visually coupled image.

7.9.3 The Boeing VSX: Operations with virtual aircraft in a virtual environment

The Virtual Space Experimental (VSX) craft is a demonstration of how virtual environment systems could be applied to the design of aircraft and other complex systems involving human interaction. The user of a virtual environment design system would be an engineer or a pilot who wants to evaluate an aircraft's design. Issues such as operability, maintainability and manufacturability can be investigated, even though it exists only as a computer representation. The VSX is the result of a collaborative programme between the Boeing Advanced Technology Center, Seattle, USA and the Human Interface Technology Laboratory at the University of Washington, USA.

The VSX is a 3-D virtual model of the interior and exterior of a tilt-rotor aircraft in virtual space that allows the user to interact with items such as the maintenance hatch and cargo ramp. The user can rearrange the flight deck to a limited extent, interact with the flight controls to start the rotors and rotate the engines, and then take off. Additionally, it is possible to rearrange passenger and cargo area. The VSX is based around VPL EyePhones and a VPL DataGlove. The DataGlove allows the user to point with one or two fingers in order to fly towards or away from any point in the virtual world at a variable speed. Buttons can be pushed using the appropriate hand gestures normally used. Objects such as hatches and throttles can be grabbed by the user by making a fist and inserting it into the object to be manipulated.

7.9.4 Virtual Environment Computer Aided Design (VECAD): The next generation

Computer aided design has completely revolutionized the manufacturing business and several companies have dispenced with paper drawings completely. The concept of a paperless aircraft design has even been suggested (Shaw, 1992).

Provided virtual environment technologies start to deliver their claimed performance, we could face another technological revolution. The author can foresee a time when a total design process, from conception through to the end product, is conducted on a virtual environment system. For example:

- The designer can visualize the design.
- The customer can verify that the design meets the required specifications.
- The manufacturer can test build the product.
- The manufacturer can check 'assemblability' of the product.
- The customer can train his staff, or the end user, with a virtual equivalent of the product.

All this could be achieved long before the product is made. The potential cost savings and risk reductions are obvious. When a complex product is being designed, such as an aircraft or ship, the cost savings would be significant.

7.10 Product visualization

Virtual environments have tremendous potential in the manufacturing business, from the initial marketing stages through to manufacture and post-delivery support. Manufacture of complex systems or products usually involves making expensive mock-ups or facsimiles of the finished article. It is necessary to build mock-ups to verify the design and check out issues such as human factors. New designs often involve the construction of a range of mock-ups to check out various aspects of the design. Although these mock-ups are expensive, it is a lot easier to correct design flaws at an early stage.

If we take the design of a new car as an example, it may come as a surprise to many readers that several mock-ups are made long before the car is ever built. These mock-ups are full size models, which allow stylists to visualize the final product. Modifications at this stage can still be quite expensive. Full-size models are also fabricated to allow interior design to be investigated. It is interesting that even in this age of computer systems, designers still resort to full-scale mock-ups. This suggests that computer design tools are unable to fulfil the designer's visualization needs. It is very hard to simulate all the implicit detail in a computer model that can replace all the information that is available in a real model. There appears to be no substitute for the look, touch and feel of a product.

Once a product design has been completed it is often desirable to perform dummy installation procedures to ensure that the individual components of the product go together. In complex systems such as aircraft or ships it is necessary to perform operations such as pipe layout investigations. It is possible to design a hydraulic pipe that is easy to install at the assembly stages of the product line but which becomes impossible to replace when maintenance is necessary. Logistics support is extremely important from a customer's point of view and it is up to the manufacturer to ensure that his product can be adequately maintained (at minimal cost) without major overhauls.

Virtual environments have the potential to allow the customer, marketeer, designer, maintenance engineers and many others to visualize any product throughout the product life cycle.

To demonstrate the potential benefits (and current disadvantages) of virtual environments in a product life cycle a demonstration was performed. A virtual Rover 400 car interior was set up on a virtual environment rapid prototyping facility. A decision was taken to employ a range of virtual environment technologies, including helmet-mounted displays, tracking systems, virtual hand controllers, graphic systems and a 3-D audio localization system. A further objective of the exercise was to build a fully interactive demonstration where all the features of the interior could be rearranged by the designer. The objects of the car interior were designed using a CAD package and included seats, steering wheel, gear stick, indicator stalks, rear view mirror, windscreen wipers, hand brake, door handles, car radio, car heater and telephone. (The majority of these components could be re-positioned by the user by means of a DataGlove.) To interact with the virtual objects, a virtual hand controller (a VPL DataGlove) was used. The user employed the DataGlove to grab hold of the virtual objects, this being facilitated by means of gesture control. A series of gestures were programmed into the system and whenever a gesture was made an appropriate action was taken. For instance, to grab an object and move it into another position the hand was pushed into the object and a fist gesture was made. This signalled to the virtual environment system that the object had been grabbed. The graphics system, or more correctly the virtual systems processor, attached the grabbed virtual object to the hand. When the hand changed position (or orientation), the object replicated this movement.

7.11 Virtual environment laboratory

7.11.1 Justifications for a virtual environment laboratory facility

The availability of technologies that can be integrated into a virtual environment is increasing at a great pace (Kalawsky, 1991a). There are discrete systems whose functional requirements and specifications are driven by perception of the market demand and a function of their manufacturing capability. This 'bottom up' design approach is totally unacceptable from an integration point of view. Many manufacturers do not care how their system will be used; their prime objective is to make a product that sells, for the maximum profit, and with a minimum of effort and risk. To the designer, higher up in the design life cycle, this situation is intolerable. The risks are transferred to the designer and manufacturer of the integrated product. Manufacturers of discrete enabling systems do not seem to realize that if the integrated product fails, then their market will also collapse.

Successful manufacturers of products involving integration of several discrete enabling technologies use test rigs or comprehensive laboratory facilities (Kalawsky, 1991c). These not only test the integration philosophy but also drive the specification of the component technologies.

Virtual environments are no exception: test rigs and laboratory facilities are used. A virtual environment system will generally have more variables than any other product. Therefore, it is vital to understand and control the effect of each variable within task and cost constraints. There is no doubt that virtual environments will play an important part in our lives in the future. The high profile this technology has achieved as a result of press coverage has resulted in many people and organizations jumping on the 'Virtual Reality band-wagon' hoping to make a quick profit. These initiatives are likely to fail unless they realize that they are dealing with a complex subject involving both human factors and engineering constraints. It is particularly important to capture the user's requirements and ensure that the product is matched to them. Often with new technologies the customer may not know what his/her requirements are, or at least may not be able to specify them in a way that is understandable to the manufacturer. Rapid prototyping involving the customer and the manufacturer working together has emerged as an extremely effective way of encapsulating the end user's requirements in engineering terms.

It has to be acknowledged that many virtual environment technologies are emerging that have been developed without consideration of the end application. These various products have been developed from manufacturers' perceptions of what is required. A quick cursory examination will reveal the limited extent of human factors research that has been conducted. Not unexpectedly, manufacturers are producing ambiguous specifications that are very inaccurate or, at worst, completely untrue. It is very disappointing that even though the fundamental technologies behind virtual environments have been around for many years, we still cannot produce a set of consistent definitions. Perhaps this situation has arisen out of the multidisciplinary nature of the subject. Manufacturers are working in areas that are completely new to them. This can be illustrated by an example. The majority of manufacturers of head-mounted displays for virtual environment applications simply take the display resolution figure quoted by the LCD manufacturer and claim that their display has this resolution. In doing so they make a fundamental error because they are quoting the total number of individual primary colour dots on a display. This is not the conventional way of expressing resolution. What they should quote is the number of pixels on the display. That is, a composite of red, green and blue elements. Misquoting in this way gives a false impression of the actual display resolution; the resolution is really much lower than that specified.

7.11.2 Requirements of a virtual environment laboratory

Before describing a specific virtual environment facility it is best to consider what are the requirements of a generic facility, and develop the discussion around that. The aim of a generic facility is to ensure flexibility without being too specific. If the facility were to be configured for a particular application then it could become very difficult to address other ideas as they emerge. Care must be taken at all costs to avoid the temptation to lock a specific technology into the facility, otherwise, as new developments come on line they may not integrate without a major rewrite of the interface software. It should be remembered that one of the greatest costs of maintaining a flexible facility, apart from the hardware cost, is that of software. Therefore, the use of software tools must be considered from the outset, not only to keep overall development costs down but also to improve productivity. If the right development tools are chosen it should be possible to provide a certain level of isolation against the graphics platform that will be used. There is no doubt that the computer graphics business is moving at a very fast pace and new products are continually being launched that overcome the problems of their predecessors. Too many products have emerged from the research laboratories that have required major redesign and development before they can be exploited.

It is probably unlikely that a single virtual environment laboratory facility will meet the needs of all virtual environment products. It may even be necessary to employ several facilities throughout the life cycle of a single product. To keep development costs to an acceptable level, migration of the concept from the prototype stage to the production line must be undertaken very carefully, in a seamless manner.

A few of the requirements are:

- Rapid prototyping.
- Flexibility – reconfigurable.
- Investigation of human factors issues.
- Establishment of a series of system performance metrics.
- Validation of system design.
- Concept demonstration.
- Generation of specification and performance requirements.
- Assessment facility.
- Upgradable – technology independent.
- Technology independent.

If the virtual environment laboratory is required to support a range of different applications it is even more important to get the configuration of the laboratory right. It is easy to buy certain virtual environment type peripherals off the shelf and put them together to create a so-called virtual environment system. However, it is likely that this will have limited usefulness because it has not been designed for a specific application. Limitations in performance, especially of the cheaper peripherals, can lead to very disappointing results. This does not mean that only the most expensive equipment must be purchased before research work can be considered. However, it is very important to examine the type of work that is to be addressed and to ensure that the technology is not limiting the necessary extent of the research programme. Careful consideration of the performance specifications for the virtual environment equipment to be used will reduce the risks normally associated with leading edge research programmes. Moreover, it is important to have an idea of the potential end user's needs. The material presented in the earlier chapters of this book will have given the reader an insight into the problems and technology limitations of today's virtual environment equipment. Although many of these will be overcome by further research and product developments, the basic human factors issues will not change. This means that the establishment of a virtual environment laboratory must take cognisance of the human factors requirements.

When building a multipurpose facility that allows the introduction of state of the art virtual environment technology, particular attention must be given to issues such as interfacing standards. By careful specification of the equipment at an early stage in the construction of the facility, it is possible to accommodate future generation virtual environment equipment when it becomes available. This is clearly desirable in a field such as virtual environment where considerable developments are likely to take place. For example, the author's facility at British Aerospace, Brough can accommodate any of the helmet-mounted displays that are available today. Future designs of helmet-mounted displays can even be simulated or emulated to explore the ideas before the actual hardware becomes available. This important aspect will be discussed later.

7.11.3 Simple virtual environment laboratory

Figure 7.10 shows the architecture of a simple virtual environment laboratory combining a visual system and virtual hand controller interfaces. The absolute minimum of equipment is some form of helmet-mounted display, high performance computer graphics system and the best head position tracker that funds will buy. To produce a stereoscopic image the researcher has to decide whether it is better to:

1. Buy two single-channel graphics systems.
2. Use a single-channel graphics system and multiplex the output to drive two channels of the display.
3. Use two separate graphics systems.

Obviously there are both cost and performance trade-offs. The two-channel graphics system will generally offer the better performance but cost will be higher. Additionally, care has to be taken to ensure that both channels are synchronized when they execute drawing operations. It is visually disturbing to be presented with a stereo image pair where the two channels are updated at a slightly different rate or are out of synchronism. Under certain circumstances the scene complexity can vary from one graphics channel to another. While this is not a problem with the single-channel system using a video splitter/multiplexer, overall update rate can be seriously affected. For those working on a shoestring budget the possibility of working with a biocular (same image presented to each eye with 100% overlap) system should not be overlooked. True depth perception derived from stereoscopic cues will be missing but the motion parallax cues produced as a result of using the head tracking device can sometimes more than compensate for lack of stereo information.

While it would be easy to recommend a range of different graphics platforms and peripheral devices to put together a simple virtual environment laboratory, it is better to start by considering what type of work the facility will be required to address. This will essentially dictate the type of equipment and, more particularly, the performance requirement. Given that even the best technology today may not meet all the performance requirements of a virtual environment system, it is unwise to assume that high performance can be achieved with a simple set up. Many people have 'lashed up' a system only to be very disappointed. However, if the facility is to be used to address some small aspect of a virtual environment system, then it is perfectly feasible to use a minimal system.

When designing a laboratory facility one should have at the back of one's mind that the visually coupled system part of the facility will place the greatest demands on performance. Consequently, it will be necessary to couple the head tracker to the visual system with the minimum of intervening hardware or software. Particular care must be exercised if the graphics are part of a large general purpose network. General network communications can introduce series delays into the system, in which case it is better to use a small local area network or detach from the general network at run-time.

In terms of a software development environment, providing one has access to one or more Silicon Graphics platforms, four very good packages are available: MR Toolkit, WorldToolKit, Division's dVS/AMAZE or MultiGen/GVS, as described in Chapter 5. The MR Toolkit is available in the public domain for non-commercial research.

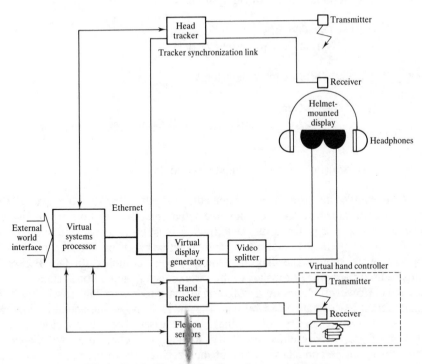

Figure 7.10 Simple virtual environment laboratory.

7.11.4 A comprehensive virtual environment laboratory

In order to understand the full implications of an integrated virtual environment system it is necessary to have access to a facility where the system can be rapidly prototyped to identify key issues.

Features of a comprehensive virtual environment laboratory should include :

- Visual world systems

    - Range of head mounted displays (low, medium, and high resolution).
    - Range of space tracking systems (different manufacturers and performance).
    - Range of high performance graphics systems (software migratable across all platforms).

- Auditory world systems

    - Sophisticated digital sound synthesis system.
    - 3-D audio localization.
    - Speech recognition system.
    - Speech synthesizer system.

- Haptic/kinaesthetic world systems

    - DataGlove.
    - Virtual environment joystick.

- Virtual world development tools

    - MultiGen.
    - VPL RB2 comprising Swivel, Body Electric and Isaac.
    - Others.

- Performance measuring/modelling tools

Figure 7.11 shows the top level architecture of the British Aerospace Virtual Environment Laboratory. It does not show the actual interface relationships between the various equipments. For instance, the head tracker must be synchronized to the position tracker which is used to determine hand position and orientation. If all such interconnects were shown, the diagram would be very complex. In fact Figure 7.11 looks misleadingly simple. For instance, the virtual display generator is shown as a pair of processors. However, there are a range of virtual processors that can be used, each offering different performance capabilities. Figure 7.12 shows the actual configuration of graphics systems (at the time of writing). One can see that it is possible to use any combination of graphics systems. Similarly, a range of helmet-mounted displays are available which can be connected to any of the graphics platforms via a video matrix. The video matrix is a definite advantage in this configuration because it allows any video input to be routed to any output. All outputs can be driven by just one of the inputs. The specification of the video matrix is such that it will handle video standards such as NTSC, PAL and the high resolution standard of the Silicon Graphics platforms. Apart from avoiding the need to continually recable the facility whenever a different helmet-mounted display is used, it allows simultaneous comparison between different helmet-mounted displays. This level of flexibility is particularly important for research or evaluation experimentation environments.

The facility has been designed from the outset to allow for evaluations to be undertaken on a range of virtual environment technologies such as helmet-mounted displays. Many existing helmet-mounted displays can be easily integrated with minimal interfacing. This also applies to the software that must be executed in the graphics processors. Figure 7.12 shows the sort of reconfiguration that can be accommodated with different helmet-mounted displays. One should note that it is not just a case of rerouting video to the appropriate display. Each display generally requires a different video standard, ranging from composite NTSC, RGB NTSC and PAL RGB through to different high resolution video standards. Achieving this level of compatibility calls for a video routing device that can handle these different standards and corresponding video bandwidths. Furthermore, the graphics systems must be capable of being reprogrammed to produce the appropriate video output. Finally, the application software must be designed to accommodate different spatial resolutions, fields of view and occasionally some peculiar transformations, to take into account optical distortions.

Plate 10 shows part of the author's research facility, comprising helmet-mounted display drive units, DataGlove, Convolvotron, EMAX digital sound synthesizer and chroma processing system.

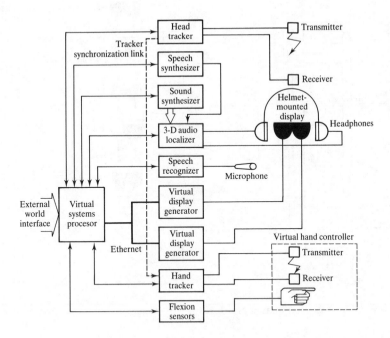

Figure 7.11 Full virtual environment laboratory.

Plate 11 shows part of the computing resource behind the author's Virtual Environment Laboratory. The Silicon Graphics SkyWriter is shown in the background.

A major requirement of a comprehensive virtual environment laboratory is the means to perform assessments on specific equipment. Very few laboratories seem keen to 'bolt' together virtual environment type systems and write software without questioning the performance specified by the manufacturer. As indicated in Chapter 6, manufacturers are unable to agree on even the basic definitions. This leads to misinterpretation of specifications. The user at the end of the chain is the one that ends up suffering the consequences. The author is undertaking a detailed study into the critical aspects of visually coupled displays (Kalawsky, 1992) involving the facilities at British Aerospace, Brough and at the University of Hull. The aim of this work is to produce detailed performance figures and transfer functions for a range of virtual environment equipments. Extremely accurate motion platforms are being used to assess the dynamic performance of systems such as space tracking systems. By deriving accurate transfer characteristics for each component part of a virtual environment system it will be possible to model the performance of the virtual environment system from end to end. A similar study is being undertaken by the NASA Ames Research Center (Ellis, 1992).

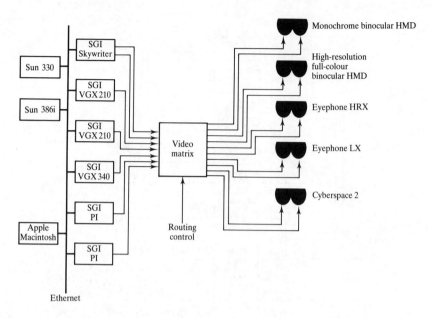

Figure 7.12 Achieving maximum flexibility by means of a video matrix router.

7.12 Very low cost virtual environment system

The cost of virtual environment systems is probably out of the reach of the average researcher or academic institution but it is recognized that many people will want to become involved in this technology. The system to be presented will put this exciting new technology within the reach of anyone operating on a reduced budget. Overall performance will be very poor compared to the more powerful system. However, many problems that have been described in the earlier sections of this book can be investigated. The total cost of the low cost virtual environment system should not exceed £2,500 (1993 figure).

The basis of all virtual environment systems is a visually coupled system. To produce a low cost visually coupled system, performance must be sacrificed. This implies that a reduction in accuracy, resolution and update rate must be accepted.

Figure 7.13 shows a suggested configuration for the low cost virtual environment system. The display is based on the Private Eye display described in Chapter 4. This system provides a monochrome, reasonably high resolution image. For approximately £500 this device offers remarkable value for money. Even though the Private Eye is a monocular system this does not detract from its usefulness. To determine head position a 3-D mouse is used, such as the one manufactured by Logitech.

7.12.1 Logitech 2D/3D mouse

Logitech's 2D/3D Mouse provides an extremely cost effective three-dimensional, spatial input system for a computer system. The mouse can operate as a conventional desktop mouse or as a true three-dimensional input system that provides position information (*x*, *y* and *z*) and three angular positions (pitch, azimuth and roll). The mouse system comprises four components: a control unit, an ultrasonic radiator assembly, a mouse and a power supply. The control unit has a microprocessor that controls the generation of ultrasonic signals and decodes the resulting reception of ultrasonic signals received by a receiver. The microprocessor derives position and orientation information. The ultrasonic radiator assembly consists of three ultrasonic transmitters that are cycled in sequence. The mouse is free to move in three dimensions and is equipped with microphones that receive sound from the radiator assembly. The mouse must be in the line of sight of the radiator assembly in order to work. A cable from the mouse provides the acoustic signal to the control unit. The control unit communicates to a host computer via a conventional EIA RS232C compatible interface at data rates of up to 19,200 baud.

The mouse operates using a right-handed, three-dimensional rectangular (Cartesian) coordinate system (in 6D mode). The *x* axis is positive in the right direction, the *y* axis is positive in the up direction and the *z* axis is positive in the reverse direction. The user can select the form in which the position and orientation data is output, from Euler and quaternions. In Euler mode (default) roll, pitch and azimuth are calculated from the radiator's reference plane. The order of calculation is important – pitch, azimuth and finally roll. The quaternions output mode provides an alternative output format based on points on the surface of a four-dimensional sphere.

The operating volume is a 2' cube and the resolution within the active area along the *x*, *y* and *z* axes is 200 dpi (1/200"). Angular resolution within the active area is 0.1°. Update rates are typically 50 samples per second. Outside the active area lies a further operating area which extends 8" in each direction. This area is known as the fringe area and has a lower resolution, typically 50 dpi (1/50") for position and 0.5° for angular. When the device is operated in the fringe region a signal is sent to the host computer to warn of the lower resolution. When the mouse is out of range a different signal is transmitted. A tracking speed in excess of 30" per second will also be signalled to the host computer.

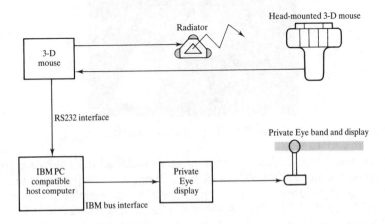

Figure 7.13 Low cost virtual environment system.

Table 7.1 Specifications for Logitech 2D/3D Mouse.

Azimuth, elevation and roll	360°
Angular accuracy	0.1°, 0.5° in fringe area, 0.5°in extended range mode
Position x, y, and z	+/- 3.5'
Positional accuracy	1/200", 1/50" in fringe area, 1/50" extended range mode
Phase lag	Not specified
Tracking speed	30" per second
Update rate	50 Hz, 25 Hz in extended range mode
Reporting modes	Demand, incremental and stream
Reporting formats	Euler and quaternions
Tracking area	2' cube, 2'8" cube in fringe area

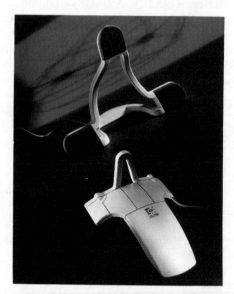

Figure 7.14 Logitech 2D/3D mouse.

The mouse has an additional operating mode which allows an extended operating range of approximately 2.13 m (7') in each direction. A consequence of the extended operating range is a lowering of the update rate to 25 samples per second and a resolution of 50 dpi (1/50"). The angular resolution is also reduced to 0.5°.

The data output from the control unit can be output in incremental mode, demand reporting mode or stream reporting mode. In head tracking applications, either the incremental or stream reporting modes should be used. These modes produce an output whenever the mouse changes position, or changes continuously.

7.13 Entertainment and leisure applications

Entertainment simulators are becoming increasingly complex, with greater realism being a driving factor. Apart from the demand for realistic visuals there is also a move towards motion simulation. Whether motion simulation needs to be completely representative for an entertainment system is unclear. Nevertheless, there is no doubt that a visual system can be enhanced from the point of view of thrill inducement by the addition of a limited movement motion base. A simple coupling of the motion base may be adequate for the lay person. This will give false cues to heighten the experience.

If, on the other hand, the user is a highly trained individual, such as a pilot, then any unnatural cues will be very apparent and may lead to a complete breakdown of the virtual illusion.

The entertainment's business seems to be a subtle combination of addictive experiences coupled with heightened fear expectations. Some of the more recent fun parks (such as Alton Towers, UK) are extremely safe, but they have been designed with fear in mind. The public feels that they are being very brave and fearful when 'riding-on' one of the enormous and fast rides, which more often than not soars through the air, leaving one's stomach behind! It seems strange to the author that people pay quite high prices to be scared out of their wits, just to boast that they have subjected themselves to such terror! As they become accustomed to these 'white-knuckle' rides they demand new extremes, but because the larger rides are almost impossible to re-engineer it is more cost effective to rebuild.

Fun parks or theme parks where one pays a single entry fee are gaining in popularity and to keep the total cost down (including items such as maintenance and replacement) they are designed for large numbers of people.

Not surprisingly, low cost virtual environment based simulators have entered these fun and theme parks, as well as amusement arcades. They are low performance systems, providing little in the way of realistic cues. In one sense they bring virtual reality to the public, but because many users will not realize that virtual environment has many serious applications, they will leave the fun parks associating virtual environment just with entertainment.

Several companies have already entered the virtual environment entertainment field. The main one in the United Kingdom is W Industries. Larger simulation companies, including Hughes Rediffusion, UK and Evans and Sutherland, USA have also declared their hand in this potentially enormous market.

7.14 Summary

Since the introduction of computer technology we have moved from batch or card input to interactive input via a mouse and graphics display. Some portable computers allow a user to write directly onto a display screen with a special plastic pen and the computer reads the user's handwriting. Speech recognition systems have been available for many years but are now slowly finding their way into computer based systems. Since the introduction of the 'Windows' environments for personal computers we are now starting to see multimedia systems being used, employing both visual and audio interfaces. The next step is a virtual interface that will embody many of the technologies described in this book. The use of virtual environment technologies in the entertainments business will soon become commonplace and the users of these systems will expect similar interactivity in their office or work systems.

Many of the problems identified in the previous chapter will ultimately be solved as manufacturers begin to understand the requirements of the technology and how it must be matched to a particular application. This will lead to considerable improvements in the technology that acts as the interface between the human and the machine. Computer graphics technology is being driven by many other applications, which will lead to remarkable performance even by today's standards. No attempt has been made to cover all potential applications because there are just too many. The aim has been to describe several obvious applications to demonstrate that the field of virtual environments is here to stay. The reader will probably be able to think of many others.

8   Concluding remarks

Objectives

This final chapter brings together the main points discussed throughout the book. Interest in virtual environments, or 'virtual reality' as it is more commonly called, has grown rapidly during the past two or three years. Amid some wild speculations about the technology and its capabilities, there have been very important breakthroughs in our understanding of the underlying principles and the enabling technologies. Although many applications require the use of high performance graphics systems, the price of these systems is falling sharply. The potential rewards in user productivity and reduction in manufacturing time (while maintaining a cost competitive edge) ensures that the field of virtual environments will continue to have a growing impact on our lives. Outstanding areas of research are discussed to direct the energies of interested scientists and researchers. Finally, a few philosophical points are mentioned, which have been developed from the author's research in virtual environment systems and from preparatory work for this book.

8.1 Conclusions

This book has taken the reader interested in virtual environment systems from the first stage of design and development of helmet-mounted displays and the tactile glove, through to the technology of the present day.

It can be seen that from the late 1950s, when the Philco Corporation were developing their Headsight System (a closed circuit television surveillance system used with a helmet-mounted display), up to the 1980s, research was very slow.

By the late 1980s, research had started to accelerate. Technology reached the required level of computational performance necessary to produce visually coupled systems, and developments in liquid crystal television displays enabled low cost helmet-mounted displays to be built. However, development in space tracker technology has been slow in achieving the required accuracy and dynamic performance.

In 1987, *Scientific American* featured an article on a virtual hand controller glove called the DataGlove. It was manufactured by a company called VPL Inc. The article aroused considerable interest. The DataGlove, an optical flex sensing glove with a space tracking system built on the back of it, gave hand orientation as well as finger flexure. It was received by the general public with amazement.

One of the founder members of VPL Inc., Jaron Lanier coined the phrase 'virtual reality'. The DataGlove, along with the term 'virtual reality' caught the attention and imagination of the press and media. From then on, virtual reality has received unprecedented coverage. The term is now known worldwide.

The general public's interest in virtual reality has spread as a result of media coverage. The development of virtual environment arcade games and movies such as 'The Lawnmower Man' have heightened interest.

At the present time (1993) the press and media have really exhausted themselves covering games and films, and are now turning their attention to the more serious sides of science that virtual environment systems can be applied to. Some ideas are already being developed, such as those described in Chapter 7, but other ideas are beyond present day technology. Much more research needs to be undertaken, particularly in the field of human factors, because at present there are no metrics to work from. Understandably, the human factors related issues will drive the technology, as will a fuller understanding of the human visual, auditory and haptic/kinaesthetic systems.

Virtual environment systems will weave their way into our lives without us realizing it. For instance, our cars, homes and cities will be designed and prototyped by virtual environment systems, and we may even be trained within a virtual environment system.

I hope this book provides the reader with adequate information concerning the concept, formation and capabilities of virtual environments, and that it points the way ahead for further research in this exciting technological field.

To those who are cynical about the technology – it must be pointed out that there will always be those who are cynical, those who doubt, those who criticize and those who just cannot envisage life or science changing from the stage that they are living in. In the same way, if people living only 100 years ago had been told about forthcoming technologies such as the television, washing machine, video camera, computer, aircraft and Space Shuttle, they too would have been cynical and would have doubted. How many of us would have believed 20 years ago that it would become routine at maternity hospitals to view a monitor screen and watch an unborn child moving in its mother's womb? Cynics, doubters and critics should stop and think.

The applications for virtual environments are all-embracing. Research scientists must build on existing knowledge and move forward in a coherent manner. In this way mankind will benefit from a concept that will interact with our lives and enrich it.

There is one thing that is reality: the scientist came into this life with nothing, and he will leave with nothing, but if his life's research work benefits mankind, then his life will not have been in vain.

8.2 Outstanding Research Issues

This book has dealt with a vast array of issues that relate to a virtual environment system. While our understanding in many areas is quite advanced, our overall understanding of the requirements of a virtual environment system is less clear. Even though we may not necessarily need to achieve virtual reality in the truest sense, we are unable to quantify the requirements of lesser systems.

It is tempting to jump on the virtual reality band-wagon and deal only with the technology aspects of the field. However, if the technology is to move forwards then it will be necessary to examine the application to which the technology is to be applied. Only by doing this will it be possible to consider what attributes a virtual environment system brings to the application that cannot be achieved by alternative, lower cost solutions. A business analysis will almost certainly be undertaken which will examine (to a 'first-order' assessment) the technological problems that may be encountered. In many respects the business case will provide the necessary justification for employing a virtual environment system in the application.

8.2.1 Human perception in virtual environments

Our understanding of human perception and human factors issues regarding virtual environments is still in its infancy. A considerable amount of research in this area is very important because it is needed to focus the development of enabling technologies. Major research areas include:

Visual perception

1. Spatial resolution: what display spatial resolution is required for a particular task?

2. Field of view is a difficult parameter to specify. However, to achieve an immersive virtual environment a field of view of 100° or more may be required. To achieve a wide field of view a very large optical system is required. The main aim will be to determine what field of view is required to perform the task effectively.

3. Binocular overlap: this parameter is related to the total display field of view. To achieve stereo displays a degree of binocular overlap is required. Partial overlapping binocular fields may be used to produce a very wide field of view. However, the amount of binocular overlap is

important and must be 'tuned' to suit the application. Perceptual and human performance studies must be undertaken to determine whether a partial overlap solution is appropriate.

4. Temporal resolution: what display update or refresh rate is acceptable for a given task? The higher the update requirement the greater the computational performance required.

5. Visual representation of the virtual environment must be investigated to determine the nature of the scene to be used for the application. Some applications may require very high fidelity displays while simplified, cartoon-like images may suffice for other applications. Obviously, there are large differences between these visual representations. How 'real' should the virtual environment appear? The answer must address the spatial and temporal fidelity of the virtual environment. Cost will be a determining factor.

6. Is an immersive or desktop system required? This question can only be answered after consideration of the task, the complexity of the system and the cost.

Auditory perception

1. In auditory environments the area that requires a great deal more research is the field of 3-D audio localization. Generation of spatialized sound can be achieved with high performance digital signal processors. However, individual differences in pinnae shape can lead to errors when non-personalized head related transfer functions (HRTF) are used. Occasionally a sensation of non-externalization can be experienced. This means that the listener does not perceive the sensation that the sound originates outside the head. Further work is required in characterizing HRTFs and determining the causes of lack of externalization in some subjects. Simpler 3-D audio localizer systems do not take account of effects such as reflection and reverberation. These are characteristics of a real environment. Therefore, work must be undertaken to examine the importance of accurate modelling of the acoustical environment. Sound in a real environment undergoes multiple reflections from a range of material types before it reaches the ear. Moreover, sound can be received from a single source via a direct path and many indirect routes. These sound waves combine in the ear to give a very complex waveform. The importance of the secondary reflections and indirect path sound signals must be quantified. If these characteristics have to be modelled it will be important to develop second generation audio localizer systems with an order of magnitude improvement in performance.

2. Improved HRTF: to achieve an acceptable degree of spatial auditory localization it is necessary to determine the individual's HRTF and use this in the audio localization system. Ideally, a more generalized solution

is required that works for many users and eventually becomes user-independent.

3.   Cues for range and localization: it is known that to determine both range and orientation of the sound signal the type of auditory cue presented to the listener is very important. This is particularly true when first time recognition of sound is required.

4.   Externalization: many users of spatial sound systems complain that the sound appears to be localized within the head. In other words, externalization does not occur. This effect may be a function of the HRTF not being compatible with the listener.

Haptic/kinaesthetic systems

1.   In comparison to visual and auditory environments, haptic environments are still in their infancy. To maintain a high degree of presence in the virtual environment it is probable that there will have to be direct contact with virtual objects. Discrete approaches are currently being undertaken to stimulate the tactile and kinaesthetic senses. These are largely confined to force reflecting joysticks, hand/arm exoskeletons and tactile feedback gloves. On investigation, the human haptic system is considerably more complex than one realizes. To convey haptic stimulations it is necessary to take account of surface skin and subsurface physical properties of the tissues.

2.   The human haptic/kinaesthetic systems need to be characterized and consideration must be given to temporal variations. Manipulation strategies in real-world systems should be determined for a range of tasks. Object characteristics such as compliance and roughness must be defined in such a way that these parameters can be encapsulated in a CAD/virtual environment modelling program. To provide computer synthesized haptic responses it will be necessary to develop a computational model of the physical properties of the skin and underlying tissues.

3.   In order to apply forces to the hand and arm it is necessary to use a form of exoskeleton into which the hand and arm is inserted. The problem of safety must be addressed because forces of the order of 10 Newtons will be applied. There seems to be no alternative to the exoskeleton but to couple haptic and kinaesthetic forces to the operator.

4.   Work is required in the development of lightweight sensors and actuators to keep the overall mass of the exoskeleton at an acceptable level. The bandwidth and frequency response of a force reflecting system needs to be quantified by careful experimentation. Current tactile stimulation systems are essentially stand-alone demonstrations of a field of mechanically activated (or pneumatic) 'points'. Depending on the

technology used they either provide small reactive areas (each area covering several square millimetres) or an array of extendable points at a density of 1/2 mm.

5. A key element to the development of a haptic display system is a complete analysis of the biomechanical properties of the skin.

6. Bandwidth: to perceive detailed surface texture information it is important to characterize the haptic and kinaesthetic system in terms of bandwidth and dynamic response. If a haptic actuator system is to be built it must have a bandwidth that exceeds that of the human perception system. A similar requirement exists for force reflective devices, except that the problems of supporting an exoskeleton must be addressed. The actuation system must not only provide the right level of force feedback but it must also overcome the mass, inertia and friction of the exoskeleton system.

7. Resolution: equally important to the bandwidth of the haptic system is the resolution of the actuator system used to convey the sensation of touch. The spatial resolution and dynamic range are important parameters.

8. Strategies performed by the human with haptic tasks must be analysed in a way that allows the actuator technology to be simplified. It is probably impractical to replicate all the cues provided by picking up an object. Therefore it will be necessary to isolate the dominant cues and ensure that these are presented with a sufficient level of fidelity.

Performance metrics

The area of performance metrics is extremely important for determining the effectiveness of a particular virtual environment solution. Without any form of metric it is very difficult to match the human operator to the virtual environment. Moreover, it will be almost impossible to optimize the man–machine interface because we have to rely on subjective opinion. The problems of defining suitable performance metrics are not unique to the field of virtual environments. Indeed the whole field of man–machine interfacing is desperately in need of a set of standard performance criteria. If a suitable set of metrics were to exist then it would be easy to quantify the benefits that a virtual environment system brings, compared to alternative approaches. The author encourages researchers to think very carefully about the advantages of applying a series of metrics to the field of virtual environments. Once a set of metrics has been established then hesitant potential investors may be convinced of the real benefits brought by virtual environment technology.

Virtual environment technology

1. Displays: urgent research is required to assist the development of true 1000 × 1000 pixel colour displays. These should be full colour, with a

high update rate and contained within a small package size of about 25.4 mm square. Future display resolution requirements are likely to approach the limiting resolution of the eye (1 minute of one) with several minutes of arc being a more practical requirement. It is well known that the human eye has excellent visual acuity in the region of the fovea. Outside this area the spatial resolution falls off dramatically. It may be possible to develop a display system that is matched to the resolution of the human eye. This will mean using an eye slaved high resolution insert. Eye slaved high resolution patches seem to offer the necessary resolution over relatively small angular subtenses. However, there is a question regarding the performance of the eye tracking technology and the dynamic response of the high resolution patch deflection system. Displays embodying this approach will be expensive.

2. Space tracking technology: low phase lag. Without doubt, one of the critical areas of space tracking systems (and virtual environments) is the requirement for low phase lag. The phase lag will probably have to be less than 5 ms if the lags are not to affect the performance of the operator. Particular care has to taken when interpreting what is meant by phase lag, as described in Chapter 6. Resolution requirements for tracking systems probably do not need to exceed 0.1 mm in translation and 0.01° in angular terms. For many applications translation resolution of the order of 1 mm and angular resolution of 0.1° may be quite adequate.

3. Multiple object tracking: it will be desirable to track multiple objects within a virtual environment, for example, the user's head and possibly both hands. With most current tracking systems the effective update rate of each tracked object is divided by the number of tracking sensors used. This reduction in update rate is due to the synchronization or multiplexing of trackers in the system. Unfortunately, this is a consequence of the technology used in the tracking system. A better method of tracking multiple objects is required that does not use multiplexed sensors. Moreover, if the whole body is to be tracked in terms of limb position this amounts to a considerable number of sensors. Apart from the update problems, the large number of cables connecting the sensors to the tracking electronics becomes a significant problem. Ideally, a wireless tracking system should be used. In the future, image processing systems may be able to determine the position of multiple objects without the need to cable up the participant. However, this will demand considerable processing performance and high resolution imaging sensors.

4. Image generators: virtual environments place severe timing constraints on image generation systems. While very high performance can undoubtedly be achieved there is a concern that the architectures of these systems do not lend themselves to the demanding performance required. As described in Chapter 6, the key parameter is the system throughput time. This figure must be considerabiy better than the current values of

40–100 ms. Apart from designing graphics system architecture to suit the virtual environment application, benefits can also be obtained by employing predictive filtering techniques. Different algorithms must be studied to determine whether they offer any real advantage.

Low latency architectures: current graphics platforms may need to be redesigned with low latency architectures in mind. This requirement derives from the need to couple head tracking systems to the later stages of the graphics system. It is tempting to employ the standard RS232 interface of the graphics system for the space tracking system. Unfortunately, this interface is not usually designed for real-time applications. As a consequence, attempts to send large amounts of high speed data through this interface result in an unacceptable interrupt load on the host processor. This means that more time is spent servicing the interrupt than in dealing with graphics drawing operations.

Update rate: the question of update rate is an interesting one. At the moment the computer graphics industry is concerned with increasing the spatial resolution of a display in preference to display update rate. However, for a virtual environment application this may be the complete opposite of what is required. Spatial resolution could be secondary to display update rate. Urgent research is required to determine whether high frame rate displays should be used in preference to high resolution displays. One factor in favour of the high frame display is the limitation in display resolution of current helmet-mounted displays. There seems to be little point in wasting computational effort when the display device cannot resolve the fine detail.

Motion prediction: there is some merit in being able to use motion prediction methods to compensate for inherent system lags. Provided the motion of an object can be expressed by means of a motion equation, it is possible that previous motion data can be used to predict where the object will be during the next few iterations. Parameters such as velocity and acceleration profiles are used in the prediction process. It will be necessary to determine the dynamics of the human head. Kalman filters could be used to predict where the object or head would be during the next few frames.

Virtual environment software engineering

1. Visual programming languages: to build the synthetic environment from a collection of library routines, the majority of software tools for virtual environment applications rely on a competent 'C' programmer being available. In contrast to this the VPL RB2 virtual environment programming tools rely on visual programming techniques, which allow people with fairly minimal computer literacy to create and maintain a virtual environment. With these tools it is possible to create a fully interactive virtual environment without writing any software. The visual

programmer constructs the virtual environment by linking objects in the virtual environment with behaviourial constructs. These are represented on screen by icons and simple 'wiring diagrams'. While the highest performance virtual environments will be programmed at a basic level, the use of a visual programming language will be of great benefit to the person interested in rapid prototyping. As computer graphics systems become more powerful, the performance difference between visual programming languages and conventional programming techniques will converge. As virtual environments become larger, visual programming techniques may result in significant cost savings that far outweigh conventional approaches.

2. Database standards: all virtual environment systems rely on an underlying database standard on which to represent the objects of the environment. In some ways the database is rather like a CAD-type database standard. (Some virtual environment software packages are actually based on well-known CAD standards.) However, a virtual environment system will generally require considerably more data to describe the environment. Not only is it necessary to describe the geometrical and spatial relationships of objects, but other parameters such as behaviour must be specified. This includes responses to external events or stimuli such as collisions and also includes mass and feel. To date, there are no standards in this area. A virtual environment standard is an obvious requirement.

3. Virtual environment modelling: the whole area of modelling for virtual environments needs attention. At the moment there are no standards, and there is a danger that future virtual environment systems will have to support multiple standards. If some measure of standardization does not come soon then organizations will have invested effort in their chosen standard and will be reluctant to move to another. With a virtual environment it will be necessary to store additional attribute information about an object such as texture (feel), weight, compliance and so on. Therefore, we have an opportunity to develop an open standard that can be used by everyone.

4. Multiple participants: in order to create multiple participant virtual environments, it will be necessary to develop communication protocols so that consistent databases can be maintained for each user. This means that if one participant moves an object in his virtual environment, then the corresponding object in another participant's environment is updated accordingly. The problems of networking in database systems should be reasonably well understood. However, some work will be required to ensure that efficient protocols are developed that allow real-time operation.

5. Use of virtual environments inside the virtual environment systems: the high level of interactivity within a virtual environment is one of the strengths of the technology. However, this interactivity will only be of

value if the design work that is undertaken within the virtual environment can be used outside the virtual environment.

8.3 Philosophical reflections

It is easy to become excited by virtual environments and the potential they offer. However, it is very important to resist this initial burst of enthusiasm and direct one's attention to the task of determining what the key issues of the system should be. It will be necessary to address the nature of the user interface and to understand the system requirements. Only when this has been undertaken should consideration be given to the type of technology that should be employed. Care must also be taken to address the human factors issues inevitably associated with complex man–machine interfaces.

An equally important issue that must be addressed along with the human factors and the associated engineering is a thorough business analysis. Nearly all ventures in high technology systems will fail unless the business issues have been properly addressed. From the author's perspective, many people who having heard of the term virtual reality believe that the subject is all about helmet-mounted displays and glove-like devices. However, virtual reality or virtual environments is much more than that. The business decision makers must be made to understand the wider issues of virtual environments. They must realize that a virtual environment is a synthetic computer generated representation of a physical system; a representation that allows a user to interact with the synthetic environment as if it were real. One of the distinct advantages of this is that the user is not bounded by limitations presented by the real world. For instance, virtual environments could be used to prototype a product during the early part of its life cycle. The interactivity of a virtual environment would allow the user to explore alternative configurations before the product is manufactured. This approach means that design and development risks could be removed early in the manufacturing life cycle. In many respects the world is already moving towards rapid prototyping systems or synthetic design environments. The benefits of these systems are already established. A virtual environment system addresses the totality of such design and rapid prototyping systems by allowing the user to achieve a higher level of interactivity than can be afforded by CAD systems. It would be wrong to suggest that every prototyping system will require total immersion in the virtual environment. Some design tasks may be better served by a traditional CAD system, but during the latter stages of design a more immersive system may be required. Therefore, a key requirement is the ability to move between these different prototyping systems by providing the designer with the right level of immersion for the task. Ideally, the transition between the different prototyping stages would be seamless and would extend into the manufacturing process. The concept of assessing ease of manufacture and ease of assembly is extremely exciting. This could be further extended into customer product training while the product is being manufactured. Manufacturing processes based on a virtual environment could revolutionize the way we design and manufacture things in the future.

8.4 Recommendations for the way ahead

There is little doubt that current generation virtual environment peripherals are limited in terms of resolution. However, by conducting research into the human factors requirements it will be possible to match the technology to the human interface. The affordable high resolution full colour helmet-mounted display is already on its way and so too are the high performance computer systems. Advances in the other technologies such as tracking systems and haptic/kinaesthetic feedback display systems are moving at a slightly slower pace. As people recognize the importance of virtual environments, improvements will be made. From a virtual environment scientist's point of view it will be necessary to provide human factors' guidelines so that the technology may be developed appropriately. Would-be developers of the technology (including software) are advised to consider the standardization of interfaces. This will make it easier to take advantage of improved technology as it emerges. It is hoped that this book will act as a baseline of knowledge, upon which we can all build up our understanding of the next generation human–machine interface.

Recommended further reading

(1992). Research directions in virtual environments. *Computer graphics*, 26 (3).

VR News, Cydata Ltd, PO Box 2515, London N4 4JW, UK

Presence: *Teleoperators and Virtual Environments*. (Quarterly journal) Cambridge, MA: MIT Press

Bibliography

Objectives

This bibliography is in two parts. Part 1 is in alphabetical order, and Part 2 is in keyword order, and is a re-grouping into major topic headings of Part 1. This will facilitate the reader who has a specific interest in a given subject.

Part 1: Bibliography in alphabetical order

Ackerman D. (1990). *A Natural History of the Senses*. New York: Random House, pp. 80–1

Adelstein B.D. and Rosen M.J. (1992). Design and implementation of a force reflecting manipulation for manual control research. In *ASME Winter Annual Meeting*, Anaheim CA, November 1992

Adelstein B.D., Johnston E.R. and Ellis S.R. (1992). A testbed for characterizing dynamic response of virtual environment spatial sensors. In *Proc. UIST '92: 5th Annual ACM Sym. on User Interface Software and Technology*, Monterey, CA, 15–18 November 1992

Airey J.M, Rohlf J.H and Brooks F.P. (1990). Towards image realism with interactive update rates in complex virtual building environments. In *Symposium on Interactive 3D Graphics (SIGGRAPH '90)*

Akin D.L., Minsky M.L., Thiel E.D. and Kurtzman C.R. (1983). *Space Applications of Automation, Robotics, and Machine Intelligence Systems (ARAMIS). Phase II* vol. 3: Executive Summary, MIT, Contract NAS 8-34381, NASA Marshall Space Flight Center

Applewhite H. (1991a). *Design of Acoustic Ranging Systems*. Technical Report 91-02, Piltdown Incorporated: Beaverton OR

Applewhite H. (1991b). Position-tracking in virtual reality. In *Proc. 2nd Annual Virtual Reality Conference and Exhibition*, San Francisco, CA, 23–25 September 1991 (Helsel S.K., ed.). Westport CT: Meckler Corporation

Arnheim R. (1969). *Visual Thinking*. Berkeley CA: University of California Press

Baltzley D.R., Kennedy R.S., Berbaum K.S., Lilienthal M.G. and Gower D.W. (1989). The time course of postflight simulator sickness symptoms. *Aviation, Space, and Environmental Medicine*, **60**, 1043–8

Barlow H.B. and Mollon J.D. (1982). *The Senses*. Cambridge University Press

Barlow J. (1990). Life in the DataCloud: Scratching your eyes back in. In *Mondo 2000*, Summer, 1990, p. 36

Batter J.J. and Brooks F.P., Jr. (1972). GROPE-1. In *Proc. IFIP '71*, p. 759

Baudrillard J. (1983). *Simulations*, p. 2. New York: Semiotest(e)/Columbia University Press

Beard N. (1992). Tunnel vision. *Personal Computer World*, December, 374–82

Bergman L., Fuchs H., Grant E. and Spach S. (1986). Image rendering by adaptive refinement. In *Proc. SIGGRAPH '86*

Bergson H. (1911). *Creative Evolution*, p. 139. New York: Henry Holt (translated by Arthur Mitchell)

Bettelheim B. (1987). The importance of play. *The Atlantic Monthly*, March

Bevan M. (1992). BAe merges real and virtual environments. *VR News*, **1**(7)

Biocca F. (1992). *Will simulation sickness slow down the diffusion of virtual reality technology?* Working Paper Series: Communication Technology and Cognition Group, Center for Research in Journalism and Mass Communication, University of North Carolina

Bishop G. (1984). Self-Tracker. A smart optical sensor on silicon. *Doctoral Dissertation* TR84-002, Department of Computer Science, University of North Carolina at Chapel Hill

Bishop G. and Fuchs H. (1984). The Self-Tracker: A smart optical sensor on silicon. In *Proc. 1984 MIT Conference on Advanced Research in VLSI*, pp 65–73. Dedham MA: Artech House

Blauert J. (1983). *Spatial Hearing: The Psychophysics of Human Sound Localisation*. Cambridge MA: MIT Press

Bolt R. (1984). *The Human Interface: Where People and Computers Meet*. Belmont CA: Lifetime Learning Publications

Boynton R.M. (1979). *Human Color Vision*. New York: Holt, Rinehart and Winston

Brand S. (1987). *The Media Lab: Inventing the Future at MIT*. New York: Viking

Breglia D.R. and Oharek F.J. (1984). *Head Position and Orientation Sensor*, US Patent 4 446 480 (filed 14 December 1981)

Brennan S. (1990). Conversation as direct manipulation. In *The Art of Human-Computer Interface Design* (Laurel B., ed.), pp. 394-5. Menlo Park CA: Addison-Wesley

Bricken W. (1990). *Virtual Environment Operating System: Preliminary Functional Architecture*. TR-HITL-M-90-2, Human Interface Technology Laboratory, University of Washington, Seattle

Bronowski J. (1978). *The Origins of Knowledge and Imagination*, p. 18. New Haven: Yale University Press

Brooks F.P., Jr. (1975). *The Mythical Man-Moth: Essays in Software Engineering*. Reading MA: Addison-Wesley

Brooks F.P., Jr. (1977). The computer scientist as toolsmith: Studies in interactive computer graphics. In *Information Processing '77* (Gilchrist B., ed.), pp. 625–34. Amsterdam: North-Holland

Brooks F.P., Jr. (1988). Grasping reality through illusion: Interactive graphics serving science. In *Proc. CHI*, pp. 1–11. Reading MA: Addison-Wesley

Brooks F.P., Jr., Ouh-Young M., Batter J.J. and Kilpatrick P.J. (1990). Project GROPE – Haptic Displays for Scientific Visualization. *ACM Computer Graphics*, **24**(4), 177–85

Bryson S. (1991). Interaction of objects in a virtual environment: A two point paradigm. In *Stereoscopic Displays and Applications II, SPIE Proceedings* vol. 1457

Burdea G. (1991). *Portable Dextrous Force Feedback Master for Robot Telemanipulation*, US Patent 5 004 391

Burdea G. and Speeter T. (1989). Portable dextrous force feedback master for robot telemanipulation. In *Proc. 1989 NASA Conf. on Space Telerobotics* vol. 2, Pasadena CA, pp. 153–61

Burdea G., Zhuang J., Roskos E., Silver D. and Langrana N. (1991). Direct drive force feedback control for the DataGlove. In *Proc. European Robotics Intelligent Systems Conf.*, Corfu, June 1991

Burdea G., Zhuang J., Roskos E., Silver D., Langrana N. (1992). A portable dextrous master with force feedback. *Presence*, **1**(1), 18–28

Burgess P. (1984) *Scientific American*, September

Burgess P. (1988). *MacWEEK*, 2 August, p. 38

Bush V. (1945). As we may think. *The Atlantic Monthly*, August

Cadoz C. and Ramstein C. (1990). Capture, representation, and composition of the instrumental gesture. In *Proc. ICMC '90*, Glasgow

Cadoz C., Jean-Loup F. and Annie L. (1984). Responsive input devices and sound synthesis by simulation of instrumental mechanisms: the CORDIS system. *Computer Music Journal*, **8**(3), 60–73

Cadoz C., Lesez L. and Jean-Loup F. (1990). Modular feedback keyboard. *Computer Music Journal*, **14**(2), 47–51

CAE Electronics (1984). *Wide Field of View, Helmet Mounted Infinity Display Systems Development*, AFHRL-TR-84-27, AF Systems Command, Brooks AFBTX

Calhoun G.L., Arbak C.J. and Boff K.R. (1984). Eye controlled switching for crew station design. In *Proc. Human Factors Society, 28th Annual Meeting*, 1984

Calhoun G.L., Valencia G. and Furness T.A., III (1987). Three-dimensional auditory cue simulation for crew station design/evaluation. In *Proc. Human Factors Society, 31st Annual Meeting*, 1987, pp. 1398–1402

Campbell J. (1988). Day of the dead lecture. *Magical Blend*, **16**, 58–62

Canfield Smith D., Irby C., Kimaball R. and Harslem E. (1982). The Star user interface: An overview. In *Office Systems Technology*, El Segundo CA, Xerox Corporation

Canon L.K. (1970). Intermodality inconsistency of input and directed attention as determinants of the nature of adaption. *Journal of Experimental Psychology*, **84**, 141–7

Carroll J.M., ed. (1987). *Interfacing Thought: Cognitive Aspects of Human-Computer Interaction*. Cambridge MA: MIT Press

Carroll J.M. and Thomas J.C. (1982). Metaphor and the cognitive representation of computing systems. *IEEE Transactions on Systems, Man and Cybernetics*, **12**(2), 107–16

Carroll J.M., Mack R.L. and Kellogg W.A. (1988). Interface metaphors and user interface design. In *Handbook on Human-Computer Interaction* (Helander M., ed.). Amsterdam: Elsevier

Chavel P. and Strand P. (1984). Range measurement using Talbot diffraction imaging of 9 gratings. *Applied Optics*, **23**(6), 862–70

Chen S.E. (1990). Incremental radiosity: An extension of progressive radiosity to an interactive image synthesis system. In *Proc. SIGGRAPH '90*

Cherri A. and Cooper P. (1989). *Visual Environment Simulator for Mobile Viewer*, US Patent 4 807 202 (filed 17 April 1986)

Chung J., Harris M., Brooks F., Kelly M.T., Hughes J.W., Ouh-young M., Cheung C., Holloway R.L. and Pique M. (1989). Exploring virtual worlds with head-mounted displays, non-holographic 3-dimensional display technologies. In *SPIE Proc. on Non-holographic 3-dimensional display technologies*, Los Angeles CA, 15-20 January

Church E. (1945). *Bulletin of Aerial Photogrammetry*, **15**, Syracuse University

CIE (Commission Internationale de l'Eclairage) (1970). *CIE Document on Colorimetry (Official Recommendations)*. Publ. 15

Cohen M.F. and Greenberg D.P. (1985). The Hemi Cube: A radiosity solution for complex environments. In *Proc. SIGGRAPH '85*

Cohen M.F, Chen S., Wallace J. and Greenberg D.P. (1988). A progressive refinement approach to fast radiosity image generation computer graphics. In *Proc. SIGGRAPH '88*

Danielou A. (1984). *Shiva and Dionysus: The Religion of Nature and Eros*. New York: Inner Traditions International (translated by K.F. Hurry)

Davidson C. (1991). European astronauts to fly in virtual space. *Computer Weekly*, 28 November

Delaney B. (1991). On line. *CyberEdge Journal*, May/June, 2

Dewitt T. (1989). Rangefinding by the diffraction method. *Laser and Optics*, **8**(4), 119–24

Ditlea S. (1990). Grand illusion. *New York Magazine*, 6 August, 32

Doherty R. (1990). DC magnetic fields guide 6D pointer. *Electronic Engineering Times*, 20 August

Doll T., Gerth J., Engleman W. and Folds D. (1986). *Development of Simulated Directional Audio for Cockpit Applications*, USAF Report AAMRL-TR-86-014

Eglowstein H. (1990). Hands on under the hood: Can we talk? *Byte*, July, 288–9

Ellis S.R. (1989). Visions of visualization aids: Design philosophy and observations. In *Proc. SPIE-Int. Soc. Optical Engineering Sym. on Three Dimensional Visualization of Scientific Data*, Los Angeles CA, 15–20 January

Ellis S.R., ed. (1991a). *Representation in Pictorial and Virtual Environments*. London: Taylor and Francis

Ellis S.R. (1991b). Nature and origins of virtual environments: A bibliographical essay. *Computing Systems in Engineering*, **2**(4), 321–47

Endo T. and Hiroshi I. (1989). *NTT Human Interface Laboratories*, NTT publication, Kanagawa, Japan

Engelbart D. (1963). A conceptual framework for augmenting man's intellect. In *Vistas in Information-Handling* vol. 1 (Howerton P.W. and Weeks D.C., eds.), pp. 1–29. Washington DC: Aparton Books

Ferranti Defence Systems (1987). Ferranti helmet pointing system (HPS). In *The Royal Aeronautical Society, Aircrew Helmets and Helmet Mounted Devices Proc.* 10 February, pp. 6.1–6.15

Ferrin F.J. (1991). Survey of helmet tracking technologies. In *SPIE Proc. Large-Screen-Projection, Avionic, and Helmet-Mounted Displays* vol. 1456

Fisher S. (1982). Viewpoint dependent imaging: An interactive stereoscopic display. In *Processing and Display of Three-Dimensional Data, SPIE Proceedings* vol. 367

Fisher S. (1986). Telepresence master glove controller for dextrous robotic end-effectors. In *Advances in Intelligent Robotics Systems, SPIE Proceedings* vol. 726 (Casasent D.P., ed.)

Fisher S. (1989). Panel Session. Virtual environments and interactivity: Windows to the future. In *SIGGRAPH '89 Panel Proc.*, Boston MA, 31 July 1989

Fisher S. (1990). Virtual environments, personal simulation and telepresence, multimedia review. *Journal of Multimedia Computing*, **1**(2)

Fisher S. and Marion A. (1983). Real time computer graphics from body motion. In *Optics in Entertainment, SPIE Proceedings* vol. 391, pp. 59–63

Fisher S. and McGreevy M. (1986). Virtual workstation: A multi-modal, stereoscopic display environment. In *Advances in Intelligent Robotics Systems, SPIE Proceedings* vol. 726 (Casasent D.P., ed.), pp. 517–522

Fisher S., McGreevy M., Humphries J. and Robinett W. (1986) Virtual environment display system. In *ACM Workshop on Interactive 3D Graphics*, University of North Carolina, Chapel Hill, 23–24 October, pp 77–87

Flannery J.B., Jr. (1973). Light controlled light valves. *IEEE Transactions on Electronic Devices*, **20**(11), 941–53

Foley J.D. (1987). Interfaces for advanced computing. *Scientific American*, **257**(4): October, 126–35

Fox B. (1991). 3D video doubles up on tape. *New Scientist*, (1772), 8 June

Friedman n M., Starner T. and Pentland A. (1992). Synchronization in virtual realities. *Presence*, **1**(1), pp 139–44

Fuchs H., Poulton J., Eyles J. and Greer T. (1988a). Coarse-grain and fine-grain parallelism in the next generation pixel planes graphics system. In *Proc. International Conference and Exhibition on Parallel Processing for Computer Vision and Display*. New York: Springer-Verlag

Fuchs H., Pizer S.M., Creasy J.L., Renner J.B. and Rosenman J.G. (1988b). Interactive, richly cued shaded display of multiple 3D objects in medical images. In *Proc. SPIE Medical Imaging II Conference* vol. 914(2)

Fuchs H., Poulton J., Eyles J., Greer T. *et al.* (1989). A heterogeneous multiprocessor graphics system using processor enhanced memories. In *Proc. SIGGRAPH '89*

Furness T.A., III (1986a). Fantastic voyage. *Popular Mechanics*, December, 63–5

Furness T.A., III (1986b). The super cockpit and its human factors challenges. In *Proc. of the Human Factors Society, 30th Annual Meeting*, 1986

Furness T.A., III (1988). Harnessing virtual space. *Society for Information Display Digest*, 4–7

Geldard F. (1957). Adventures in tactile literacy. *American Psychologist*, **12**(3), 117

George D.W., Sillion F.X. and Greenberg D.P. (1990). Radiosity redistribution for dynamic environments. *IEEE Transactions on Computer Graphics and Applications*, July

Giacalone A, Heller J. *et al.* (1989). VERITAS: Visualization environment research in the applied sciences. In *Three Dimensional Visualization and Display Technologies, SPIE Proceedings* vol. 1083, pp. 127–33

Gibson J.J. (1950). *The Perception of the Virtual World*. Boston: Houghton Mifflin

Gibson J.J. (1966). *The Senses Considered as Perceptual Systems*. Boston: Houghton-Mifflin

Gibson J.J. (1979). *The Ecological Approach to Visual Perception*. Boston: Houghton-Mifflin

Gibson W. (1984). *Neuromancer*. New York: Berkeley Publications

Goral C.M., Torrance K.E., Greenberg D.P. and Battaile B. (1984). Modelling the interaction of light between diffuse surfaces. In *Proc. SIGGRAPH '84*

Greenfield H., Vickers D., Sutherland I., Kolff W. and Reemtsma K. (1971). Moving computer graphic images seen from inside the vascular system. *Transactions of the American Society of Artificial Internal Organs*, **17**, 381–5

Gregory R.L. (1989). Seeing by exploring. In *Spatial Displays and Spatial Instruments* (Ellis S.R., Kaiser M.K. and Grunwald A., eds.), pp. 5–11. NASA Conference Publication 10032

Grimsdale C. (1991). dVS-distributed virtual environment system. In *Proc. Computer Graphics '91 Conference*, London (ISBN 0 86353 282 9)

Guedry F.E., Lentz J.M. and Jell R.M. (1978). Visual-vestibular interactions: I. Influence of peripheral vision on suppression of the vestibulo-ocular reflex and visual acuity. *Aviation, Space, and Environmental Medicine*, **50**, 205–11

Gullichsen E. and Randal W. (1989). Cyberspace: Experimental computing. In *Nexus '89 Science Fiction and Science Fact*

Haber R.N. (1986). Flight simulation. *Scientific American*, **255**(1), 96, 103

Haber R.N. and Hershenson M. (1973). *The Psychology of Visual Perception*. New York: Holt, Rinehart and Winston

Hannford B. (1989). A design framework for teleoperators with kinesthetic feedback. *IEEE Transactions on Robotics and Automation*, **5**(4)

Hatada T., Sakata H. and Kusaka H. (1980). Psychological analysis of the 'sensation of reality' induced by a visual wide-field display. *Journal of the Society of Motion Picture and Television Engineers*, **89**, 560–9

Hatamura Y. and Miroshita H. (1990). *Direct Coupling System between Nanometer World and Human World,* Department of Mechanical Engineering for Production, The University of Tokyo, Japan

Hartley R.V.L. and Fry T.C. (1921). The binocular localisation of pure tones. *Physics Review*, 2nd ser., **18**, 431–42

Hay J.C. (1974). Motor transformation learning. *Perception*, **3**, 487–96

Hay J.C. and Goldsmith W.M. (1973). Space-time adaption of visual position constancy. *Journal of Experimental Psychology*, **99**, 1–9

Heeter C. (1992). Being there: The subjective experience of presence. *Presence*, **1**(2)

Heilig M. (1955). *The Cinema of the Future*. Mexico City: Espacios

Heilig M. (1960). *Stereoscopic Television Apparatus for Individual Use*, US Patent 2 955 156 (filed 4 October 1960)

Heilig M. (1962). *Sensorama Simulator*, US Patent 3 050 870 (filed 28 August 1962)

Heinlein R. (1965). *Three By Heinlein: The Puppet Masters; Waldo; Magic, Inc.* Garden City NY: Doubleday

Held R. (1965). Plasticity in sensorimotor systems. *Scientific American*, **213**(5), 84–94

Held R. and Durlach N. (1991). Telepresence, time delay, and adaption. In *Representation in Pictorial and Virtual Environments* (Ellis S.R., ed.). London: Taylor and Francis

Held R., Efstathiou A. and Greene M. (1966). Adaption to displaced and delayed visual feedback from the hand. *Journal of Experimental Psychology*, **72**(6) 887–91

Henderson J., McKellar C.J., Price M. and Venning R. (1992). Visualisation as a practical tool. In *National Lighting Conference '92 Proceedings* (in press)

Herot C. (1980). Spatial management of data. *ACM Transactions on Database Systems*, **5**(4)

Hettinger L.J., Berbaum K.S., Kennedy R.S., Dunlap, and Nolan (1990). Vection and simulator sickness. *Military Psychology*, **2**(3), 171–91

Hill J.W. (1967). *The Perception of Multiple Tactile Stimuli*, Stanford Electronics Laboratory Technical Report No. 4823-1, Stanford University, CA

Hochberg J. (1986). Representation of motion and space in video and cinematic displays. In *Handbook of Perception and Human Performance* vol. 2. (Boff K., Kaufmann L. and Thomas J., eds.), pp. 1–64. New York: Wiley

Hodges L.F. (1991). Basic principles of stereographic software development. In *Stereoscopic Displays and Applications II, SPIE Proceedings* vol. 1457

Hollis R.L., Salcudean S. and Abraham D.W. (1990). *Toward a Tele-Nonrobotic Manipulation System with Atomic Scale force Feedback and Motion Resolution,* IBM Thomas J. Watson Research Center, Yorktown Heights, NY

Iwata H. (1990). Artificial reality with force-feedback: Development of desktop virtual space with Compact Master Manipulator. *Computer Graphics*, **24**, 165–74

Jacobson A.D. (1975). A new television projection light valve. *SID Digest*, 27

Jau B. (1991). *Technical Support Package on Anthropomorphic Remote Manipulator for NASA TECH BRIEF 15(4)*. *#127*, JPL Invention Report, Report No. NPO-17975/7222, JPL Technology Utilization Office, Pasadena CA, April

Johnson-Laird P. (1983). *Mental Models*. Cambridge MA: Harvard University Press

Kajiya J.T. (1986). The rendering equation. In *Proc. SIGGRAPH '86*

Kalawsky R.S. (1991a). Pilot integration and the implications on the design of advanced cockpits. In *Conf. on the Man-Machine Interface in Tactical Aircraft Design and Combat Automation*, Agard, Stuttgart

Kalawsky R.S. (1991b). State of virtual reality in the UK. In *IEE Colloquium on Real World Visualisation - Virtual World-Virtual Reality*, London

Kalawsky R.S. (1991c). From visually coupled systems to virtual reality: An aerospace perspective. In *Proc. Computer Graphics '91*, Blenheim Online

Kandebo S.W. (1988). Navy to evaluate Agile Eye helmet-mounted display system. *Aviation Week and Space Technology*, 15 August, 94–6

Kaufman A. and Bakalash R. (1989). The Cube system as a 3D medical workstation. In *Three-Dimensional Visualization and Display Technologies, SPIE Proceedings* vol. 1083, pp. 189–94

Kaufman A., Yagel R. and Bakalash R. (1990). Direct interaction with 3D volumetric environment. In *Proc. SIGGRAPH '90*, pp. 33–4

Kay A. (1977). Microelectronics and the personal computer. *Scientific American*, **237**(3), 230

Kay A. (1984). Computer software. *Scientific American*, September

Kay A. (1990). User interface: A personal view. In *The Art of Human-Computer Interface Design* (Laurel B., ed.), p. 192. Menlo Park CA: Addison-Wesley

Kennedy R.S. and Fowlkes J.E. (1990). *What does it mean when we say that simulator sickness is polygenic and polysymptomatic?* Paper presented at E1/IMAGE V Conference, Phoenix AZ, June 1990

Kennedy R.S., Hettinger L.J. and Lilienthal M.G. (1987). Simulator sickness. In *Motion and Space Sickness* (Crampton G., ed.), pp. 317–41. Boca Raton FL: CRC Press

Kertesz A.E. and Sullivan M.J. (1978). The effects of stimuli size on human cyclofusional response. *Vision Research*, **18**, 567–71

Knowlton K. (1975). Virtual pushbuttons as a means of person-machine interaction. In *Proc. Conf. Computer Graphics, Pattern Recognition and Data Structure*, 14–16 May 1975

Knowlton K.C. (1977). Computer displays optically superimposed on input devices. *Bell System Technical Journal*, **56**(3), 367–83

Kobayashi Y. (1989). *Artificial Intelligence Department 1988 Special Report*, Advanced Telecommunications Research Institute International, Communication Systems Research Laboratories, Kyoto, Japan

Kramer J. and Leifer L. (1989). The Talking Glove: A speaking aid for non-vocal deaf and deaf-blind individuals. In *Proc. RESNA 12th Annual Conf.*, Louisiana, pp. 471–2

Krueger M. (1977). Responsive environments. In *Proc. National Computer Conf.*, pp. 423–33

Krueger M. (1983a). *Virtual Reality*. Reading MA: Addison-Wesley

Krueger M. (1983b). *Artificial Reality*. Reading MA: Addison-Wesley

Krueger M. (1985). VIDEOPLACE: A report from the Artificial Reality Laboratory. *Leonardo*, **18**(3)

Kulpers J. (1975). *Object Tracking and Orientation Determination Mean, System, and Process*, US Patent 3 868 565 (filed July 1973)

Kulpers J. (1976). *Tracking and Determining Orientation of Object using Coordinate Transformation Means, System, and Process*, US Patent 3 983 474 (filed February 1975)

Kulpers J. (1977). *Apparatus for Generating a Nutating Electromagnetic Field*, US Patent 4 017 858 (assignee: Polhemus Navigation Sciences, Inc., 12 April 1977)

Laboratoire d'Informatique Fondamentale et d'Intelligence Artificielle (1990). Brochure published by l'Institut d'Informatique et de Mathematiques Appliquees de Grenoble

Laurel B. (1986a). Interface as mimesis. In *User-Centered System Design: New Perspectives on Human-Computer Interaction* (Norman D.A. and Draper S., eds.). Hillsdale NJ: Lawrence Erlbaum Associates.

Laurel B. (1986b). Towards the design of a computer-based interactive fantasy system. *PhD Dissertation*, Ohio State University

Laurel B. (1991). *Computers as Theatre*. Menlo Park, CA: Addison-Wesley

Leifer L., Van der Loos M. and Michalowski S. (1990). Telerobotics in rehabilitation: Barriers to a virtual existence. In *Conf. on Human-Machine Interfaces for Teleoperators and Virtual Environments*, Santa Barbara CA, 4–9 March, sponsored by the Engineering Foundation

Levine H. and Rheingold H. (1987). *The Cognitive Connection*, pp. 232–33. New York: Prentice-Hall

Levinthal C. (1966) Molecular model-building by computer. *Scientific American*, **214**(6), 42–52

Liang J., Shaw C. and Green M. (1991). On temporal-spatial realism in the virtual reality environment. In *Proc. 4th Annual Symposium on User Interface Software and Technology*, Hilton Head SC, pp. 19–25

Licklider J.C.R. (1960). Man-computer symbiosis. *Institute of Radio Engineers Transactions on Human Factors in Electronics*, **1**, 4–11

Lippman A. (1980). Movie-Maps: An application of the optical videodisc to computer graphics. *Computer Graphics*, **14**(3)

Lipton L. (1964). Sensorama. *Popular Photography*, July

Logitech (1991). *Logitech 2D/6D Mouse Technical Reference Manual*

Mann R., Rowell G., Conati F., Tetwsky A., Ottenheimer D. and Antonsson E. (1981). Precise, rapid, automatic 3D position and orientation tracking of multiple moving bodies. In *Proc. VIII International Congress of Biomechanics*, Nagoya, Japan, July

McCauley M.E., ed. (1984). Simulator sickness. In *Proc. Workshop*. Washington, DC: National Academy Press

McGreevy M.W. (1991). Virtual reality and planetary exploration. In *29th AAS Goddard Memorial Symposium*, Washington DC, March 1991

McKim R.H. (1980). *Thinking Visually*, p.7. Belmont CA: Lifelong Learning Publications

McLuhan M. (1964) *Understanding Media: The Extensions of Man*. New York: McGraw-Hill

McLuhan M. (1969). Interview. *Playboy*, March

Menn A. and Krimerman J. (1990). *System for Measuring the Angular Displacement of an Object*, US Patent 4 896 962 (filed 26 May 1986)

Minsky M. (1979). *Toward a Remotely-Manned Energy and Production Economy*, Massachusetts Institute of Technology, Artificial Intelligence Laboratory, AI Memo No. 544, September

Minsky M., Ouh-Young M., Steele O., Brooks F.P., Jr. and Behensky M. (1990). Feeling and seeing: Issues in force display. *ACM Computer Graphics*, **24**(2), 235–43

Monkman G.J. (1992). An electrorheological tactile display. *Presence*, **1**(2), 219–228

Morishima A. and Speeter T.H. (1989). *Teleoperator Control of the Utah/MIT Dextrous Hand - A Functional Approach*, AT&T Bell Laboratories, Technical Report No. CUCS-474-89

Murray P.M. and Barber B. (1985). Visual display research tools. In *AGARD Conf. Proc.* vol. 408(2), pp. 1–8

Negroponte N. (1970). *The Architecture Machine*. Cambridge MA: MIT Press

Negroponte N. (1981). Media Room. *Proceedings of the Society for Information Display*, **22**(2), 109–13

Nelson T. (1980). Interactive systems and the design of virtuality. *Creative Computing*, November/December, 56–62

Nemine K. and Ellis S.R. (1991). Optic bias of perceived eye level depends on structure of the pitched optic array In *Psychonomic Society, 32nd Annual Meeting*, San Francisco CA, 22-24 November

Newquist H. (1991). A computer generated suspension of disbelief. *AI Expert*, 34–9

Nishijima M. and Kijima Y. (1989). Learning a sense of rhythm with a neural network: The Neuro-Drummer. In *Proc. 1st International Conference on Music Perception and Cognition*, Kyoto, Japan, October, pp. 77–80

Noar D., Arnon O. and Avnur A. (1987). A light weight innovative Helmet Airborne Display And Sight (HADAS). In *Display System Optics, SPIE Proceedings* vol. 778, pp. 89–95

Noll M. (1972). Man-machine tactile communication. *Journal of the Society for Information Display*, July/August

NTT Visual Media Laboratory (1988). *Annual Report*

Pagels H. (1988). *The Dreams of Reason*. New York: Simon and Schuster

Papert S. (1980). *Mindstorms: Children, Computers, and Powerful Ideas*, pp. 21, 76. New York: Basic Books

Pausch R. (1991). Virtual reality on five dollars a day. In *ACM SIGCHI Conf. Proc.*, New Orleans, 1991, pp. 265–70

Perkins D.N. (1979). *Pictures and the Real Thing*, Project Zero, Harvard University, Cambridge MA

Perry Barlow J. (1990). Being in nothingness. In *Mondo 2000*, Summer, p. 44

Pfeiffer J.E. (1982). *The Creative Explosion: An Inquiry into the Origins of Art and Religion*, p. 205. Ithaca NY: Cornell University Press

Polhemus (1991). A Kaiser Aerospace and Electronics Company, Colchester VT (trade literature)

Pollack A. (1989). What is artificial reality? Wear a computer and see. *New York Times*, 10 April, p. 1

Pollack A. (1990). Coming soon: Data you can look under and walk through. *New York Times*, 14 October

Posnick-Goodwin S. (1988). Dreaming for a living. *Peninsula*, July, p. 58

Posselt C., Schroter J., Opitz M., Divenyi P. and Blauert J. (1986). Generation of binaural signals for research and home entertainment. In *Proc. 12th ICA*, Toronto, Paper B1-6

Potter R.J. (1961). *Journal of the Optical Society of America*, **51**, 1079–89

Pund M.L. (1986). *Stereoscopic Display*, US Patent 4 649 425 (filed 16 January 1986)

Raab F. (1977). *Remote Object Position Locator*, US Patent 4 054 881 (filed 26 April 1976)

Raab F.H., Blood E.B., Steiner T.O., Jones R.J. (1979). Magnetic position and orientation tracking systems. *IEEE Transactions on Aerospace and Electronic Systems*, **15**(5), pp 709–718

Rayleigh, Lord (1945). *Theory of Sound* 2nd edn, vol II, pp. 440–3. New York: Dover

Reason J.R. and Brand J.J. (1975). *Motion Sickness*. London: Academic Press

Rebo R.K. and Amburn P. (1989). A helmet-mounted environment display system. In *Helmet-Mounted Displays, SPIE Proceedings* vol. 1116, pp. 80–4

Redding G.M. (1973a). Simultaneous visual adaption to tilt and displacement: A test of independent processes. *Bulletin of the Psychonomic Society*, **2**, 41–2

Redding G.M. (1973b). Visual adaption to tilt and displacement: Same or different processes? *Perception and Psychophysics*, **14**, 193–200

Redding G.M. (1975a). Decay of visual adaption to tilt and displacement. *Perception and Psychophysics*, **17**, 203–8

Redding G.M. (1975b). Simultaneous visuomotor adaption to optical tilt and displacement. *Perception and Psychophysics*, **17**, 97–100

Rediffusion (1985). Flight simulation. In *AGARD Conf. Proc.* vol. 408

Rheingold H. (1976). The ultimate cashflow. *California Living*, 26 September

Rheingold H. (1985). *Tools for Thought*, pp. 260–1. New York: Simon and Schuster

Rheingold H. (1991). *Virtual Reality, the Revolutionary Technology of Computer-Generated Artificial Worlds – and How it Promises and Threatens to Transform Business and Society*. New York: Summit Books

Rifkin A. (1982). Mort Heilig's Feelie Machine. *L.A. Weekly*, 12–18 March, p. 10

Roberts L. (1966). The Lincoln Wand. In *AFIPS Conf. Proc., 1966 Fall Joint Computer Conference*, November, pp. 223–7

Robinett W. and Rolland J.P. (1992). A computational model for the stereoscopic optics of a head mounted display. *Presence*, **1**(1), 45–62

Rock I. (1990). *The Perceptual World*. New York: W.H. Freeman and Co.

Rodgers A.G. (1991). Advances in head tracker technology – A key contributor to helmet vision system performance and implementation. In *Society for Information Display International Symposium, Digest of Technical Papers*, 6–10 May, pp. 127–30

Roscoe S.N. (1980). *Aviation Psychology*. Ames IA: Iowa State University Press

Roscoe S.N. (1984). Judgments of size and distance with imaging displays. *Human Factors*, **26**, 617–20

Roscoe S.N. (1985). Bigness is in the eye of the beholder. *Human Factors*, **27**, 615–36

Roscoe S.N. and Jensen R.S. (1981). Computer-animated prediction displays for microwave landing approaches. *IEEE Transaction on Systems, Man and Cybernetics*, **11**, 760–5

Roscoe S.N., Hasler S.G. and Dougherty D.J. (1966). Flight by periscope: Making takeoffs and landings: The influence of image magnification practice and various conditions of flight. *Human Factors* **8**, 13–40

Roscoe S.N., Olzek L.A. and Randle R.J. (1976). Ground-referenced visual orientation with imaging displays: monocular versus binocular accommodation and judgments of relative size. In *Proc. AGARD Conf. on Visual Presentation of Cockpit Information Including Special Devices for Particular Conditions of Flying*, Neuilly-sur-Seine, France, pp. A5.1–A5.9. North Atlantic Treaty Organization

Roskos E. (1991). *Towards a Distributed, Object-Oriented Virtual Environment*, Report to the National Science Foundation (NSF), Grant CCR89-09197, 18 pp., November 1991

Rumelhart D.E., Hinton G.E. and Williams R.J. (1986). Learning internal representations by back-propagating errors, *Nature*, **323**, 533-6

Schmandt C. (1982). Interactive three-dimensional computer space. In *Processing and Display of Three-Dimensional Data, SPIE Proceedings* vol. 367, pp. 155-9

Schoenberger K. (1990). Nintendo investing in research on children. *Los Angeles Times*, 16 May

Shaw A.L. (1992). Paperless aircraft – Vision of the future. In *SERC/IMechE Annual Expert Meeting, Information Technology and Product Design*

Sheff D. (1990). The virtual realities of Timothy Leary. *Upside*, April, p. 70

Shenker M. (1987). Optical design criteria for binocular helmet mounted displays. In *Display System Optics, SPIE Proceedings* vol. 778

Sheridan T.B. (1992). Musings on Telepresence and Virtual Presence. *Presence*, **1**(1), 120-25

Sillion F. and Puech C. (1989) A general two-pass method integrating specular and diffuse reflection. In *Proc. SIGGRAPH '89*

Skidmore R.A. and Pulliam R. (1986). *A Simulation Capability for Future Space Flight*, SAE Technical Paper Series, No. 861784, October

Spain E.H. and Coppock D. (1989). Toward performance standards for remote manipulation. In *Proc. 11th Annual Meeting of the IEEE Engineering in Biology and Medicine Society*, Seattle WA, vol. IV, pp. 923-4

Speeter T.H. (1992). Transforming human hand motion for telemanipulation. *Presence*, **1**(1), 63-70

Srinivasan M.A. (1988). *Tactile Sensing in Humans and Robots: Computational Theory and Algorithms*, Neuman Laboratory for Biomechanics and Human Rehabilitation, Department of Mechanical Engineering, MIT Technical Report, October

Srinivasan M.A., Whitehouse J.M. and LaMotte R.H. (1990). Tactile detection of skip: Surface microgeometry and peripheral neural codes. *Journal of Neurophysiology*, February

Stanton A.N., (1956) *Headgear mounted cathode ray tube and binocular viewing device*. US Patent 3,059,519

Starks M. (1991). Stereoscopic video and the quest for virtual reality: An annotated bibliography of selected topics. In *Stereoscopic Displays and Applications II, SPIE Proceedings* vol. 1457

Stone R. (1990). Human Factors Research at the UK National Advanced Robotics Research Centre. *The Ergonomist*, (239), May

Stone R. (1991a). Advanced human system interfaces for telerobotics using virtual reality and telepresence technologies. In *Proc. 5th Int. Conf on Advanced Robotics*, Pisa, Italy, 1991

Stone R.J. (1991b). Applications focus: Telepresence. In *Proc. Virtual Reality '91 (Impacts and Applications). Day 2: Real World Applications of Virtual Reality*, June 1991

Stone R.J. and Dalton G.D. (1991). Virtual reality and telepresence: Creating visual worlds from non-visual sensors. In *Proc. ORIA '91: Telerobotics In Hostile Environments*, Marseille, France, December 1991

Sutherland I. (1965). The ultimate display. In *Proc. IFIP Congress* vol. 2, pp. 506-8

Sutherland I. (1968). A head-mounted three-dimensional display. In *Proc. Fall Joint Computer Conference, AFIPS Conf. Proc.* vol. 33, 757–64

Tachi S., Tanie K., Komoriya K. and Kanego M. (1984). Tele-existence (I): Design and evaluation of a visual display with sensation of presence. In *Proc. RoManSy '84, 5th CISM-IFToMM Sym.*, Udine, Italy, June, p. 245. London: Hermes Publishing/Kogan Page

Tachi S., Arai H. and Maeda T. (1989). Development of an anthropomorphic tele-existence slave robot. In *Proc. Int. Conf. on Advanced Mechatronics*, Tsukuba Science City, Mechanical Engineering Laboratory, MITI, May, p. 385

Takagi A., Takaoka H., Oshima T. and Ogata Y. (1990). Accurate rendering technique based on colorimetric conception. In *Proc. SIGGRAPH '90*

Teitel M.A. (1990). The Eyephone, a head mounted stereo display. In *Stereoscopic Displays and Applications, SPIE Proceedings* vol. 1256

Thompson S.L. (1987). The big picture. *Air and Space*, April/May, pp. 75–83

Thorpe J.A. (1987). The new technology of large scale simulator networking: Implications for mastering the art of warfighting. In *9th Interservice Industry Training Systems Conf.*

Triesman M. (1977). Motion sickness: An evolutionary hypothesis. *Science*, **197**, 493–5

Uttal W.R. (1989). Teleoperators. *Scientific American*, December, 124–9

Vance D.W. and Keenan P.B. (1975). Light valve projection displays for information system terminals. *SID Digest*, 23

Vickers D.L. (1971). Sorcerer's Apprentice: Head-mounted display and wand. *PhD Dissertation*, University of Utah

Vogel S. (1990). Smart skin. *Discover*, April

VPL Research, Inc. (1989). *Virtual Reality at Texpo '89*, Redwood City CA: VPL Research, Inc.

Waite R. (1990). Thatcher lends a hand. *Observer* (Sunday Supplement Magazine), 4 March, pp. 44–6

Waldern J.D., Humrich A. and Cochrane L. (1986). Studying depth cues in a three dimensional computer graphics workstation. *International Journal of Man-Machine Studies*, **24**, 645–57

Walker J. (1988). *Through the Looking Glass*. Sausalito CA: Autodesk, Inc.

Walker J. (1990). Through the looking glass. In *The Art of Human-Computer Interface Design* (Laurel B., ed.). Menlo Park CA: Addison-Wesley

Wallace J.R., Elmquist K.A. and Haines E.A. (1989). A ray tracing algorithm for progressive radiosity. In *Proc. SIGGRAPH '89*

Walser R. (1990). Elements of a cyberspace playhouse. In *Proc. National Computer Graphics Association '90*, Anaheim CA, March

Wang C., Koved L. and Dukach S. (1990). Design for interactive performance in a virtual laboratory. In *Proc. SIGGRAPH '90*, pp. 39–40

Wang J. (1990). A real-time optical 3D tracker for head-mounted display systems. *Doctoral Dissertation*, R90-01 1, University of North Carolina at Chapel Hill

Wang J.F., Chi V. and Fuchs H. (1990a). A real-time 6D optical tracker for head mounted display systems. *Computer Graphics*, **24**(2)

Wang J.F., Azuma, Bishop, Chi V., Eyles and Fuchs H. (1990b). Tracking a head-mounted display in a room-sized environment with head-mounted cameras. In *SPIE Technical Sym. on Optical Engineering and Photonics in Aerospace Sensing: Helmet-Mounted Displays II, SPIE Proceedings* vol. 1290, Orlando FL, 16–20 April

Ward G.J, Rubinstein F.M and Clear R.D. (1988) A ray tracing solution for diffuse interreflection. In *Proc. SIGGRAPH '88*

Ward M., Azuma R., Bennett R., Gottschalk S. and Fuchs H. (1992). A demonstrated optical tracker with scalable work area for head-mounted display system. In *Proc. 1992 Sym. on Interactive 3D Graphics*, Cambridge MA, 29 March–1 April

Ware C. and Osborne S. (1990). Exploration and virtual camera control in virtual three dimensional environments. In *Proc. SIGGRAPH '90*, pp. 175–83

Waters F. (1970). *Masked Gods*, pp. 170–1. New York: Ballantine

Weigenbaum (1976). *Computer Power and Human Reason*. San Francisco: Freeman

Welch R.B. (1978). *Perceptual modification: Adapting to Altered Sensory Environments*. New York: Academic Press

Welch R.B. and Shenker M. (1984). The fibre optic helmet mounted display. In *Image Conf. III*, AFHRL

Wells J.M., Venturino M. (1990). Performance and head movements using a helmet-mounted display with different sized fields-of-view. In *Optical Engineering*, Vol 29, No 8 pp 870-77

Wenzel E.M. (1992). Localization of virtual acoustic displays. *Presence. Teleoperators and Virtual Environments*, 1(1), 80-107

Wenzel E.M., Wightman F.L. and Foster S.H. (1988). A virtual acoustic display for conveying three-dimensional information. In *Proc. Human Factors Society, 32nd Annual Meeting*

Wenzel E.M., Foster S.H., Wightman F.L. and Kistler D.J. (1989a). *Real-time synthesis of localized auditory cues*. Presented at meeting of the Association for Computing Machinery, Special Interest Group, Computer-Human Interface (SIGCHI)

Wenzel E., Foster S. and Wightman D. (1989b). Realtime digital synthesis of localized auditory cues over headphones. In *IEEE Workshop on Applications of Signal Processing to Audio and Acoustics*, 15–18 October

Wesolowicz K.G. and Sampson R.E. (1987). Laser radar range imaging sensor for commercial applications. In *Laser Radar II, SPIE Proceedings* vol. 783, pp. 152–61

Westheimer G. and McKee S.P. (1978). Stereoscopic acuity for moving retinal images. *Journal of the Optical Society of America*, **68**, 450–5

Whitted T. (19) An improved illumination model for shaded display. *Communications of the ACM*, **23**(6)

Wightman F.L. and Kistler D.J. (1989a). Headphone simulation of free-field listening I: stimulus synthesis. *Journal of the Acoustical Society of America*, **85**, 858–67

Wightman F.L. and Kistler D.J. (1989b). Headphone simulation of free-field listening II: psychophysical validation. *Journal of the Acoustical Society of America*, **85**, 868–78

Wiker S.F., Kennedy R.S., McCauley M.E. and Pepper R.L (1970). *Reliability, Validity, and Application of an Improved Scale of Assessment of Motion Sickness Severity*, USCG Technical Report No. CG-D-29-79, US Coast Guard Office of Research and Development, Washington DC

Wilbur R.B. (1979). *American Sign Language and Sign Systems*. Baltimore: University Park Press

Winograd T. (1984). Computer software for working with languages. *Scientific American*, September, p. 59

Wright W.D. (1941). The sensitivity of the eye to small colour differences. *Proceedings of the Physical Society (London)*, **53**, 93-112

Wright W.D. (1946). *Researches on Normal and Defective Colour Vision*. London: Henry Kimpton

Wright W.D. (1965). *The Measurement of Colour* 3rd edn. London: Hilger and Watts

Yamaguchi H., Akiro T. and Kobayashi Y. (1989). *Proposal for a Large Visual Field Display Employing Eye Movement Tracking*, ATR Communication Systems Research Laboratories, Kyoto, Japan

Yeaple F. (1986). Live video and animated graphics are interfaced effortlessly. *Design News*, 18 August, pp. 98-102

Young L.R. and Sheena D. (1975). Survey of eye movement recording methods. *Behavior Research Methods and Instrumentation*, **7**(5), 397–429

Zeevi Y. and Hileemrath O. (1990). *Single Camera Three Dimensional Head Position Sensing System*, US Patent 4 956 794 (filed 16 October 1989)

Zeltzer D. (1992). Autonomy, interaction, and presence. *Presence*, **1**(1), pp 127–132

Zuboff S. (1988). *In the Age of the Smart Machine: The Future Work and Power*, pp. 71-3. New York: Basic Books

Part 2: Bibliography in keyword order

The second part of the bibliography is a regrouping of the Part 1 references into major topic headings. This will help the reader who has a specific interest in a given subject.

Auditory localization, binaural stereo, speech recognition

Blauert J. (1983). *Spatial Hearing: The Psychophysics of Human Sound Localisation.* Cambridge MA: MIT Press

Cadoz C., Jean-Loup F. and Annie L. (1984). Responsive input devices and sound synthesis by simulation of instrumental mechanisms: the CORDIS system. *Computer Music Journal*, **8**(3), 60–73

Calhoun G.L., Valencia G. and Furness T.A., III (1987). Three-dimensional auditory cue simulation for crew station design/evaluation. In *Proc. Human Factors Society, 31st Annual Meeting*, 1987, pp. 1398–1402

Doll T., Gerth J., Engleman W. and Folds D. (1986). *Development of Simulated Directional Audio for Cockpit Applications*, USAF Report AAMRL-TR-86-014

Eglowstein H. (1990). Hands on under the hood: Can we talk? *Byte*, July, 288–9

Hartley R.V.L. and Fry T.C. (1921). The binocular localisation of pure tones. *Physics Review*, 2nd ser., **18**, 431–42

Posselt C., Schroter J., Opitz M., Divenyi P. and Blauert J. (1986). Generation of binaural signals for research and home entertainment. In *Proc. 12th ICA*, Toronto, Paper B1-6

Rayleigh, Lord (1945). *Theory of Sound* 2nd edn, vol II, pp. 440–3. New York: Dover

Wenzel E.M. (1992). Localization of virtual acoustic displays. *Presence. Teleoperators and Virtual Environments*, **1**(1), 80–107

Wenzel E.M., Wightman F.L. and Foster S.H. (1988). A virtual acoustic display for conveying three-dimensional information. In *Proc. Human Factors Society, 32nd Annual Meeting*

Wenzel E.M., Foster S.H., Wightman F.L. and Kistler D.J. (1989a). *Real-time synthesis of localized auditory cues*. Presented at meeting of the Association for Computing Machinery, Special Interest Group, Computer-Human Interface (SIGCHI)

Wenzel E., Foster S. and Wightman D. (1989b). Realtime digital synthesis of localized auditory cues over headphones. In *IEEE Workshop on Applications of Signal Processing to Audio and Acoustics*, 15–18 October

Wightman F.L. and Kistler D.J. (1989a). Headphone simulation of free-field listening I: stimulus synthesis. *Journal of the Acoustical Society of America*, **85**, 858–67

Wightman F.L. and Kistler D.J. (1989b). Headphone simulation of free-field listening II: psychophysical validation. *Journal of the Acoustical Society of America*, **85**, 868–78

Colour

Boynton R.M. (1979). *Human Color Vision*. New York: Holt, Rinehart and Winston

CIE (Commission Internationale de l'Eclairage) (1970). *CIE Document on Colorimetry* (Official Recommendations). Publ. 15

Wright W.D. (1941). The sensitivity of the eye to small colour differences. *Proceedings of the Physical Society (London)*, **53**, 93–112

Wright W.D. (1946). *Researches on Normal and Defective Colour Vision*. London: Henry Kimpton

Wright W.D. (1965). *The Measurement of Colour* 3rd edn. London: Hilger and Watts

Displays

Fisher S. (1982). Viewpoint dependent imaging: An interactive stereoscopic display. In *Processing and Display of Three-Dimensional Data, SPIE Proceedings* vol. 367

Fisher S., McGreevy M., Humphries J. and Robinett W. (1991) Virtual environment display system. In *ACM Workshop on Interactive 3D Graphics*, University of North Carolina, Chapel Hill, 23–24 October, pp 77–87

Flannery J.B., Jr. (1973). Light controlled light valves. *IEEE Transactions on Electronic Devices*, **20**(11), 941–53

Gregory R.L. (1989). Seeing by exploring. In *Spatial Displays and Spatial Instruments* (Ellis S.R., Kaiser M.K. and Grunwald A., eds.), pp. 5–11. NASA Conference Publication 10032

Heilig M. (1960). *Stereoscopic Television Apparatus for Individual Use*, US Patent 2 955 156 (filed 4 October 1960)

Hodges L.F. (1991). Basic principles of stereographic software development. In *Stereoscopic Displays and Applications II, SPIE Proceedings* vol. 1457

Jacobson A.D. (1975). A new television projection light valve. *SID Digest*, 27

Knowlton K.C. (1977). Computer displays optically superimposed on input devices. *Bell System Technical Journal*, **56**(3), 367–83

Murray P.M. and Barber B. (1985). Visual display research tools. In *AGARD Conf. Proc.* vol. 408(2), pp. 1–8

Pund M.L. (1986). *Stereoscopic Display*, US Patent 4 649 425 (filed 16 January 1986)

Robinett W. and Rolland J.P. (1992). A computational model for the stereoscopic optics of a head mounted display. *Presence*, **1**(1), pp 45–62

Stanton A.N., (1956) *Headgear mounted cathode ray tube and binocular viewing device*. US Patent 3,059,519

Starks M. (1991). Stereoscopic video and the quest for virtual reality: An annotated bibliography of selected topics. In *Stereoscopic Displays and Applications II, SPIE Proceedings* vol. 1457

Thompson S.L. (1987). The big picture. *Air and Space*, April/May, pp. 75–83

Vance D.W. and Keenan P.B. (1975). Light valve projection displays for information system terminals. *SID Digest*, 23

Eye tracking

Calhoun G.L., Arbak C.J. and Boff K.R. (1984). Eye Controlled Switching for Crew Station Design. In *Proc. Human Factors Society, 28th Annual Meeting*, 1984

Yamaguchi H., Akiro T. and Kobayashi Y. (1989). *Proposal for a Large Visual Field Display Employing Eye Movement Tracking*, ATR Communication Systems Research Laboratories, Kyoto, Japan

Young L.R. and Sheena D. (1975). Survey of eye movement recording methods. *Behavior Research Methods and Instrumentation*, **7**(5), 397–429

Force feedback, haptic feedback, glove devices, remote manipulation

Adelstein B.D. and Rosen M.J. (1992). Design and implementation of a force reflecting manipulation for manual control research. In *ASME Winter Annual Meeting*, Anaheim CA, November 1992

Batter J.J. and Brooks F.P., Jr. (1972). GROPE-1. In *Proc. IFIP '71*, p. 759

Brooks F.P., Jr., Ouh-Young M., Batter J.J. and Kilpatrick P.J. (1990). Project GROPE – Haptic Displays for Scientific Visualization. *ACM Computer Graphics*, **24**(4), 177–85

Burdea G. (1991). *Portable Dextrous Force Feedback Master for Robot Telemanipulation*, US Patent 5 004 391

Burdea G. and Speeter T. (1989). Portable dextrous force feedback master for robot telemanipulation. In *Proc. 1989 NASA Conf. on Space Telerobotics* vol. 2, Pasadena CA, pp. 153–61

Burdea G., Zhuang J., Roskos E., Silver D. and Langrana N. (1991). Direct drive force feedback control for the DataGlove. In *Proc. European Robotics Intelligent Systems Conf.*, Corfu, June 1991

Burdea G., Zhuang J., Roskos E., Silver D., Langrana N. (1992). A portable dextrous master with force feedback. *Presence*, **1**(1)

Cadoz C., Lesez L. and Jean-Loup F. (1990). Modular Feedback Keyboard. *Computer Music Journal*, **14**(2), 47–51

Fisher S. (1986). Telepresence master glove controller for dextrous robotic end-effectors. In *Advances in Intelligent Robotics Systems, SPIE Proceedings* vol. 726 (Casasent D.P., ed.)

Hannford B. (1989). A design framework for teleoperators with kinesthetic feedback. *IEEE Transactions on Robotics and Automation*, **5**(4)

Held R., Efstathiou A. and Greene M. (1966). Adaption to displaced and delayed visual feedback from the hand. *Journal of Experimental Psychology*, **72**(6) 887–91

Hill J.W. (1967). *The Perception of Multiple Tactile Stimuli*, Stanford Electronics Laboratory Technical Report No. 4823-1, Stanford University, CA

Hollis R.L., Salcudean S. and Abraham D.W. (1990). *Toward a Tele-Nonrobotic Manipulation System with Atomic Scale force Feedback and Motion Resolution*, IBM Thomas J. Watson Research Center, Yorktown Heights, NY

Iwata H. (1990). Artificial reality with force-feedback: Development of desktop virtual space with Compact Master Manipulator. *Computer Graphics*, **24**, 165–74

Jau B. (1991). *Technical Support Package on Anthropomorphic Remote Manipulator for NASA TECH BRIEF 15(4)*. #127, JPL Invention Report, Report No. NPO-17975/7222, JPL Technology Utilization Office, Pasadena CA, April

Kaufman A., Yagel R. and Bakalash R. (1990). Direct interaction with 3D volumetric environment. In *Proc. SIGGRAPH '90*, pp. 33–4

Knowlton K. (1975). Virtual pushbuttons as a means of person-machine interaction. In *Proc. Conf. Computer Graphics, Pattern Recognition and Data Structure*, 14–16 May 1975

Kramer J. and Leifer L. (1989). The Talking Glove: A speaking aid for non-vocal deaf and deaf-blind individuals. In *Proc. RESNA 12th Annual Conf.*, Louisiana, pp. 471–2

Krueger M. (1977). Responsive environments. In *Proc. National Computer Conf.*, pp. 423–33

Minsky M., Ouh-Young M., Steele O., Brooks F.P., Jr. and Behensky M. (1990). Feeling and seeing: Issues in force display. *ACM Computer Graphics*, **24**(2), 235–43

Monkman G.J. (1992). An electrorheological tactile display. *Presence*, **1**(2), 219–228

Morishima A. and Speeter T.H. (1989). *Teleoperator Control of the Utah/MIT Dextrous Hand – A Functional Approach*, AT&T Bell Laboratories, Technical Report No. CUCS-474-89

Nishijima M. and Kijima Y. (1989). Learning a sense of rhythm with a neural network: The Neuro-Drummer. In *Proc. 1st International Conference on Music Perception and Cognition*, Kyoto, Japan, October, pp. 77–80

Noll M. (1972). Man-machine tactile communication. *Journal of the Society for Information Display*, July

Spain E.H. and Coppock D. (1989). Toward performance standards for remote manipulation. In *Proc. 11th Annual Meeting of the IEEE Engineering in Biology and Medicine Society*, Seattle WA, vol. IV, pp. 923–4

Speeter T.H. (1992). Transforming human hand motion for telemanipulation. *Presence*, **1**(1), pp 63–70

Srinivasan M.A. (1988). *Tactile Sensing in Humans and Robots: Computational Theory and Algorithms*, Neuman Laboratory for Biomechanics and Human Rehabilitation, Department of Mechanical Engineering, MIT Technical Report, October

Srinivasan M.A., Whitehouse J.M. and LaMotte R.H. (1990). Tactile detection of skip: Surface microgeometry and peripheral neural codes. *Journal of Neurophysiology*, February

Vogel S. (1990). Smart skin. *Discover*, April

Wilbur R.B. (1979). *American Sign Language and Sign Systems*. Baltimore: University Park Press

Winograd T. (1984). Computer software for working with languages. *Scientific American*, September, p. 59

Gesture

Cadoz C. and Ramstein C. (1990). Capture, representation, and composition of the instrumental gesture. In *Proc. ICMC '90*, Glasgow

Graphics, graphic systems, realism, techniques

Airey J.M, Rohlf J.H and Brooks F.P. (1990). Towards image realism with interactive update rates in complex virtual building environments. In *Symposium on Interactive 3D Graphics (SIGGRAPH '90)*

Bergman L., Fuchs H., Grant E. and Spach S. (1986). Image rendering by adaptive refinement. In *Proc. SIGGRAPH '86*

Chen S.E. (1990). Incremental radiosity: An extension of progressive radiosity to an interactive image synthesis system. In *Proc. SIGGRAPH '90*

Cohen M.F. and Greenberg D.P. (1985). The Hemi Cube: A radiosity solution for complex environments. In *Proc. SIGGRAPH '85*

Cohen M.F, Chen S., Wallace J. and Greenberg D.P. (1988). A progressive refinement approach to fast radiosity image generation computer graphics. In *Proc. SIGGRAPH '88*

Fox B. (1991). 3D video doubles up on tape. *New Scientist*, (1772), 8 June

Fuchs H., Poulton J., Eyles J. and Greer T. (1988a). Coarse-Grain and Fine-Grain parallelism in the Next Generation Pixel Planes Graphics System. In *Proc. International Conference and Exhibition on Parallel Processing for Computer Vision and Display*. New York: Springer-Verlag

Fuchs H., Pizer S.M., Creasy J.L., Renner J.B. and Rosenman J.G. (1988b). Interactive, richly cued shaded display of multiple 3D objects in medical images. In *Proc. SPIE Medical Imaging II Conference* vol. 914(2)

Fuchs H., Poulton J., Eyles J., Greer T. *et al.* (1989). A heterogeneous multiprocessor graphics system using processor enhanced memories. In *Proc. SIGGRAPH '89*

George D.W., Sillion F.X. and Greenberg D.P. (1990). Radiosity redistribution for dynamic environments. *IEEE Transactions on Computer Graphics and Applications*, July

Giacalone A, Heller J. *et al.* (1989). VERITAS: Visualization environment research in the applied sciences. In *Three-Dimensional Visualization and Display Technologies, SPIE Proceedings*, vol. 1083, pp. 127–33

Goral C.M., Torrance K.E., Greenberg D.P. and Battaile B. (1984). Modelling the interaction of light between diffuse surfaces. In *Proc. SIGGRAPH '84*

Greenfield H., Vickers D., Sutherland I., Kolff W. and Reemtsma K. (1971). Moving computer graphic images seen from inside the vascular system. *Transactions of the American Society of Artificial Internal Organs*, **17**, 381–5

Henderson J., McKellar C.J., Price M. and Venning R. (1992). Visualisation as a practical tool. In *National Lighting Conference '92 Proceedings* (in press)

Herot C. (1980). Spatial management of data. *ACM Transactions on Database Systems*, **5**(4)

Kajiya J.T. (1986). The rendering equation. In *Proc. SIGGRAPH '86*

Sillion F. and Puech C. (1989) A general two-pass method integrating specular and diffuse reflection. In *Proc. SIGGRAPH '89*

Takagi A., Takaoka H., Oshima T. and Ogata Y. (1990) Accurate rendering technique based on colorimetric conception. In *Proc. SIGGRAPH '90*

Waldern J.D., Humrich A. and Cochrane L. (1986). Studying depth cues in a three dimensional computer graphics workstation. *International Journal of Man-Machine Studies*, **24**, 645–57

Walker J. (1988). *Through the Looking Glass*. Sausalito CA: Autodesk, Inc.

Walker J. (1990). Through the looking glass. In *The Art of Human-Computer Interface Design* (Laurel B., ed.). Menlo Park CA: Addison-Wesley

Wallace J.R., Elmquist K.A. and Haines E.A. (1989). A ray tracing algorithm for progressive radiosity. In *Proc. SIGGRAPH '89*

Ward G.J, Rubinstein F.M and Clear R.D. (1988) A ray tracing solution for diffuse interreflection. In *Proc. SIGGRAPH '88*

Whitted T. (19) An improved illumination model for shaded display. *Communications of the ACM*, **23**(6)

Helmet-mounted displays

CAE Electronics (1984). *Wide Field of View, Helmet Mounted Infinity Display Systems Development*, AFHRL-TR-84-27, AF Systems Command, Brooks AFBTX

Chung J., Harris M., Brooks F., Kelly M.T., Hughes J.W., Ouh-young M., Cheung C., Holloway R.L. and Pique M. (1989). Exploring virtual worlds with head-mounted displays, non-holographic 3-dimensional display technologies In *SPIE Proc. on Non-holographic 3-dimensional display technologies*, Los Angeles CA, 15-20 January

Kandebo S.W. (1988). Navy to evaluate Agile Eye helmet-mounted display system. *Aviation Week and Space Technology*, 15 August, 94-6

Noar D., Arnon O. and Avnur A. (1987). A light weight innovative Helmet Airborne Display And Sight (HADAS). In *Display System Optics, SPIE Proceedings* vol. 778, pp. 89-95

Rebo R.K. and Amburn P. (1989). A helmet-mounted environment display system. In *Helmet-Mounted Displays, SPIE Proceedings* vol. 1116, pp. 80-4

Shenker M. (1987). Optical design criteria for binocular helmet mounted displays. In *Display System Optics, SPIE Proceedings*, vol. 778

Sutherland I. (1965). The ultimate display. In *Proc. IFIP Congress* vol. 2, pp. 506-8

Sutherland I. (1968). A head-mounted three-dimensional display. In *Proc. Fall Joint Computer Conference, AFIPS Conf. Proc.* vol. 33, 757-64

Teitel M.A. (1990). The Eyephone, a head mounted stereo display. In *Stereoscopic Displays and Applications, SPIE Proceedings* vol. 1256

Vickers D.L. (1971). Sorcerer's Apprentice: Head-mounted display and wand. *PhD Dissertation*, University of Utah

Welch B. and Shenker M. (1984). The fibre optic helmet mounted display. In *Image Conf. III*, AFHRL

Miscellaneous, philosophical

Ackerman D. (1990). *A Natural History of the Senses*. New York: Random House, pp. 80-1

Arnheim R. (1969). *Visual Thinking*. Berkeley CA: University of California Press

Barlow J. (1990). Life in the DataCloud: Scratching your eyes back in. In *Mondo 2000*, Summer, 1990, p. 36

Bergson H. (1911). *Creative Evolution*, p. 139. New York: Henry Holt (translated by Arthur Mitchell)

Bettelheim B. (1987). The importance of play. *The Atlantic Monthly*, March

Bolt R. (1984). *The Human Interface: Where People and Computers Meet*. Belmont CA: Lifetime Learning Publications

Brand S. (1987). *The Media Lab: Inventing the Future at MIT*. New York: Viking

Brennan S. (1990). Conversation as direct manipulation. In *The Art of Human-Computer Interface Design* (Laurel B., ed.), pp. 394-5. Menlo Park CA: Addison-Wesley

Bronowski J. (1978). *The Origins of Knowledge and Imagination*, p. 18. New Haven: Yale University Press

Brooks F.P., Jr. (1975). *The Mythical Man-Moth: Essays in Software Engineering*. Reading MA: Addison-Wesley

Brooks F.P., Jr. (1977). The computer scientist as toolsmith: Studies in interactive computer graphics. In *Information Processing '77* (Gilchrist B., ed.), pp. 625-34. Amsterdam: North-Holland

Brooks F.P., Jr. (1988). Grasping reality through illusion: Interactive graphics serving science. In *Proc. CHI*, pp. 1-11. Reading MA: Addison-Wesley

Burgess P. (1984) *Scientific American*, September

Burgess P. (1988). *MacWEEK*, 2 August, p. 38

Bush V. (1945). As we may think. *The Atlantic Monthly*, August

Campbell J. (1988). Day of the dead lecture. *Magical Blend*, **16**, 58–62

Danielou A. (1984). *Shiva and Dionysus: The Religion of Nature and Eros*. New York: Inner Traditions International (translated by K.F. Hurry)

Delaney B. (1991). On line. *CyberEdge Journal*, May/June, 2

Furness T.A., III (1986). Fantastic voyage. *Popular Mechanics*, December, 63–5

Geldard F. (1957). Adventures in tactile literacy. *American Psychologist*, **12**(3), 117

Gullichsen E. and Randal W. (1989). Cyberspace: Experimental computing. In *Nexus '89 Science Fiction and Science Fact*

Hatamura Y. and Miroshita H. (1990). *Direct Coupling System between Nanometer World and Human World,* Department of Mechanical Engineering for Production, The University of Tokyo, Japan

Heilig M. (1955). *The Cinema of the Future*. Mexico City: Espacios

Heinlein R. (1965). *Three By Heinlein: The Puppet Masters; Waldo; Magic, Inc.* Garden City NY: Doubleday

Kay A. (1977). Microelectronics and the personal computer. *Scientific American*, **237**(3), 230

Kobayashi Y. (1989). *Artificial Intelligence Department 1988 Special Report*, Advanced Telecommunications Research Institute International, Communication Systems Research Laboratories, Kyoto, Japan

Laboratoire d'Informatique Fondamentale et d'Intelligence Artificielle (1990). Brochure published by l'Institut d'Informatique et de Mathematiques Appliquees de Grenoble

Laurel B. (1986). Towards the design of a computer-based interactive fantasy system. *PhD Dissertation*, Ohio State University

Laurel B. (1991). *Computers as Theatre*. Menlo Park CA: Addison-Wesley

Levine H. and Rheingold H. (1987). *The Cognitive Connection*, pp. 232–33. New York: Prentice-Hall

Licklider J.C.R. (1960). Man-computer symbiosis. *Institute of Radio Engineers Transactions on Human Factors in Electronics*, **1**, 4–11

Lippman A. (1980). Movie-Maps: An application of the optical videodisc to computer graphics. *Computer Graphics*, **14**(3)

Lipton L. (1964). Sensorama. *Popular Photography*, July

McKim R.H. (1980). *Thinking Visually*, p.7. Belmont CA: Lifelong Learning Publications

McLuhan M. (1964) *Understanding Media: The Extensions of Man*. New York: McGraw-Hill

McLuhan M. (1969). Interview. *Playboy*, March

Minsky M. (1979). *Toward a Remotely-Manned Energy and Production Economy,* Massachusetts Institute of Technology, Artificial Intelligence Laboratory, AI Memo No. 544, September

Negroponte N. (1970). *The Architecture Machine*. Cambridge MA: MIT Press

Negroponte N. (1981). Media Room. *Proceedings of the Society for Information Display*, **22**(2), 109–13

Nelson T. (1980). Interactive systems and the design of Virtuality. *Creative Computing*, November/December, 56–62

Pagels H. (1988). *The Dreams of Reason*. New York: Simon and Schuster

Papert S. (1980). *Mindstorms: Children, Computers, and Powerful Ideas*, pp. 21, 76. New York: Basic Books

Perkins D.N. (1979). *Pictures and the Real Thing*, Project Zero, Harvard University, Cambridge MA

Perry Barlow J. (1990). Being in nothingness. In *Mondo 2000*, Summer, p. 44

Pfeiffer J.E. (1982). *The Creative Explosion: An Inquiry into the Origins of Art and Religion*, p. 205. Ithaca NY: Cornell University Press

Pollack A. (1989). What is artificial reality? Wear a computer and see. *New York Times*, 10 April, p. 1

Pollack A. (1990). Coming soon: Data you can look under and walk through. *New York Times*, 14 October

Posnick-Goodwin S. (1988). Dreaming for a living. *Peninsula*, July, p. 58

Rheingold H. (1976). The ultimate cashflow. *California Living*, 26 September

Rheingold H. (1985). *Tools for Thought*, pp. 260–1. New York: Simon and Schuster

Rheingold H. (1991). *Virtual Reality, the Revolutionary Technology of Computer-Generated Artificial Worlds – and How it Promises and Threatens to Transform Business and Society*. New York: Summit Books

Rifkin A. (1982). Mort Heilig's Feelie Machine. *L.A. Weekly*, 12–18 March, p. 10

Schoenberger K. (1990). Nintendo investing in research on children. *Los Angeles Times*, 16 May

Sheff D. (1990). The virtual realities of Timothy Leary. *Upside*, April, p. 70

Sheridan T.B. (1992). Musings on Telepresence and Virtual Presence. *Presence*, 1(1), pp 120–25

Waite R. (1990). Thatcher lends a hand. *Observer* (Sunday Supplement Magazine), 4 March, pp. 44–6

Walser R. (1990). Elements of a cyberspace playhouse. In *Proc. National Computer Graphics Association '90*, Anaheim CA, March

Waters F. (1970). *Masked Gods*, pp. 170–1. New York: Ballantine

Weigenbaum (1976). *Computer Power and Human Reason*. San Francisco: Freeman

Yeaple F. (1986). Live video and animated graphics are interfaced effortlessly. *Design News*, 18 August, pp. 98–102

Zeltzer D. (1992). Autonomy, interaction, and presence. *Presence*, 1(1), pp 127–132

Zuboff S. (1988). *In the Age of the Smart Machine: The Future Work and Power*, pp. 71–3. New York: Basic Books

Physiology

Baltzley D.R., Kennedy R.S., Berbaum K.S., Lilienthal M.G. and Gower D.W. (1989). The time course of postflight simulator sickness symptoms. *Aviation, Space, and Environmental Medicine*, 60, 1043–8

Biocca F. (1992). *Will simulation sickness slow down the diffusion of virtual reality technology?* Working Paper Series: Communication Technology and Cognition Group, Center for Research in Journalism and Mass Communication, University of North Carolina

Canon L.K. (1970). Intermodality inconsistency of input and directed attention as determinants of the nature of adaption. *Journal of Experimental Psychology*, 84, 141–7

Carroll J.M., ed. (1987). *Interfacing Thought: Cognitive Aspects of Human-Computer Interaction*. Cambridge MA: MIT Press

Engelbart D. (1963). A conceptual framework for augmenting man's intellect. In *Vistas in Information-Handling* vol. 1 (Howerton P.W. and Weeks D.C., eds.), pp. 1–29. Washington DC: Aparton Books

Gibson J.J. (1966). *The Senses Considered as Perceptual Systems.* Boston: Houghton-Mifflin

Gibson J.J. (1979). *The Ecological Approach to Visual Perception.* Boston: Houghton-Mifflin

Guedry F.E., Lentz J.M. and Jell R.M. (1978). Visual-vestibular interactions: I. Influence of peripheral vision on suppression of the vestibulo-ocular reflex and visual acuity. *Aviation, Space, and Environmental Medicine*, **50**, 205–11

Hatada T., Sakata H. and Kusaka H. (1980). Psychological analysis of the 'sensation of reality' induced by a visual wide-field display. *Journal of the Society of Motion Picture and Television Engineers*, **89**, 560–9

Hay J.C. (1974). Motor transformation learning. *Perception*, **3**, 487–96

Hay J.C. and Goldsmith W.M. (1973). Space-time adaption of visual position constancy. *Journal of Experimental Psychology*, **99**, 1–9

Heeter C. (1992). Being there: The subjective experience of presence. *Presence*, **1**(2)

Held R. (1965). Plasticity in sensorimotor systems. *Scientific American*, **213**(5), 84–94

Hochberg J. (1986). Representation of motion and space in video and cinematic displays. In *Handbook of Perception and Human Performance* vol. 2. (Boff K., Kaufmann L. and Thomas J., eds.), pp. 1–64. New York: Wiley

Johnson-Laird P. (1983). *Mental Models.* Cambridge MA: Harvard University Press

Kennedy R.S. and Fowlkes J.E. (1990). *What does it mean when we say that simulator sickness is polygenic and polysymptomatic?* Paper presented at E1/IMAGE V Conference, Phoenix AZ, June 1990

Kennedy R.S., Hettinger L.J. and Lilienthal M.G. (1987). Simulator sickness. In *Motion and Space Sickness* (Crampton G., ed.), pp. 317–41). Boca Raton FL: CRC Press

Nemine K. and Ellis S.R. (1991). Optic bias of perceived eye level depends on structure of the pitched optic array, poster presentations. In *Psychonomic Society, 32nd Annual Meeting*, San Francisco CA, 22–24 November

Redding G.M. (1973a). Simultaneous visual adaption to tilt and displacement: A test of independent processes. *Bulletin of the Psychonomic Society*, **2**, 41–2

Redding G.M. (1973b). Visual adaption to tilt and displacement: Same or different processes? *Perception and Psychophysics*, **14**, 193–200

Redding G.M. (1975a). Decay of visual adaption to tilt and displacement. *Perception and Psychophysics*, **17**, 203–8

Redding G.M. (1975b). Simultaneous visuomotor adaption to optical tilt and displacement. *Perception and Psychophysics*, **17**, 97–100

Roscoe S.N. (1980). *Aviation Psychology.* Ames IA: Iowa State University Press

Roscoe S.N. (1984). Judgments of size and distance with imaging displays. *Human Factors*, **26**, 617–20

Roscoe S.N. (1985). Bigness is in the eye of the beholder. *Human Factors*, **27**, 615–36

Roscoe S.N. and Jensen R.S. (1981). Computer-animated prediction displays for microwave landing approaches. *IEEE Transaction on Systems, Man and Cybernetics*, **11**, 760–5

Roscoe S.N., Hasler S.G. and Dougherty D.J. (1966). Flight by periscope: Making takeoffs and landings: The influence of image magnification practice and various conditions of flight. *Human Factors* **8**, 13–40

Roscoe S.N., Olzek L.A. and Randle R.J. (1976). Ground-referenced visual orientation with imaging displays: monocular versus binocular accommodation and judgments of relative size. In *Proc. AGARD Conf. on Visual Presentation of Cockpit Information Including Special Devices for Particular Conditions of Flying*, Neuilly-sur-Seine, France, pp. A5.1–A5.9. North Atlantic Treaty Organization

Triesman M. (1977). Motion sickness: An evolutionary hypothesis. *Science*, **197**, 493–5

Welch R.B. (1978). *Perceptual modification: Adapting to Altered Sensory Environments*. New York: Academic Press

Wiker S.F., Kennedy R.S., McCauley M.E. and Pepper R.L (1970). *Reliability, Validity, and Application of an Improved Scale of Assessment of Motion Sickness Severity*, USCG Technical Report No. CG-D-29-79, US Coast Guard Office of Research and Development, Washington DC

Simulation

Baudrillard J. (1983). *Simulations*, p. 2. New York: Semiotest(e)/Columbia University Press

Haber R.N. (1986). Flight simulation. *Scientific American*, **255**(1), 96, 103

Hettinger L.J., Berbaum K.S., Kennedy R.S, Dunlap, and Nolan (1990). Vection and simulator sickness. *Military Psychology*, **2**(3), 171–91

McCauley M.E., ed. (1984). Simulator sickness. In *Proc. Workshop*. Washington, DC: National Academy Press

Reason J.R. and Brand J.J. (1975). *Motion Sickness*. London: Academic Press

Rediffusion (1985). Flight simulation. In *AGARD Conf. Proc.* vol. 408

Thorpe J.A. (1987). The new technology of large scale simulator networking: Implications for mastering the art of warfighting. In *9th Interservice Industry Training Systems Conf.*

Software

Bricken W. (1990). *Virtual Environment Operating System: Preliminary Functional Architecture*. TR-HITL-M-90-2, Human Interface Technology Laboratory, University of Washington, Seattle

Grimsdale C. (1991). dVS-distributed virtual environment system. In *Proc. Computer Graphics '91 Conference*, London (ISBN 0 86353 282 9)

Kay A. (1984). Computer software. *Scientific American*, September

Roskos E. (1991). *Towards a Distributed, Object-Oriented Virtual Environment*, Report to the National Science Foundation (NSF), Grant CCR89-09197, 18 pp., November 1991

Skidmore R.A. and Pulliam R. (1986). *A Simulation Capability for Future Space Flight*, SAE Technical Paper Series, No. 861784, October

Telepresence, teleoperation

Akin D.L., Minsky M.L., Thiel E.D. and Kurtzman C.R. (1983). *Space Applications of Automation, Robotics, and Machine Intelligence Systems (ARAMIS). Phase II* vol. 3: Executive Summary, MIT, Contract NAS 8-34381, NASA Marshall Space Flight Center

Held R. and Durlach N. (1991). Telepresence, time delay, and adaption. In *Representation in Pictorial and Virtual Environments* (Ellis S.R., ed.). London: Taylor and Francis

Leifer L., Van der Loos M. and Michalowski S. (1990). Telerobotics in rehabilitation: Barriers to a virtual existence. In *Conf. on Human-Machine Interfaces for Teleoperators and Virtual Environments*, Santa Barbara CA, 4–9 March, sponsored by the Engineering Foundation

Stone R.J. (1991). Applications focus: Telepresence. In *Proc. Virtual Reality '91 (Impacts and Applications). Day 2: Real World Applications of Virtual Reality*, June 1991

Stone R.J. and Dalton G.D. (1991). Virtual reality and telepresence: Creating visual worlds from non-visual sensors. In *Proc. ORIA '91: Telerobotics In Hostile Environments*, Marseille, France, December 1991

Tachi S., Tanie K., Komoriya K. and Kanego M. (1984). Tele-existence (I): Design and evaluation of a visual display with sensation of presence. In *Proc. RoManSy '84, 5th CISM-IFToMM Sym.*, Udine, Italy, June, p. 245. London: Hermes Publishing/Kogan Page

Tachi S., Arai H. and Maeda T. (1989). Development of an anthropomorphic tele-existence slave robot. In *Proc. Int. Conf. on Advanced Mechatronics*, Tsukuba Science City, Mechanical Engineering Laboratory, MITI, May, p. 385

Uttal W.R. (1989). Teleoperators. *Scientific American*, December, 124–9

Tracking systems

Adelstein B.D., Johnston E.R. and Ellis S.R. (1992). A testbed for characterizing dynamic response of virtual environment spatial sensors. In *Proc. UIST '92: 5th Annual ACM Sym. on User Interface Software and Technology*, Monterey, CA, 15-18 November 1992

Applewhite H. (1991a). *Design of Acoustic Ranging Systems*. Technical Report 91-02, Piltdown Incorporated: Beaverton OR

Applewhite H. (1991b). Position-tracking in virtual reality. In *Proc. 2nd Annual Virtual Reality Conference and Exhibition*, San Francisco, CA, 23-25 September 1991 (Helsel K., ed.). Westport CT: Meckler Corporation

Bishop G. (1984). Self-Tracker. A smart optical sensor on silicon. *Doctoral Dissertation* TR84-002, Department of Computer Science, University of North Carolina at Chapel Hill

Bishop G. and Fuchs H. (1984). The Self-Tracker: A smart optical sensor on silicon. In *Proc. 1984 MIT Conference on Advanced Research in VLSI*, pp 65–73. Dedham MA: Artech House

Breglia D.R. and Oharek F.J. (1984). *Head Position and Orientation Sensor*, US Patent 4 446 480 (filed 14 December 1981)

Chavel P. and Strand P. (1984). Range measurement using Talbot diffraction imaging of 9 gratings. *Applied Optics*, **23**(6), 862–70

Church E. (1945). *Bulletin of Aerial Photogrammetry*, **15**, Syracuse University

Dewitt T. (1989). Rangefinding by the diffraction method. *Laser and Optics*, **8**(4), 119–24

Ditlea S. (1990). Grand illusion. *New York Magazine*, 6 August, 32

Doherty R. (1990). DC magnetic fields guide 6D pointer. *Electronic Engineering Times*, 20 August

Ferranti Defence Systems (1987). Ferranti helmet pointing system (HPS). In *The Royal Aeronautical Society, Aircrew Helmets and Helmet Mounted Devices Proc.* 10 February, pp. 6.1–6.15

Ferrin F.J. (1991). Survey of helmet tracking technologies. In *SPIE Proc. Large-Screen-Projection, Avionic, and Helmet-Mounted Displays*, p. 1456

Kulpers J. (1975). *Object Tracking and Orientation Determination Mean, System, and Process*, US Patent 3 868 565 (filed July 1973)

Kulpers J. (1976). *Tracking and Determining Orientation of Object using Coordinate Transformation Means, System, and Process*, US Patent 3 983 474 (filed February 1975)

Kulpers J. (1977). *Apparatus for Generating a Nutating Electromagnetic Field*, US Patent 4 017 858 (assignee: Polhemus Navigation Sciences, Inc., 12 April 1977)

Logitech (1991). *Logitech 2D/6D Mouse Technical Reference Manual*

Mann R., Rowell G., Conati F., Tetwsky A., Ottenheimer D. and Antonsson E. (1981). Precise, rapid, automatic 3D position and orientation tracking of multiple moving bodies. In *Proc. VIII International Congress of Biomechanics*, Nagoya, Japan, July

Menn A. and Krimerman J. (1990). *System for Measuring the Angular Displacement of an Object*, US Patent 4 896 962 (filed 26 May 1986)

Raab F. (1977). *Remote Object Position Locator*, US Patent 4 054 881 (filed 26 April 1976)

Raab F.H., Blood E.B., Steiner T.O., Jones R.J. (1979). Magnetic position and orientation tracking systems. *IEEE Transactions on Aerospace and Electronic Systems*, **15**(5), pp 709–18, September

Roberts L. (1966). The Lincoln Wand. In *AFIPS Conf. Proc., 1966 Fall Joint Computer Conference*, November, pp. 223–7

Rodgers A.G. (1991). Advances in head tracker technology – A key contributor to helmet vision system performance and implementation. In *Society for Information Display International Symposium, Digest of Technical Papers*, 6–10 May, pp. 127-30

Wang J.F. (1990). A real-time optical 3D tracker for head-mounted display systems. *Doctoral Dissertation*, R90-01 1, University of North Carolina at Chapel Hill

Wang J.F., Chi V. and Fuchs H. (1990a). A real-time 6D optical tracker for head mounted display systems. *Computer Graphics*, **24**(2)

Wang J.F., Azuma, Bishop, Chi V., Eyles and Fuchs H. (1990b). Tracking a head-mounted display in a room-sized environment with head-mounted cameras. In *SPIE Technical Sym. on Optical Engineering and Photonics in Aerospace Sensing: Helmet-Mounted Displays II, SPIE Proceedings* vol. 1290, Orlando FL, 16-20 April

Ward M., Azuma R., Bennett R., Gottschalk S. and Fuchs H. (1992). A demonstrated optical tracker with scalable work area for head-mounted display system. In *Proc. 1992 Sym. on Interactive 3D Graphics*, Cambridge MA, 29 March–1 April

Wesolowicz K.G. and Sampson R.E. (1987). Laser radar range imaging sensor for commercial applications. In *Laser Radar II, SPIE Proceedings* vol. 783, pp. 152–61

Zeevi Y. and Hileemrath O. (1990). *Single Camera Three Dimensional Head Position Sensing System*, US Patent 4 956 794 (filed 16 October 1989)

User interfaces

Canfield Smith D., Irby C., Kimaball R. and Harslem E. (1982) The Star user interface: An overview. In *Office Systems Technology*, El Segundo CA, Xerox Corporation

Carroll J.M. and Thomas J.C. (1982). Metaphor and the cognitive representation of computing systems. *IEEE Transactions on Systems, Man and Cybernetics*, **12**(2), 107–16

Carroll J.M., Mack R.L. and Kellogg W.A. (1988). Interface metaphors and user interface design. In *Handbook on Human-Computer Interaction* (Helander M., ed.). Amsterdam: Elsevier

Kay A. (1990). User interface: A personal view. In *The Art of Human-Computer Interface Design* (Laurel B., ed.), p. 192. Menlo Park CA: Addison-Wesley

Laurel B. (1986). Interface as mimesis. In *User-Centered System Design: New Perspectives on Human-Computer Interaction* (Norman D.A. and Draper S., eds.). Hillsdale NJ: Lawrence Erlbaum Associates.

Stone R. (1991). Advanced human system interfaces for telerobotics using virtual reality and telepresence technologies. In *Proc. 5th Int. Conf on Advanced Robotics*, Pisa, Italy, 1991

Virtual environment systems, virtual reality

Bevan M. (1992). BAe merges real and virtual environments. *VR News*, **1**(7)

Bryson S. (1991). Interaction of objects in a virtual environment: A two point paradigm. In *SPIE Stereoscopic Displays and Applications II* vol. 1457

Cherri A. and Cooper P. (1989). *Visual Environment Simulator for Mobile Viewer*, US Patent 4 807 202 (filed 17 April 1986)

Davidson C. (1991). European astronauts to fly in virtual space. *Computer Weekly*, 28 November

Ellis S.R., ed. (1991a). *Representation in Pictorial and Virtual Environments*. London: Taylor and Francis

Ellis S.R. (1991b). Nature and origins of virtual environments A bibliographical essay. *Computing Systems in Engineering*, **2**(4), 321–47

Endo T. and Hiroshi I. (1989). *NTT Human Interface Laboratories,* NTT publication, Kanagawa, Japan

Fisher S. (1989). Panel Session. Virtual environments and interactivity: Windows to the future. In *SIGGRAPH '89 Panel Proc.*, Boston MA, 31 July 1989

Fisher S. (1990). Virtual environments, personal simulation and telepresence, multimedia review. *Journal of Multimedia Computing*, **1**(2)

Fisher S. and Marion A. (1983). Real time computer graphics from body motion. In *Optics in Entertainment, SPIE Proceedings* vol. 391, pp. 59–63

Fisher S. and McGreevy M. (1986). Virtual workstation: A multi-modal, stereoscopic display environment. In *Advances in Intelligent Robotics Systems, SPIE Proceedings* vol. 726 (Casasent D.P., ed.), pp. 517–22

Foley J.D. (1987). Interfaces for advanced computing. *Scientific American*, **257**(4): October, 126–35

Friedmann M., Starner T. and Pentland A. (1992). Synchronization in virtual realities. *Presence*, **1**(1), pp 139–44

Furness T.A., III (1986). The Super Cockpit and its Human Factors Challenges. In *Proc. of the Human Factors Society, 30th Annual Meeting*, 1986

Furness T.A., III (1988). Harnessing virtual space. *Society for Information Display Digest*, 4–7

Gibson J.J. (1950). *The Perception of the Virtual World*. Boston: Houghton Mifflin

Gibson W. (1984). *Neuromancer*. New York: Berkeley Publications

Greenfield H., Vickers D., Sutherland I., Kolff W. and Reemtsma K. (1971). Moving computer graphic images seen from inside the vascular system. *Transactions of the American Society of Artificial Internal Organs*, **17**, 381–5

Gregory R.L. (1989). Seeing by exploring. In *Spatial Displays and Spatial Instruments* (Ellis S.R., Kaiser M.K. and Grunwald A., eds.), pp. 5–11. NASA Conference Publication 10032

Heilig M. (1962). *Sensorama Simulator*, US Patent 3 050 870 (filed 28 August 1962)

Kalawsky R.S. (1991a). Pilot integration and the implications on the design of advanced cockpits. In *Conf. on the Man-Machine Interface in Tactical Aircraft Design and Combat Automation*, Agard, Stuttgart

Kalawsky R.S. (1991b). State of virtual reality in the UK. In *IEE Colloquium on Real World Visualisation – Virtual World – Virtual Reality*, London

Kalawsky R.S. (1991c). From visually coupled systems to virtual reality: An aerospace perspective. In *Proc. Computer Graphics '91*, Blenheim Online

Kaufman A. and Bakalash R. (1989). The Cube system as a 3D medical workstation. In *Three-Dimensional Visualization and Display Technologies, SPIE Proceedings* vol. 1083, pp. 189–94

Krueger M. (1983a). *Virtual Reality*. Reading MA: Addison-Wesley

Krueger M. (1983b). *Artificial Reality*. Reading MA: Addison-Wesley

Krueger M. (1985). VIDEOPLACE: A report from the Artificial Reality Laboratory. *Leonardo*, **18**(3)

Liang J., Shaw C. and Green M. (1991). On temporal-spatial realism in the virtual reality environment. In *Proc. 4th Annual Symposium on User Interface Software and Technology*, Hilton Head SC, pp. 19–25

McGreevy M.W. (1991). Virtual reality and planetary exploration. In *29th AAS Goddard Memorial Symposium*, Washington DC, March 1991

Newquist H. (1991). A computer generated suspension of disbelief. *AI Expert*, 34–9

NTT Visual Media Laboratory (1988). *Annual Report*

Pausch R. (1991). Virtual reality on five dollars a day. In *ACM SIGCHI Conf. Proc.*, New Orleans, 1991, pp. 265–70

Stone R. (1990). Human Factors Research at the UK National Advanced Robotics Research Centre. *The Ergonomist*, (239), May

VPL Research, Inc. (1989). *Virtual Reality at Texpo '89*, Redwood City CA: VPL Research, Inc.

Wang C., Koved L. and Dukach S. (1990). Design for interactive performance in a virtual laboratory. In *Proc. SIGGRAPH '90*, pp. 39–40

Ware C. and Osborne S. (1990). Exploration and virtual camera control in virtual three dimensional environments. In *Proc. SIGGRAPH '90*, pp. 175–83

Vision

Barlow H.B. and Mollon J.D. (1982). *The Senses*. Cambridge University Press

Ellis S.R. (1989). Visions of visualization aids: Design philosophy and observations. In *Proc. SPIE-Int. Soc. Optical Engineering Sym. on Three Dimensional Visualization of Scientific Data*, Los Angeles CA, 15–20 January

10 Glossary

Abberation of light The passage of light by paths other than those making for the efficiency of an optical system (including that of the eye), and exclusive of the effect of poor adjustment of focus.

Accomodation The change in shape of the lens of the eye to bring objects of varying distances into focus. Relatively weak cue and limited to a maximum of 6–9m.

Achromatic Lacking in hue and saturation. Achromatic colours vary only in brightness, from black to white.

Acuity, visual The ability of the eye to perceive form and detail in a plane perpendicular to the line of sight.

Adaption A change in sensitivity to a stimulus following continuous exposure to the same stimulus.

Aerial Perspective Attenuation of light and change in hue produced by particles in the atmosphere. Normally noticeable only at substantial distances except in cases of heavy haze and smog.

Ambient (illumination) Encompassing on all sides.

Anisometropia Unequal refractive power in the two eyes.

Aphakia Absence of the crystalline lens.

Aqueous humour A transparent, watery fluid, which fills the space between the cornea and the lens in the anterior part of the eye.

Astigmatism A defect of the eye. Two types are recognized: regular, in which the error is due to a greater curvature of a refractive surface (chiefly the cornea) in one meridian, and which may be corrected by a cylindrical lens; and irregular, in which the refraction is irregularly unequal within the pupillary area and which is not correctable except by contact lenses.

Attenuation The decrease of an electrical signal; the process of decreasing the power of an electrical signal.

Attitude   The aspect that an aircraft presents at any given moment, as determined by its inclinations about its three axes. Also attributively, as in attitude indicator, attitude instrument.

AudioSphere   A 3-D real-time sound rendering signal processor that converts monaural sounds into fully spacialized stereo, manufactured by Crystal River Engineering.

Aural signal   A signal which must be heard by the ear and be interpreted without benefit of visual instruments.

Azimuth   A bearing in the horizontal plane, usually expressed as an angle, and in air navigation measured clockwise from true north, grid north, or magnetic north, from 0° to 360°.

Binocular field   The field of vision of the two eyes acting conjointly.

Blind spot   A small area in the retina, where the optic nerve leaves the eyeball. The blind spot is not sensitive to light stimulation.

Body Electric (BE)   A program for controlling the behaviour of objects in virtual reality, animation, or teleoperations. It was written by VPL and runs on the Macintosh. Body Electric can read model files created with Swivel 3D or Swivel Professional.

Brightness   (1) Attribute of visual sensation determined by intensity of light radiation reaching the eye. Sometimes called lightness, tint or value. Refers to variations along the achromatic scale of black to white.
(2) Photometric measure of light emission per unit area of a luminous body or of a translucent or reflective surface, i.e. candlepower per unit area.

Candle   Unit of light intensity. At a distance of one foot, one candle produces an illumination of one foot-candle (equivalent to one lumen per square foot) upon a surface normal to the beam.

Cathode-ray tube (CRT)   A vacuum tube in which the deflection of an electron beam indicates on a fluorescent screen instantaneous values of the actuating voltages or currents.

Chiasma   The junction point of the optic nerves, from which they again diverge and pass to the respective cerebral hemispheres. In the human eye, the fibres from the nasal half of each retina cross at this point, the remainder going to the hemisphere on the same side.

Choroid   The intermediate of the three layers of the eyeball, situated between the sclera and the retina.

Chroma   Synonym for colour saturation.

Ciliary body An annular mass of unstriped muscle fibres, which surrounds the eye-lens and regulates its curvature, thereby accommodating (focusing) the eye for vision at various distances.

Cladding The coating of glass or plastic surrounding a fibre optic core and having a lower refractive index.

Colorimetry A method for measuring colours and specifying them in numerical of definite symbolic terms.

Colour Visual sensation determined by interaction of wavelength, intensity, and mixture of wavelengths of light. The corresponding attributes of colour are hue, brightness, and saturation.

Complementary colour Colour which, when combined with another colour, and acting together with it on the retina, cancels out the hue and saturation of the second colour, so that the total effect of the combination matches an achromatic stimulus, giving a white or grey sensation.

Cones Structures found in the retina of the eye that constitute specific receptors for vision at high levels of illumination and for colour.

Contrast Difference in brightness between two portions of visual field, usually expressed in experimental procedures as a change in apparent brightness of colour of a visual field as a result of recent stimulation of this field or a neighbouring one; the effect is to enhance opposing characteristics.

Convergence The inward rotation of the eyes as the object of fixation approaches from visual infinity (9 m). Eye position is sensed from feedback from muscle contractions controlling eye movement. Provides little or no information beyond 3.6 m.

Core The inner portion of a fibre optic cable, having a higher refractive index.

Cornea The transparent portion of the outer coat of the eyeball, situated in front of the iris and constituting the first of the refractive media of the eye.

Correlation The tendency of certain paired measures to vary concomitantly, so that knowledge of the value of one measure gives information as to the mean value of all measures paired with that measure.

Critical angle The smallest angle of incidence in a medium of greater refractive index for which light is totally reflected.

Cues Stimuli which guide the organism's responses, e.g. highlights and shadows in depth perception. Sometimes referred to as clues.

Dark adaption Process whereby the eye attains greater sensitivity to light placed in an illumination lower than that to which it was previously exposed.

Data Flow Network (Net) The data processing program that is written with Body Electric. A net is comprised of raw inputs, DMs, points and the connections between them.

DataGlove A VPL product for sensing hand gestures. Position and orientation are measured by a Polhemus attached to the DataGlove. The angles of the two joints per finger are measured by fibre-optic flex sensors.

Data Massage Module (DM) The part of a network that processes data. Data Massage Modules take inputs from Raw Inputs or other Data Massage Modules and outputs to Points or other Data Massage Modules.

Decibel Log unit expressing relative levels of intensity or power.

Decollimation Spreading of light by a fibre optic cable due to various internal and end effects.

Desktop VR Desktop virtual reality has emerged from animated computer aided design (CAD). With desktop virtual reality the user views and interacts with the computer-represented image on a traditional computer graphics screen. Whether or not this is virtual reality or just a more sophisticated version of CAD is an interesting philosophical question.

Diffraction Bending of a portion of the wave-front behind the edge of an obstacle.

Diopter Measurement of the focusing power of a lens according to the reciprocal of the focal length of the lens. A lens of one diopter focuses parallel rays at 1 m.

Diplopia Any condition of the ocular mechanism in which a single external object is seen double.

Divergence The turning of two eyeballs outward with respect to each other, or their movement from a position of greater convergence to one of less.

Enmetropic The normal condition of the ocular refractive system, in which rays from distant objects are focused sharply on the retina of the eye, while accommodation is relaxed.

Extrafoveal Outside of the fovea.

EyePhone A display device worn over the eyes and ears for viewing and hearing in stereo. It contains two tiny TV monitors, one for each eye, earphones, and a Polhemus for sensing the position and orientation of the user's head.

Fixation point Point in the visual field at which the observer is looking directly. It is the point whose image falls on the centre of the fovea.

Flicker, visual A rapid periodic change in a visual impression, due to a corresponding rapid cyclic change in the intensity or some other characteristic of the stimulus.

Flight simulator A device that simulates any or all of the conditions of actual flight, used especially for training purposes; specifically, any ground trainer. In a broad sense, the term could be applied to a centrifuge or to a low-pressure chamber.

Focal length A characteristic of a lens or other focusing optical system, being the focal distance for parallel entering rays.

Fovea A small depression in the central region of the retina, containing only cones.

Genlocked It is sometimes necessary to synchronize two video signals together o that they can be overlaid on top of each other. Whenever two or video signals have to mixed together it is extremely important to ensure that they are synchronized from a common source of synchronization signals. The process of synchronizing one video source to another is often called genlocking.

Heterophoria The tendency of either eye to deviate abnormally from its position of fixation when fusion of the two images is prevented; muscular imbalance.

Heterotropia The failure of one of the two eyes to take its proper position of binocular fixation with reference to the other, due to defect or lack of control of the extrinsic ocular muscles.

Hue The attribute of colour determined primarily by the wavelength of light entering the eye. Spectral hues range from red through orange, yellow, green, and blue to violet.

Hyperopia Synonym for farsightedness; a defect of the eye such that, with accommodation relaxed, parallel rays of light focus behind the retina.

Illuminance The flux striking a surface, measured in lumens per unit area.

Illusion A misinterpretation of certain elements in a given experience, so that the experience does not represent the objective situation.

Intensity (1) The quantitative attribute or value of a sensory process or unit, correlated in general with the intensity of the physical stimulus.
(2) Flux per solid angle from a point source measured in lumens per steradian.

Interposition or superposition An object whose form or outline is obscured by another object is seen as behind or further in depth than the object whose complete outline is visible.

Inverse square law Illumination varies inversely as the square of the distance of receiving plane from point source.

Iris A flat, ring-shaped structure situated within the eyeball immediately in front of the lens, containing unstriped muscle-fibres whose contraction and relaxation regulate the amount of light admitted through the pupil.

Isaac The program that renders the stereo images displayed on the EyePhone. It is initialized with a model exported from Swivel. It receives real-time input of changes to the model from Body Electric and runs on fast graphics computers such as the Silicon Graphics machines.

Isopter All the points at which a threshold level of performance is obtained, plotted on a chart of the visual field so that they form an irregular ring around the centre of vision.

Just noticeable difference (jnd) The least amount of a stimulus which, added to or subtracted from a standard stimulus, produces a just noticeably different experience.

Keratoconus Conically bulging cornea.

Lambert Unit of brightness; it is the brightness of a perfect diffusing surface giving out one lumen per square centimetre of surface area.

Landlot ring A ring with a small gap at one point, used to test visual acuity by having the observer report the orientation of the gap.

Lens The transparent body, convex on its front and back surfaces, situated just behind the iris and pupil of the eye; it serves, through changes in its shape brought about by the action of the ciliary muscles, to focus the eye for different distances.

Light Radiant energy that arouses visual sensations.

Linear perspective The apparent convergence of parallel lines with distance toward a vanishing point at visual infinity. This cue is intimately tied to relative size and can be used to create a strong impression of depth on two-dimensional surfaces such as line drawn images on a computer graphics display. Angular relationships and ratios of objects and dimensions also provide depth cues.

Lumen Unit of luminous flux; luminous flux emitted per second by a point source of one candle intensity through a solid angle of one steradian.

Luminous emittance The flux emitted in all directions from each unit area of an extended source, measured in lumens per unit area.

Luminous flux Analogous to rate of transfer of energy, it is the total visible energy emitted by a source per unit time.

Meniscus A lens, one of whose refracting surfaces is convex and the other concave.

Minimum distinguishable acuity Least change in form that can be identified visually, i.e. the least lateral displacement in the ends of two lines that will result in the experience of discontinuity. It is measured in terms of the angle subtended by the object, measured at the eye.

Minimum perceptible acuity Smallest object that is visible. It is measured in terms of the angle subtended by the object, measured at the eye.

Minimum separable acuity Smallest space between two lines that can be discriminated as a gap. It is measured in terms of the angle subtended by the gap, measured at the eye.

Minimum visible acuity Least area of a uniform brightness that can activate the eye. It is measured in terms of the angle subtended by the area, measured at the eye.

Monocular field Field of vision with one eye alone.

Motion parallax The direction of movement and apparent angular velocity of objects in the visual field vary as a function of distance, linear speed and slant angle. The peripheral streaming of ground texture during a landing approach is an example of motion parallax.

Myopia Refractive defect of the eye, such that, with the lens relaxed, parallel rays of light are brought to a focus before they reach the retina.

Numerical aperture (NA) A measure of the light gathering power of a fibre optic component (or other optical device), usually equal to the sine of the acceptance angle.

Optic disc A small, low eminence on the inner surface of the retina, within the eyeball, formed by the nerve fibres of the retina, as they collect just before emerging from the eyeball to form the optic nerve.

Optic nerve The second cranial nerve, which connects the retina of the eye with the visual centres.

Orthophoria Condition in which an eye may continue to look toward an object even if the object is hidden.

Orthorater Commercial apparatus for determining visual acuity at both near and far accommodations, but with distance factor induced by a system of lenticular prisms.

Parallactic angle The angle between the two lines drawn from a single point on an object to the two eyes.

Perception The awareness of external objects, qualities, or relations, which ensues directly upon sensory processes.

Perimeter An instrument for determining the discriminative powers of different parts of the retina.

Phosphor A substance applied to the inner face of a cathode-ray tube which fluoresces during bombardment by electrons, and phosphoresces after bombardment.

Photometer An optical device that utilizes equations of brilliance to permit the measurement of a photometric quantity, such as candle power, illumination, or brightness.

Photometry The measurement of visible radiation on the basis of its effect upon the eye under standard conditions, and usually involving an adjustment of two contiguous parts of the visual field, either to identify or to determine a minimal difference.

Photopic Vision under illumination sufficient to permit the discrimination of colours. Sometimes called daylight vision.

Presbyopia A condition of the eye characterized by ability to see distant objects clearly and inability to obtain a clear picture of nearby objects, due to inelasticity of the lens, with consequent reduction of accommodation, which develops with advancing age.

Pseudo-isochromatic test A colour-blindness test in which the plates contain two colours which can be distinguished by the normal eye, but not by the colour blind eye.

Pyschophysical methods Standardized procedures for presenting stimulus material to a subject for judging and for recording of results. Originally developed for determining functional relations between physical stimuli and correlated sensory responses, but now used more widely.

Pupil The circular opening in the iris, which forms the diaphragm of the optical system of the eye, regulating the amount of light admitted to the eye by contracting as the light increases, or the expanding as the light decreases.

Reality Built for Two (RB2) The virtual reality system manufactured by VPL for creating and running virtual realities for one or more people. RB2 is comprised of computers, special I/O devices, and the software that controls them. RB2 can integrate data from the real world (such as video via VideoSphere) or artificial data (such as computer graphics via Swivel) into virtual reality.

Reduced eye A simple schematic system designed to have the same optical properties as the average unaccommodated human eye.

Reflectance Ratio of luminous flux reflected from a surface to luminous flux striking it.

Refraction A change in the angle of propagation of a wave in passing from one medium to another of different density of elasticity.

Refractive index A numerical expression indicating the degree to which the path of light or radiant energy is bent in passing from one transparent medium into another.

Response The muscular contraction, glandular secretion, or any other activity of an organism which result from stimulation.

Retina Inner coating of the eyeball, which receives the image formed by refraction of light rays at the cornea and lens; it is made up of rods and cones, the receptor cells for vision.

Retinal disparity The difference which exists between the images formed in the right and left eyes when a solid object is viewed binocularly.

Rhodopsin A substance found in the rods of the dark-adapted eye, which bleaches rapidly on exposure to light, and is believed to be the substance underlying scotopic or twilight vision.

Rods Structures found in the retina of the eye which constitute specific receptors for vision at low levels of illumination. They do not produce sensations of colour.

Saccadic movements Sudden movement of the eyes from one fixation point to another.

Saturation Extent to which a chromatic colour differs from a grey of the same brightness, measured on an arbitrary scale from 0% to 100% (where 0% is grey).

Sclera The white outer fibrous coat of the eyeball, primarily a supporting or skeletal structure.

Scotoma A blind or partially blind area in the visual field.

Scotopic vision Vision which occurs in faint light, or after dark adaption. Sometimes called twilight or night vision. Hues and saturations cannot be distinguished.

Sensation Subjective response or any experience aroused by stimulation of a sense organ.

Servo system Control system with feedback. The behaviour of a servo is governed, not by the input signal alone, but by the difference between the input and some function of the output.

Simulator Any machine or apparatus that simulates a desired condition or set of conditions, such as a flight simulator.

Specular surface One that scatters little of the flux striking it.

Stereopsis The horizontal separation of the eyes causes objects at different depths to fall on non-corresponding parts of each retina with the magnitude of separation a function of the difference in depth of the objects. When two-dimensional scenes containing disparity are presented to the eyes, they fuse to form a striking impression of depth or volume. Stereopsis does not provide a cue to absolute distance unless other cues are present.

Stimulus Energy, external or internal, which excites a receptor.

Swivel 3D & Swivel 3D Professional Programs for modelling three-dimensional objects as well as movement constraints between pieces. The programs were developed at VPL and are published by Paracomp. They run on Macintosh computers.

Telepresence A term to cover the situation where the remote operator receives sufficient information about the environment and the teleoperator such that the remote operator feels physically immersed in the environment of the teleoperator.

Threshold A barely noticeable environmental energy level (absolute threshold) or energy change (differential threshold).

Transmittance Ratio of transmitted to incident luminous flux (expressed as a percentage).

Total internal reflection Reflection of light at angles of incidence greater than the critical angle between two optical media of different refractive indexes.

Visual angle The angle subtended by an object of vision at the nodal point of the eye. The magnitude of this angle determines the size of the corresponding retinal image, irrespective of the size or distance of the object.

Visual field That part of space that can be seen when head and eyes are motionless, (or) the totality of visual stimuli which act upon the unmoving eye at a given movement.

Vitreous humour The transparent, jelly-like mass which fills the eyeball from the concave surface of the retina as far forward as the lens.

Wavelength The distance in metres travelled by an electromagnetic wave during the interval covered by a cycle.

Zonule fibres The set of bands which extend from the ciliary body to the equator of the lens of the eye, constituting its suspensory ligament.

Index